Religious change in Zambia

Monographs from the African Studies Centre, Leiden

Religious change in Zambia

Exploratory studies

Wim M. J. van Binsbergen

Kegan Paul International
London and Boston

306.6
B614r

First published in 1981
by Kegan Paul International
39 Store Street,
London WC1E 7DD and
9 Park Street,
Boston, Mass. 02108, USA
Set in Press Roman by
Hope Services
Abingdon, Oxon
and printed in Great Britain by
The Thetford Press Ltd
Thetford, Norfolk

British Library Cataloguing in Publication Data

Binsbergen, Wim M. J. van

Religious change in Zambia. – (Monographs/Leiden
African Studies Centre).
1. Zambia – Religion
I. Title
306'.6   BL2470.Z3   80–041964

ISBN 0-7103-0000-X
ISBN 0-7103-0012-3 Pbk

Contents ___

Contents

Illustrations

Plates

Figures

Maps

Tables

ndaba bapashi banakana

Map 1 Religious change in Zambia: localities and ethnic groups

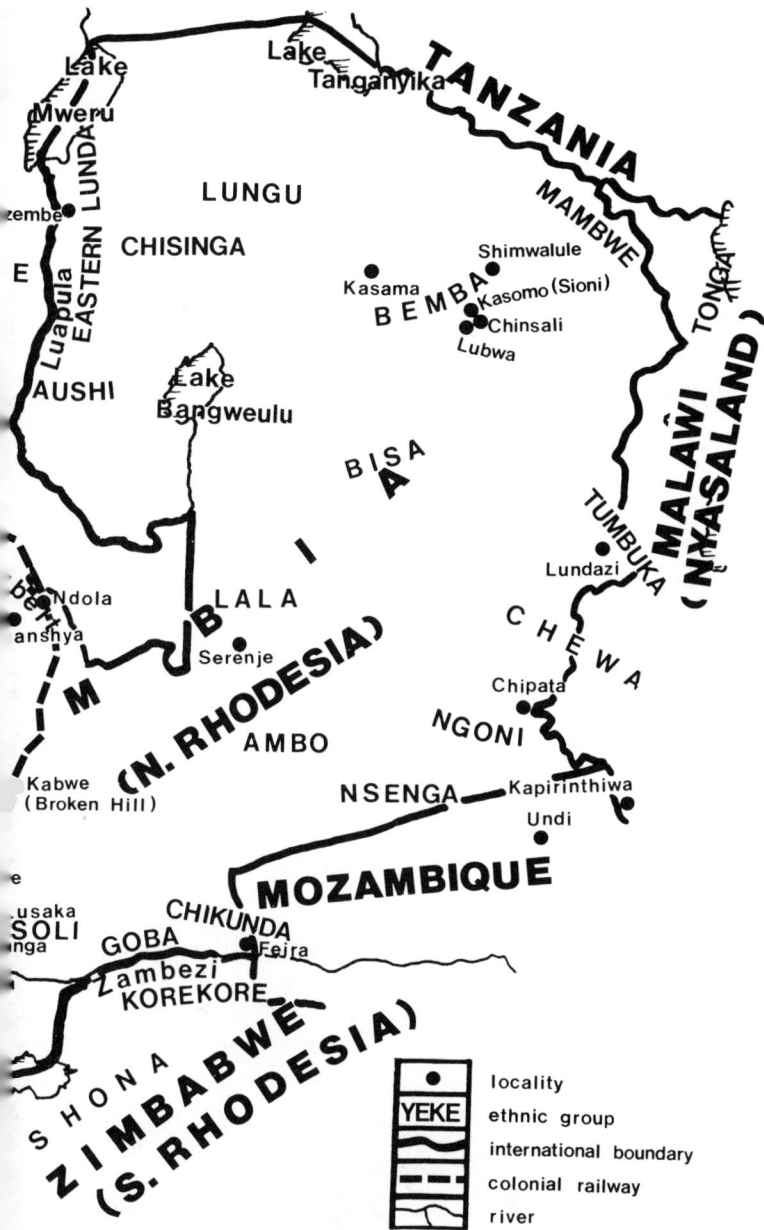

Lake Mweru

Lake Tanganyika

TANZANIA

EASTERN LUNDA

LUNGU

CHISINGA

MAMBWE

zembe

Luapula

E

AUSHI

Lake Bangweulu

Shimwalule

Kasama

BEMBA

Kasomo (Sioni)

Chinsali

Lubwa

BISA

TONGA

MALAWI (NYASALAND)

TUMBUKA

Ndola

Lundazi

beri

BALA

CHEWA

anshya

M

Serenje

Chipata

W

(N. RHODESIA)

AMBO

NGONI

Kabwe
(Broken Hill)

NSENGA

Kapirinthiwa

Undi

MOZAMBIQUE

e

usaka

CHIKUNDA

SOLI

GOBA

Fejra

nga

Zambezi

KOREKORE

SHONA

ZIMBABWE
(S. RHODESIA)

●	locality
YEKE	ethnic group
	international boundary
- - -	colonial railway
	river

0   200 km

Preface and acknowledgments

This volume brings together seven studies of religious change in Zambia which were written between 1972 and 1979. During these eight years, our factual knowledge of social and religious phenomena in Central Africa increased considerably. Moreover, these years saw profound changes in the theory and methodology of the disciplines studying these phenomena: anthropology and sociology, history and political science. Structural functionalism virtually disappeared from the academic scene. It was partly supplanted by a Marxist approach stressing modes of production, the penetration of capitalism and processes of class formation. The historical study of societies and periods about which no written records exist became an established speciality. And finally, the bounded ethnic group or tribe, once considered a viable unit of social analysis, gave way to regional approaches transcending the comfortable political and cultural boundaries within which anthropologists used to carve out their little empires.

My introductory chapter indicates how these general trends were reflected in the studies presented here. As I struggled to unearth the scarce and stubborn data of Zambian religious change, the process of interpretation of these data forced me constantly to re-evaluate and revise my theoretical perspective. I started out with the approach to which my anthropological training at the University of Amsterdam had introduced me: a mild version of structural functionalism, tending towards transactionalism, yet stressing cross-cultural comparison between local social systems conceived as bounded and integrated units, and certainly underrating wider regional and historical dimensions. Such an approach had proved feasible in my earlier analysis of popular religion in a rural community in north-western Tunisia, where I did my first field-work (1968). However, my extensive Zambian field-work,

1

both in urban compounds and in a remote village community, as well as the intellectual exchanges into which I was meanwhile drawn, profoundly challenged this initial positition. I was brought to stress process rather than institutions; regional linkages rather than a single bounded ethnic group; and material aspects (production, expropriation, control) of social phenomena, in addition to institutional and normative aspects. The theoretical and conceptual difficulties involved in the painful transition from a more or less classic anthropology to my present theoretical position were solved only gradually and partially. Each of the following studies therefore represents a momentary stage in a complex argument, which I built up in the course of nearly a decade. What on the surface might appear a puzzling lack of consistency between the chapters turns out to be a sustained intellectual process, the outlines of which I have sketched in the Introduction (chapter 1).

The general trends in Central African studies, as reflected in the present volume, took shape through a series of specific debates, which formed the substance of a number of conferences and edited books. Most of the papers included here have been written, and partly published, within such specific settings, in which certain problems, certain concepts, certain approaches, were to be stressed rather than others. While the body of data expanded only slowly, I was forced to re-examine these data and my theoretical position in the light of, respectively: the concept of the territorial cult; the study of witchcraft, sorcery, and the problem of evil; regional cults theory; the relation between nationalism and religious innovation; and the paradigm of the articulation of modes of production. The chapters in this volume link up with a series of current debates which in themselves are implied rather than fully discussed within each individual study, and whose significance for the overall argument is made clear in the introduction. The sequence of different approaches in these chapters reflects both general trends in Central African studies and my own intellectual development, but mediated through the market mechanisms of academic production.

Even though this book constitutes one complex and sustained argument, some of the earlier parts would look very different if I were to write them today. For various reasons, however, I have not re-written these chapters in the light of my present theoretical position. Instead, the introduction and the postscript to chapter 8 deal at length with such substantial alterations as I would now make. Frankly, it turned out to be impossible to rewrite the original arguments. For it is implied in the exploratory nature of these studies that they contain a fair amount of speculative deduction and thought experiments. It seems to me that such value as these studies may have derives from the interpretative imagination underlying them, much more than from the presentation of a new and complete set of factual data. This interpretative imagination is intimately linked to the theoretical premises I held at the time. A different theoretical position would have led the exploration, in any of the chapters, in a rather different direction. While one can explicitly acknowledge this, an attempt to build later theoretical premises into the earlier arguments can only cause the latters' destruction. The original creative moment, rendering a measure of plausibility to my hypothetical and controversial models, would be lost. The second reason for leaving the texts largely as they are is that in their original form they have given rise to published debate. Rather than falsifying this debate by producing, in this book, more readily available but greatly revised versions of the original studies, I have taken the opportunity offered by this volume of replying to my critics, both in the Introduction and in a Postscript.

All this means that the present volume is less rigorously integrated than a book written to reflect a scholar's views at one well-defined moment in his intellectual development. Yet the present approach may have advantages as well as disadvantages. This volume of themes and variations on Zambian religious change may provide a telling illustration of the problems of theory and method with which so many of us Africanists have struggled in the 1970s. And anyway, when dealing with historical processes (such as religious change in Zambia), it is no great shame if our analysis of these processes in itself reflects the process of our own intellectual development.

While all this may justify the specific *form* in which the individual studies have now been collected, it says nothing about this collection as such. One justification is that some of the studies included have not yet been published, or have had rather limited circulation. The major justification, however, lies in the fact that these studies appear to constitute the only extensive and systematic attempt so far to come to terms with the data on religious change in Zambia. Underneath my evolving methodological and theoretical position, underneath even the deficiencies that others (reflecting on the separate constituent articles) have pointed out, these studies form the result of a concerted effort to pull together the data on Zambian religious change and to suggest directions for a theoretical interpretation of these phenomena. Tentative, inchoate, incomplete as they are, these studies may yet represent a base-line from which future studies can start. They are exploratory

3

studies in the literal sense of the word. And, as in all exploration, the immediate gains have been very uneven.

To place these studies in their proper perspective, let me indicate when and in what context they were written. The Introduction and the Postscript were produced in 1979, specifically for this collection. An earlier draft of the Introduction was presented at the Afrika-Studie-centrum Conference on Recent African Religious Studies, Leiden, December 1979. Chapter 2 was read at the 1972 Lusaka Conference on the History of Central African Religious Systems (organized jointly by the Institute for African Studies, University of Zambia, and the Center for African Studies, University of California, Los Angeles). The paper has since circulated, along with the other papers of that conference, in sets made available by the Institute for African Studies. Chapter 3 was commissioned by Matthew Schoffeleers in 1972 as an overview on Zambian territorial cults for his collection *Guardians of the Land: Essays on Central African Territorial Cults*. The chapter was completed in 1973. The international energy crisis, and subsequent economic decline, greatly delayed publication of the book; it finally appeared in 1979 (Gwelo: Mambo Press, pp. 47–88). In 1977, when R.S. Roberts finalized the text of the Schoffeleers book for publication, I gratefully took the opportunity to update the references and to correct a few factual and stylistic errors.

Chapter 4 was originally written as a final section of chapter 3. In 1973 Terence Ranger requested a much expanded and rewritten version for his planned collection entitled *The Problem of Evil in Central and East Africa*. A final version was submitted in 1974. That book was haunted by similar problems as the Schoffeleers book, and when towards the end of 1975 no progress had been made towards publication, I withdrew my chapter. A greatly condensed version was subsequently published in *Ufahamu*, 6, 3, 1976, pp. 69–87. The chapter is published here in the original form as submitted for the Ranger book, with the addition of a few paragraphs from the *Ufahamu* version.

Chapter 5 was written in 1976 on request from Richard P. Werbner, for his book *Regional Cults* (ASA Monograph 16, London: Academic Press, 1977, pp. 141–75). This book was the result of the 1976 Manchester Conference on Regional Cults and Oracles, organized by the Association of Social Anthropologists of Great Britain and the Commonwealth. My chapter is in part a re-examination of material earlier presented at the 1972 Lusaka Conference, in a paper entitled: 'Bituma: Preliminary Notes on a Healing Movement among the Nkoya of Kaoma District and of Lusaka, Zambia'. The paper originally presented at the 1976 Manchester conference was entirely different, and has not yet been published.

Chapter 6 was drafted in 1975. It was presented in the same year at a seminar of the Antropologisch-Sociologisch Centrum, University of Amsterdam; a revised version was published in *Cultures et développement*, 8, 1976, pp. 195-218.

Successive drafts of chapter 7 were presented at the Institute for African Studies, University of Zambia (1977), the Amsterdam Work-Group on Marxist Anthropology (1978 and 1979), the Leiden Africa Seminar (1979), and the Department of Social Anthropology, University of Manchester (1979). A Dutch version is to be included in a publication of the Amsterdam Work-Group, *De Koppeling van Produktiewijzen*, Leiden, Afrika-Studiecentrum, in press. Chapter 8 was written in 1976-7, and published in a volume which I edited with Robert Buijtenhuijs: *Religious Innovation in Modern African Society* (African Perspectives, 1976/2, Leiden, Afrika-Studiecentrum, pp. 101-35).

As I have already indicated, these studies appear here in what is essentially their original form. However, I corrected printing errors, and altered a few words and sentences for the sake of style, readability and clarity. Without substantial rewriting of the original texts, it is inevitable that some overlap occurs between the chapters in the present volume. The original cross-references between the articles have been retained here, but in addition the relevant chapters of the present volume are indicated. For this book, a uniform system of footnotes and references has been adopted for all chapters, with a cumulative bibliography at the end. Only such acknowledgments have been retained in the footnotes to the separate chapters as are not yet covered in this preface.

It is to these acknowledgments that I shall now turn. If this book reflects an exploration, it has not been a solitary one. Many people have accompanied me for longer or shorter stretches of the road.

For all their abstraction and attempts at synthesis, and their partial reliance on archival and secondary sources, these studies are yet very much the work of a fieldworker. Urban field-work was carried out on a part-time basis in Lusaka from February 1972 to August 1973; after shorter research trips in February and May–June 1973, rural field-work was conducted in Kaoma district from August 1973 to April 1974. I followed up both the rural and the urban ends of the research in September–November 1977, and in August 1978. It was in the field that I began to formulate my first hypotheses about the possible

5

historical dimensions of the contemporary religious phenomena I was studying. It is therefore proper that my first acknowledgments should be to the people who greatly contributed towards my field-work. Henny van Rijn, my wife, shared loyally in much of the urban and most of the rural field-work, helping to establish and maintain productive relationships with informants (up to the point of designing and sewing ceremonial white garments for priestesses of the Bituma cult!), putting up with a division of domestic labour blatantly different from our original agreements, and forming a partner in those crucial preliminary discussions upon which research can thrive.

Dennis K. Shiyowe, my sometime research assistant and friend ever since, introduced me to non-Christian urban cults, and to the Nkoya ethnic group upon which my urban and rural research in Zambia was to concentrate. Many of the ideas underlying the present book sprang from the fieldwork we conducted together in Lusaka and Kaoma district. The very great contribution he, and the members of his family and wider kin-group, made towards my research cannot be expressed in full. Almost as a matter of course we were allowed to be present at, and take part in their day-to-day life and their rituals. Without this prolonged first-hand involvement at a profound personal level, I would never have had the ambition nor the courage to probe for the historical dimensions of contemporary Zambian religion.

Pat A. Mutesi, once a student of mine and since long a graduate of the University of Zambia, was my assistant in two surveys (of urban religious organization, and of the religious dimension in marriage and urbanization) which we conducted in Lusaka in 1972 and 1973. Although the material of these surveys remains to be written up, this joint work has given me a much wider background in Lusaka society and Zambian Christianity than the Nkoya research alone could have done, and I am grateful to Mr Mutesi for his contribution in this respect. In 1977 and 1978, when I returned to the field with new questions reflecting my growing interest in class formation, political and economic rural history, and the use of song texts for anthropological and historical analysis, I was fortunate to benefit from the knowledge and untiring energy of Davison Kawanga; he has been feeding me with exciting new material ever since. More limited, but significant contributions to the data collection were made by Masuku Malasha, Hamba H. Mwene and Dickson K. Makiyi.

All the efforts of those mentioned would have been in vain but for the trustful co-operation of hundreds of Zambian informants both in Lusaka and in Kaoma district. The majority of these belonged to the

Nkoya people. By thanking their traditional leaders Mwenekahare Kabam-bi and the late Mwenemutondo Kapulikila, as well as the Hon. J.K. Kalaluka, Member of Parliament, it is understood that my gratitude extends to all those men and women who went out of their way to accommodate us and explain their way of life and their rituals to us. They may be disappointed that in the present volume relatively little of their own social and ritual experience will be described and analysed in its own right, as the past and present of the Nkoya, rather than as typical for more general trends which have obtained throughout Zambia. Therefore, while acknowledging their contribution to the present study, let me make it clear that this is not the book with which I hope to discharge my debt towards the Nkoya people. Writings on Nkoya history, and on contemporary Nkoya life, are now in an advanced stage of preparation, and will soon be published.

Beyond such companionship as marriage can offer, an anthropologist doing field-work in the kinship-dominated and natalistic environment of Central African society is lucky if his own family provides him with a recognizable human face. Despite her very tender age at the time, our daughter Nezjma did help us through the ups and downs of field-work, spreading charm and joy (in a toddler's version of three Zambian languages) no matter how heavily our physical and mental resources were taxed. And our empathy with Zambian life, its hopes and anxieties, its material and spiritual struggles, interpersonal tensions, and above all its warmth and pride, owed a very great deal to our own childhood experiences in our families of orientation, as we grew up in a mobility-conscious working-class environment not so fundamentally different from that of our Zambian urban informants. And this is only one reason why our relatives may properly be mentioned in these acknowledgments.

On the institutional side these studies owe much to the stimulating intellectual environment of the University of Zambia, where I held an appointment in sociology in 1971-3, and where subsequently I was a Research Affiliate at the Institute for African Studies in the years 1973-4, 1977 and 1978. A research grant from the University of Zambia in 1972 enabled me to get a first footing in the religious life of Lusaka; out of this first project developed the research upon which these studies have been based. I am particularly indebted to H. Jack Simons, sometime Head of Sociology, and to successive Directors of the Institute for African Studies: Jaap van Velsen, Mubanga E. Kashoki and Robert Serpell. They and their academic and administrative staff all made an effort to extend to me such intellectual and logistic support,

7

as well as friendship, as were essential for my research. In addition, Jaap van Velsen took an active part in the planning of my Nkoya research, and spurred me on with advice and with challenging and incisive criticism.

In the course of my research in Zambia, I greatly benefited from the hospitality, advice, and assistance extended to me by: the Cabinet Office; the Ministry of Home Affairs (Registrar of Societies); the District Governors, Kaoma and Lusaka; the District Secretaries, Kaoma and Lusaka, and their staff; the Regional Secretaries, United National Independence Party (UNIP), both in Lusaka and in Kaoma, and many party officials at the Branch and Section level; the Zambia National Archives; the University of Zambia Library, particularly the Special Collection on Zambia, and the Microfilm Department; the senior staff at the Nkeyema scheme, Tobacco Board of Zambia; the Medical Officers and staff of Kaoma Government Hospital, Luampa Hospital and Mangango Hospital; officials and members of a large number of Zambian Christian Churches, among which should in particular be mentioned the Evangelical Church of Zambia (and the associated Africa Evangelical Fellowship), the Reformed Church of Zambia, the Roman Catholic Church, the Watchtower Bible and Tract Society, the Apostolic Faith Church, the Holy Gospel Church, the Apostolic Faith Holy Gospel Church, and the inter-denominational Mindolo Ecumenical Foundation. Numerous individuals made vital practical contributions. Let me thank them all through Edward Kahare (who miraculously turned our car, which looked like a total loss after an accident, into a vehicle still suitable for field-work along the rough roads of his home area); and Leo and Aafke van den Berg, our own 'homeboys' in Lusaka (who, among many things, by minding our daughter, enabled me to conduct at least archival research during the desperate weeks when very serious illness had put a premature end to our rural field-work).

After I left Zambia in 1974, the Netherlands Foundation for the Advancement of Tropical Research (WOTRO) offered me a writing-up grant for 1974-5, during which period several of the present studies were written or revised. I am indebted to André J.F. Köbben for his guidance during that period. In 1975-7, when I was acting in the chair of Sociology and Cultural Anthropology of Africa at Leiden University, this institution enabled me to carry on with my research into Zambian religious change, and provided funds for my participation in the 1976 Manchester Conference, which led to one of the studies included here. Finally, shorter visits to the field were made possible, and several chapters including the Introduction were written or prepared for publication, under the stimulating conditions of my current appointment with the Afrika-Studiecentrum, Leiden. I am greatly indebted to Gerrit Grootenhuis, Managing Director, for encouragement and advice; and to Wilma Freeke and Ria van Hal for excellent secretarial assistance towards the production of the present volume.

It has been my great good fortune that, ever since the 1972 Lusaka Conference, my work on religious change in Zambia has developed in a context of immensely stimulating, largely informal exchange with a number of prominent scholars in this field. It is here that my intellectual debts in the present volume mainly lie. The first person to be mentioned in this connection is Terence Ranger, who since the late 1960s has done more than anyone else to stimulate and deepen the study of religious change in central and east Africa. Without his incessant encouragement most of the studies presented here would simply never have been written.

Matthew Schoffeleers's powerful grasp on the past and present of the religion in southern Malawi enabled him to play a leading role in the study of Central African territorial cults, and of the exchanges between African historical religion and Christianity. Thus he has continuously inspired my own work along these lines. I am very grateful for his generous advice and criticism towards the production of the present volume. Particularly, his encouragement as well as his profound personal interest in the complex problems involved enabled me to overcome, to some extent, the difficulties attending the writing of the most difficult part of this collection, the introduction.

Robert J. Papstein, Maud Muntemba, Keith Rennie and Marcia Wright were at crucial stages in my own research engaged in similar work and, as historians, helped me to ask what still appear to be the right sort of question. Jean-Loup Calmettes made available to me his various writings on the Lumpa Church; although our views continue to differ, the postscript I added to my Lumpa study makes sufficiently clear how much I benefited from this exchange. With his knowledge of the religion of Zimbabwe and Botswana, and his efforts to rescue African religious studies from the dead-ends of single-tribe approaches and naïve correspondence theory, Richard Werbner has been a most stimulating critic of my work ever since 1974.

Another network of intellectual exchange I have been fortunate to draw upon was that of the Amsterdam Work-Group for Marxist Anthropology, comprising Simon Simonse, Klaas de Jonge, Peter Geschiere, Jos van der Klei, Reinie Raatgever and Johan van der Walle, in addition to myself; most of these are or were my colleagues at the Afrika-Studiecentrum. It is to this Work-Group's collective efforts that I am largely indebted for such Marxist overtones as my approach has acquired in recent years.

Although I (and they themselves) have moved a long way from the anthropology they taught me in the 1960s, this list would not be complete without acknowledgment of the great intellectual and personal debts I owe to my teachers at the University of Amsterdam, foremost André Köbben, Douwe Jongmans, and Jeremy Boissevain. Bonno Thoden van Velzen was still a very young lecturer, and I a first-year student, when we were engaged in a formal teacher/student relationship at that same university. But whenever our paths crossed in later years (in Lusaka, 1972 and for the ASA work on regional cults), I have benefited from his sound judgment, inspiring discussions, and friendship; I am therefore grateful for his recent critical contributions towards the production of this volume.

Finally, I wish to thank Franc Knipscheer, Henrik Barends and D. Allen for their editorial and graphical contributions to this book.

Two chapters had already been dedicated in their original form: one to Max Gluckman, who helped me formulate a crucial dimension of my research and who died shortly after the first draft of chapter 6 had been written; and one to Jack Simons, whom a common colleague at the University of Zambia aptly described as 'an ageing South African exile, a bull of a man who I understand is still breathing fire and brimstone upon the tragical and farcical situation in these troubled parts of Africa' (P.O. Nsugbe, in *African Social Research*, no. 24, December 1977, p. 340). It is striking that both Gluckman and Simons should be white South Africans by birth, loyal interpreters of modern African life by profession, and left-wing activists by political and moral conviction. They are examples of the type of Africanist scholar a non-African in the 1970s might aspire to be.

Dedicating the volume as a whole is a different matter, though. However much this collection developed out of an intellectual exchange whose co-ordinates I have attempted to outline in this preface (so as to discuss its substance in the Introduction), its most fundamental inspiration lies elsewhere: in a few hauntingly vivid images dating mainly from the early stages of my Zambian research. These images have been with me ever since, forcing me time and again to return to the inspiration, and the intellectual and emotional puzzles, which the confrontation with contemporary Zambian religion produced in me, a European apostate Christian:

After nightfall, together on one tiny Honda moped, my assistant and I arrive at the outskirts of an outlying Lusaka squatter compound, in order to meet the leader-founder of an independent Christian church. We are welcomed by the leader's brother, himself a senior official in the church. Through the darkness (no street-lights here, of course), across puddles and a muddy path, and somewhat surprised at the tranquillity of the place and the absence of passers-by, we are taken up to the house, where after prayer we conduct a first interview, in an incredible atmosphere of serenity, wisdom and warmth.

In the early morning, while some members of the audience are still asleep and others are too drunk to pay attention, the drums start again in the middle of the fenced yard – in another squatter compound, by now fully familiar to me. Mary and Jenita, the two young women we have got to know best among the urban Nkoya, have been engaged in possession dancing throughout the night, with a short break during the last few hours before dawn. Now they make up to reach the paroxysms of ecstasy, through violent bodily rhythms, their faces distorted with what looks like immense fear more than anything else, their bare breasts shaking wildly, the fly-switch in their hands beating in the air. Their legs and knees furrow in the soil, as they slowly advance in a kneeling position. Then, when their crisis has subsided, we all line up and squeeze, one after the other, the juice from sacred, boiled waterlily leaves onto their bare backs and breasts – thus collectively acknowledging, as it were, the cathartic drama they have just gone through, and sharing responsibility for it.

In her house at the fringe of Matero township, during a first interview again, the widow of the prophet Simbinga unties a cloth in which, for twelve years, she has kept her deceased husband's sacred paraphernalia. Squatting beside us, she displays the items on the floor, and explains their meaning and origin with almost clinical precision. The afternoon light filters through the door and the small window. From outside, the sounds of the compound penetrate, including the noise of heavy motor traffic on the tar road adjacent to the house. Her children enter the room: a relative has arrived from the rural areas, with vegetable produce she has to sell for him. She

11

efficiently deals with these interruptions and returns to work with us.

And the most powerful memory of them all:

At Mindolo Ecumenical Centre, working through some forgotten file of newspaper clippings on the Lumpa rising, I realize for the first time the full extent of the Lumpa tragedy, when I hit upon a newspaper photograph of a missionary we have befriended in the previous months. Perceptibly younger, he is shown carrying away from the battlefield a small child whose mother, a Lumpa adherent, has been killed in battle with state troops, only minutes before the picture was taken.

Very little of the intensity of these and similar personal, emblematic images pierces through the academic surface of the studies in this collection. Some of my other articles, and particularly my books of poetry, are less reticent on these points. Yet, on looking back I can see this volume as the result of a persistent effort to create, in the idiom of scientific analysis, discursive arguments whose complexity and originality at least does some justice to the existential force underlying both Zambian religious innovation and my own experiences with it. Erecting, within these pages, small memorial shrines for such great visionaries as Mupumani and Simbinga, it seems proper to dedicate the book as a whole to the memory of the greatest prophetess Zambia has yet seen, Alice Lenshina Mulenga. And this I would have done, were it not that such a gesture would most likely be mistaken for an act of paternalism, if not betrayal (for I am a UNIP member myself), in the eyes of the bureaucratic bourgeoisie with whom her church fought a final battle. Tragic as this episode was, and puzzlingly ambiguous when assessed in terms of class struggle (see below, Postscript to chapter 8), this should not blind us to the very real positive achievements of Lenshina, and of the category of Central African religious innovators to which she belonged. They had the courage and the vision to use and reshape symbolic material so as to redefine the world fundamentally, both conceptually and through action. Thus their significance transcends the obvious limitations of their communities, and becomes paradigmatic for the predicament, and the potential, of modern man. Although we cannot adopt their solutions, we may yet derive inspiration, and hope, from their efforts.

Amsterdam, June 1979

Chapter 1

Introduction: Towards a theory of religious change in Central Africa[1]

The background of the present studies

In the early 1970s, when I started my research into Central African religious change, this field of enquiry was in what we might call a state of 'great expectations'. It was the time when established anthropological and historical approaches to Africa were beginning to be challenged by new work pursuing new questions with a combination of old and new data.

Anthropology had become fully aware of the limitations of single-tribe studies, but was still looking for a theory and a method capable of dealing with the unmistakable regional similarities, the permutations of a limited number of recurrent structural themes, as emerging from the accumulation of anthropological work done on specific areas and subcontinents. The method of cross-cultural comparison[2] seemed to offer one possible solution. It attempted to itemize the societal elements identified at a given place and time, and to compare their distribution across societies, apparently without challenging the assumptions (usually holistic and structural-functionalist) underlying the original descriptions of such items in the single-tribe monographs they had been gleaned from. Regional studies calling for a less mechanical and more structural approach to the problem of societal comparison were not lacking, particularly not in the field of Central and Southern African studies,[3] but they had not yet proceeded far beyond the stage of programmatic statements and tentative explorations. Comprehensive, more-than-single-tribe anthropological studies of Central African *religion* were virtually absent, although the few studies dealing with urban religion[4] reflected the fact that Central African towns were of multi-ethnic composition.

Through its association with the Rhodes-Livingstone Institute and its post-Independence heir (the Institute for Social Research, later Institute for African Studies, University of Zambia, Lusaka), Max Gluckman's Manchester School dominated Zambian social research. Whatever the strengths and weaknesses of the evolving Manchester approach,[5] it had no strong interest in religion, nor in regional studies. No doubt, this research tradition did produce several deservedly classic analyses of a single rural religious system in Central Africa.[6] But however brilliant these contributions were, they were conceived within the framework of a unique local social structure, whose similarities with the structures prevailing in adjacent geographical areas were hardly investigated. And while synchronic comparison was ignored, these religious studies would also hesitate to explore the historical dimensions of the religious phenomena they dealt with, or to interpret the synchronic material in a context of social change.[7] Such depth as Manchester religious studies achieved lay in their tracing of ramifications of religious phenomena within the overall structure of local group processes, or (especially in the case of Turner) in the unprecedented exploration of fundamental patterns of ritual and symbolism which, from the purely local, immediately proceeded to a universal human plane (colour symbolism, liminality, the opposition between 'structure' and 'communitas'), regardless of historical or regional communalities. Meanwhile, the intensive coverage of Zambia by anthropological research, coupled with the significance of religious phenomena in many aspects of Zambian life during the colonial and post-colonial period, produced an abundance of shorter anthropological discussions of aspects of religion in Zambia – many of which will be referred to in the present book.

In the field of history, around 1970 the transition took place from a Central African historiography still largely based on documentary evidence, to one in which a variety of non-documentary sources (derived from archeology, linguistics, the examination of ethnographic distribution patterns, and particularly oral evidence) enables us to chart areas and periods for which no written records are available. Documentary historiography had produced some insights into aspects of religion in Zambia during the colonial period.[8] However, the scope of these studies was limited, and as pioneer studies they were still unable to analyse convincingly forms of missionary or independent Christianity against the context of evolving economic and political structure of colonial society, or to make the link with non-Christian Central African religious forms. In these respects the earlier Zambian studies were inferior, both to Shepperson and Price's classic on Malawi, *Independent African*, and to Zimbabwean studies appearing around 1970: Murphree's analysis of contemporary Shona religion, and especially Daneel's masterly *Old and New in Shona Independent Churches.*[9]

In 1971 Werner,[10] preparing for historiographic field-work in the extreme north-east of Zambia, published a seminal article in which he tried to reconstruct processes of change in pre-colonial Bemba religion, on the basis of such documentary sources as were then available. By that time a few other historians had already begun to conduct intensive oral-historical research in Zambia.[11] Although none of them concentrated on religion, they produced the first tentative and necessarily crude analyses of the changes the historical religious systems in this part of Africa might have undergone prior to colonial times.[12] The most brilliant of these researchers, Roberts, did not concentrate much on religion, but happened to be doing field-work in north-eastern Zambia at the time of the Lumpa rising; his analysis of the history of Lumpa[13] is one of the most comprehensive and sophisticated studies yet to appear not only on the Lumpa church but also on religious innovation in Zambia in general.

Specific historical field-work into aspects of the pre-colonial religious history of Zambia was undertaken only after 1970.[14] These projects were greatly influenced by Terence Ranger, who in the period 1969–74 was the recipient of a Ford Foundation grant for the development of African religious research. Ranger organized a number of eminently successful and inspiring conferences; interested some of his PhD students in religion and related topics; founded and virtually filled the pages of the excellent though short-lived journal *African Religious Research*; and through numerous articles, conference papers and reviews kept the world constantly informed of the new and exciting advances that were being made in this field. His own major contribution to the development of Central and Southern African religious studies prior to the early 1970s was his full-length study of *Revolt in Southern Rhodesia 1896–1897,*[15] based on colonial archives. In this study he developed some of the themes which were to provide paradigms and objects for criticism for a decade or more:[16] the model of a centrally organized southern African High God cult of considerable scope and antiquity; the identification of the religious basis of colonial protest, and of colonial protest in religious movements; and the persistence and resilience of historical African religious institutions, despite the imposition of colonial rule, the advent of Christianity, and (as one would phrase it in the 1970s) the penetration of capitalism.

By 1972, when unpublished papers of several of Ranger's conferences were frantically being circulated, and the Lusaka conference was imminent, the first volume to come out of these conferences was published: *The Historical Study of African Religion*.[17] The title sounded like a programme, and was meant to. It was the contention of the editors that African religious systems did not represent undifferentiated 'traditional beliefs', but instead had a rich and traceable history; and the time had come to try to write that history. The book was a proud statement of such advances as had recently been made in the field of non-documentary historiography. On the other hand, many of the contributions showed how scarce the data still were, and how difficult it was to make sense of them.

Not surprisingly, many of the tentative models employed to organize and interpret the data had an anthropological origin. Turner's approaches to symbolism and ritual were discussed by Shorter, Alpers, Posnansky and Ranger and Kimambo;[18] Lewis's studies of spirit possession and peripheral cults, and Beattie and Middleton's attempts at systematizing similar material,[19] were likewise advertised by the editors of *The Historical Study of African Religion*;[20] so was Horton's intellectualist theory of African conversion, and of African religious change in general.[21] De Heusch's structural approach to myths formed a major inspiration for Gilsenan's discussion of the historical analysis of African myths.[22] Finally, Marcia Wright could set her more historical approach to Nyakyusa political leadership against the models developed by the Wilsons.[23] Significantly, out of the fourteen contributors to *The Historical Study of African Religion* only seven were originally trained as historians; and of the remaining seven, three were anthropologists – who together contributed four papers. A study of African religion was developing where the historically-minded anthropologist could feel at home; where the models and theories of his discipline were eagerly but not uncritically welcomed as possible aids towards the structuring of the gigantic tasks the historians had set for themselves; and where the anthropologists were tempted to explore geographical expanses and time depths of a scope and perhaps relevance that contrasted favourably with what had become almost routine anthropological research in one or other thoroughly mapped rural backwater in post-colonial Africa.

For despite all the specificity of the historical and ethnographic data, it was clear that the patterns which slowly emerged from painstaking data collection and exciting debate were seldom entirely confined to the period and the small part of Africa covered by any single field-work project. It could hardly have been mere perspectival distortion that led to the recognition of broad similarities in process and structure over large areas and long time-spans. Ranger contributed even more than his enthusiasm, organizing skill, elegance of style, dexterity in summarizing, and access to funds. By constantly searching for, reporting on, and commenting on patterns which to him seemed to have a wider than merely local occurrence,[24] he continued to inspire and partly direct the complex debate to which anthropologists could contribute as much as historians, political scientists, and missiologists, and of which the present book is one of the outcomes.

This was the background against which the earliest studies in the present book (chapters 2 and 3) were conceived. Since I have actively participated in the subsequent developments in the study of Zambian religious change during the 1970s, there is little need to trace these developments at this point in my argument. Such more recent work as is directly relevant for the present book will be discussed in the polemical parts of this Introduction, and throughout the other chapters. However, my aim is certainly not to write a representative review of the entire field; and since not all religious studies deal primarily with religious change, some of the significant recent work on central African religion falls outside the scope of this book.[25]

Possible anthropological contributions to the study of Central African religious change

Within the context sketched in the preceding section, what could be the contribution of the anthropologist? The papers collected in the present volume suggest three major dimensions: the examination of historically-relevant distribution patterns of ethnographic traits; the development of new or better conceptual and analytical tools; and the development of theoretical models of religious change.

There is, however, a fourth dimension, which is much less stressed in this book but which yet most anthropologists and historians working on African religion would consider crucial: the anthropologist's ability to act as a medium through which the religious concepts of African people are made accessible to a western-educated audience, in Africa and elsewhere. Patterns of distribution, analytical tools and theoretical models of change are all rather remote from the immediate reality of the participants' experience and conceptualizations. The anthropologist, through his techniques of participant observation and interviewing, through the intimacy with a particular community which he builds up over his years of field-work, is in a position to describe and translate these immediate data on African religion, and to explain the significance they have for the participants themselves – before these data become systematized, and more likely than not violated, in the process of scientific generalization and abstraction.

Throughout the chapters of this book, my emphasis is on such generalization and abstraction. In so far as I, as an anthropologist, have insights to offer on Central African religion, these insights are mainly on the level of the contextualization of this religion, i.e. the way it operates within a wider social, political and economic field. Contrary to many studies of African religion, there is little to be found here in the way of an intra-religious symbolic analysis, and then only in so far as religious symbols can be argued to have specific, detectable relations with that wider field.[26] Yet, like Turner,[27] we do well to heed Monica Wilson's reminder that 'any analysis not based on some translation of the symbols used by people of [a specific] culture is open to suspicion'.[28] Therefore, while accepting the limitations which my approach to African religion so manifestly contains, I shall have to come back to the problems of symbolic translation in the course of this introductory chapter. But let us first consider what an anthropologist's contribution to the problem of contextualization might consist of.

Examination of distribution patterns of ethnographic traits

The simplest anthropological contribution would be extracting, from the existing anthropological literature, the scattered and fragmentary references to religion and religious change as are available in abundance. When we collate these fragments so as to form broad distributional patterns, it is most likely that systematic similarities and differences emerge that lend themselves to historical interpretation.[29] I followed this approach in chapters 3 and 4, where I traced the geographical and historical distribution of various types of shrine cults, prophetic movements, and cults of affliction. The systematic patterns which became visible could be interpreted through an analogy with geological layers that have been formed one after the other.

In contemporary rural society, various religious sub-systems exist side by side. They revolve around different, mutually irreducible conceptions of the supernatural (ancestors, spirits of the wilds, alien affliction spirits, the High God, the evil powers of sorcerers); and around mutually fairly unrelated forms of religious organization (various more or less permanent and more or less local structures of religious inter-action, ranging from the *ad hoc* relationship between the healer and patient, via local and inter-local congregations such as involved in cults of affliction and prophetic cults, to fully-fledged Christian church organizations). A first step towards historical interpretation of this synchronic pattern is: to interpret the *horizontal* co-occurrence of these sub-systems as a *vertically layered* composite structure, where each layer (characterized by a specific type of supernatural entity, specific ritual and specific organization) represents a complex that is *historically* distinct from the other main layers or strata. The ancestral cult is an example of one such stratum. The next step is to trace the wider distribution over the geographical region or sub-continent – not of the total combined structure comprising several religious strata, but of each stratum separately. The third step would be to assign a particular time depth to each stratum, and to explain the succession of these strata in time.

Exciting as the exercise is, and encouraging as I think the results are in the case of chapters 3 and 4, a major difficulty is, of course, that one deals essentially with synchronic material, collected mainly during the present century. As Gwyn Prins writes in a recent methodological article, inspired by historiographic research in western Zambia:[30]

> The principal methodological obstacle looming before each historian who seeks to understand social dynamics over time is to know where he may and where he may not legitimately *extrapolate* backwards from the perceivable *present* form of the society in his interpretation of archival and oral materials.

The methodological problems involved are so formidable that one might shun any attempt at historical analysis along these lines. Take for example ancestral worship as I studied it in the 1970s among the Nkoya people of central western Zambia.[31] Established anthropological theory offers us an interpretational framework within which this religious complex can be meaningfully linked to economic, residential and political relations within the local rural community. As will be clear from chapters 3 and 4, the Nkoya ethnographic pattern is strikingly similar to that described for other groups in western Zambia. In the present volume, I treat ancestral worship as a particularly ancient layer in Central African religion, part of an ideal-typical primordial situation (in itself only the end-product of many millennia of religious change). In the course of the second half of the present millennium, chiefly cults, cults of affliction, prophetic cults, etc. were superimposed upon this ancestral layer, in close association with processes of state formation, the growth of long-distance trade and the penetration of capitalism. But what was the historical form of ancestor worship, 'before everything started to change'? For lack of good historical information, we are prompted to assume, as a working hypothesis, that this form was basically that of contemporary ancestor worship. To calm our protesting conscience, we might try to delete from our model of ancestor worship any elements that manifestly refer to contemporary conditions. For example, it is only recently that offerings of meal and beer are dispensed from enamel receptacles imported from the People's Republic of China. Beyond these superficialities, we must search intently for signs (in the ritual, symbolism, and cultic organization) of inconsistencies and contradictions that might be suggestive of heterogeneous historical elements within the same overall institution.

So far I have been unable to detect any in contemporary Nkoya ancestor worship. The contemporary institution is concerned with kinship obligations and morality within the small local group. It emphasizes hunting as a way to communicate with nature as well as with the ancestors. The hunter's luck or failure is taken as an indication of how the ancestors feel about him: and when confronted with a choice that is crucial to the life of the local group (e.g., acceptance or rejection of a particular candidate for village headmanship), the sex of an animal killed by a hunter is held to convey the ancestors' decision. Both the consistency of the institution as a whole and its relative insulation from more recently emerged economic concerns that have come to play a considerable role in village life today (cash cropping, labour migration) do suggest that here we are actually dealing with an archaic and not fundamentally transformed institution. But this remains only a working hypothesis, and a very doubtful one.[32] In the Nkoya case, the availability of oral traditions[33] which, in passing and without contextual emphasis, mention village shrines and ancestral ritual, does provide some slight corroboration for this hypothesis – but what if these traditions, collected in modern times just like the ethnographic distribution data, simply project contemporary ritual complexes into the past? Moreover, there is firm evidence that twentieth-century forms of religious innovation directed attacks against the institution of ancestor worship in western Zambia.[34] On the one hand this seems to confirm the archaic nature of this institution; but on the other hand it is unlikely that under the force of these attacks the institution retained a perfect elasticity, ready to resume its historical form once these attacks had subsided. All we can do is to formulate the hypothesis of essential continuity explicitly in the case of ancestor worship; build this hypothesis into our models of religious change; and continue our quest for data which would upset our hypothesis, as well as for theory which may lead us beyond this unfortunate methodological position.[35]

A related methodological problem, equally essential for a historical analysis based on an examination of ethnographic patterns of distribution, goes back to Galton's famous dilemma in cross-cultural comparison.[36] Comparative anthropologists have, since Tylor, struggled with the idea that similarities between institutions might not spring from similarity between attending social-structural conditions in the distinct societies within which these institutions were encountered; for they might also spring from common historical origins, and have diffused across structurally different societies. For purposes of historical reconstruction, we would tend to reverse the argument and ask: if in a synchronic analysis we find a cluster of neighbouring societies having similar religious forms (e.g., ancestor worship of the western Zambian pattern), may we really presume a common underlying historical layer, or should the similarities be explained mainly by reference to similar social-structural conditions obtaining in all these societies? Specifically, if in the twentieth century the Nkoya, Ndembu, Kaonde, Luvale, Tonga, Lamba, etc. can all be shown to have similar ancestral cults, can we then safely presume the existence of a common underlying historical pattern?

There is a well-defined alternative. Similar overall transformations have worked upon these different peoples: the introduction of a world religion inimical to ancestor worship; incorporation of local village communities focusing on ancestral shrines, in a much wider social formation defined by tributary and capitalist modes of production. Why not maintain that these similar transformations produced a similar end-product (twentieth-century ancestor worship) on the basis of what, several centuries ago, may have been very different institutions of ancestral veneration? Convergence of historically dissimilar cultural forms under the impact of capitalist and colonial transformations is by no means exceptional in Central Africa. We only need to cite the case of Zambian chieftainship. There is evidence[37] that the pre-colonial forms of political leadership showed very considerable variation; yet the external form of the incapsulated, neo-traditional chieftainship in colonial (and post-colonial) Zambia has become rather similar throughout the country, since it was defined by colonial and post-colonial political and economic structures emanating from and controlled by the centre, more than by local historical institutions in the periphery.

In the light of these methodological difficulties, perhaps we had better abandon the attempt to arrive at historical insights through the analysis of ethnographic distributions. The position adopted in this book is a more audacious, if more risky one. In an exploratory phase, methodological problems should not be ignored; our methodological choices should be made explicit, especially when they are so elementary and naïve as those underlying my own analyses in chapters 3 and 4. Yet, having made these choices, for better or worse, let us proceed and see where they take us. Methodology should not be allowed to become an aim in itself. I am not betraying a secret when I say that even the most sophisticated and validated approaches in modern social science can, on close scrutiny, be shown to contain very major methodological flaws. The researcher has to strike a balance between the risk of committing methodological blunders, and the risk of letting excessive methodological concern paralyse his conceptual and theoretical imagination.

Sharpening our tools

Even before the anthropologist can set out to contribute to the analysis of religious change by an examination of patterns of ethnographic distribution, he has to define the phenomena whose distribution in time and space he is to analyse. In this connexion it is good to realize that anthropologists' style of definition tends to differ from historians'. Whereas many anthropologists would attempt to arrive at definitions that are sufficiently abstract to transcend a particular social group and a particular period (though seldom his own!), many historians would find such definitions have little meaning, and would suggest that it is precisely within a specific historical setting that a particular phenomenon under study defines itself. Both approaches have their advantages and disadvantages. The anthropologist may become over-confident of his definition, and include qualitatively different phenomena into a single category on the basis of superficial, nominal similarities. The historian, on the other hand, may become so engrossed in the logic of a phenomenon at one specific place and time, that comparison is virtually ruled out.

In the studies presented in this volume, there appears to be a gradual shift from more strictly anthropological definitions, to definitions taking into account the specificity of historical settings, and the historical processes to which the defined phenomena themselves have been subject; the definition of religion is a case in point.[38] However this may be, throughout the book there is a constant concern with definition. The models I try to evoke by a combination of concepts thus defined, may soon be supplanted by better ones (which is what these models are meant for in the first place). Yet the many definitions propounded throughout this book, and the typologies derived from them, are useful, perhaps necessary, tools for the analysis of Central African religious change. The main analytical concepts thus drawn into the orbit of my analysis are the following: cult of affliction, shrine, shrine cult, chiefly cult, territorial cult, regional cult, possession, mediumship, prophet, High God, mode of production, and articulation.[39] Few of these definitions are entirely original. But I have tried to adapt them to the specific requirements of theory and evidence which my topic posed. They are at the root of the theoretical models to which we shall now turn.

The search for theoretical models

In his stimulating methodological article already quoted above, Prins claims: 'Since African history began to be produced in quantity one-and-a-half academic generations ago, there have rarely been shortages of new explanatory theory'.[40]

Looking at the study of Central African religious change, I think this statement calls for considerable qualification. Where is all the explanatory theory here? Admittedly, in my overview of developments up to the 1970s I could cite a number of anthropological approaches which were beginning to have an impact on historiography. But few of these were sufficiently comprehensive in scope to illuminate the patterns that were becoming manifest in the data, or to reveal, with considerable time depth and geographical extension, patterns that previously had not yet been recognized. The studies collected in this book have been written in order to provide such models, where previously there were virtually none.

If this is the major contribution an anthropologist could hope to make to the study of Central African religious change, it seems to derive from his possessing systematic models of how real societies 'work'; and how real human actors, in social settings, tend to act. Evidence on Central African religious history is fragmentary and scattered. New and more systematically collected material is unlikely to be unearthed, unless we have made up our minds as to the direction in which we should look. This requires the formulation of explicit models in which the available data, which in themselves are too defective to conjure up a total picture, are fitted, at strategic points, into an otherwise hypothetical construction. The extent to which the construction makes sense can be assessed by application of common methodological and theoretical tools which general anthropology can offer. The extent to which this construction can be taken as a plausible model of actual historical processes depends on the extent to which available fragments of evidence can be accommodated within the construction. The procedure is similar to that of an archeologist trying to reconstruct the most likely form of an earthen vessel of which only a few tiny sherds have been dug up. Most of his reconstructed model may consist of contemporary modelling clay, but the few actual sherds must be made to fit smoothly into the curvature of the reconstructed vessel, and the model's overall shape must be moulded in accordance with general archeological insights concerning the area and period from which the sherds are likely to derive. A combination of craftsmanship, imagination, courage and scepticism is what is required for this sort of undertaking.

In this book I have tried to fit a handful of potsherds relative to Central African religious change into a succession of more or less likely models. The formulation, testing out, and revision of these models constitute the book's main substance. Hence, there is probably no better way of introducing the book than a discussion, chapter by chapter, of the main models brought to bear upon the data. This will also offer the opportunity to discuss wider theoretical and polemical issues.

Evolving models of Central African religion and religious change

Beyond deprivation

The earliest study in this book (chapter 2) was primarily intended as a terminological and theoretical exercise, in which I pulled together the scattered material on possession and mediumship in Zambia. The theoretical model examined in that study is the structural-functional interpretation of the relation between religion and the society in which that religion occurs, as either a relation of correspondence, or one of compensation. The deprivation thesis is one of the most common forms in which religious analysis stressing compensation is cast. The thesis claims that people, particularly in a context of rapid social change, would adopt a particular form of religious behaviour so as to find compensation for deprivation they are experiencing in secular life. Contrary to views rather popular in the 1960s and early 1970s,[41] I claimed that the deprivation hypothesis was not a meaningful way of dealing with possession, mediumship or cults of affliction in Central Africa.

After a discussion of the theoretical deficiencies of the deprivation thesis, that chapter offers an overview of the available material on possession and mediumship in Zambia, and indicates ways in which this material might be used to gain historical insights. Much of the research programme formulated there was actually filled in by my subsequent studies as presented in this book.[42] In the meantime, satisfied with my dismissal of the deprivation interpretation of possession phenomena, I did not yet re-examine the data in the light of new insights coming up in the literature. While possession may have little to do with deprivation as consciously experienced by the possessed, yet there are various indications now for a relation between possession and *domination*; or, as McKillop Wells puts it in a recent paper, 'interaction with non-familial groups which impinge on individual autonomy'.[43] Similarly, Bourgignon[44] and Greenbaum[45] have offered cross-cultural comparisons of the standard Murdock/Human Relations Area Files type, in which it was suggested that the occurrence of possession beliefs is associated with the level of complexity and rigidity of society, and the occurrence of social stratification. Already in 1970 Mary Douglas,[46] not an admirer of deprivation theory herself, made tentative remarks in the same direction. A fresh look at the history of Central African possession and cults of affliction along these lines might still produce interesting results, particularly since they can now proceed beyond the mechanical superficiality of cross-cultural statistics. However, this is a line of enquiry I did not pursue.

Shrines, chiefs and myths

Having thus familiarized myself with some of the data on Zambian religious change, I could then, in the later articles, explore the extent to which other models could illuminate the problems which the deprivation thesis apparently left unsolved.

Turning to an analysis of shrine cults in Zambia, I faced the double task of accounting for the ubiquitous occurrence of individual and village shrines, and explaining the more limited geographical distribution of royal or chiefly shrines in this part of Africa. My earlier work on popular-Islamic shrine cults in Tunisia[47] had made me aware of the fact that there was virtually no systematic anthropological theory of shrines, and of cults focusing on shrines. Several years later, the ASA monograph *Regional Cults*[48] was to mark the beginning of a collective attempt, by several more or less prominent scholars in the field of religious anthropology, to formulate such a theory. My ventures in chapter 3 could not have been but very preliminary. Yet I managed to throw some light on the ecological aspects of shrines (i.e., aspects concerning man's relations with nature, through hunting, agriculture, doctoring, etc.); on the communal aspects of shrines within the village community; and on the political aspects peculiar to higher levels of inter-community organization.

The concept of royal shrines serving political legitimation of rulers (by providing foci of their claims to ritual authority over the land, its fertility, and meteorological events, as well as manifesting their legitimate links with the previous incumbents of their office) had been a recurrent theme in the Central African studies available at the time.[49] However, in order to construct a model of the emergence of these royal, ecological shrine cults, I had to contrast them with a non-royal pattern as described by Colson[50] for the Tonga, and by Smith and Dale, and Jaspan, for the Ila.[51] Application of the model of a non-royal, inter-local shrine cult as described for North Africa by Gellner,[52] suggested some of the political implications of the non-royal cults, and helped me to appreciate the changes brought by the introduction of royal cults. Thus, both the underlying similarity, and the specific regional differences in the Zambian material could be fitted into a single historical model.

This model hinged on a postulated conflict over ritual authority between aspirants to political leadership who came in from parts of the Central African savanna closer to the equatorial forest in the north, and shrine priests administering pre-existing inter-local shrine cults. My argument does not conceal the fact that in the Zambian case the evidence for these inter-local priestly cults, and for the priest/ruler confrontation, is slight and largely circumstantial. The immigration of militant small groups trying to impose a new political style seemed at the time a well-established historical fact.[53] Vansina's masterly synthesis of Central African history[54] was still being used as a key text. Since then various critical studies have called for a less literal and more symbolic interpretation of the oral traditions,[55] have advocated a revision of Vansina's too shallow chronology, and have proposed to view the Luba-Lunda diaspora not so much as a circulation of actual people, but as a circulation of prestigious titles and political ideas.[56]

26

These debates were still gaining momentum when chapter 3 was written. Nor have these debates yet led to some sort of agreement. Meanwhile, my own subsequent work on oral traditions from western Zambia, and its convergence with, e.g., Papstein's work on north-western Zambia,[57] confirms my view that the reconstruction as offered in chapter 3 is still tenable, and can certainly still serve the heuristic purposes for which it was primarily meant.

The model of chiefly encroachment upon pre-existing territorial cults primarily derived from areas of Central Africa outside Zambia. In Malawi, Zimbabwe and Zaïre the evidence for such intrusion is extensive, and convincing.[58] More seems involved here than an accidental lack of data, in the Zambian case. It would appear as if the new, chief-centred political and religious structures which came to be superimposed upon the territorial organizational structures of Central Africa, in Zambia somehow managed to gain a stronger hold, supplanted the pre-existing structures more fully than in the surrounding areas. In chapter 3 I argue that among the Zambian Tonga and Ila, chiefly penetration was far less successful, and non-chiefly territorial cults survived to a far greater extent, than in other parts of Zambia; and tentatively I attribute this not to the weakness or remoteness, but to the viability and strength of ecological and economic structures prevailing in the Ila and Tonga areas in the second half of the present millennium. What the immigrant prospective chiefs brought was not only new conceptions of political office and ritual, but also and primarily, new relations of production: a tributary mode of production within which the surpluses of direct producers in the village communities would be expropriated and used to keep up royal establishments and tributary networks between aristocrats.[59] What were the differences, in relations of production and in productive forces (ecological conditions, agricultural and hunting techniques, available manpower, etc.) between the Tonga and Ila areas on the one hand, and most of Zambia on the other? What were the similarities between the Tonga and Ila areas, and areas in Malawi, Zimbabwe, and Zaïre? Part of an answer seems to lie in the peculiar nature of relations of production in a cattle economy. At any rate, there is an obvious case here for further materialist analysis of the distributional patterns of Central African religion. My emphasis in chapter 3 on the ecological aspect of territorial cults foreshadowed such a materialist theory, but still lacked the theoretical framework required for consistent elaboration. The outlines of such a framework are presented in the later chapters. But first another theoretical model of African religious change must be discussed.

The shattered microcosm

In chapter 4 the major anthropological model employed (if largely implicitly) is that of Robin Horton's Intellectualist Theory of African religious change.[60] Horton's theory has been the subject of so much published debate[61] that a concise summary is sufficient here. For Horton, African religion is primarily an instrument with which people try to interpret the world; it is a theory of causation. The qualities attributed to the supernatural entities featuring in a religious system are analogous to the scope of the human life-world over which these entities are supposed to hold sway. Lesser spirits (ancestors, spirits of the wilds) belong to the microcosm of the household, the village, the small rural community. More formidable spirits are proper to larger organizational complexes: states, trade networks, the entire world as known to a local population. In the 'typical traditional cosmology' in Africa[62] a 'two-tiered arrangement of unobservables' obtained. The daily life of individuals was largely contained within the microcosm, and was considered to be administered by the lesser spirits. However, with the growth of trade, with state formation, and finally the imposition of colonial rule, the boundaries of the microcosm broke down and more people were, as part of their daily experience, involved in aspects of the macrocosm: as traders, slaves, migrants, soldiers, peasants whose production and consumption was involved (albeit peripherally) in large networks of tribute, trade, taxation, etc. Spirits of the macrocosm could rise to greater prominence. A shift towards ever more formidable and all-encompassing concepts of spirit was 'in the air' by the time the two world religions, Islam and Christianity, penetrated Africa effectively, introducing the monolatry of the High God, and supplanting the latter's previously otiose connotations by those of active presence and intervention. The success of the world religions in Africa was, according to Horton, largely attributable to the fact that they had come at just the right time.

Horton's theory was met with considerable enthusiasm among those working on African religious change. It tied in with ideological commitments which many Africanists shared at the time: the emphasis on essential continuity in African societies, where earlier studies had stressed so heavily the sharp break created by colonial rule and the introduction of a 'money economy', i.e. capitalism; and the emphasis on the African as actively shaping and reshaping his own social and ritual world – instead of being the mere recipient of ideas and commodities introduced from the metropolitan areas. There may have been a third undercurrent. Although Horton[63] is critical of what he calls

28

the 'devout opposition' of committed Christian scholars of African religion (including H. W. Turner, V. W. Turner, B. Idowu and E. Evans-Pritchard – he might have added M. Wilson[64]), yet a Christian audience (and Christians are still a majority among the contemporary students of African religion[65]) could derive comfort from a scholarly theory which, on apparently objective grounds, discovers that when all is said and done, Christianity (along with Islam, admittedly) constitutes the best option for modern Africa.

I certainly shared the first two commitments (but by no means the third) when, for my analysis of the dynamics of religious change in western Zambia, I constructed a model strikingly parallel to Horton's. Based on intensive participatory research into the contemporary religious scene of central western Zambia, augmented by comprehensive oral-traditional and archival research, my analysis showed a remarkable correspondence with Hortonian ideas, as Ranger pointed out.[66]

Chapter 4 discusses the major religious forms such as have manifested themselves in western Zambia during the twentieth century. These forms are then traced back in history. Chiefly cults are pictured as having imposed themselves upon the 'primordial village religion' (revolving on the interlocking concerns of production and illness, and taking shape in beliefs highlighting environmental spirits, ancestors, and sorcery[67]). A considerable variety of other religious forms enter into the picture: non-ancestral cults of affliction; prophets presenting new messages concerning the land, affliction, the imminent end of the world, or the High God; movements centring on the search for new medicines; the emergence, in the 1920s and 1930s, of preachers and dippers (advocates of ritual immersion) within or outside the wide-spread ideologies of popular African Watchtower and the *mchape* witch-cleansing movement; and finally the introduction of mission Christianity. What is added in typological scope and complex dynamics here, necessarily goes in at the expense of geographical scope and historical depth. Although there are minor excursions into adjacent areas and earlier periods, chapter 4 essentially deals with central western Zambia, from the late nineteenth century onwards.

The main argument of the chapter is that the many and apparently very different forms of religious innovation which occurred in that region in recent times have so much in common that they can be said to be aspects of the same, overall process of religious change, in which the religious system prevailing in the area in the nineteenth century is consistently redefined along at least five converging dimensions: the conception of time; the attitude *vis-à-vis* nature; the conception of dominant supernatural entities; the conception of community; and the explanation of evil in terms of sorcery. In a fashion not unlike that in which the argument in the present book develops from chapter to chapter, each new innovatory religious movement in western Zambia represents a further step along one or more or these five dimensions, often at the expense of such progress made by immediately preceding movements along one or more other dimensions. The process of religious change is shown to be *dialectical*, not always cumulative, faltering at times, but yet unmistakable and systematic when viewed in a somewhat wider regional and historical perspective. It is suggested that this overall process corresponds with processes of economic and political change well documented for the same period: the emergence of chiefly states, the imposition of colonial rule, the penetration of the capitalist economy through labour migration and the introduction of manufactured commodities.

The concrete mechanics of the relationship between these economic and political changes, and religious change, receive little specific discussion except the largely implicit reliance on the Hortonian scheme. None the less, an attempt is made to indicate social situations in which, as new steps in the overall process of religious change, new discrete innovatory movements are most likely to materialize. Thus, three categories of people are suggested to form a potential *avant-garde* of religious innovation: those who are, more than others, involved in the new economic and political opportunities that arise during the period covered; those who are, as religious specialists, more than others involved in the religious forms of a previous stage of religious innovation; and those who belong to segments of society previously oppressed and who now, under changing political and economic conditions, stir with the hope (initially expressed in a religious idiom) of improving their social position. Despite the thinness of the data, repeated attempts are made to reconstruct and understand the thought-processes of the people involved in these innovations – and the consciousness imputed to them has definite Hortonian overtones.

The approach to Central African religious change as presented in chapter 4 contrasts strongly with the main other elaborate model, as presented recently by De Craemer, Vansina and Fox.[68] The thrust of their model is clear from the following quotation:[69]

> The culture common to Central Africa that existed in precolonial times can be called 'classical'. Its core elements have remained remarkably intact in the face of the enormous changes that

Central Africa has undergone in the past century, which includes
the colonial and postcolonial periods. . . . The common religion
has been remarkably stable, perhaps for millenia. Specific religious
movements rise and fall over periods of time ranging from a
quarter to more than half a century. Changes in the membership
and organization of a movement occur; different time scales
are involved. Social scientists and historians who study such movements should specify both the nature of the change with which
they are dealing and its concomitant time scale. Statements with
regard to fundamental changes in the common religion should not
be made on the basis of short-term intervals, since this deep-seated,
comprehensive part of the cultural tradition changes very slowly.

Fernandez[70] sees the analysis of De Craemer *et al.* mainly as a
stronger statement of my own idea that 'the same symbolic materials
seem to be manipulated within narrow limits in diverse movements'.[71]
But the essential difference between my approach and theirs is that,
despite all continuity, and despite the essentially dialectical nature of
the process of religious change, in my view this process is far from
cyclical. On the contrary, there is a very real cumulation of change
along the five dimensions I have indicated, as is most vividly illustrated
by Table 4.1. The process displays much more irreversibility and
accretion that De Craemer *et al.* suggest – at least in western Zambia
in the nineteenth and twentieth centuries; but the innovations
recorded then and there show considerable parallels with the Zaïrese
material on which De Craemer *et al.* base their views.[72]
Of course I am flattered by Ranger's judgment, that[73]

Binsbergen's analysis remains the most fully worked out but
neither his western Zambian data nor his interpretation of it can
be regarded as idiosyncratic. It is becoming clear that the overall
process of religious and conceptual change in many other regions
of East and Central Africa has taken place in much the same sort
of way and moves in much the same sort of direction.

Yet the four chapters following chapter 4 do more than clarify or
extend specific elements of my overall analysis. Certainly, there is such
clarification and extension as well. Chapter 5 offers a much more
elaborate analysis of the dynamics of one particular class of religious
phenomena contained in the overall analysis of chapter 4: cults of
affliction, which are explicitly placed against the background of the
overall process of religious change. In chapter 6 and 7 I explore *urban*

31

cults of affliction in Zambia against partly the same background. And in chapter 8 I refer to this background in order to assess the innovatory originality, as well as the specific development, of the Lumpa Church, in a very different part of Zambia. But essentially these remaining four chapters represent attempts to go beyond the limitations of the Hortonian approach as pursued in chapter 4.

Some of the limitations of my overall analysis are at the empirical level, and can only be overcome by further data collection. One such problem is the periodization of cults of affliction. Various authors have claimed that in Central Africa cults of affliction are of great antiquity.[74] On the other hand, it is my contention that they are only a recent phenomenon in the specific form in whch they represent a dominant feature of the religion of central western Zambia in the late nineteenth and early twentieth centuries: the veneration, in non-communal congregations, of non-anthropomorphic illness-causing spirits endowed with connotations of alienness and foreign ethnic groups. All the evidence I collected in western Zambia points in that direction, as do the references in the literature.[75] However, further analysis is needed of the relations between these new cults of affliction and pre-existing possession cults associated with chiefs, diviners and spirits of the wilds, conceived within the local life-world and venerated on a communal basis. In western Zambia, the *muba* and *mayimbwe* cults seem to derive from this older stratum;[76] but they were subsequently transformed so as to become powerful cults of the new, non-communal idiom.

Still on the level of empirical data, a much more serious short-coming of my argument in chapter 4 is the following. Although I claim an overall process of religious change that has been going on for centuries, my evidence has only a time span of a century or less. What I analyse and project back into the past may very well have been the later stage of a development that was much more complex, erratic, and determined by chance circumstance as much as by systematic process. The point has been made repeatedly,[77] most recently by Ranger.[78] Ranger speaks of my argument in chapter 4 as[79]

> a bold attempt to pull together all the scattered data for religious change in Western Zambia, for a period when cults of affliction had lost their corporate character and cults of the earth were in danger of losing theirs.

Thus Ranger sees the process stipulated by my model as the end phase of a long historical development, about whose outlines he gleans suggestions from the oral-historical data provided by Vansina,[80] Miller,[81] Anne Wilson[82] and Janzen.[83] However, these various studies concern different areas far away from central western Zambia, and with considerable differences in the process of state formation and long-distance trade. (In western Zambia these processes gained momentum only during the nineteenth century.) The applicability of these studies to western Zambia may be more limited than Ranger is suggesting. Particularly, there is no reason to assume, as he does, that the cults of affliction I dealt with developed out of anything like the massive, corporate, in origin royal, *lemba* cult which Janzen described for lower Zaïre. All the same, it is necessary to extend the historical base of the argument in chapter 4 further into the past.

The new attempt at synthesis which Ranger presented in his 1979 paper developed not only out of dissatisfaction with the cyclical approach of De Craemer *et al.*,[84] but also out of a rethinking of the Hortonian implications of my own analysis as offered in chapter 4:[85]

[Van Binsbergen's] model of change was really derived from the idea of the transition from closed societies to open ones. In so far as one can begin to see outlines of historical change in Central African religion they suggest a less consistent, more particular, more fully *historical* set of processes.

I shall have to come back to this criticism towards the end of this introductory chapter, when we shall have considered the Marxist reformulation of the model presented in chapter 4 – a reformulation which would appear to be even more open to criticism, exposing elements of unilinear evolutionism, and the utilization of too simple societal ideologies. Meanwhile, the transition Ranger refers to here, is really at the root of the Hortonian analysis. Let us therefore review, at this point, some of the more theoretical questions which that approach raises.

The philosophical status of Horton's approach has been discussed at length by Skorupski.[86] Skorupski's argument makes only one passing reference[87] to Horton's specific theory of African religious change and conversion,[88] and anyway would deserve a much fuller treatment than I could accommodate within the confines of this introduction. But what Skorupski certainly makes clear is the limitation of an approach that stresses only the cognitive, intellectual, explanatory side of African religion, without paying systematic attention to symbolic representation and ritual. This ties in with Fernandez's criticism: he rebukes both

Horton's work[89] and my own[90] for imposing our own, western academic, 'imageless' thought upon the dynamics of African symbolic activity. What we do, Fernandez says,[91]

> is not intellectual enough because it ignores the dynamic relation of images and ideas – that is, it ignores how ideas are squeezed out of images and how they can be again embedded in them – and it ignores the difficult problem of the coding in thought of images and symbolic forms.

It would be difficult to disagree totally with Fernandez. Of course, what is really at the heart of African religion comes through only dimly in such comparative and synthetic model building as Horton and I myself have engaged in. These models are painfully far removed from the drama and intensity of African ritual, and of our own participatory field experiences with that ritual. But while we are sacrificing so much that is dear to us, are we not gaining something in return?

No one, perhaps, has come closer to an understanding of the synchronic symbolic dynamism of African religion in a rural context than Victor Turner in his writings on the Ndembu; just as few analyses of contemporary religious movements in urban Central Africa have reached the level of symbolic and perhaps existential penetration which characterizes the work of Jules-Rosette.[92] The sorts of insights offered there are not available in studies like Horton's and mine. But for an understanding of African religion we also need other sorts of insights, those having to do with the way in which observed, and lived-through, ritual and symbolism, at a given time and place, reflect broad historical processes which have affected a whole region or sub-continent. Such criticism of Turner's work as the present book contains is precisely on this point. While it is impossible to provide the insights Fernandez asks for, and which to some extent Turner's and Jules-Rosette's works do provide, without total immersion in the ritual and symbolic idiosyncrasies of one particular human group or one particular movement, it is equally impossible to arrive at the broader insights, with greater geographical scope and historical depth, without considerable abstraction from the specific ideas and symbols encountered in specific ethnographic settings. Perhaps the crudeness of Horton's and my own approach can be surmounted in future, as a result of more profound reflexion on the methodological and philosophical requirements of a 'history of symbols', and of a symbolic yet dynamic cross-cultural comparison of African religion. For the time being, I would not know how to confront the research tasks we have set ourselves, without recourse to analytical, 'etic', 'imageless' thought.

34

Yet the abstract and non-culture-specific statements we make about the structure and development of the religious ideas of the Africans we are writing about may be somewhat closer to what actually goes on in their minds, than Fernandez suggests:[93]

> In an earlier article[94] Horton recognized that statements about belief in Africa had to be taken from the occasions in which they were expressed. He recognized that belief as such was rarely volunteered and that it was through participation in events that men most often came to know and believe. He recognized that vehicles of problem solving in Africa were the various spiritual images, ghosts, demons, and magical objects in African religion. In his conversion argument he has abandoned these insights, becoming too converted to a 'philosophy of science' argument and too exclusively attentive to relatively rare occasions of volunteered thought. . . . [Here] we prefer the Horton of the 1960s.

Horton can speak for himself. But since Fernandez's criticism of my own work is in a similar vein, I take the freedom to point out the shortsightedness underlying his allegations. The synthetic models Horton and I have tried to build for African religious change are the work of people who for years have conducted participatory field-research into specific African religions. This background, the empathy it generates in the researcher's mind and heart, and the implicit aware-ness of underlying local concepts and structures of thought, are not suddenly abandoned when the same researchers try their hand at a synthesis extending, in time and place, beyond the confines of their field experiences. The existence of broad regional and historical patterns in African religion warrants that these specific field experiences are likely to have considerable relevance for a wider region and period than that in which they were thrust upon the researchers. Far from being (in this respect) the naïve, Eurocentric model-builders Fernandez takes us to be, I would submit that without the profound, prolonged, and in my case certainly traumatically existential exposure to field experiences, we would have been altogether incapable of arriving at our more synthetic views.[95]

Contrary to Fernandez's allegations, we are not estranged from[96]

> the intellectual . . . constituency that matters most, at least for the anthropologist whose primary constituency it is or should be . . . That constituency is the local one, the peoples and cultures who are the subjects of study. It is entirely possible that

35

conceptualizations which are ingrained within a Western intellectual tradition may not capture their imaginations.

It is possible. Yet (leaving aside the fact that one could not pursue *any* kind of anthropology *outside* a western intellectual tradition, for whether we like it or not anthropology is very much a part of that same tradition) I think that Fernandez underestimates the extent to which generalized, abstract statements such as found in Horton's and my synthesis, do yet (through the years of field-work that underpin them) reflect some of the basic orientations which local religious systems express, no doubt more adequately, in their local symbolic idiom, imagery, and ritual discourses.

The 'thought experiments' Horton speaks of, and which also occur throughout the present book, are not so much the projection of analytical thought into African religious systems, but rather the reformulation, in more general (and, I admit, analytical, i.e. 'image-less') terms, of principles which are, implicitly or explicitly, already part of these systems. Our analytical imagination is not that of the armchair anthropologist, but that of field-workers who (as all field-workers do all the time) apply and extrapolate such elements of the local system as they have already understood, in order to illuminate aspects of the local (or wider) system they do not yet understand, or lack specific data on. This has been my approach, for instance, when analysing the principles underlying Central African ecological shrines (chapter 3), the dynamics of witchcraft and sorcery in the context of new economic opportunities (chapter 4); or the problems of alienation and superstructural reconstruction (chapter 8). They are, to a considerable extent, generalizations from culture-specific insights, and from actual and lived-through social dramas, which were part of my Zambian field-work.

Admittedly, this approach is beset with enormous methodological problems. If our tentative analytical views derive from our personal (and probably idiosyncratic) internalization of an African local religious and social system, what checks are there on the plausibility of our interpretations, based on empathy and introspection as they partly are?

To come back to the problem of the translation of culture referred to earlier in this chapter, the point is not so much that we do not translate, but that we do not, in our published arguments, provide the 'raw' data (participants' vernacular terms, etc.) on the basis of which our translations could be checked and be found valid. For instance, in chapter 4 I trace the changing attitudes towards nature, and the changing concept of time, which I claim can be detected in ten forms of religious innovation in central western Zambia. Both 'nature' and 'time' are abstract analytical, western concepts which, *on the level of the symbolic contents of the religious forms described,* have no clear-cut equivalents in the Nkoya language (nor, probably, in any other western Zambian language as employed on the village level). So, while my argument does provide a symbolic analysis of some kind, it is an analysis performed not on the raw symbolic material as encountered in the field (the sort of material Turner has taught us to analyse), but on the 'processed' symbols, after translation, generalization, and abstraction. At the same time, it is only by virtue of this processing that we can compare the symbolic material of so many different religious forms, from several ethnic and linguistic western Zambian groups; and that we can detect an underlying similarity, the permutation of the same limited selection of symbolic material. I would maintain that, as a method of analysis, this approach is legitimate and leads to valuable insights. But I would be the first to admit that its underlying methodology should be made much more explicit, and that ultimately not just the results of the processing, but also the raw data should be presented.

This leads on to a further problem which I find extremely difficult to solve. The religious concepts and beliefs we are discussing in this book are largely those of illiterate people. These religious notions are not enshrined, standardized and immobilized in written texts, but have a strong situational aspect. As Fernandez rightly points out and as I myself stress repeatedly, they take shape, and alter, in concrete ritual actions mainly.[97] Such actions, and the religious notions which emanate through such actions, are therefore very specifically bound to concrete settings of time and place, to the relationships existing between the concrete people involved in a specific ritual situation, to the specific crises they go through, and to the creatively evolving symbolizing these people are engaged in. This means that it is already a very risky undertaking to make definite, comprehensive statements about the symbolic content of any one religious form, e.g., ancestor worship, or the Bituma cult, among the contemporary Nkoya – religious forms with which my field-work has familiarized me. Even on the level of a single-tribe study, a generalized ethnographic account of a symbolic system is likely to produce artefacts of abstraction and systematization, which are far removed from actual, dynamic ritual practice. Again, Turner's work, and especially *The Drums of Affliction,*[98] represents a sustained effort to overcome these difficulties. But at what hopeless level of extreme artificiality are we then operating if we attempt a regional and historical analysis of symbolic contents each of which is tied to the situational specificity of myriads of concrete social and ritual settings? And finally, how justified are we at all to project our ethnographic knowledge of any contemporary symbolic system back into the past?

It is important to make all these methodological problems explicit. Neither Horton's nor my own work comes yet anywhere near providing the methodological solutions that are so urgently required here. At the same time, this does not seem to make our tentative models entirely worthless. With the certainty that these models are based on a personal and empirical understanding of the dynamics, including situational aspects, of at least some concrete ritual settings in the regions we discuss, and thrilled by the deceptive illumination that even our present crude models can provide, we shall just have to keep working on methodological refinement.

Beyond the Intellectualist Theory of African religous change

My own growing dissatisfaction with a Hortonian approach to the study of Central African religious change clearly does not converge with Fernandez's. My criticism has to do not with religious images and ideas as such, but with their relation to aspects of social structure. And then I do not mean to contribute to the exchange between Ifeka-Moller[99] and Horton and Peel[100] on social-structural factors in African conversion to the world religions. What I am concerned with here is not the social-structural background which makes individuals adopt or reject a particular form of religious innovation. It is the social-structural requirements for such innovation itself.

The first point I wish to make is that, for a religious innovation to establish itself, it needs not only to satisfy the intellectual requirements such as posed by individual minds reflecting on the changing world order with which they are confronted. In addition, the new ideas and rituals have to surround themselves by new and viable forms of *religious organization.* The idea of alien, affliction-causing spirits does not automatically, through some process of logical deduction, lead to the specific non-regional cult organization characteristic of the new cults of affliction dealing with these spirits. Nor does the High God's rise to greater prominence really imply the creation of churches as organizational bodies, or (in the context of cults of affliction) the creation of centralized, hierarchically organized inter-local cult organizations like Nzila or early Bituma. The Intellectualist Theory has little to say on the organizational dimension of religious innovation.

Stimulated by the emerging theory of regional cults,[101] I grappled with this problem in chapter 5. In western Zambia, such cults as Nzila and Bituma were recently founded by prophets; they managed to build up (and partly retain) a very extensive regional hierarchical organization. These cults I showed as having developed out of a common and widespread substratum of non-prophetic non-regional cults of affliction. Under specific circumstances, which obtained in the case of Bituma, the prophetic cults virtually returned to this non-regional substratum. Under more favourable circumstances, however, a cult like Nzila was able to develop into a very large independent church. A comparison between the Nzila and Bituma cults of affliction, placed against the general context of religious innovation in the area, enabled me to discern some of the organizational dynamics involved, in relation to conceptual and ritual changes. I stressed, as background variables, on the one hand the leadership styles displayed by the prophet-founders, and on the other the specific demographic, economic and ethnic structures of the geographical regions which these cults transformed into cultic regions.[102] Later criticism by Gwyn Prins suggests that for an understanding of the organizational dynamics a more complex model is needed than that of (a) non-regional substratum, (b) regional outgrowth, (c) non-regional decline which I proposed. A closer study particularly of the Nzila side of my comparison may be necessary.[103]

The second social-structural problem in the Hortonian approach has to do with the analytical typology used to characterize the social context within which religious ideas and rituals exist, and within which they change. Neat as Horton's juxtaposition of microcosm/macrocosm may have been, it was a little too simple to be true. This becomes very clear when, in reply to Fisher's[104] incisive (and I must say, rather convincing) criticism of the 1971 version of Horton's theory, the latter in his rejoinder starts juggling with the concept of microcosm so that it encompasses anything between the tiny rural village and the large-scale kingdom.[105] Obviously, we would need to define microcosm and macrocosm in a much more rigid way. Only then could we begin to discuss the nature of microcosmic boundaries meaningfully, and their weakening or breakdown. But in addition, we need to re-examine the place of religious ideas and actions within the economic, social and political structure of the units enclosed by these boundaries. Horton's approach gives the impression that a sharp distinction between the religious and the secular (i.e., economic, social, political) is meaningful;

39

thus, as secular structures widen, religious ideas follow suit. Ultimately, the intellectualist approach is yet another, and rather blunt, version of the classic correspondence theory in the social-scientific study of religion.[106] Beliefs and rituals are held to be systematically isomorphic to the social structure, so that, for example, expansion of the latter is reflected in the emergence of more exalted spirits in the former. There is very little room for anything but one-to-one correspondence. A dialectical view, in which, for instance, newly emerging religious ideas might constitute the negation rather than the reflexion of a penetrating macrocosm, is nowhere considered in the Hortonian scheme. Yet I am sure that a theory that allows for the religious negation of macrocosmic encroachment into the microcosm would make much more sense than the straightforward correspondence version, when we try to apply a Hortonian line of analysis to developments in the popular religion of North Africa or Europe.[107]

What underlies the Hortonian approach is a rather common, but unsatisfactory, theory of social change. Non-religious factors of change are claimed to penetrate from outside through some sort of mechanical process (diffusion?); these factors break down microcosmic boundaries, and the people who thus find themselves exposed to the wider world adapt themselves to the altered social-structural conditions by devising or adopting more universalist religious ideas. It is as if the only way in which economic and political changes could penetrate to the religious plane is through the exclusive medium of the conscious and deliberate reflexion of human participants. Horton's stress on causal explanations (lack of enthusiasm for such explanations is what he rebukes the 'devout opposition' for) presupposes a certain compartmentalization between religion and non-religious aspects of society, as well as one-way traffic between these aspects. When Fisher suggests that it may not have been state formation which led towards more massive adoption of Islam in West Africa, but Islam which led to state formation,[108] Horton has to plod through virtually the entire history of West African *jihads* to prove him wrong – without being properly convincing, I am afraid.[109] A similar compartmentalization between religion and society, and reluctance to admit that under certain circumstances religion might be a primary factor in social change, can surely be detected in my chapter 4 and in some other parts of the present volume.

If religion and secular structure are neatly compartmentalized, and the former is only a secondary reflexion of the latter, one does not need a very elaborate theory of social, political and economic change in order to understand religious innovation. All one needs to know is how, and for which section of a given population, microcosmic boundaries started to break down. But this is not good enough. It is more likely that there is a more profound and direct relationship between religious and secular change, and that this relationship is enacted largely (though by no means entirely) irrespective of the conscious reflexion of individuals. In order to identify such a relationship over time, one needs a powerful theory of economic, social and political change, and of the ways in which religious and non-religious aspects are *intertwined* within an evolving social structure.

Here we hit on a third shortcoming of the intellectualist approach, which again applies to my own version of it. Although there is considerable common-sense plausibility in the idea that lesser spirits administer the microcosm, and greater spirits the macrocosm, one would require a fully-fledged theory of religious symbolism in order to arrive at a real systematic understanding of this relationship. How does one relate, in a theoretical sense, the geographical or social extension of human spheres of action (in politics, trade, warfare, pilgrimage, agriculture, animal husbandry, residential mobility), to a set of qualitatively very different phenomena: the notions participants have concerning the nature of supernatural beings? How does one relate the shape and texture of interactional and communication structures to the structure of ideas people involved in these structures have? This is a fundamental problem, for which Horton's work, or my own, does not provide the solution.

My chapters 6, 7, and 8 are attempts, along different lines, to confront the problems of social structure, theory of change and (to a lesser extent) symbolism indicated in the preceding paragraphs. The arguments in all these three chapters reflect a Marxist inspiration. But as my awareness of Marxist theory, its potential and limitations, grew over the years, the arguments in these chapters are inevitably rather dissimilar.

Chapter 6 is mainly a theoretical exercise about the relations between ritual and society. Its contribution to the social-structural and symbolic interpretation of Central African religious change is mainly negative. It argues against current dominant approaches: versions of a Durkheimian correspondence theory, which try to place religious phenomena in the very centre of a unique, total and integrated social structure. I indicate the inapplicability of this approach to a cult like Bituma; although this cult primarily operates among members of the Nkoya ethnic group, it cannot be analysed in terms of 'Nkoya society' – since that is only a part-society, incorporated in the wider economic and political structures of Zambia, and the world system at large.[110] But neither can the Bituma cult be directly relegated to this wider structure. Even though Bituma ritual is performed in multi-ethnic urban environments far away from the Nkoya homeland, Bituma symbolism and ritual show no strong correspondence with the basic structure of that wider society. As a way out of this dilemma, I suggested that religion should not be considered as the expression or reflexion *par excellence* of any prevailing social structure. If there is to be a primary symbolic referent, it should be sought in the individual human experience, much more than in specific social structures. Meanwhile, as I claimed in chapter 6, ritual can play a role in the social structure, even if it does not reflect it: through Bituma, social and economic ties are maintained between Nkoya urban migrants, and between these migrants and their home villages. Bituma's continued existence seems to be based not on any profound symbolic relationship with the social structure, but on the fact that it provides a useful organizational setting in the context of migrancy.

The negative part of chapter 6, the criticism of the dominant approach in religious anthropology, which also is one of the foundations of the Hortonian approach, seems of more lasting value than the positive solutions (transactionalism *cum* universal human experience) it comes up with.[111] Thus the argument does precisely what I criticize Turner's work for: it jumps from the purely local to the universal human place, without considering the intermediate level of historical and regional communalities.

However, chapter 6 cleared the way towards a serious exploration of an alternative model that, on the empirical level, would be compatible with the synthesis provided in chapter 4, yet on the theoretical level would proceed beyond the shortcomings of the Hortonian model, and of such structural-functionalist orientation as is present in the older analyses contained in this book. Such a solution, I think, may be at hand in the emergent Marxist theory of modes of production and their articulation.[112]

Religious change and the articulation of modes of production

Without entering into the many debates surrounding recent Marxist anthropology, the following minimal definition of mode of production could be acceptable to many writers in this field:[113]

A mode of production is a model that stipulates a specific arrangement according to which the productive forces (means of

production, resources, labour and knowledge) existing at a
particular time and place, are subject to specific relations of
production such as define forms of expropriation and control
between the various classes of people involved in the
production process.

Regulation of production is the crucial aspect of a mode of production. But this does not mean that the mode of production realizes
itself only at the level of what is conventionally called the economy. In
many societies, specific relations of expropriation and control are
defined through the systems of kinship, marriage, clanship, political
organization, law and religious organization. While the basic social
problem of meeting the material requirements of human life has to be
solved by any society, different modes of production represent different
solutions, within the range of variation that a particular level of development of the productive forces allows for. In order to persist over time
(a precondition for the regulation of production), a mode of production
must be capable of reproducing itself: materially (so that the necessary
productive forces are available), demographically (in order to have
human personnel), organizationally and ideologically. Meanwhile,
in most societies more than one mode of production coexists with other
modes. Modes of production can be said to be articulated ('linked') to
one another if surpluses generated in one mode are expropriated so
as to serve the reproduction of another, dominant mode. In this context
the concept of 'social formation' is preferred over that of society, the
latter suggesting an extent of monolithic integration, boundedness and
historical maturity rather at variance with the structural reality of
diverse and mutually subordinating modes of production at various stages
of their internal development.

Thus, over the past few centuries, western Zambia[114] has seen the
emergence of three new modes of production which have imposed
themselves upon the social formation such as existed in the late eighteenth century. Despite its complexity, that social formation was then
dominated by a domestic mode of production, revolving on agriculture,
and having the dominance of the old over the young (reinforced by the
dominance of men over women) as the central contradiction governing
the production process. In the early nineteenth century, a tributary
mode of production emerged, which thrived on the basis of extraction
of surpluses from the domestic mode, and whose central contradiction
was that between rulers and courts on the one hand, and local communities on the other. As this tributary mode of production established

itself, long-distance trade penetrated into the region, and the local domestic and tributary modes were articulated to the mode of production of mercantile capitalism, such as prevailed in the distant North Atlantic metropolises. Around 1900 the imposition of colonial rule set the conditions under which both the tributary and the mercantile-capitalist mode (as represented by long-distance trade) could be largely destroyed, and with the rise of labour migration the domestic mode became articulated to industrial capitalism, as located in the sub-metropoles along the Zambian line of rail, in Zimbabwe, and South Africa.

In chapter 7 I suggest that the processes of religious change which have been identified in the preceding chapters might be regarded as aspects of this articulation process. Particularly the emergence of cults of affliction in the late nineteenth and early twentieth centuries, their subsequent development into prophetic cults, and back into non-prophetic cults, keeps pace with the triple sequence of articulation indicated above. The emergence of non-prophetic non-regional cults of affliction in western Zambia in the nineteenth century is seen as an aspect of the articulation of mercantile capitalism and the domestic mode of production. Bituma and Nzila, as prophetic regional cults, developed in the 1930s out of the substratum of non-regional cults of affliction, when mercantile capitalism had effectively given way to industrial capitalism. Urban-rural relations between urban migrants from rural western Zambia, and their home communities, are an aspect of the articulation between the domestic and the industrial-capitalist mode of production. According to Meillassoux's penetrating analysis of circulatory labour migration,[115] urban immigration of workers (raised in the village, and likely to retire in the village whenever they are expendable in the capitalist sector) represents a major device through which the capitalist mode of production, in Zambia as elsewhere in Africa, reproduces itself at the expense of the domestic mode which is mainly located in distant rural villages. The extensive regional cults of affliction (such as Nzila) may be more appropriate to a situation closer to definite proletarization (i.e., when urban migrants no longer define themselves by reference to the domestic mode of production, and *de facto* have been divorced from the rural means of production). Alternatively the fragmentation of a prophetic, regional cult into a form reminiscent of the earlier non-regional cults of affliction (such as happened in the case of Bituma), may be more appropriate to migrants in the earlier stages of proletarization, i.e., when they still rely heavily on the domestic mode of production.

44

It is not difficult to see how this approach, however tentative and in need of much further theoretical development, yet provides some of the answers to the questions raised in chapter 6. The notion of one, unitary, integrated social structure is supplanted by that of a composite, internally contradictory social formation, consisting of various modes of production which each have their own logic and which are linked to each other in relations of dominance and superordination.

Some religious forms as discussed in chapters 3 and 4 are clearly part of the internal logic of one such mode of production. The ancestral cult forms an integral, even essential part of the domestic mode, much as the chiefly or royal cults are implied in the logic of the tributary mode of production. But some other religious forms, and particularly the cults of affliction in their various prophetic and non-prophetic forms, are not part of any one specific mode, but instead are aspects of the articulation between modes of production. Therefore they cannot show clear-cut correspondence *vis-à-vis* the non-religious aspects of any one mode. They reflect the rural communities just as little as they reflect long-distance trade or urban industrial capitalism: their symbolic and interactional elements are borrowed from all these modes, and integrated into a form that resembles none or all.

This implies that there is a systematic formal relationship between the symbols selected as elements for a new cult constituting articulation of modes of production, and the symbols which pertain to these various modes themselves. Here the articulation approach departs from the theory of the arbitrary nature of the sacred.[116] If the symbolic imagery in Bituma employs elements (e.g., references to hunting and gathering) which seem out of place in the urban environment, this is not because religious symbols are arbitrary anyway, but because Bituma revolves on the articulation between the mainly rural-based domestic mode of production (where hunting and gathering are eminently significant), and the largely urban-based industrial-capitalist mode, where other forms of production prevail, notably wage-labour within formal, bureaucratic settings.

At the same time these cults of affliction do have an essential structural significance which makes the solution offered in chapter 6 untenable. They are *not* just 'a secondary reflexion, an expression, comment, adornment, etc., of whatever other more fundamental and central aspects of society',[117] nor do they directly refer to the timeless, universal human predicament as such. Dealing with the human predicament *in the specific context of articulation*, they reveal, and even constitute, fundamental social-structural patterns. While negating

45

each of the constituent modes of production within the social formation, these cults confirm the articulation between these modes. A cult like Bituma contains in itself the dialectical structure of articulation which is crucial for the total social formation in which both urban and rural, capitalist and pre-capitalist structures are contained. Bituma does not just *express* articulation, it *is* articulation, since (as the description in chapter 7 shows) the cult provides (to an extent rivalled only by the marriage system) the material and ideological links out of which articulation consists: the circulation of people and money between urban and rural areas, between male wage-earners and those males and females who do not themselves participate in capitalist relations of production.

If articulation of modes of production is the principle behind some of the major changes in Zambian religion, and if cults of affliction, more than ancestral or chiefly cults, are pertinent to the total, articulated structure of the rapidly expanding social formation which came into being in Zambia since the early nineteenth century, then this provides a justification for devoting such a substantial part of this volume (chapters 2, 5, 6, 7) to the study of the dynamics of possession, mediumship, and cults of affliction. However, it remains to be seen to what extent other forms of religious innovation, besides cults of affliction, can be analysed within the same theoretical framework. The synthesis in chapter 4 deals, along with cults of affliction and affliction prophets, with ecological and eschatological prophets, the search for new medicines, witchcraft eradication movements, and various types of independent and mission Christianity. My argument would lose much of its meaning if all these, too, while emerging in the same colonial period, were to be treated as undifferentiated aspects of articulation. If the concept applies at all to these other forms, we have to explain why in their cases articulation precipitated very different religious forms. Before this is done, the overall process of religious change as posed in chapter 4 may be rather well established at the descriptive level, but we can certainly not maintain to have identified, in the notion of the articulation of modes of production, the general motor behind that process. What seems most needed in this connexion, again, is a theory of symbolism, which links the material aspects of production, expropriation and control (around which modes of production and their articulation revolve), to the ideological level at which ideas concerning the supernatural are generated, maintained, and revised. Chapter 7 contains only the most rudimentary and implicit embryo of such a theory, when I try to make plausible that the cults of affliction, in the relations they stipulate between cult leaders and followers, and in their beliefs concerning affliction-causing entities, unite contradictory principles which are partly taken from the domestic mode of production, partly from the mercantile-capitalist mode, and partly from remnants of the tributary mode. But very much more theoretical work has to be done on this point, before even the specific argument in relation to the cults of affliction will satisfy the sceptical reader.

The argument in chapter 7 leads on to a further problem: why should articulation between modes of production be expressed along religious lines, e.g., in a cult of affliction such as Bituma?

On the level of general, systematic theory the following answer might seem sufficient; it is in fact a recasting, in terms of the modes-of-production approach, of the tentative answer to this question as presented in chapter 8.[118] The articulation process characteristic of the social formation of Kaoma district since the 1930s involved, along with industrial capitalism, the encapsulation of other modes of production in which (contrary to capitalism) religion is an integral, infrastructural part. So along with economic and social linkages (the traffic of remittances, bridewealth, manufactured articles, food, male migrant workers, wives and visitors) between towns and villages, there also had to be a religious aspect to this articulation.

In the Nkoya case a more specific answer seems to be required. For the argument as put forth in chapter 7[119] suggests that, from the 1950s onward, cults of affliction along with the marital structure form the main contexts in which town-earned cash can be syphoned back to the rural areas. Here it seems that the peculiar situation of the Nkoya should be taken into account. They form a small ethnic minority, ranking very low in the national prestige scale of ethnic groups, having a rather heavily declined production system in their homelands, and possessing very little of a foothold in the urban areas or in national and provincial politics. Their situation is certainly very different from that of the mass of Eastern Province immigrants in Lusaka, or Bemba-speaking immigrants in the Copperbelt towns. If articulation in the Nkoya context shows a marked religious emphasis, as compared with urban ethnic majorities (and this is a hypothesis which is confirmed by my field impressions but awaits further quantitative testing), then this is very likely to be related to the minority status of the Nkoya. Given the extreme insecurity of their urban foothold, they have to rely rather more heavily than urban ethnic majorities on such refuge as rural ties can offer them. At the same time, given their low urban prestige, the few successful Nkoya in town would be particularly prone to shed their Nkoya ethnic identity, and to adopt instead some other, more prestigious label (e.g., Lozi or Bemba).[120] This is not the place to try to sort out the intricacies of the contemporary predicament of the Nkoya. However, if in this apparently exceptional situation ideological elements (such as the Bituma cult) are stressed over more directly economic associations and transactions between the capitalist and the domestic mode of production, we should be careful not to generalize too readily our interpretation of Nkoya cults of affliction in the context of urban-rural relations.

The problems raised by my argument in chapter 7 are further illuminated by my attempt to apply, in chapter 8, Marxist-inspired concepts such as mode of production, class conflict and alienation, to a form of Central African religious innovation that is very different from the cults of affliction of western Zambia: the Lumpa Church, founded by Alice Lenshina in north-eastern Zambia in the mid-1950s, and dissolved after violent clashes with the Zambian state in 1964. It is to this analysis that I shall now turn. Among other things, this may help us to assess the potential of my emerging theory in a social context (that of the Bemba, one of Zambia's largest and most powerful ethnic groups) very different from the enclosed ethnic minority of the Nkoya.

Superstructural castles in the air

Chapter 8 carries the treatment of religious change in Zambia further towards the present than any of the other chapters. It deals with a form of religious innovation (an independent Christian church) which according to the general argument in chapter 4 would be considered the most advanced form of religious innovation available in Central Africa in modern times.[121] While there are thus very good reasons to place this chapter at the end of the book, its theoretical argument is less consistently Marxist than that of chapter 7. It represents, instead, much in the way of chapter 6, a rather idiosyncratic experiment with Marxist-inspired concepts and theories not yet illuminated by recent Marxist theoretical literature.

After an introductory discussion of various interpretations of the Lumpa church, the 1964 conflict, and its aftermath, in the eyes of the Zambian elite and academic writers, the argument deals with two topics: the emergence of the Lumpa Church against the overall background of religious innovation in Zambia; and the process through which the

Lumpa Church came into violent conflict with the state. The two parts of the argument are linked by a complex theoretical discussion, which hinges on the concept of *superstructural reconstruction.* I make a distinction between a society's superstructure and its infrastructure. The superstructure is[122]

> the total arrangement . . . [of] explicit and mutually shared ideas members of a society have concerning the universe, society, and themselves – ideas supported by implicit, often unconscious cognitive structures. . . . [The] superstructure defines a society's central concerns, major institutions, and basic norms and values. . . . [It] is the central repository of meaning. On the other hand . . . the infrastructure [is] the organization of the production upon which the participants' lives depend, and particularly such differential distribution of power and resources as dominate the relations of production.

In a relatively stable situation, infrastructure and superstructure are supposed to be attuned to each other, but in situations of rapid change the relative autonomy of each becomes more pronounced, they grow out of touch, and the participants experience alienation as a result.[123] It is the fundamental assumption of my argument in this chapter that people in such a situation will attempt, through a process of super-structural reconstruction (which in some cases may be accompanied by attempts to alter the infrastructure) to restore the disrupted link between superstructure and infrastructure, thus regaining their grasp on the world.

In Zambia, religious innovation has been a major form of super-structural reconstruction, as a response to the infrastructural changes taking place with the emergence of the tributary and the capitalist modes of production. In chapter 8 I assume that the overall process of religious change, as identified in chapter 4 for central western Zambia, *grosso modo* also applies to northern Zambia, where the Lumpa Church originated. I claim that the distinct individual forms of religious innovation, of which the overall process of religious change consisted, were so many attempts at superstructural reconstruction. They were first formulated by gifted individuals, and subsequently tried out, adopted or rejected in a wider popular response, among people who were subject to the same processes of infrastructural change as the religious innovators in their midst.

Ultimately, the motor behind superstructural reconstruction is claimed to be an ideological form of class struggle. Local rural

49

communities were confronted with the encroachment of: pre-colonial rulers imposing a tributary mode of production; traders (often in alliance with rulers) imposing, through long-distance trade, a mercantile-capitalist mode of production; and colonial administrators, labour recruiters and capitalist employers in the Central and Southern African sub-metropolises, imposing the industrial-capitalist mode of production. I argue that the forms of religious innovation which emerged in this context (particularly witchcraft eradication, Watchtower and other independent churches, and prophets other than those dealing with affliction) represent an attempt to reconstruct the integrity of the local rural community assaulted by these various incorporation processes.

The penetration of new modes of production attempted to reduce the villagers of northern Zambia to peasants and proletarians. Peasants could then be defined as agricultural producers who, while retaining some control over their means of production, are involved in a complex social formation within which part of their product is expropriated so as to reproduce a tributary or capitalist mode within the same social formation; proletarians are producers who have no control over their means of production (land, industrial plants, etc.), and therefore have to sell their labour power in a capitalist labour market.[124] I argue that the religious forms of superstructural reconstruction are in essence attempts to resist the process of class formation, by curbing peasantization and proletarization, and by reviving, at least at the superstructural level, the rural community as the matrix of a domestic mode of production. I show how the emergence of the Lumpa Church ties in with the wider patterns of religious change. Lenshina's prophetic message consists of a new permutation of the same symbolic and ritual material underlying the forms of religious innovation discussed throughout this book.

In order to understand the evolution of the Lumpa church in relation to Zambian nationalism and the Zambian state, I found it necessary to distinguish between a proletarian and a peasant stream of super-structural reconstruction. In the colonial period, the proletarian stream was characteristic of what could be called the 'intensive contact situation', where Africans were directly and painfully exposed to capitalist relations of production, including their political and ideological aspects. In this context religious responses like Watchtower and other African independent church movements must be located. The unmistakable element of anti-colonial protest manifest in this stream after the Second World War led to a secular nationalist movement. This movement aimed not at reversing proletarization nor at the dissolution of industrial capitalism in the direction of an ideal of viable socialist relations of production. Its proclaimed aim was to seize the state as a possible instrument to improve the conditions of life of African proletarians, with the implication of leaving the overall structure of peripheral capitalism intact. In the peasant stream of superstructural reconstruction, protest against the relatively distant colonial and industrial powers was much less pronounced, and instead reconstruction concentrated on the ideological reconstruction of the rural community. Despite the extensive interactions between the proletarian and the peasant stream (due mainly to circulatory labour migration), each stream retained its basic orientation.

The Lumpa Church, as a rural response yet located at a centre of Christian missions, initially straddled both streams, to such an extent that Lumpa functioned as a platform for nationalist propaganda. However, Lumpa developed more and more into an exclusive peasant movement. In the struggle against local chiefs, the attempts to gain control over land, and the imposition upon the countryside of northern Zambia of new economic and judicial relations, it even went some way towards the development of infrastructural conditions capable of counteracting the process of peasantization. Thus elements from the proletarian stream were increasingly alien to this religious movement. In the face of massive labour migration and of the presence of the colonial state at the rural administative centres and (indirectly) chiefly courts, peasant incorporation had become an almost inescapable reality. The growth of a rural religious community that opted out of that reality was even less acceptable to the nationalist movement, and particularly the United National Independence Party (UNIP), than it was to the colonial state. Violent feuding arose between rural UNIP branches in northern Zambia, and the Lumpa Church. The latter was forced into a defensive position, and into more and more extreme, eschatological attitudes *vis-à-vis* the nationalists and the state (which was controlled by UNIP as from the creation of the transition government in 1963, one year before territorial independence). The killing of police officers investigating a stockaded Lumpa settlement triggered the Lumpa rising. The confrontation between Lumpa adherents on the one hand, and state troops and non-Lumpa villagers on the other, resulted in hundreds of casualties, and in the exodus of thousands of Lumpa adherents from the countryside of northern Zambia.[125]

The moment of the rising could not have been a coincidence: it occurred a few weeks before the creation of the post-colonial state controlled by a nationalist African elite, whose power base was UNIP.

An analysis of Lumpa in terms of class formation (i.e., villagers resisting being turned into a peasant class) would not be complete without an analysis of nationalism and the post-colonial state in similar terms. However, my original argument provides such an analysis only in a very partial form: as a discussion of the legitimation problems of the post-colonial state. Here the Marxist inspiration gives way to a Weberian one. I argue that the major, established Christian churches in Zambia provide an ideological framework that, given state-church alliances, may help to legitimize the post-colonial state. However, many other churches, including smaller, independent churches but also Watchtower which is one of the largest churches in Zambia, are regarded with suspicion by the Zambian state and the ruling elite. These churches often belong to a theocratic tradition opposed to the secular state, and therefore cannot provide additional legitimation for the state. Church-state tensions reminiscent of the Lumpa conflict continue to exist, although now, nearly twenty years after Independence, the elite's hold of the state is so firm that an escalation of religious conflict to dimensions similar to those of the Lumpa uprising is very unlikely.

Work on the Lumpa church by J.-L. Calmettes[126] gives us a much better insight in the internal dynamics of that Church, and allows us (despite Calmette's critcism of my own earlier conclusions) to draw the analysis of this form of religious innovation much closer to the line of argument pursued in chapter 7. In view of the length and specificity of my debate with Calmettes, I decided not to include it in this Introduction; instead, I devote a separate postscript to it.

What is important at this stage, however, is to point out one major weakness in the argument of chapter 8: the much too rigid distinction between superstructure and infrastructure.

In the capitalist mode of production the separation of workers from their means of production, and consequently the reduction of labour, products, and virtually all other aspects of human life to the status of commodities which have their price and can be bought and sold in a market, has led to a very marked prevalence of the economy over all other levels (politics, ideology, religion) within the mode of production. Here the economy could properly be called the infrastructure, from which the other levels within the mode of production are largely secondary reflexions or negations; in other words, superstructural elements. It is a weakness of my analysis in chapters 6 and 8 that I did not sufficiently realize that in social formations where capitalist relations of production have not yet become absolutely dominant in all aspects of life (and contemporary Zambia is still a clear example of such a social formation) – that there the make-up of the infrastructure is unlikely to be primarily economic in the narrower sense (revolving on the process of material production and the circulation of surpluses). The point has been made repeatedly, e.g., by Godelier.[127]

In the Zambian situation it is perfectly clear that, for instance, the cult of the ancestors is not just a secondary, superstructural reflexion on secular institutions which are in themselves 'more' infrastructural. The cult is, on the contrary, one of the pivotal elements in a kinship order which, in itself, defines crucial relations of production within the domestic community. This is particularly clear when, as among the Nkoya, the ancestral cult stipulates the distribution of the hunter's bag over close kinsmen, creating a structure of powerful supernatural sanctioning over processes of circulation which are, also materially, absolutely vital. Similarly, when emergent kings and chiefs try to wrench ritual control over the land from the hands of pre-existing territorial cults (chapter 3), this is not a mere superstructural extension of some other 'real' power realized at the infrastructural level (in the form of tributary relations of production and circulation); it is, instead, an attempt to redefine the religious basis in order to appropriate that aspect of the infrastructure that links ownership and material control to ritual control over the land. In the past I have reproached a colleague studying the overall transformation of Zambian society, for projecting into non-capitalist aspects of that social formation the make-up of our own capitalist life-world.[128] It now appears as if, in the distinction between infrastructure and superstructure, I have been guilty of doing just that.

With regard to this distinction, Werbner[129] remarked that the 'cumbersome dichotomy between superstructure and infrastructure . . . . would sink a less agile analysis' – writing the full extent of his criticism between the lines. Fernandez[130] discusses my dichotomy in detail. He remarks approvingly (but somewhat incorrectly) that it has a 'Godelierian ring'; for Fernandez it 'has a very contemporary 1970s feel to it'.[131] But all the same Fernandez takes me to task for imposing alien analytical categories and distinctions upon the images out of which, he claims, African cultural systems exist. And in the case of this dichotomy, I think his criticism is justified.

What I mainly tried to capture with my opposition between infrastructure and superstructure, was this. One of the significant consequences of the articulation of modes of production (and one that is of particular interest to the student of religion), is that beliefs, norms, values and cosmologies pertaining to an earlier phase in the development of the social formation, and tied up with a mode of production forced into a subservient position within that formation, yet live on, even although new relations of production have emerged which have their own ideological dimensions. Decades ago, Ogburn and Nimkoff[132] discussed this well-known phenomenon, coining the phrase 'cultural lag'. Marxists would tend to discuss the same phenomenon under the heading of 'relative autonomy'. This capability of aspects of the symbolic order to survive with a measure of relative autonomy *vis-à-vis* the new relations of production (including new ideological elements) that surround them, suggests that also in the pre-articulation phase a certain dialectical tension has existed between ideology and practice. Once again, only a full-size theory of the symbolic dimension of modes of production and their articulation can offer the precision that is urgently needed on this point. Not yet possessing such a theory, I was lured into representing the tension between symbol and material process, *within* one and the same 'infrastructure', as the opposition *between* 'infrastructure' and 'superstructure'. It seems possible to rewrite the argument in chapter 8 in this sense, without destroying it. Meanwhile, we should realize that the increasing dominance of capitalism in the recent history of the social formation of Zambia, even although it has not yet attained the level characteristic of the social formation of the North Atlantic region in the nineteenth and twentieth centuries, implies that narrowly economic structures increasingly determine the infrastructure, forcing ideological elements gradually into the superstructure. So, although the distinction between superstructure and infrastructure such as presented in chapter 8 does not apply to, say, 1800, it does apply somewhat better to the most recent period.

Towards a Marxist theory of Central African religious change

The arguments in chapters 7 and 8, despite the fact that they contain many fundamental similarities, are contradictory in several other respects. Do they merely represent abortive attempts to arrive at something better than Horton's intellectualist theory of Africn religious change? Or is it possible, by comparing both arguments and proceeding still beyond them, to arrive at the first outlines of such a more viable theory? In order to answer these questions, which are truly fundamental to this whole book, let me first contrast the argument in both chapters, and then confront the tentative insights we have gained thus with the general theoretical and methodological problems raised in the course of this Introduction, particularly with reference to the intellectualist approach.

Articulation and dialectics

While the argument in both chapter 7 and chapter 8 revolves around the articulation of modes of production (chapter 8 deals with the principle without mentioning the concept itself), the treatment of religious innovation in that context is rather different. In chapter 7, cults of affliction in their successive developmental forms are claimed to be religious forms which *express*, and at the same time *constitute*, articulation. In chapter 8, witchcraft eradication, prophetic movements, Watchtower, and an independent church like Lumpa, while likewise springing from a context of articulation, are claimed to be much more specific responses in that context: they are said to be religious forms through which villagers and migrants *militate* against the form articulation has taken (or is about to take) in their lives. These people try to influence, even to reverse, the processes of class formation to which the articulation of modes of production is giving rise. The attempt to arrive at an all-encompassing insight, and enthusiasm about the vistas opening up in either of these arguments, have perhaps seduced me, within these chapters, to attribute all forms of religious innovation to either articulation (chapter 7), or class struggle against articulation (chapter 8). On re-reading, I find both arguments convincing up to a point. They represent genuine attempts to identify the principles behind the overall mechanism of Zambian religious change over the past few centuries. Chapter 8, in its emphasis on the reconstruction of a symbolic order ('superstructure')[133] in the minds of individual religious innovators, whose visions are subsequently tested out in the popular response, remains rather close to the earlier overview as presented in chapter 4. Chapter 4 asserts that individual innovatory visions, and their impact upon the wider population, were closely associated with overall processes of political and economic change – but whereas it does identify three *avant-garde* situations that are structurally prone to produce religious innovators, the psychological processes of innovative symbolization are hardly explored there. Chapter 8 provides an explicit (though tentative) theory of a possible mechanism in this connexion, and applies this theory to a well-documented case. Thus while in chapters 4 and 8 some emphasis is put on the creative efforts of individual innovators, in chapter 7 individual visionaries are played down, and the cults of affliction are presented as arising almost automatically, by blind necessity, out of the context of articulation. The biographies of such affliction prophets as Simbinga, Chana and Moya (as presented in chapter 5) may be invoked to stress that, at least in the reshaping of cults of affliction into prophetic and regional cults, a similar creative moment can be detected in the processes that form the subject matter of chapter 7. But chapter 8 brings out much more the dialectical relation between religious innovation and articulation. Here religious innovation is the negation of the reality of articulation. This negation exists at the ideological level and, in the Lumpa case, even at the level of relations of production. On the other hand, in chapter 7 articulation and religious innovation much more coincide and correspond; the dialectical negation is not between religious innovation and articulation, but between religious innovation and the various distinct modes of production of which the social formation consists.

Identification of the articulation of modes of production as the crucial condition governing religious innovation, clearly does not provide the full answer we need – although it does go a long way towards such an answer. Now we must go further, and admit that articulation gives rise to a number of fundamentally *different* types of religious response. (a) Sometimes religious innovations are produced which, in their internal structure, show almost one-to-one correspondence with the secular aspects of the structure of the new, dominant mode of production imposing itself upon the pre-existing social formation. The clearest case in point is the emergence of chiefly or royal cults, as discussed in chapter 3 (but not in terms of articulation, and with rather too little attention to the material basis of pre-colonial state formation). (b) Under different conditions, articulation produces a religious response which reflects, not the secular structure of any one of the various modes of production involved in the articulation process, but articulation as a whole. The example is the emergence of cults of affliction, as discussed in chapters 2, 5, 6 and 7 of this book. (c) Under different conditions again, articulation produces a variety of religious responses (ranging from witchcraft eradication movements, through eschatological and ecological prophets, to independent churches like Watchtower and Lumpa), which like the cults of affliction direct themselves to the overall articulation process more than to any one of the distinct modes of production involved, but which do not express or constitute articulation, but instead deny and counteract it. Some of these innovations of the third type attempt to counteract articulation by the revival, at the symbolic level, of a domestic community such as it was supposed to have been prior to articulation. In that case, the religious innovation produced must not be mistaken for an expression of the domestic mode of production; instead, it is the very reality of articulation which makes people long for a viable and self-sustained domestic community now lost forever.

The dialectics between objective relations of production such as exist at a given time and place, and people's consciousness of these relations, has constituted the main problem in the analysis of class conflict ever since Marx. Under what conditions does a 'class in itself' become a 'class for itself', one which is conscious of the relations of production in which it is involved, engaging in class struggle on the basis of this class consciousness? Looking at Central African religious change in terms of the articulation of modes of production amounts to a class analysis. Every mode of production revolves around one central class-like contradiction; and the articulation of modes of production is a process in which new class-like contradictions are superimposed upon those contradictions governing pre-existing modes. Since religion is so often studied mainly or exclusively at the level of people's consciousness, it is proper that we now turn to a consideration of the potential of the modes-of-production paradigm for an understanding of varieties of consciousness, in a context of changes both in religion and in relations of productions.

With this in mind, let us look at the three types of dialectical relation between religious aspects and the structure of articulated modes of production such as identified in the preceding paragraphs: (a) Simple correspondence (e.g., royal cults); (b) the total structure of articulation is positively reflected, but each constituent mode of production is now reflected, now negated according to a dialectical logic (e.g., prophetic, regional cults of affliction) – for lack of a better term, let us call this syndrome 'dialectical correspondence'; (c) the total structure of articulation is negated, which often leads to a positive confirmation of one *idealized* constituent mode of production (cf. Lumpa): by analogy with (b), let us call this syndrome 'dialectical compensation'. The implication of these relations at the level of consciousness seems fairly straightforward. Simple correspondence (a) implies acquiescence, or even positive support, *vis-à-vis* the new relations of production which are being imposed in the course of the articulation process. Specifically, royal cults legitimate, conceal, perhaps even deny the fundamental class contradiction between rulers and local communities upon which the tributary mode of production is based. A similar case could be made for ancestral worship, which likewise leads members of the local community to affirm the domestic relations of production, and expels from their consciousness the underlying class-like contradictions at the village level (contradictions between elders and youth, men and women).

Dialectical correspondence (b) implies, at the level of consciousness, an element of ambivalence not conducive to the emergence of a class consciousness that is politically manifest. The religious forms proper to this type negate the constituent modes of production within the total articulation structure, but at the same time they reflect, and thus affirm, this overall structure. Such symbolic ambivalence is characteristic of the modern cults of afflictions (chapters 2, 5, 6, 7). These cults, borrowing elements from the various religious sub-systems that each correspond with one mode of production, integrate these elements in such a way that only the total structure of articulation is reflected and affirmed. Contained within a new symbolic and ritual structure which has its own logic (that of the cults of affliction), the elements borrowed from the various modes of production, if still recognizable as such, mock or negate these modes, but only implicitly or symbolically so. Thus the use of chiefly paraphernalia (e.g., hourglass drums, fly-switches) in cults of affliction at the symbolic level challenges chiefly prerogatives. But this does not instill in the people's mind a critical consciousness of the tributary mode of production and its exploitative nature. At the same time, the functioning of these cults in the context of urban-rural relations affirms and actually helps to shape the articulation between industrial capitalism and the domestic community, without the presence even of recognizable symbolic references to this articulation in the imagery of these cults.

In this way it becomes possible to rephrase the argument of chapter 2 within the conceptual framework utilized in the more recent work collected in this volume. We are now beginning to see further, and probably more fundamental, reasons why possession and mediumship (as pursued in Central African ancestral cults, chiefly cults and cults of affliction) cannot be meaningfully analysed with the model of relative deprivation. These religious forms simply do not contain that element of protest which analysts read into them in the 1960s and early 1970s. At the same time, however, we should recognize such elements of protest as are manifested in other forms of Central African religious innovation.

Protest, a stirring of class consciousness even if confined to a religious idiom, is a major aspect of those religious innovations which relate to the articulation structure through dialectical compensation (c). Lumpa as analysed in chapter 8 is a case in point. However, as I argued there, the protest element in Lumpa was not of the type stressed by academic supporters of African nationalism in the 1960s (e.g., Ranger, Rotberg). In this respect my analysis in chapter 8 is a continuation of a theme developed in some of the other chapters of the book: the attempt to arrive at a more balanced assessment of Central African religious protest. Lumpa's protest was not primarily against the colonial state (although in the first years, when the Church served as a platform for the nationalist movement, there was this element too); Lumpa primarily opposed the total structure of articulation through which rural producers had been relegated to the status of peasants and proletarians.

Thus we have tentatively established a trichotomy of acquiescence, symbolic ambivalence and protest, as descriptions of the state of consciousness belonging to simple correspondence, dialectical correspondence and dialectical compensation respectively between aspects of religion, and the overall articulation structure within the social formation.

Interestingly, in Schoffeleers's recent work he arrives, independently and along very different lines, at similar views.[134] As his 1978 fieldwork reveals, acquiescence, symbolic ambivalence and protest are useful keywords to describe and contrast the three religious responses that currently dominate the religious scene in the Lower Shire Valley, Malawi. These responses are: missionary Christianity; cults of affliction and the independent churches that are supplanting them (not unlike Nzila as described in chapter 5); and, finally, what Schoffeleers tentatively calls nativistic movements, which try to revive the earlier religious forms of the local community. His explanation for this trichotomy likewise tends towards an analysis of the relations of each of these responses to the overall structure of articulation.

Meanwhile Schoffeleers's other work[135] suggests that there is a fourth type: one which explicitly rejects one constituent mode of production, without at the same time challenging the total structure of articulation; thus combining aspects of dialectical correspondence and compensation. The only example of this so far available for Central Africa is the M'bona cult of redemptive martyrdom, which emerged in a context of the imposition of a particularly violent and oppressive variant of the tributary mode of production, in southern Malawi around 1600. The M'bona cult, according to Schoffeleers's analysis, 'calls into being a dual antithetical value system', which neither affirms chiefly prerogatives nor incites class struggle against them, but transcends these prerogatives by offering an alternative, underdogs' model of power and achievement in the person of M'bona the Martyr.

Introduction

What, specifically, are those conditions under which the overall context of articulation leads to such very different specific forms of religious innovation? I suspect that the material presented in this volume could already form the basis for an answer; but at the same time I would submit that an attempt at an answer should be made in a separate study. With several theoretical studies now becoming available in which the potential of the paradigm of the articulation of modes of production, for purposes of religious analysis, is being explored,[136] the enormous theoretical problems involved here may come closer to a solution within a few years.

But while fundamental problems in the historical sociology of Zambian religion await further treatment, we have made some progress towards a better understanding of the relation between religion and the non-religious aspects of the society in which that religion is found. Part of the answer lies in a rethinking of the concept of society. Far from being the bounded, internally integrated monolithic whole that classic anthropology dreamed about, the historical societies we encounter in Central Africa in the second half of the present millennium are a composite of mutually irreducible (though interconnected, 'articulated') sub-systems: modes of production. None of these modes of production is static in itself. All go through their own development, whereas their process of articulation to one another is also dynamic. Within this complex whole, whose internal dynamism and historical process is so aptly captured by the term of 'social formation', it is rather meaningless to try and define, once for all, the nature and function of religion.

In this respect the studies in this volume represent a process of theoretical growth, and illustrate the ways in which a historical perspective can enrich our anthropology – which is not a facile gambit after this long exposition, in the course of this Introduction, of how anthropology can help history!

Throughout the structure of the overall social formation, there are aspects (now of greater, now of lesser significance in the total whole) which are imbued with religious elements. Some religious elements are integral parts of the various modes of production within the formation; some elements are about articulation – directly, as I have argued for the cults of affliction, or dialectically and through negation, as I have argued for, e.g., the Lumpa church. In some of these elements (notably those incorporated within a single mode of production) a high degree of correspondence between religious aspects and non-religious aspects of the same constituent structures could be expected. Correspondence theory, the main stock-in-trade of the dominant, classic

60

tradition in religious anthropology, would find here a lot that argues in its favour. But then we would be dealing with correspondence, not between the total religion and the total social structure within a tribe, ethnic group, or polity regarded as a bounded monolithic whole, but instead correspondence between constituent part-structures, both religious and non-religious, within the total evolving social formation. However, in those religious elements where negation and dialectical opposition prevail correspondence theory would be rather inapplicable, and instead elements of symbolic experiment and creativity, protest, 'counter-points'[137] would loom large in our analysis. Wholesale rejection of classic correspondence theory would be just as superficial and premature as wholesale adoption of correspondence as the fundamental dogma in religious studies; needless to say, many researchers of religion still believe in precisely this dogma.

It would appear that the definition of a society (in terms of social formation) and the definition of religion within that social formation could only be achieved in a dynamic fashion, by trying to capture the historical development of various, and essentially heterogeneous, religious elements within an evolving social formation. It is in the light of this insight that I can now see that the way in which the problem of the relation between religion and society was formulated in the earliest study in this collection (chapter 2), was essentially wrong – in its assumption that a timeless definition of 'a society' and 'its religion' is possible. But in so far as this initial study led to all the other chapters, it was a good way of opening up the enquiry.

Meanwhile all this may appear to the sceptical reader as a clever way of avoiding, throughout this book, a fundamental issue: the definition of religion 'as such', outside the context of change, and outside the specific historical and social settings in which we come upon manifestations of Central African religion. Must I explicitly state that, to my mind, such a definition would be meaningless? On this point I have adopted a common-sense approach, which on the whole accepts the religious nature of such phenomena as ancestor worship, cults of affliction, etc. Those pressing for a more formal approach I must refer to the classic texts and reference works on religious anthropology, where abstract, non-contextualized definitions of religion can be found by the dozen.

The potential of the emerging theory

Horton's summing up of the evolving structure of African societies by the simple opposition between microcosm and macrocosm can no longer be maintained. Instead, I submit that the actual units of social structure on which both secular and religious aspects of social change hinge are modes of production. In its purest form, Horton's microcosm could be equated with the domestic mode of production. Far from being internally undivided, it is characterized by processes of expropriation and control between elders and youth, and between men and women. Religious beliefs and practices underpin as well as constitute (and sometimes perhaps negate) these domestic relations. Social and political change in Africa over the past few centuries can be understood as the process through which these domestic communities became articulated to other, more complex modes of production: the tributary mode, mercantile capitalism, and industrial capitalism. The breakdown of microcosmic boundaries, in Horton's terms, was nothing but this articulation process. The ascendance of new and more formidable spirits is no longer part of a fluid and gradual process of local microcosms opening up to, and trying to come to terms with, the wider world; nor are these spirits merely the outcome of conscious reflexion by participants. Instead, the new spirits are an important aspect, either of the new modes of production articulating themselves to the domestic mode, or of this articulation process itself. As in the case of the domestic mode of production, the new beliefs and new rituals are not just ideological expressions of an underlying, more primary material reality: in so far as they impose new networks for the flow of people and goods (tribute, pilgrims' offerings, healers' fees, etc.) over wider areas, they actually take part in shaping the new, supra-local relations of production themselves.

Let us now look again at the three ideological attractions I claimed the intellectualist approach to have: the idea of essential continuity between colonial and pre-colonial period; the image of African Man the Active Religious Innovator; and apparently scientific apologetics for the presence and expansion of two world religions in Africa.

In the modes-of-production approach, the imposition of colonialism would not in itself constitute a sharp break. Colonialism would be interpreted as a phase in the penetration of capitalism, and particularly as the creation of peripheral, metropole-controlled state structures which, by mediating a new type of class domination in the peripheral economies, allowed for the transition from mercantile to industrial capitalist relations of production. The point, however, is that modes of production are essentially and fundamentally different from each other. There is no gradual continuity between them, but only absolute discontinuity. For each mode of production is based on a different central contradiction.[138] Thus the process of articulation, and the attending religious changes, introduce essentially new economic, social and religious forms – which should be discovered underneath the appearance of continuity. The tributary mode of production (organized around kings, chiefs, tribute, often also slaves), the capitalist mode of production (of which colonialism was a secondary instrument) – both represented fundamental changes in the relations of production in which local African populations were involved. Far from being a sign of commitment to the interests of the African masses, in terms of freedom, identity or self-esteem, it is a denial of the fundamental class relations in which these masses have been involved for centuries when we ignore this discontinuity in their social and economic history, and indeed their religious history. The actual historical processes by which each mode of production defined itself and articulated itself to pre-existing modes may have been gradual and prolonged; but in these gradual changes real qualitative changes took shape that were central to the whole organization and ideology of the social formation.[139]

Similarly, the modes-of-production approach would see religious change not exclusively, perhaps not even primarily, as the result of gifted individuals struggling with the interpretation of life, society, and the widening or contracting cosmos. Of course, there is that element too; and it would be foolish not to recognize the achievements of such great religious innovators as, for instance, Central Africa has seen in the course of the twentieth century. But through these individuals, less individual and less conscious processes of profound structural change were at work, processes which the religious innovators and their followers scarcely perceived or comprehended. However great African prophets have been, a Great Men theory does not really help us to understand them. Neither does a Blind Structure theory, of course, but the latter takes us slightly further, while we are waiting for a symbolic theory to solve it all.

As to the place of Christianity in modern Africa, I cannot say that the modes-of-production approach has really advanced beyond Horton's view. There does seem to be a major correspondence, or at least compatibility, between nineteenth and twentieth century Christianity and capitalism. Once a systematic symbolic theory has been formulated, we shall be able to pinpoint this correspondence convincingly. At the same time there does seem to be considerable room for dialectics here. Mission education prepared many thousands of Africans for a career within capitalist relations of production: how many carpenters, bricklayers, clerks, teachers, nurses, derived their specific skills and

63

their overall adjustment to wage labour within formal bureaucratic organizations, from early mission experience? But the same education also provided thousands of people with the intellectual background and the attitudes to *challenge* capitalism and colonialism. The success of the world religions in Africa is a firm datum in the study of the religious transformation of Africa; and if Horton's explanation is no longer good enough, the theory advocated here is not yet sufficiently mature to provide a better answer.

However, many problems I discussed above in connexion with the intellectualist approach do come closer to a solution with the modes-of-production approach. No longer do we need to juggle with the concept of a microcosm comprising anything between a small rural village and a large kingdom. The unit carrying a specific, distinct religious complex is not the microcosm or the macrocosm (ultimately a unit of experience), but the mode of production -- a unit defined by such primary determinants of experience as labour, production, reproduction, control, and expropriation. The specific pattern a composite religious system takes at a given point in time and place, links up with the specific pattern of mutually articulated modes of production within the social formation -- which is altogether more complex and more fundamental than the admixture of macrocosmic and microcosmic elements within a society. Nor is the extreme compartmentalization between religious and secular aspects of society a necessary assumption for all phases of religious change. In so far as religious elements are part and parcel of the relations of production (and this is clearly the case in all modes of production except capitalism), the relation between religious and social change is no longer solely enacted through the individual consciousness of religious innovators and their followers. This relation also takes place at a much deeper structural level, beyond individual reflexion. Since religious change is also a matter of shaping new relations of production, the organizational aspect which the intellectualist approach could not accommodate, becomes much less problematic. Religious change creates not just new structures of thought, dealing with the explanation of causation; it also creates new structures of extraction and circulation, and thus new class-like structures between those involved in the new religious forms in different, complementary roles (e.g., as followers versus leaders). Even the tantalizing problem posed in chapter 6 has come much closer to a solution: the practice of a particular cult, like Bituma, in geographically and structurally very different settings within the same wider society (modern Zambia), becomes understandable once we realize that we should not try to relate such a cult exclusively to either the total 'local rural society' or the total 'wider society' – but that the cult could be an aspect of the articulation process between the domestic and the capitalist modes of production as contained, in the form of evolving and mutually subservient sub-structures, within the same overall social formation.

Finally, the image of contemporary Central African religion as a composite of layers, each with its own historical background yet retained and integrated within a complex present, now opens up for more incisive theoretical and methodological analysis. Most layers represent a distinct mode of production. Ancestor worship has been retained, since the domestic mode of production of which it forms an integral part, is still a more or less viable structure within the overall social formation.[140]

The same applies to chiefly ritual, and the cult of the High God. The picture gets more complicated once we realize that some religious layers of sub-systems refer manifestly not to any one distinct mode of production, but to the process of their articulation, as I have claimed to be the case for the cults of affliction in western Zambia. But at any rate, the modes of production to which the various religious forms belong no longer function as they did when their basic structure defined itself. They have been articulated to each other, and in the course of the present century have been effectively subjugated to the capitalist mode of production. Also, their present articulation, under general dominance of the capitalist mode, is no longer what it was prior to the penetration of industrial capitalism. Thus, the articulation between the neo-traditional, encapsulated domestic and tributary modes (in other words, between rural villages and chieftainship) in Zambia in the 1970s is likely to be very different from the articulation between the domestic and tributary modes in the early nineteenth century.[141]

Methodologically, this way of looking at religious change has one major drawback. What changes did this process of articulation and subjection produce within each mode? What likely transformations did this process effect in the religious aspects of each mode? These crucial questions can now be asked, and both the theoretical and the empirical spade-work towards answering them is now in full progress. Whatever the ultimate answers, it seems likely that we shall have to consider those layers in contemporary Central African religion which pertain to other modes of production than capitalism, as the results of recent transformations, which only after systematic decoding (but we have yet to find the key) can be used as historical evidence (cf. note 32). This, again, places some of the analyses in this book on shifting grounds – but such is the way of scientific discovery.

Conclusion

The primary aim of the studies presented here has been to create a regional and historical framework within which the data on Central African religion and religious change could be integrated and interpreted. That, after the initial application of different models, a modern Marxist model turned out to be the most appropriate, was largely for two reasons. A historical yet explicitly theoretical approach is built into Marxism; and the recent emphasis on modes of production and their articulation enables us to rise above single-tribe approaches, and to see the underlying economic, social and political patterns that, stretching over much of Central Africa, appear to form the background to the amazing similarity of the religious forms and innovations that have manifested themselves in that region over the last few centuries.

To conclude this introductory chapter, I shall discuss some of the remaining problems and tasks associated with this emergent Marxist approach. This may help to clarify its status in the light of the methodological, theoretical and philosophical concerns of a much wider community of scholars than Marxists alone.

The empirical identification of modes of production

One of the main problems in current research on Central African society and history is that of the unit of study. Single-tribe approaches no longer meet the requirements imposed by our increasing body of data and our increasing theoretical sophistication in this field. To what extent does the adoption of the mode of production as the main unit of study represent a real advance? Is it not the return, under a fashionable label, to what essentially amounts to a model of bounded ethnic groups? Recent French Marxist authors, with the notable exception of Amin, have tended to apply the modes-of-production approach to the analysis of social formations which seem to be confined to a single ethnic group. An example are the Gouro of the Ivory Coast, first described by Meillassoux, and subsequently the subject of heated debate when Terray re-analysed Meillassoux's interpretation of the Gouro economy.[142] Not only is the problem of ethnic boundaries in relation to the boundaries of modes of production still awaiting exhaustive discussion in the French Marxist literature. We also have to admit that the level of concrete operationalization of the high-sounding theoretical catchwords of this anthropological school leaves much to be desired. How does one go about the actual spade-work of identifying and demarcating a particular mode of production in the course of anthropological or historiographic research? When our French colleagues working in the Marxist tradition get down to specific discussions of empirical material, the theoretical concepts would often seem to be less powerful than in broad theoretical *tours de force*.[143] On this point a cross-fertilization seems required between French theorizing and the canons of data collection and handling as developed in British, American and other schools of anthropology and historiography.

It is my contention that the problems attending the operational definition of modes of production in the Central African context can be solved, even if such a solution is not yet available. The normal definition of a mode of production as employed in this volume points to concrete relationships of production, expropriation and control, that are clearly manifest on the grass-root level where ethnographic and historical data are collected. In fact, many researchers have collected and analysed data of this nature, but usually, without already casting their analyses in the idiom of the modes-of-production approach. This approach looks for fields of economic, social and political relationships, and it is, on the level of data-collection, not so very different from established approaches cast in terms of economic, social or political structure. However, the emphasis on material production and circulation enables us to see patterns and fields that are by no means peculiar to the many bounded ethnic groups we have come to distinguish in the Central African region. The domestic mode of production among the Nkoya and the Bemba may be slightly different, especially on the level of social organization and ideology,[144] but on the level of production and circulation it certainly falls within the same overall category extending over the whole of Central Africa. Likewise the emergence of the tributary mode, while displaying a considerable amount of local variation,[145] revolves around the same few processes of extraction and circulation, and has created similar structures of equally wide geographical extension. The industrial-capitalist mode of production is not even confined to the Central African social formation. The processes of extraction it represents have fairly similar forms in much of Africa and in the Third World at large. Only for convenience's sake could we limit a case study of the modes of production to specific geographical areas, or to the ethnic and linguistic groups, and administrative divisions, occupying those areas. In the same way, there is only very slight justification for equating the domestic mode of production mainly with rural areas and the capitalist mainly with urban areas, in Central Africa. In actual fact we are dealing with fields of domestic, tributary and capitalist relationships which overlap in any one of these demarcated geographical, ethnic or administrative spaces, and which may well extend beyond the more or less arbitrary boundaries defined in that space. And it is precisely for this reason that a modes-of-production approach fits in with a regional perspective that extends beyond bounded ethnic groups. Another reason why the mode of production, rather than the ethnic group, can serve as a unit of study particularly with regard to pre-colonial Central Africa, is that many ethnic groups are of recent origin anyway.[146] They have become pronounced, regrouped, in some cases they have even come into being, in response to the dynamics of regional competition within the overall administrative and political framework imposed by the colonial state.

The remaining heuristic potential of discarded models

Does the adoption of a Marxist perspective (in chapters 6, 7 and 8 of this book), and the reflexion on the methodological and theoretical potential and limitations of such a perspective (as in this introductory chapter), mean that the potential of the earlier, non-Marxist models has been reduced to nothing? I do not think so. The systematic, explicit models, both Marxist and non-Marxist, that are applied in this book were adopted for two reasons: because they seemed to make sense of the available, limited body of data; and because they could guide us in the collection of more and better data. While I argue that the interpretative power of the Marxist approach is superior, the heuristic value of the alternative models has by no means been exhausted. However, in order to make further collection of data along the lines of the non-Marxist models meaningful as contributions to the emergent Marxist framework, it is necessary that these models are reformulated in Marxist terms. In the course of this introduction I have already indicated some possible reformulations, e.g., by incorporating the analysis of protest within a more comprehensive framework of the types of consciousness that are associated with the dynamics of the articulation of modes of production; and by presenting the postulated confrontation between immigrant rulers and earlier territorial cults, as the rise of a tributary mode of production. However, on this point some more work will have to be done.

This line of argument would seem to contain an invitation to eclecticism. If so, it would be eclecticism of a hierarchical kind, where other approaches are brought in only to the extent to which they can be integrated into a primarily Marxist framework. This is the theoretical strategy pursued by Godelier.[147] The present chapter shows that it is possible, even necessary, to compare and contrast various possible approaches, and select the one that best fits the expanding body of data. It is not for dogmatic reasons that I have opted for a Marxist perspective, but for reasons of empirical analysis, which are discussed in detail in chapters 6, 7 and 8 as well as in the preceding sections of this Introduction. At the same time I have tried to make the great limitations of this perspective very explicit. The single main limitation is that the Marxist approach does not yet offer a viable, convincing theory of symbols capable of confronting the Central African religious data on the level of symbolic analysis itself. We cannot just take our pick among the existing non-Marxist approaches to symbolism, and graft the approach of our choice onto a Marxist analysis of economic and political aspects. What we do need is a new, *Marxist* theory of symbols, which does full justice to the relative autonomy of the symbolic order (and which therefore can fully benefit from the many and valuable insights non-Marxist researchers have attained), but whose real power and originality would lie in the fact that it succeeds in presenting an explicit analysis of the relations and transformations forward and backward between the symbolic and the material order, devising typologies and dynamic patterns for these relations and transformations, and indicating under which specific conditions which types will occur.

Discussion of the relations between the symbolic and the material orders leads on to two major objections which tend to be raised against a Marxist approach: economic determinism, and the idea of a unilinear evolution of social forms, which realizes itself irrespective of human freedom and of the unpredictability implied therein. A general discussion of these formidable themes can hardly be expected here. Let us instead discuss them briefly and with exclusive reference to this book's argument.

Economic determination of the symbolic order, and the latter's relative autonomy

I reject a conception of the symbolic order which attributes to it a dynamic existence all of its own, entirely divorced from the processes of production, control and expropriation which create and reproduce the material conditions for human life and for society at large. With Marx, Althusser and perhaps all Marxist writers, I am inclined to view these material processes as *determining*, in the last analysis, the totality of social phenomena. On the level of religious research this means that, if one wishes to penetrate to the essence of religion, only a contextualized analysis is meaningful, that is, one that takes into account not just religious phenomena, but also non-religious ones.

When has one arrived at 'the last analysis'? The processes of material production which take place within the various modes of production, take shape on a number of levels, which we could provisionally identify as economy, social relations, politics and ideology. These levels do possess a considerable degree of relative autonomy *vis-à-vis* the material processes that may well be their ultimate determinants. The various levels are autonomous to such an extent that in all modes of production except the capitalist one, the *dominant* level turns out to be *not* the economic level. Processes of production (which in themselves are constrained by the degree of development that the productive forces have attained) set the confines for a mode of production; the latter's actual shape and texture is dominated by the nature of social relations within the domestic community, by the nature of political relations within a tributary system, etc. Therefore, the link between material processes on the one hand, and social relations, politics and ideology on the other, is not of the nature of an absolute dependence, as might be claimed by some extra-scientific dogma. Instead, the nature of this link is to be assessed by painstaking and prolonged empirical research.

At many places in this book[148] I stress the relative autonomy of the symbolic order (i.e. the ideological level) and the freedom this autonomy implies in terms of symbolic experimentation, creativity, free variation, exuberance. This opens the door to the development of a mature theory of symbols. African religious innovators are eminently worth studying, their activities are moving and inspiring, not because they slavishly obey the laws governing processes of material production; for that is precisely what these innovators do not do. Perhaps their main significance is that they actively confront the contradictions around which these processes of material production are organized, contradictions which relate to the social, political and ideological level in all sorts of complex ways. This confrontation takes the form of the creation of new symbols, or at least of new combinations of symbols, to such an extent that in some cases (e.g. Lumpa) the very production process is shaken to its foundations.

What is so fascinating in religion, African and otherwise, is not that it is a true reflexion of processes of material production, but that it tries (in vain?) to transcend these processes, thus displaying something of unique value: not, I should say, a spark of the divine, but at least courage on a truly human scale. It appears to me that an adequate theory of symbols, capable of dealing with religious phenomena, should also be able to cope with artistic and esthetic aspects of human life. Beauty is perhaps the ultimate consequence of the symbolic order's capability of transcending the limitations and humiliations of material production. And such beauty (man's reward for a creative and passionate handling of symbols?) as well as the powerful emotion it produces, is present in African ritual in abundance. An approach like the one advocated in this book neither denies nor defiles this side of religion. At most it contains the suggestion that we are not ready yet for an analysis on this exalted level. For the time being so little has been researched with regard to the material constraints of the symbolizing process, that the latter deserve priority in our research strategy.

Chapters 4, 5, 7 and 8 suggest that, in the Central African context, new symbols are being invented, or new combinations of existing symbols are being forged, within a fairly limited creative space, and in rather close interplay with changes in the processes of material production. The same symbols crop up time and again, and innovations take place along the same few dimensions. But this does not mean that the human symbolizing activity is swept under the carpet. Rather, our attention is focused, in addition to symbolic analysis in itself, on fundamental material conditions which probably have a wider scope and contain profounder tragedy than the idealist categories that so often figure in analyses based on the assumption of the primacy and the absolute autonomy of the symbolic order.

A unilinear evolutionism?

The idea of the relative autonomy of the symbolic order, which implies a considerable degree of free play in religious innovation, already rules out *a priori* a model of religious innovation as a process of unilinear evolution, taking place out of blind necessity, and in absolute dependence on processes of material production and the changes therein. On the concrete level of the analyses offered in this book, it will be clear that the very chapters which show the limitations of the creative space as well as the importance of material processes in religious innovation also stress the complex and unpredictable nature of religious innovation. Admittedly, empirical analysis suggests that religious innovation in Central Africa has revolved around the permutation of the same, limited selection of symbolic material. There is a certain degree of accumulation of the results of earlier innovations. For a very limited part of Central Africa (notably, central western Zambia), and for a relatively short period (not much more than two centuries), an 'overall process of religious change' is claimed to have manifested itself through many different religious movements. But this image of convergence and, perhaps, unilinearity, appears only at the level of data; it will be discarded without hesitation as soon as more and better data will turn out to point in a different direction. This convergence is in no way a deduction from some preconceived theory. And as to the actual historical processes through which this overall convergence manifests itself, I stress in chapter 4[149]

> its strikingly dialectical nature. Innovation along the five dimensions would not be accumulated from movement to movement in a simple, one-way fashion: rather than consistently following up the themes that an earlier movement had emphasized, a later movement might show a relapse to a less advanced state of these particular themes, and instead emphasize other themes.

The social mechanisms which trigger each of the distinct religious movements are indicated (the three types of religious *avant-garde*). There is nowhere the suggestion of a predestined evolutionary process seeking to break through at all costs. Also when this model is reformulated in the Marxist version of chapters 7 and 8 and of this Introduction, it never becomes a simple, self-validating deduction from theory; its dialectical (i.e. historical) element increases rather than decreases. The identification of three main modes of production, and the periodization of the process of their articulation, may be crude, but it is based on some evidence at least. Moreover, the model of the various modes of production existing side by side in the same social formation, each going through its own development, and each being articulated to the other modes, is too complex for it to lend itself to simple unilinear evolutionism. Shifts and swings from one type of religious form, one type of consciousness, to another remain possible. In fact, my analysis of the development of the Nzila, Bituma and Moya cults indicates precisely such shifts. The future developments in the field of religious innovation cannot be predicted from the evolving analytical model. There remains plenty of room for prophets propounding real, original forms of innovation.

Above I discussed Ranger's recent criticism of my approach, and his call for an analysis suggestive of 'a less consistent, more particular, more fully historical set of processes'.[150] I wonder to what extent Ranger's point implies, after all, a fundamental difference of opinion as to the nature of historical analysis. My own primary aim has been

to arrive at an explicit and systematic social theory which takes historical dimensions into account. Ranger, and most historians with him,
would seem to be after a form of historiography that is, no doubt,
enriched by the application of social-scientific concepts and insights,
but that yet retains its proper identity as a discipline, and that, particularly, objects to too much theory, too much systemization, too much
explanation in other than common-sense terms.

There is an element of irony in this. Ten years ago the data on
Central African religious change were scarce and scattered beyond hope,
and no one could have predicted the emergence of systematic, regional,
integrated approaches such as offered by, e.g., Schoffeleers's collection
Guardians of the Land,[151] or the present volume. Now that these
approaches are finally becoming available (largely as a result of Ranger's
immensely stimulating efforts), they are deemed too systematic, too
little historical. I suppose this is a passing phase in the development of
this field of studies. The analyses presented here were not meant to be
final.[152] What we should do now is to try to improve on the theoretical
and methodological deficiencies of the emerging models; and, perhaps
even more urgent, go out and collect, in the light of these as yet deficient
models, the finely-grained historical data that are to give our models
a much sounder empirical basis, and that, we hope, would endow
them with those elements of historicity which they are now still lacking.
It would be best if professional historians took over again. Meanwhile
the possible contribution of archeology should not be overlooked. The
materialist overtones in the more recent models might well provide
the missing link between the artefacts that can still be unearthed, and
the irretrievable religious concepts and activities of an earlier age.

'The essence of religion'

I wish to conclude with a couple of questions that many researchers
steeped in more traditional approaches to African religion are likely
to raise. Does a highly contextualized approach to African religion, like
the present one, really bring us closer to an understanding of the
'essence of religion'? Does it help us understand the religious experience
of Africans, or of mankind as a whole? Or does it get stuck in superficialities, in secondary phenomena that may explain the concrete
formal modifications of African religion, but that do not touch on its
essence? What did the writer do, after all, with those 'hauntingly
vivid images' he presented as a kind of credentials in the preface, only
to write, in the remainder of the book, on anonymous structures and

processes in which the real men and women engaged in ritual and religious innovation appear to get drowned – if not the writer himself. Or, in my own words,[153]

> What is it (if anything) the adepts communicate with, when the drumming and the medicinal vapours they inhale, lead them (though rarely) to paroxysms of ecstatic transport?

After the abortive argument in chapter 6, this question does get a tentative answer in chapters 7 and 8, and in the course of this introduction; and that answer may cast light on the other questions as well.

The adepts find themselves in a situation of articulation of modes of production which affects every aspect of their lives, resulting in a very low level of fulfilment of material needs, as well as limiting these people's capability of understanding their own situation and changing it. Given all this, against the background of my view that a cult of affliction like Bituma is in itself a form of articulation, I am inclined to suggest that in the ritual the adepts communicate primarily with symbols in which the specific historical development of the social formation they belong to lies stored, in a condensed, coded and de-historicized form. The emotions stimulated by the ritual, seem to stem from the adepts' encounter, in a symbolic form, with the precipitate of the succession and articulation of modes of production, and thence with the nature of the contradictions, the mechanisms of expropriation and control, and (on the subjective level) the misery and humiliation, which constitute those modes of production.

Among other things, religion seems to be a means for people to expose themselves to their collective history in a coded, de-historicized (fossilized?) form. And the scientific study, in other words the decoding, of religion is an undertaking which, among other disciplines, belongs to the science of history, not so much because religious forms have a history, but because religion is history.

This may be the sort of outré statement an anthropologist trained in a-historical approaches would make once he has discovered history. At the same time it seems to sum up, for better or worse, the theoretical content of this book rather adequately.

Chapter 2

Possession and mediumship in Zambia: towards a comparative approach

Introduction[1]

Since the first comparative studies in anthropology that were not only comprehensive (in the old tradition of Tylor and Frazer) but that also followed a systematic comparative method,[2] anthropology has gone through a long and heated debate over the uses and limitations of cross-cultural comparison. I do not intend to raise here, once again, all the well-known arguments.[3] My treatment would be biased anyway by the fact that my own academic training[4] all but turned me into the kind of comparativist who, even when he is studying a single society, is not happy with his explanations of structure and process therein, unless he has tested these out cross-culturally, with a representative sample of the world's societies, and preferably with the use of some inferential statistics.

This position may be difficult to accept for some historians and anthropologists. At any rate, it is not a very comfortable one in the field of the study of religion – where Swanson's ambitious pioneer work *The Birth of the Gods*,[5] with all its methodological flaws and superficial theorizing, is still about the only full-size cross-cultural study we have. And certainly this position is extremely awkward in the field of possession, mediumship and the associated religious organizations and movements, where even the preliminary systematizing and classification of the comparative material has hardly begun.[6]

Whether a strict comparative approach to possession and mediumship will ever help us to solve the problems of description and theoretical interpretation that face us in this field, cannot be decided before such a study has actually been undertaken. Meanwhile, all I will do in this chapter is to raise a few problems (concentrating on the

75

relation between religion and the wider society in which it occurs) for the solution of which a comparative approach seems to be appropriate, and to suggest, in the remainder of the chapter, some of the lines along which such an approach could be developed.

My discussion will be limited, in most aspects, to Zambia. This is only to respect an emerging division of scientific labour, and should by no means be taken to imply that our more advanced knowledge of Zimbabwean and Malawian possession, for example, were not extremely relevant for the student of the Zambian material.

Compared with other countries in Africa, indeed in the world, the sociographic and historiographic coverage of Zambia is remarkable, both in a quantitative and in a qualitative sense. The present state of our knowledge (largely due to the excellent work done under the aegis of the Rhodes-Livingstone Institute and its post-Independence heir) offers unique opportunities for systematic, comprehensive and thorough comparative research. However, so far this opportunity has seldom been taken.

The situation of Zambian possession studies is typical for this overall situation. There is no lack of primary source material. The topic is repeatedly touched upon throughout the sociological and historical literature. There are a few monographs. But there is no general, integrated account that adequately sums up what we know (and what we still have to find out), and that complies with contemporary standards of analysis and explanation.

For the benefit of those who do not automatically subscribe to the comparativist credo, let me end this introduction by summing up the major gains that a comparative approach to the Zambian material is likely to yield:

We will attain a somewhat greater continuity with regard to the research work done before Independence.

Comparison is likely to suggest underlying, general patterns of a much wider geographical and historical distribution than can be revealed by the monographic material.

On this basis, new problems for research of specific topics and specific regions can be formulated in a more meaningful and strategic way; and new models can be devised that may have heuristic and explanatory power outside the local setting for which they were devised.

Thus the Zambian material, with its enormous potential, can on the one hand be better illuminated by, and can on the other hand better contribute to, the development of generalized theory about man and society.

Religion and society: some theoretical considerations[7]

The problem

To whatever aspect of human behaviour and human society we turn, everywhere we see a great variety.

This is particularly the case in the field of religion, partly because religion, dealing with non-empirical beings and forces, is less confined by the normal empirical conditions of space, time and efficacy which limit the range within which everyday kinship, economic and political systems can vary.[8] For instance, it is rather impractical for a kinship system to define as one's close kinsman a person who lived two thousand years ago and at the other side of the earth. But religious systems, especially in their definition of supernatural beings, are relatively unaffected by such base practicalities; and a huge variety of religious forms and contents, throughout the societies of the world, is the result.

The religion of any given society represents a particular selection from this worldwide range of religious possibilities. To what extent is this selection *random*? In other words, to what extent is the particular religious system of a society dependent on or independent of other, non-religious aspects of the same society? Is it possible to formulate general statements about what features the religion of a society will have, given the patterns of residence, kinship and marriage, given the political and economic system of that society?

What, indeed, is the relation between religion and society?

Admittedly, by the adoption of certain forms of religious activity, belief and organization, rather than other ones, societies can show a dynamic creativity that in many cases is as difficult to relate to other aspects of the same society and to its history as, say, the literary imagery of a poet can be explained away by reference to his life history and social position. Originality and some measure of uniqueness are indeed among the most fascinating aspects of any socio-cultural arrangement.

In so far as this applies, the process by which religion takes a particular shape in a society may not be totally random, but will yet follow patterns that elude a systematic, comparative approach. In many cases, however, the correspondence between aspects of religion, on the one hand, and particular social-structural and historical data, on the other, is so striking that we do not hesitate to point out the connexion.

One such case is the obvious relation between a social organization based on descent groups, and local possession beliefs in terms of ancestral spirits.[9]

Likewise, if we find that in many types of possession throughout Zambia the invisible agents to which possession is attributed are claimed to be members (especially chiefs) of neighbouring tribes, or of tribes previously occupying the same area, every sensible researcher would view this state of affairs in the light of other information about the relations (political, migratory, marital, economic) between these tribes. Depending on the historical situation, we might, for instance, regard such beliefs as the reflexion (and even, other data lacking, as evidence!) of past invasion, when the possessed's tribe ousted the previous inhabitants of the area, but was not completely successful in legitimizing its claims to the territory; the memory of the original 'owners of the land' still haunts them in the form of possession agents.

Fascinating as such an analysis may be, what is its actual value? This cannot be assessed before we thoroughly analyse the total field of related phenomena: the precise nature of the historical confrontations between the two tribes; their actual interaction at the time when such local possession beliefs were recorded; other ways in which the historical relations between the two tribes may be reflected (e.g., institutionalized joking relationships); the existence of similar possession beliefs, among the same tribe, with regard to other tribes with which it has had comparable historical experiences; and, alternatively, the absence of such beliefs in cases where the historical experiences were decidedly different.

And even so, the scientific explanation of local beliefs in terms of social-structural and historical phenomena remains very arbitrary, unless it can be incorporated (as is, yet, only very seldom the case) into a more general, systematic theory.

Basically, our problem here is that of the empirical referents of religious symbols. This has been a major problem in the social and historical analysis of religion (including possession and mediumship) ever since the middle of the last century, and may be said to be really at the basis of the emergence of sociology as a discipline.[10] Despite this long tradition in the social sciences, a general and widely accepted theory in this field (a theory of social symbols with particular reference to religion) is at present only in a nascent state. Our current theory hardly allows us more precise statements than that 'religion is a model of, and for, society'.[11] Comparative studies, which clearly show the range of variation and the general principles of the relation between religion and wider society, would surely bring us nearer to an insight. A detailed comparative analysis of the Zambian material would be relevant here. But even V. W. Turner,[12] whose profound analyses of

Ndembu society and religion form such a landmark in modern religious studies, did not manage to bridge the tremendous gap in our comparative understanding of the problem, such as it stands in the Central African region.[13]

Correspondence and compensation

So far, the literature (on Zambia and elsewhere) suggests mainly two possible relations between religion and the wider society: correspondence between one and the other, and compensation of one by the other.

Correspondence can be said to occur whenever the dominant social-structural and historical themes of a society are in agreement with dominant aspects of its religion. In the case of possession, numerous examples could be cited. I mentioned already possession by ancestral spirits in a society whose dominant organizational principle is descent. We may find possession by invisible weather-controlling agents (with a territorial rather than a descent connotation) in a society where locality rather than descent is the dominant organizational principle of economic activities.[14] Also, the measures taken within the narrower family group (as effective in the non-religious sphere) whenever one of its members is afflicted by possession, enhance the integration and identification within this group.[15] And so on.

Compensation we might call a situation where religion brings out principles that have no direct equivalents outside the ritual sphere, and which rather counteract the non-religious social arrangements. Here again many examples could be cited. Rituals of possession and mediumship are said to: provide structural remembering (anamnesis, as opposed to amnesia) of key ancestors of social groups;[16] provide social hierarchies, in the religious sphere, in a society otherwise lacking these;[17] create both interaction and identification on a supra-local scale, in a society that, in the non-religious sphere, lacks such supra-local integration.[18]

Likewise, social association and dissociation in ritual may cut across group formation in the domestic, economic, kinship and political field.[19] Ritual specialists may form a check on the excessive concentration of political and ritual authority in the hands of chiefs.[20] And possession provides a theory of causation whereby misfortune can be attributed to invisible agents outside human society (allegedly following their own whims, or in direct retaliation for human failure) rather than (as in witchcraft and sorcery) fellow-members of society.

I will not aim at any degree of completeness in this summing-up, or suggest the refinements the above approach badly needs. The more fundamental question I would like to raise is: how meaningful, how scientific, is this approach?

The resourceful researcher, reasonably well versed in both the theoretical and the descriptive literature on his subject, will seldom be at a loss when analysing aspects of religion as either correspondence or compensation of principles in the wider society he describes. If correspondence cannot be demonstrated, there is always a good chance that the compensatory aspects will clearly stand out, and vice versa. In either case he works already under the assumption that anyhow there is an identifiable relation between religion and society. Let us not overlook that this assumption in itself requires further investigation. What do we mean when we say that religion reflects society and its history?

Religion and society: configurational congruence

What we seem to mean is, essentially, the congruence, respectively incongruence, between patterns (configurations) of elements in social life – configurations in beliefs, concepts, structural arrangements, inter-action, etc. Take the fairly common situation in which religion mobilizes, for a certain ritual, roughly the same set of persons as interact with one another in non-religious activities. If for such a situation we claim that religion corresponds with social organization, all we are saying is that in the religious sphere the pattern of recruitment between individuals is more or less congruent with the pattern of recruitment in the non-religious sphere: see Figure 2.1.

Likewise, if we claim that socio-economic deprivation in the non-religious sphere is compensated by exalted religious expectations (of belonging to 'the chosen'), all we say is that the believers, either con-sciously or subconsciously, use two closely related (inversely symmetri-cal) interpretative configurations, one for the religious sphere and one for the non-religious sphere, configurations that can be summed up by Figure 2.2.

Similar representations could be devised for other cases where soci-ologists and historians have 'explained' the relation between religion and society in terms of correspondence or compensation.

This is not to demonstrate that such explanations are meaningless, but only to suggest that they are rather shallow; too shallow to be presented as sparks of original and ultimate insight.

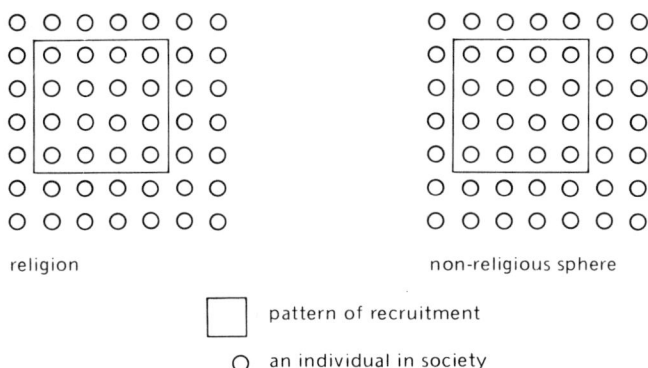

religion   non-religious sphere

□ pattern of recruitment

○ an individual in society

Figure 2.1 *Recruitment patterns in the religious and non-religious sphere*

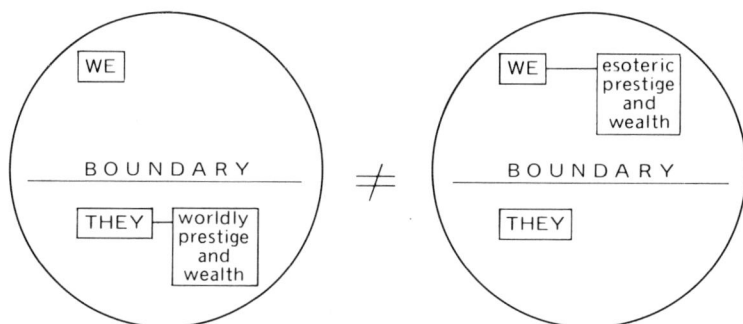

Figure 2.2 *Religious compensation for socio-economic deprivation*

Problems in the analysis of configurational congruence between religion and society

Apart from the obvious empirical problems involved in the actual description of both the religious and the non-religious field, there are several explanatory problems that I will discuss in this section.

Compare what is comparable: The social sciences have developed numerous rival approaches to classify the various aspects of social life: interaction versus values; structure versus culture; infrastructure versus superstructure; participants' level versus analytical level; the division of society into various institutional complexes (political, economic, etc);

and so on. Whichever scheme we adopt, the religious and the non-religious configurations we relate to one another should really be comparable in that they belong to the same class of phenomena. For instance, if we adopt a distinction of social phenomena into inter-action and values, a discussion of the compensatory integration as created by religion can only be meaningful if ritual interaction is compared with non-ritual interaction, or ritual values with non-ritual values. For if, in such a case, we claim that ritual interaction in itself compensates non-religious values, then we make the assumption that there is an automatic, invariable one-to-one relationship between values and interaction; and the whole of the social sciences is there to prove that such an assumption is ludicrous.

Selection and relevance of the religious and the non-religious item: Independent from whether the systematic distinctions are carefully observed, still the configurations can be chosen from widely different aspects of society, as is illustrated by the Zambian examples given in this chapter. We are never able to compare the whole of a religious system with the whole of the non-religious aspects of the society. Therefore, in our analysis we only touch upon a few salient aspects, and hope that they are typical and significant for the total society we are dealing with. The choice of these aspects is largely arbitrary: what guarantees that an author really singles out basic principles, instead of trivialities? In many cases, moreover, a religious item may have both compensatory and entirely corresponding functions, depending on with what non-religious item we choose to compare it. What is guiding our choice then? The only reliable guide would be, again, an explicit, systematic theory of the relation between religion and society – but such a theory we do not have yet.

Relevance of correspondence and compensation: We want to be sure that the religious and non-religious items we select for comparison are *in themselves* really crucial enough to justify our analytical efforts. However, the problem of relevance has yet another side. The value of our analysis depends on the extent to which the relationship of corres-pondence or compensation, *between* religious and non-religious item, is really relevant.

Let us take again a compensatory analysis in terms of the depriva-tion hypothesis. Such analysis, then, only makes sense if, among other, the following conditions are fulfilled:

1 The difference in wealth and prestige between the deprived and their reference group is really an intensely felt reality to them – and not just a humanitarian assumption made by the researcher.

2 The depriveds' access to esoteric wealth and prestige is, equally, an intensely felt reality to them, and not just a state of mind that the researcher, eagerly interpreting into their religious symbolisms, attributes to them without very good reasons.

3 The compensation is at least temporarily effective, i.e., it succeeds (albeit only during ritual) in resolving the deprivation by presenting the alternative, esoteric configuration not only as a theoretical, intellectual possibility, but also as a thoroughly felt reality for the believers. If and when such success is achieved, typical verbal and psycho-motor behaviour (symbolic action, joy, trance, ecstasy) can normally be observed. If no such success occurs, the esoteric configuration (even although it is inversely symmetrical to the socio-economic configuration) can be viewed as corresponding to, rather than compensating for, the believers' perception of their own deprivation. The existence, somewhere, of the 'new earth and new heaven' is stressed, but they remain unattainable. Much as a *fata Morgana* of shadowed oases drives home the predicament of the thirsting desert traveller, the mere image of a better life tends to underline whatever is wrong with the actual life.

Another example of the same problem (that compensatory analysis is dubious unless the relevance of the compensation itself is clearly demonstrated) may be taken, again, from Turner:[21]

> By establishing ties of co-participation in cults which operate independently of kinship and local linkages, the ritual system compensates to some extent for the limited range of effective political control and for the instability of kinship and affinal ties to which political value is attached.

Turner suggests that the adepts in the same cult identify with one another – regardless of political and kinship ties. But is this identification really followed up in the non-religious sphere, e.g., in political support, economic co-operation, establishing of marriage ties, between the adepts thus ritually linked? Neither in the passage cited here, nor in his major analysis of ritual, *The Drums of Affliction*,[22] nor in any of his other Ndembu studies, does Turner deal explicitly with this important question; and the descriptive material he provides in other contexts does not take away my impression that in actual fact this ritual identification is only of little relevance outside the religious sphere. What then is the significance of the compensation Turner claims to exist?

The degree of insulation between religion and society: Another important aspect of the problem of configurational analysis is the degree of insulation that exists between the religious sphere (including possession and mediumship) and the sphere of everyday, non-religious activities and concepts.

The absolute distinction between the sacred and the secular ('profane') which Durkheim[23] introduced into the sociology of religion, was so much a product of the philosophy, and of the wider social structure, of the highly differentiated, industrial, European nineteenth-century society, as to make its general applicability doubtful.[24] There does not seem to be so much of a problem if the same principles pervade religion and society equally (correspondence). But if religion has to counteract, rather than correspond with, the rest of society, then the religious sphere must be shielded off from the other spheres to some extent.

Within one society the degree of insulation of the religious sphere is unlikely to be fixed and inflexible. The modern descriptive material, on whatever religious system (not in the last place the perceptive analyses of Zambian religion by Turner and Colson[25]), suggests that the degree of insulation is produced, and both consciously and unconsciously manipulated by the believers, in an extremely complicated, often contradictory dialectic pattern of conceptualization and interaction. As Geertz writes:[26]

> The movement back and forth between the religious perspective
> and the common-sense perspective is actually one of the more
> obvious empirical occurrences on the social scene, though, again,
> one of the most neglected by social anthropologists.

Unless we recognize the processual nature of the relative insulation between religion and society, our general statements about the ways in which religion reflects society may be utterly irrelevant. And if we do realize this problem, how are we going to solve it, in the course of a comparative analysis of religions taken from a number of societies?

Intermezzo: an optimistic example: I am not over-confident that the comparative problem posed in the previous paragraph can easily be solved within our present cross-cultural methodology. If some solution can be found, it will become possible to formulate tentatively typical patterns of insulation and connectivity, and to relate these (as correspondence and compensation) to major aspects of societies and their history. Thus we might explore hypotheses linking the compensatory (respectively corresponding) nature of religion as mechanism of local and supra-local integration, to the average size of the political unit, in a number of (Zambian) societies: an approach reminiscent of Swanson's.[27]

The Tables below illustrate my point. In a first attempt we classify the average effective political unit in a society as small, medium size, or large (as compared to the other societies in our sample); similarly, we classify the average effective ritual unit (as defined by the number, and the geographical extension, of the people collectively mobilized by, e.g., a single possession cult). Table 2.1 gives a few examples.

There is (see Table 2.2) one compensatory belt, where the ritual unit is larger than the political one, and where the possession cult can be said to compensate the political structure by providing interaction and identification on a scale exceeding the political organization; there is a correspondence belt, where ritual and political unit virtually coincide; and another compensatory belt, where the ritual unit is consistently smaller than the political unit, and forms a ritually integrated segment within the wider political organization. This suggests that the compensatory function of ritual (provided that the compensation can be shown to be really relevant), even when we confine ourselves to such a limited aspect as political organization, can work in at least two directions: it can either break through the political boundaries, or it can, within the wider political framework, define effective smaller groups within which certain effects (such as satisfactory participation and close identification, hence psychological security) may be more readily achieved than in the wider political group.

Further exploration along these lines (extended to many other items in the field of social organization, religious concepts and interaction) is likely to show a wide variety in types of compensation – and to refine our conceptual apparatus. However, the value of such an approach largely depends on proper control of the comparative process (adequate data, typologies, and operationalization).

The explanation of correspondence and compensation: Finally, there is the problem of how this relation between religion and society (correspondence or compensation) is produced, and of how it persists

Table 2.1 *Effective political and ritual units: some Zambian examples*

		Effective ritual unit		
		small	medium	large
Effective political unit	small		Tonga (a)	
	medium			Chewa (b) Ila (c)
	large		Urban Nkoya (d) Ndembu (e) urban Independency (f) urban Pentecostal (g)	

Sources: (a) Colson (1960, 1962); (b) Langworthy (1971); (c) Smith and Dale (1920); (d) Van Binsbergen (1972a); (e) Turner (1957, 1968); (f) and (g) my urban field-notes.

Table 2.2 *Ritual reinforcement and compensation of political structures*

over time. What mechanisms can we firmly identify in this respect?

The whole approach that views religion as a reflexion of society has a definite functionalist ring about it: religion, by corresponding with, or compensating, the non-religious aspects of society, contributes to societal survival and integration; and is this postulated contribution not the main *raison d'être*, not only of the compensation or correspondence, but even of religion itself?

If this crude teleology is unacceptable to us, what else can we then suggest to be the basis for the systematic relation between religion and society? As long as we lack more adequate answers to these questions, the minute classification of ritual in terms of direct or inversed reflexion of the non-religious aspects of society, might be little more than a time-wasting intellectual game.

The deprivation hypothesis

The theoretical considerations presented here have direct relevance for what has emerged as a major interpretative model in the total field of the sociological and historical study of Central and Southern African religion: the 'deprivation hypothesis'. The basic idea in this approach is suspiciously simple: 'people will look for compensation in the religious sphere, if and when they cannot get what they want, or need, in the non-religious sphere'.

I shrink from summing up the large number of publications where this type of interpretation has been used. Its predominance in the indicated field of study seems due partly to a too one-sided interpretation of Sundkler's conclusions in the first[28] edition of *Bantu Prophets in South Africa*; and partly to Gluckman's early work on the Zulu,[29] which appears to have influenced Sundkler[30] and which certainly had a great impact on the Manchester-dominated research in Central Africa. Zambian examples of application of the deprivation hypothesis can be found in the works by Long, Watson, and Rotberg, among others.[31]

In the context of possession and mediumship the deprivation hypothesis appears, at first sight, highly applicable in many ways,[32] of which I will only mention the following: In some Zambian cases, the interpretation of certain illness behaviour as possession is resorted to only after the patient has failed to be successfully diagnosed and healed by application of more prosaic, technical, non-ritual medicine, of either African or European origin; i.e., if the patient is 'deprived' of recovery.[33] Several forms of possession have their highest incidence amongst women, who are typically regarded by the analysis as being deprived as compared with men.[34] Mediums display the tendency to be recruited from clans barred from the highest political office.[35]

Though in these and other aspects of possession the deprivation hypothesis may provide some interesting initial organization and analysis of the material, we must clearly realize that as an explanation it is very superficial indeed. Ignoring the whole range of problems as discussed above, the deprivation hypothesis presents *compensation* as the invariable, almost universal form the relation between religion and society can take, and assumes that such compensation is automatically relevant for the believers.

Further analysis is likely to show that the deprivation which the researcher initially perceived so clearly is actually much less clear-cut, and can scarcely stand against the evidence of seriously collected and analysed data. Thus the association, in Zambia as elsewhere, of certain forms of possession with male transvestitism[36] and with women's reproductory troubles[37] suggests that the preponderance of women in possession phenomena has to be explained by a thorough analysis of the total socio-cultural system of male-female relations in a society, rather than by easy reference to male domination and female deprivation.[38] Similarly, such a simple explanation as political deprivation hardly fits the Chewa historical situation, where not only the supreme rain-medium (a woman!) played a crucial political role, but where also the clan from which rain-mediums used to be recruited, far from being really deprived, actually controlled (in the burial and installation of chiefs) the basis for chiefly legitimacy, and at the same time provided the hereditary councillors that constituted the major constraint on the chief's powers.[39]

The relation between religious and non-religious aspects of society is extremely complex, and calls for thorough theoretical and empirical analysis on the basis of much more sophisticated models than the deprivation hypothesis offers. When phrased within an explicit theoretical framework, the comparative study of Zambian possession and mediumship is likely to contribute to the extrication of some of the most fascinating problems in the study of religion.

Preliminaries to a comparative approach to Zambian possession and mediumship

After the discussion of some theoretical problems, I shall now turn to the more empirical, practical aspects of a comparative approach to the Zambian material: how shall we define possession and mediumship as a field of enquiry? what typologies can help us in the identification and the first, tentative classification of material? and how can we arrange our findings in a historical perspective?

Definition of possession and mediumship

There is, in the Zambian case especially, an obvious need for more precise definition of possession and mediumship.

The descriptive literature presents a great variety of vernacular terms, taken from many different languages, and designating widespread phenomena that we might group together, without too much distortion, into a limited number of clearly defined classes. On the other hand, the non-vernacular terms used in the literature (possession, medium, patient, cult, etc.) often do not refer to the same type of empirical phenomena.

From a theoretical point of view, the words 'possession' and 'mediumship' have certain disadvantages. In order to point these out, let me recapitulate a distinction which is now almost commonplace in modern anthropology: the distinction between participants' level and analytical level. The members, or participants, of a given society have their systems of explicit categories and definitions with which they attribute meaning to their environment and their actions, and it is a major task of social-scientific (and historical) research to identify these systems and describe them in their internal coherence. However, in so far as the local participants' interpretations of themselves and their own society does not offer a complete and exhaustive analysis, the researcher tries to go beyond these interpretations, and discusses them, with their wider social-structural and historical implications, on an analytical level, where scientific terminology takes the place of the participants' concepts.

'Possession' and 'mediumship', then, do not so much give an analytical description of certain states and activities of individuals, but rather interpret these states and activities on what is essentially the participants' level: invisible agents (such as 'spirits') are supposed to 'possess' the individuals in question, and speak through their mouths. These participants' beliefs are not in themselves analytical, but call for further, scientific interpretation on the analytical level. When and why do participants interpret their own states and activities in this fashion? With what other phenomena on the participants' level are these local beliefs associated? If we confuse the two levels of social-scientific description, and treat 'possession' and 'mediumship' as analytical concepts, these concepts will have the following undesirable implications.

Because they concentrate on the participants' interpretation of their behaviour, rather than on the behaviour itself, these concepts can deal only with varieties and similarities in such behaviour to the extent to which this diversity is explicitly recognized by the participants themselves.

These concepts attribute to the participants extremely stereotyped interpretations (such as implied in the common-sense meaning of 'possession' in English), interpretations that may not meaningfully reflect the categories that are actually being used by the participants in their own language. An important aspect of this problem is the degree to which the possessing agents are considered to be personalized. As our concept of spirit possession implies a high degree of personalization, we run into difficulties when we apply this concept to the frequent Zambian cases where, in the participants' interpretation, the invisible agents involved are diffuse and essentially impersonal as in the 'modern' possession cults (see pp. 95, 97).

This is not to say that we should not analyse the local beliefs associated with possession behaviour, or that we should abolish such concepts as 'possession' and 'mediumship' altogether. For one thing, as long as we have only a very dim insight in the psychological and physiological aspects of this behaviour, there is no real alternative to the current usage. Moreover, any social impact that possession behaviour, and the people thus behaving, may have depends ultimately upon the local participants' interpretation, within their own belief system. So it is no use adding to the confusion by introducing a new conceptual framework. Still it is necessary to realize, from the outset, the implications and limitations of the accepted terminology.

We can define possession, then, as a particular state of the individual: the state of being regarded, by himself and by his social environment, as exceptionally closely associated with, and exceptionally strongly dominated by, entities other than ordinary living human beings.

Thus defined, possession shades into such adjacent concepts as: piety, religious office, illness, obsession, and insanity. Where and why local beliefs (and, for that matter, the individual ethnographers describing them) made distinctions between these concepts is a complicated semantic problem that can hardly be discussed here. The metaphysical system of local participants (not only within Zambia) tends to be considerably less coherent than the ethnographers might have wished (especially if the latter are qualified western theologians, as is the case with many early ethnographic works produced by missionaries). Within one society it is already very difficult to point out where local beliefs make the distinctions between the related concepts summed up above. Generalizations about one religion then become problematic, let alone the problem of cross-cultural comparison.

Although virtually all authors would seem to accept the above definition of possession, from their reports it is clear that at least the following types of possession states have to be distinguished:

1 Possession as an extremely momentary and very intensive state (usually accompanied by drumming, singing, sometimes smoking); here it is useful to distinguish between (a) momentary possession involving

temporary psycho-physiological changes (trance, ecstasy, speaking in tongues, unconsciousness, insensibility to pain); and (b) momentary possession not involving such changes.

2 Possession as a permanent condition with diffuse, non-intensive manifestations, but which is at intervals re-activated as under 1.

3 Possession as a permanent condition with diffuse, non-intensive manifestations, a condition reached after a short, unique period of more acute and intensive manifestations;

4 Possession as a permanent condition throughout life, with only diffuse, non-intensive manifestations.

The literature on Zambian possession often fails to distinguish between these (and possibly other) types of possession, so that the empirical facts underlying possession can be anything between a permanent backache and the most expert, breathtaking performance of less than one hour's duration.

Once these types of possession have been distinguished, we can[40] speak of *mediumship* when the state of possession involves the transmission by the possessed of messages supposed to derive from the possessing agents. Here again we have the whole range of types of possession: the medium can deliver the message in a single event, or in a process extended over time; the transmission may require a concentrated performance (possession of types 1(a) or 1(b)), – or, without a clearly demarcated ceremonial, derive from the general, permanent, possession state the medium is in.

Anthropological and historical literature on possession tends to take possession behaviour for granted. The emphasis is not on possession, but on what people and society *do* with it: reflect the social structure, compensate for deprivation, achieve prestige, make a living, etc. This is a perfectly legitimate approach, especially since few anthropologists and historians have the psychological and medical background that would enable them to study possession behaviour in itself.

Yet we need to know much more about the individual, psychological and physiological side of possession behaviour: only in contrast with such knowledge can we truly appreciate to what extent possession is something *social*.

To what extent is possession behaviour a form of social interaction: i.e., learned (formally and/or informally), sanctioned (by approval, prestige, ridicule, etc.), and part of the total interaction process by which an individual expresses himself and tries to achieve his goals in relationship with other individuals? To what extent, therefore, is possession behaviour a voluntary and conscious manifestation of the role an individual chooses to play within his social environment? Or does possession behaviour - like illness and insanity - spring from involuntary psycho-physiological conditions, with the implication that some possession behaviour (that in which these uncontrollable psycho-physiological conditions are not entirely fulfilled) must be considered as 'not genuine', as 'only simulated'? If possession behaviour is to be voluntary, what then explains the occurrence of fixed, repetitive patterns, not only in the same individual, but also between individuals? (E.g., why do many people initiated into a particular cult start trembling when the appropriate music is being played, whereas they remain unaffected when slightly different music is being played which, in its turn, is able to evoke acute possession behaviour in the members of other cults?)

For the solution of these difficult problems the distinction between permanent ('chronic') possession and momentary ('spectacular') possession may be useful.

Permanent possession seems just a participants' theory about certain diseases that are likely to occur anyway, whether the people involved want it or not, and whether they associate them with invisible possessive agents or not. With some exaggeration (for we know that even in the case of apparently strictly bodily affliction the relation between being ill and the social setting is very complex) we might say that society does not *create* chronic possession behaviour: all it does is calling this behaviour possession, and patterning it - making it the object of a cult. The theoretical problem here is analogous to the patterning of human mating (which would occur anyway) into systems of kinship and marriage. Again, we concentrate on 'what society does with it'.

Momentary possession, on the other hand, is not only secondarily patterned by society, but is much more primarily a social phenomenon. With the same exaggeration, we could say that momentary possession would not be there unless explicitly defined, recognized and institutionalized by society: it is just a form of social interaction. Here we have to ask ourselves, not only what society does do with this form of possession, but also when and why some societies produced it, whereas others do not.

Dimensions in the variety of the Zambian material

Zambian possession, as described in the literature, displays an enormous variety. Before we can make any meaningful comparisons within this material, we have to subject it to a preliminary classification, so that for each type of possession the constituent features will clearly stand out. We shall have to enumerate the whole range of possibilities that is covered within the total material. Thus, as our comparative research proceeds, we shall be able to formulate, and test, hypotheses about the relationship between various specific aspects of possession as such, and between these aspects and the specific social-structural, historical and ecological situation within which each type of possession occurs. Thus we will probably detect some of the general conditions that influence the presence and the form of certain types of possession in a certain society.

However, we should not overlook the fact that religious phenomena are somewhat more than a set of entries in a table. The comparative approach may reveal general correlations within religious systems, but such results will have to be followed up by intensive investigations of the individual cases.

Some important dimensions of the variety in Zambian possession include: the nature of the associated beliefs (the participants' interpretation of the possessing agents and of the latter's relationship with the possessed and with the community); the distinct institutional settings in which possession and mediumship can occur; and the social organization of possession and mediumship in themselves.

Not aiming at completeness, I shall briefly go through the rather tedious exercise of summing up the various possibilities along these three dimensions.

Participants' interpretation: The following types can be distinguished:
1 The possessive agents are personal invisible entities of human origin:
   (a) Earlier members of the same social group as those possessed (defined in kinship terms, territorially or politically): ancestors in general; chiefs and headmen; remarkable specialists in the fields of hunting, dancing, divining, healing; people who have died recently and who have not been treated properly after death.[41]
   (b) Earlier members of a different, but locally significant group: the original owners of the land; members of neighbouring groups (particularly chiefs and remarkable specialists).[42]
2 Personal invisible agents, not originally human:
   (a) The High God.[43]
   (b) Guardian spirits of the total community, who may derive their powers from their supposed relationship with the High God.[44]
   (c) Terrestrial spirits, whose relation with the High God is obscure.[45]

3 Impersonal, abstract, general entities (an animal species, 'guitar', 'airplane', *bindele, songo, masawe, mowa, bituma,* etc.: 'modern possession cults'; see chapters 4–7).

Institutional complexes: A usual way of linking distinct activities, and their local interpretations, to the wider society in which they occur, is to identify within this society a number of institutional settings, and then to view these activities and beliefs as embedded in one such setting.

The obvious comparative problem here is that the nature of, and the inter-relations between, such settings may widely differ from society to society, even if belonging to the same, limited geographical area (such as Central Africa). The aim of the comparative approach is to bring out and to explain systematic differences – not to deny them! So our problem is at least twofold. We have to assess whether in a certain society a particular institutional complex, defined with sufficient generality, is present or absent; and subsequently we have to describe, in as much detail as possible, the internal variations of the institutional complex in those societies where it does occur.

Thus, in the societies of Zambia, the following institutional complexes can be identified as being relevant for a discussion of possession and mediumship:

1 The institutional complexes concentrating on the interaction between man and his non-human natural environment; 'ecological' is a possible designation for this complex. Most of this interaction is of an economic nature: it consists of ways in which man uses the natural world to meet his requirements of food, shelter, clothing, implements, etc. In this context, possession can occur in three situations; these are rainmaking: ritual directed towards guardian spirits of the community;[46] hunting: ritual directed towards spirits of animals and dead hunters;[47] horticulture: ritual directed towards spirits of the arable land.[48] 'Man's selective interest in Nature'[49] does not only define that part of nature that is useful and in current use ('cultivated' – made into a part of man's society). It also defines what is not yet, or no longer, used; as well as that oppressive, dangerous part of nature that can, or should, never be used for social purposes: the abodes of malign spirits, in the forest and the water. Terrestrial spirits associated with non-cultivated, non-humanized nature are regarded as possession agents in many parts of Zambia, and they belong to the ecological complex in the possession phenomena.

2 Possession is being used, though infrequently, as a divining technique.[50]

3 Possession (either by indigenous possession agents, or by the Holy Ghost) is an aspect of Christian, or Christian-inspired denominational religion throughout Zambia.[51]

4 Although many forms of possession behaviour (especially rain-making and divining) are not in themselves locally interpreted as diseases, yet healing is the most important institutional complex within which possession occurs. It is also the most comprehensive, in that it touches on all other three complexes. The healing complex is particularly important in the 'modern' twentieth-century forms of possession in Zambia, which often took the form of those almost epidemic waves of possession 'illnesses' (*ihamba, bindele, ndeke,* etc.) that, incorporated in loosely organized cults, rapidly spread over very wide geographical areas, and that are typically associated with non-personal possession agents.[52]

It is important to note that whenever we find one of the above institutional complexes in any one Zambian society, possession and mediumship are by no means invariably part of that complex. Sometimes the absence or presence of possession in certain local forms of a particular institutional complex constitutes one of the major differences between neighbouring ethnic groups.[53] In these cases we have the opportunity to investigate the social-structural and historical conditions for the occurrence or absence of possession in a particular complex.

Identification of these major complexes within which possession and mediumship occur has also a more directly heuristic value: it can guide us in the detection of possession in other parts of Central Africa, where the same institutional complex occurs but where our sources have, so far, failed to identify possession.

Social-organizational aspects of possession and mediumship: The variations in Zambian possession sketched so far precipitate a great variety of social roles and statuses, which are often incorporated in a complex system of religious organization, with well-defined hierarchies, with specialist tasks (divinatory, curative and political), and with significant supra-local extensions. Some aspects of this variety are:

1 The social-structural principles that govern the eligibility, and the actual recruitment, of those possessed and of mediums (male versus

female; outsider versus member of the in-group, as defined in terms of descent, territoriality and/or political organization; slaves and captives versus rulers; wealth versus poverty).

2 Mode of recruitment (through personal possessive crisis and/or through apprenticeship, often including payment of a fee).

3 Organizational structure (the various distinct roles and the hierarchy, within the possession system, including related roles of those who participate but are not possessed: ritual leaders, assistants, patient's sponsors, musicians, audience, etc.; the wider geographical organization).

4 Rewards and costs in terms of prestige and wealth.

5 The degree of speciality those possessed, and mediums, represent within their community (their numerical distribution; visible paraphernalia, if any).

6 Political significance.

The literature on these subjects is very uneven and so incomplete that it does not yet allow even a tentative analysis.

The time perspective

Little do we know, as yet, about the history of particular possession cults in Zambia. Where already some work has been done (as is the case for 'modern' possession cults with impersonal agents) a review of the literature reveals an extremely confusing pattern: these cults appear alternately as well-established for centuries, or as recent innovations produced by the rapid social change of our times.[54] The concepts of diffusion and of partial reinterpretation (by the participants) may provide reasonable solutions for this dilemma, and offer topics for future historical research. The rapid spread of the modern cults over a large geographical area raises questions in the field of inter-regional contacts, trades routes and labour migration routes.

The mere fact that most of the local forms of these modern cults do have a non-local history makes their scientific analysis in terms of the expression of the immediate experiences and needs of the people concerned dubious.[55] Is a cultural item borrowed because it fulfils some deep, common need, or simply because it is new, exciting, beautiful and fashionable? The fact that the borrowers may have been in a situation similar to that of the original inventors of the modern cults (with regard to labour migration, rapid social change, exposure to missionary work, colonial administration, and white economic enterprise) can help us to understand the rapid and wide diffusion without ruling out the possibility of repeated, independent invention. This does not take away the fact that processes of cultural innovation and diffusion are too complicated to be explained by simple reference to the direct social and psychological conditions of a few individuals at a certain moment.

From the historical point of view, an adequate typology of the variety in possession along its three dimensions (participants' interpretations, institutional complexes and social organization) will form the necessary basis for further investigations inspired by the following hypothesis: that various types of possession correspond systematically to various stages in a process of social change.

For the Zambian material, this idea was advanced by White.[56] He explained the shift in Luvale possession beliefs (from ancestral agents to impersonal, non-ancestral ones) in terms of the breakdown of the traditional kinship organization, the increase of inter-regional contacts, the influx of Angolan immigrants, the growth of individualism and, generally, the new experiences brought by modernization. This interpretation is supported, though not expanded or generalized, by later writers.[57]

Along the same lines, we may compare various types of possession cults by reference to their inherent potential for adaptation to change.

It is a common observation among students of religious change that collective, communal ritual may be more open to the influence of modern changes than the intimate, solitary religious behaviour (incantations, libations) that an individual can perform all on his own. White[58] again shows the applicability of this idea to the Luvale ancestral cults.

Some interesting generalizations can also be based on Colson's detailed studies[59] of the excessive, traumatic changes produced by the creation of Lake Kariba in the late 1950s. Particularly interesting is the contrast she makes between the two protagonists in the Tonga rain ritual: the (possessed) mediums and the (non-possessed) ritual leaders. The social position of the ritual leaders, defined by hereditary attachment to a localized shrine, is more affected by, and is less able to adapt to the new resettlement situation, than the position of the mediums: possession, as the main characteristic of the medium, can come to any individual, irrespective of kinship and local background, and can gain someone a reputation as a medium far away from his home. This example demonstrates that possession seems to have an inherent flexibility in defining religious office and its incumbents. If this is a valid assumption, then we should not be surprised to find an increased emphasis on possession in times of rapid social change.[60] For if possession is open to everyone (if it forms, as it were, a crash-course in religious leadership), then it is particularly suitable whenever there is a major change in the principles (notably, membership of certain kinship, territorial and/or political groups) that historically govern eligibility to religious office.

One major form of adaptation, of course, is the incorporation and reinterpretation of possession within modern Christian, denominational religion. Published Zambian material about this topic is scarce. However, the general pattern seems essentially similar to the well-documented Zimbabwean cases.[61] A complicating factor, sometimes overlooked, is that certain new forms of possession were introduced from overseas (notably through the Pentecostal mission churches), and gave rise to patterns of innovation that compare interestingly with the typical independency-*cum*-possession syndrome of possession in independent churches, so familiar from the literature on modern Africa.

Another perspective seems equally important: that which concentrates not so much on the changes the cults themselves undergo, but which views these cults as important foci for accommodation and reorientation, even protest, in rapid social change outside the religious sphere. Here all the problems discussed in the second part of this paper are relevant. Unlike Zimbabwe,[62] Zambia still waits for its history of possession and mediumship in relation to colonial politics to be written.[63]

Moreover, even today possession cults (including those that received no Christian reinterpretation whatsoever) are still very much alive – not only in the remote rural areas, but right in the centre of Zambia's big towns, waiting for adequate sociological research.[64] Colson's observation[65] that 'a possession dance is rarely held in the immediate environment of a town' is not generally valid for modern Zambia; although much depends on how one specifies 'rarely'.

The urban cult's role in rapid social change is suggested by my own Lusaka field-work on modern cults with impersonal agents. The adepts are mainly newcomers to town in the first, strained stages of adaptation to urban life. The modern possession cults (in the urban, as well as in the rural form) are far from being a regressive lapse into traditionalism and conservatism.[66] On the contrary, they seem to perform a positive buffer function in that they provide easily accessible (though rather expensive), preliminary and perhaps superficial, but at least temporarily adequate ways of adapting to a new life situation, notably in cases where a more enduring adjustment (such as becoming a stabilized towndweller, a commercial farmer, an elder in an established Christian church) cannot yet be achieved.

This is by no means a new idea, but rather an echo of what Sundkler, on second thoughts,[67] discovered to be an important aspect of South African independent churches: 'in the city, with its rapidly industrialized civilization, they functioned as "adaptive structures" '.

Conclusion

At the present stage of the study of Central African religious systems, it is not time yet to sum up, self-contentedly, what we already know. On the contrary, what we need now is to make a thorough assessment of the enormous gaps there are still in our knowledge and particularly in our theoretical understanding; and to devise new research by which we may hope to fill these gaps, sooner or later.

In this chapter I have tried to indicate a few points at which we need a more sophisticated approach: particularly the relation between religion and wider society, the deprivation hypothesis, and the definition of possession. I have advocated a general, comparative study of the Zambian material as one of the strategies by which to gain further insight, and have finally suggested, as the basis for such comparison, a few ways in which the available material could be arranged, both sociologically and historically.

Chapter 3

Explorations in the history and sociology of territorial cults in Zambia[1]

The territorial cult in the Zambian context

Territorial cult and shrine cult

In a first attempt to apply the analytical concept of the territorial cult to Central Africa, Schoffeleers has tentatively defined this concept as[2]

> an institution of spirit veneration, proper to a land area, whose primary concern is the material and moral well-being of its population, archetypically represented by its rain-calling function, and whose immediate control is institutionally limited to an elite.

This definition identifies what in fact has been one of the main forms of religion in Central Africa. Most of the religious institutions to be discussed in this chapter comply with this definition and can conveniently be called territorial cults. However, in order to present these religious institutions, analytically and historically, in their interrelation with other institutions, I find it useful to introduce an additional analytical concept: the shrine cult.

Territorial cults as defined above are not necessarily shrine cults. The concern for the material and moral well-being of the population of a particular land area need not focus on shrines. Alternative ways in which this concern can be institutionalized are, for example, prophets who are only loosely attached, if at all, to shrines;[3] other specialists who claim magical control over rain and fertility and who are professionally employed by their individual or communal clientele whenever the need arises;[4] the concentration of power over rain, land and fertility in such movable, non-shrine-like objects as the royal bracelets of the Lunda and the Luvale.[5] Yet, as is borne out by Schoffeleers's recent collection

100

Guardians of the Land,[6] the most widespread and typical form of the territorial cult in Central Africa is that of the shrine cult.

What is a shrine? A number of characteristics seem to be relevant at the same time. First, a shrine is an observable object or part of the natural world, clearly localized and usually immobile. It is a material focus of religious activities, and perceived and respected as such by the participants. The observable features of a shrine are defined within the participants' local religious system, which entails a limited selection of material objects (man-made or not) that possibly qualify for a shrine. The material variety of shrines in the Zambian context will be discussed below. In the case of non-man-made natural shrines, particular specimens from a class of natural objects such as trees or hills are selected to become shrines in a certain community. While there is also a wide variety in man-made shrines, the most typical form here is a miniature hut-like construction. Man-made shrines in Zambia are seldom permanent; often they are short-lived, constructed for the specific occasion of placating a particular invisible entity after the latter has demonstrated his wrath.[7]

The religious activities focusing on the shrine need not occur in the present: in so far as the erection of a man-made shrine is in itself a concentrated religious activity, the shrine may fall into disuse and still remain a shrine. Religious activities include not only what the believers positively do (such as clearing a spot, erecting a shrine, offering prayers, libations and sacrifices, or manipulating sacred attributes) but also what they refrain from doing out of religious considerations (such as demolishing the shrine, removing objects from it, hunting, killing or making love near the shrine). The shrine will only cease to be a shrine, will lose its sacred nature altogether, when it has entirely ceased to instigate any such positive or negative religious activities in the participants.

The extent to which a certain shrine is effective and operative may vary considerably over time. And even within one historical period the sacred nature of the shrine is likely to have a strong situational aspect. Thus the local religious system may define times, situations and social roles in which the shrine's sacredness is particularly relevant and in which deep religious respect is to be man's main attitude when approaching the shrine; on the other hand, there may be room at other times and for people playing other social roles (such as children) for a more detached, pragmatic and even playful approach to the shrine without any offence being implied.

While identifiable by locally-defined observable features and by special treatment, the essence of the shrine lies in the fact that it refers

to non-observable beings or forces. In the midst of the empirical world
(the land, the people, the sky) a shrine is a spot which is singled out and
treated in a very special way because of its close association with events
by which entities believed to exist somewhere outside the visible order
can manifest themselves within this order – and where, therefore,
humans can communicate with these entities. This formula suggests the
enormous potential of shrines in the total field of comparative religion.
Shrine religion is not just an interesting taxonomic variant – it is one of
the main types of religion.

I have said that most territorial cults in Central Africa (as defined by
Schoffeleers) could be regarded as shrine cults. On the other hand, not
all shrines necessarily pertain to a territorial cult proper. While shrines
are normally features in the landscape, this does not imply that the
primary concern of the religious activities focusing on them can only be
the material and moral well-being of the local population. Though
concentrating on shrines in territorial cults, we shall have to discuss
in this chapter several types of shrines whose basic orientation is not
primarily, or not at all, ecological (shrines associated with chieftainship or Christianity), and shrines which, while ecological, reflect concern not so much for the total local population as for the individual
professional success of specialists. Thus the concept of territorial cult
and shrine cult intersect and indeed largely overlap, but neither is a
sub-set of the other.

General overview of the shrine cults in twentieth-century Zambia

Most available data on shrine cults in Zambia derive from twentieth-
century sources, particularly anthropological publications. This material
is fragmentary, yet it will enable us to form a picture of the recent
situation as a starting point for our historical and sociological
explorations.

Vansina has emphasized the 'considerable degree of cultural homogeneity' of the peoples of the savanna south of the equatorial forest;[8]
and while his own cursory generalizations on their religious systems[9]
are not particularly useful, it is a fact that the forms of shrine
cults, their material aspects and their rituals, are remarkably
similar at least throughout Zambia. Across the territory, similar
features of the landscape are selected as natural shrines, similar
man-made shrine structures are erected, and the same limited
range of cultic activities (assembly, prayer, offering, mediumship)
can be observed. This basic similarity, however, takes various

specific forms which I shall now examine in an attempt to construct a typology.

A general feature is that in virtually every area in Zambia there exists more than one type of shrine, each type with its own features relating to the following four basic parameters: material layout and attributes; associated ideology; organization of the cult; and nature of the associated group. A good presentation of this principle can be found in Richards's description of Bemba shrine religion,[10] where she distinguishes as many as six different types of shrine: an individual's hut,[11] the village shrine, villages of deceased chiefs, natural phenomena, chiefs' burial groves and relic shrines containing the chiefly paraphernalia. These may all be of relevance simultaneously, though each in a different way, to the same localized set of people. This multiplicity of shrine forms is by no means exceptional in Zambia and cannot be explained away by any particular religious or political characteristics of the Bemba. Any sources that go into some detail on the subject reveal a similar multiplicity for other Zambian peoples, although the concrete forms may be different, and deceased chiefs' villages and burial groves, for example, do not figure everywhere as shrines.

An overall distinction can be made between shrines that are man-made and shrines that are not. The latter include trees, groves, hills, fields, pools, streams, falls and rapids. Occasionally these natural shrines may be accentuated by the erection of man-made shrines, either permanent or temporary.[12] A transition between natural and man-made shrines occurs when trees are purposely planted in order to provide a shrine (on graves as in many parts of Zambia, and in the case of the *muyobo* tree, which is planted in the centre of the villages of southern Lunda, Luvale, Luchazi and related peoples);[13] or when rudimentary constructions such as a pile of stones,[14] two uprooted anthills placed one against the other,[15] or a branch or part of a tree trunk[16] are used as shrines. The typical form of the man-made shrine is a construction which, though often in miniature, is identical to the normal thatched dwelling-house or to the men's shelter (a thatched construction without walls, as found in the centre of villages in many parts of Zambia). Finally, graves may be used as shrines either with or without a hut-like construction on top of them.

Concerning the set of people involved in the cult of a certain shrine (through direct participation, or through reference and implication), the following possibilities exist: the cult can be limited to one individual; limited to a small group of closely related individuals; it can be extended over a village or over a neighbourhood comprising several neighbouring villages; a larger area which tends to be associated with a chief, a senior headman or a localized clan-segment; a localized ethnic group (tribe); or a group of neighbouring tribes.[17] This series represents a hierarchy of residential and political units; a quite different dimension is manifested in the cultic group, whose recruitment typically cuts across residential, kinship and political ties – as is the case with the modern cults (most of them involving shrines) which I shall discuss in the following chapters of this volume.

Ideas associated with the shrines revolve around two major issues: the goals and effects the believers hope to achieve through the activities at the shrine, and the nature of the invisible entities to whom the shrines refer.

For these goals it seems fruitful to distinguish between the domestic sphere (ranging from individual to neighbourhood) and the wider, inter-local sphere. Shrine activities in the inter-local sphere focus on two fundamentally different though frequently merging principles: concern for a land area (the territorial cult), and chieftainship. Territorial shrine cults aim at ensuring the success of the ecological activities in which the population is engaged (horticulture, fishing, hunting, animal husbandry) and hence at the material, and ultimately moral, well-being of this population. Annual planting and first-fruit ceremonies form a common (though not universal) element[18] throughout Zambia; they are supplemented by occasional ceremonies in times of crisis (drought, famine, pests). Shrines associated with chieftainship are either chiefly graves or relic shrines containing the paraphernalia (such as drums, gongs, bow-stands and axes) of deceased predecessors; access to them may be limited to the ruler himself. These chiefly shrines play a major role in accession to chieftainship; their main function is to be a source of legitimacy for the ruler. Chiefly shrines tend to assume ecological connotations, following a dialectical process which I shall explore below.

On the domestic level, village and neighbourhood shrines have primarily a territorial, ecological reference. In addition to this they may serve individual purposes as places where a living member of the village reports to the invisible, deceased members of the village community when departing for or coming back from a long journey;[19] similarly, the village shrines set the scene for rituals dealing with affliction attributed to ancestors.[20] The shrines which kinsmen erect on the grave of a deceased kinsman (usually after being summoned to do so at the latter's deathbed, or later, after dreams or illness have been divined as conveying messages from the deceased) do not primarily serve an ecological purpose but rather spring from concern for individual health and ultimately refer not to the land but to the local minimal kin-group. There is also a type of individual shrine, apparently universal in Zambia, through which the individual specialist tries to enhance his professional success by reference to direct ancestors or mythical beings associated with his skill: honey-collecting, hunting, fishing, rain-calling, iron-working, dancing, divining or healing.[21] Many of these skills have a direct ecological orientation; however, their primary concern is the ecological success of the single individual with whom they are associated rather than the general well-being of the land and of the total community.

The participants' goals and purposes in the shrine cults refer to invisible entities associated with the shrines. There exists a remarkable variety on this point: recently deceased members of the kin group; lineage spirits in general; deceased local celebrities (diviners, dancers, doctors, hunters); deceased chiefs; a class of land spirits that, lacking historical or anthropomorphic connotations, are anonymous and are normally referred to as a collectivity (such as 'ngulu',[22] 'wowa',[23]); culture heroes;[24] the High God;[25] and the abstract, rarely personified concepts that are at the core of modern cults of affliction and that sometimes merge with the anonymous collective land spirits.[26]

These ideological aspects are related to the shrine cults in such a way as to suggest a systematic pattern. First, there are hardly any non-modern shrines recorded as being directly and exclusively associated with the High God; the few examples in the literature consist of: a temporary rain shrine among the Kaonde,[27] a cursory remark on Lozi village shrines,[28] and the case of the supreme Chewa medium, Makewana, who reputedly communicated directly with the High God and whose sphere of influence extended well into Zambia – even far beyond the effective sphere of political influence of Undi's kingdom.[29] Second, cults which the participants associate with deceased kinsmen, local celebrities and lineage spirits are largely limited to the domestic level;[30] whereas, for obvious reasons, the cult of deceased chiefs belongs to the inter-local level. Third, few shrine cults are reported to unite, in their effective ritual activities and in their ideological references, more than one tribe; those that do are territorial cults associated either with land spirits[31] or with the High God.

Let us finally turn to the organizational side of shrine cults in Zambia. Usually there is a small minority of officiants as against a majority of participants or onlookers. Participation at the inter-local level (whether with ecological or with chiefly emphasis) tends to be restricted to holders of office, and the cult tends to have specialist control by priests, chiefs or both, in that the priests have to obtain the chief's permission to perform a ritual. Organization at the domestic level is more open and normally all members of the local community can participate, although women and children may be excluded; leadership, reflecting the general local authority structure, lies either with the village headman or with a ritual leader who may be the custodian of the village or neighbourhood shrine and who sometimes also practises other religious specialities, such as divining. Well described for the Tonga,[32] but probably also occurring elsewhere, is a division of labour between the secular ritual leader, responsible for the shrine and the performance of the shrine ritual, and the inspired medium who is the mouthpiece of the invisible entities with whom communication is established during the ritual. However, information on Zambian specialist mediumship other than in modern possession movements is still too scanty for this issue to be explored further.[33]

The same applies to the widespread Central African institution of the 'spirit wife': a woman (in some local variations represented by a male priest) who has never married or who has given up her marriage in order to engage in a close relationship with the spirit of the shrine. Scattered indications in the literature[34] suggest that on further research this feature may turn out to be as common in Zambia as it is in Malawi and Zimbabwe.

Tentative typology and distribution

With gross oversimplification; the above discussion leaves us with the following main types of shrine and shrine cult for twentieth-century Zambia:

1 Shrines (natural or man-made) associated with inter-local territorial concern and normally in the control of priests; they have an irregular yet widespread distribution in Zambia, apart from the northwest of the country.[35]
2 Shrines primarily associated with chieftainship (relic shrines, graves) and only secondarily with ecological functions; they are controlled by chiefs, priests or grave-keepers, and have a limited distribution.
3 Shrines primarily associated with chieftainship but having major ecological connotations at the same time; controlled by chiefs, priests or grave-keepers, they have a limited distribution.
4 Village and neighbourhood shrines, pertaining to a territorial cult

and controlled by ritual leaders (in association with mediums) and elders; though varying in physical features, this type of shrine seems to have a universal distribution in Zambia.

5 Individual shrines, controlled by the individual concerned, and associated with a particular (primarily ecological) skill; although more data are needed, this type again seems to have universal distribution in Zambia.

6 Modern shrines, controlled by either individuals or cross-cutting sections of the community, and associated with either cults of affliction or such world religions as Christianity, Islam and Hinduism; as a type, they have attained universal distribution in contemporary Zambia. They fall outside the scope of this chapter.

Despite the enormous gaps in our material, it is useful to attempt to map out the geographical distribution of those types of shrine cult that do not have universal distribution. The result of such an exercise is shown in Map 2.

The typology and map presented in this section are only starting points, suggestive of the enormous amount of research that still has to be undertaken. For the time being, they are nearly all the solid data we have; even in their very imperfect form they will have to guide us through the following sections of this chapter.

Shrines, ecology and the community

The ecological perspective

Shrine cults in Zambia tend to have a strong ecological emphasis: they tend to be territorial cults. Therefore, let us set a framework within which this emphasis can be understood and appreciated as being of literally vital importance to the cultivators, cattle-keepers, fishermen and gatherers that for many centuries have made up Zambia's population.

If there is one social science tradition which is, in more than one respect, down-to-earth, it is the one exemplified by such eminent researchers as Malinowski and Evans-Pritchard, who in their major works have attempted to describe non-industrial societies with emphasis on the close and complex links between social organization and environment: the ways in which man, with application of all his technical and organizational skill and intelligence, transforms his natural world so that it becomes livable, human, and social. Studies of systems of cultivation or food preparation may not directly appeal to the student of religion, yet they deal with a primary concern from which the participants derive much of what gives their lives meaning and orienta-

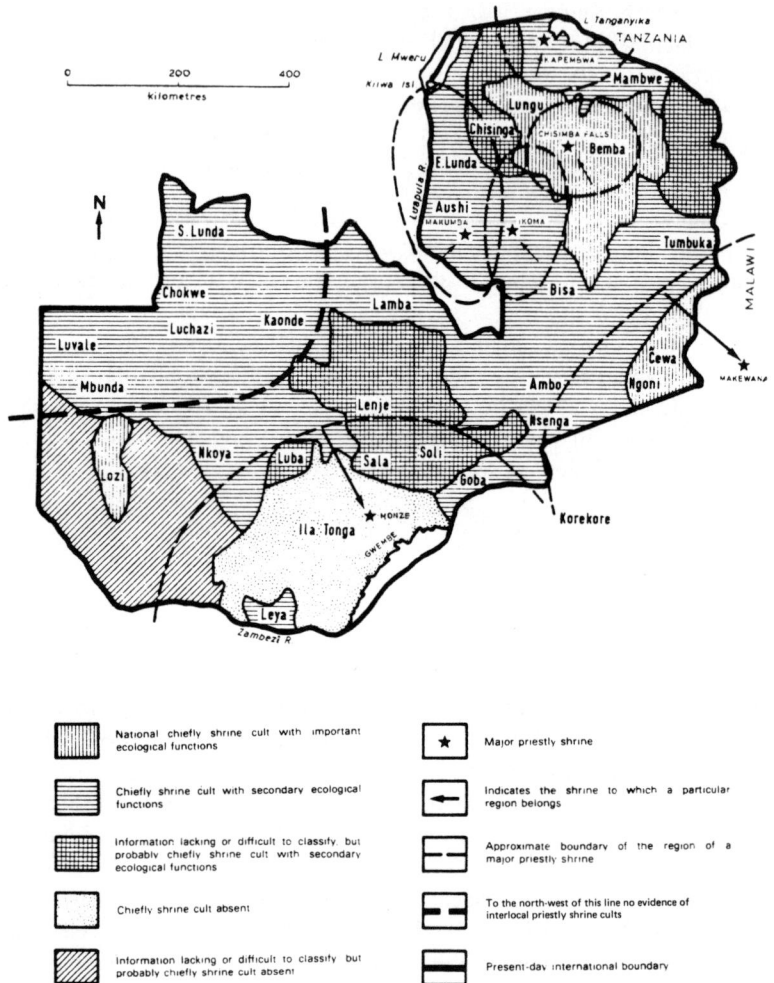

National chiefly shrine cult with important ecological functions

Chiefly shrine cult with secondary ecological functions

Information lacking or difficult to classify, but probably chiefly shrine cult with secondary ecological functions

Chiefly shrine cult absent

Information lacking or difficult to classify but probably chiefly shrine cult absent

Major priestly shrine

Indicates the shrine to which a particular region belongs

Approximate boundary of the region of a major priestly shrine

To the north-west of this line no evidence of interlocal priestly shrine cults

Present-day international boundary

Map 2 Territorial cults in Zambia

108

tion, much of their symbolism and ritual. The process of ecological transformation of nature forms a major element in the religious system of any society with a subsistence economy. In order to understand such a religion fully, we should perhaps accompany our informants to the fields, share their anxiety during a hunting expedition or even live through a minor famine with them.

It is not by accident that the first truly modern sociological study of a Zambian people (Audrey Richards's *Land, Labour and Diet in Northern Rhodesia*) focuses on ecology, but at the same time contains one of the most comprehensive accounts of a Zambian religious system.

Natural and individual shrines in the ecological perspective

The existence of natural, non-man-made shrines becomes more intelligible within the ecological perspective. In the Central African subsistence economy the landscape is never completely humanized – everywhere places remain which have never been subjected to man's ecological transformations or which, once used, have been abandoned again. These places are of great significance; they tend to represent the hidden forces on which man draws for his survival but which, on the other hand, are only too prone to harm him. 'Wild' places play a prominent part in the religions of people engaged in a subsistence economy. In order to become true foci of religious activities, all that seems necessary is that these places be localized and somehow stand out among the other natural objects in the landscape. Hills, pools, imposing trees, caves, streams, falls and rapids become associated with invisible entities, and thus become objects of veneration.

These natural objects are outside the cycle of ecological transformations and do not serve any direct utilitarian purpose for the people concerned. The opposite is true for those aspects of the ecological process that are too important and too uncertain to be left to chance. A clear example is hunting, which among several Zambian peoples[36] has acquired mystical characteristics, including: great social and sexual privileges; the development of numerous medicines to make the hunt successful (or meant for other purposes but derived from killed game); the veneration of mythical hunters; the frequent attribution of affliction cases to deceased hunters; ritual hunts as part of the healing of such affliction and as a divination technique in general; and the erection of hunters' shrines. Much of the same applies to such other important operations as fishing, honey-collecting, ironworking and doctoring (the latter is an 'ecological' operation in so far as it implies the selection and processing of raw natural material into medicine). The individual shrines commonly associated with these specialities form, in a way, the beacons that mark these essential transformations of nature.

The shrine is a spot in the landscape where a concentration takes place of activities directed to invisible entities who are supposed to be capable of influencing the visible world in one way or another. Concentrating here on shrines with strong ecological connotations, the influence of these invisible entities is associated with ecological processes, and with natural conditions necessary for such processes. Now when we arrange the everyday ecological processes (planting, hunting, fishing, collecting firewood and other forest products, building a house, etc.) and the ecological shrine activities in one schema, the result is something like Table 3.1.

Table 3.1 *Shrine ritual and everyday ecological activities compared*

	Type of activity	
	Activity directed to man-made ecological shrines (a)	Everyday ecological activity (b)
Type of area involved	Sharply localized small area	Much more extensive area, not so sharply bound as the shrine
The activity viewed as ecological transformation	No immediate effect visible; the activity only becomes meaningful through a local theory of causation which postulates invisible entities associated with the shrine	Effect is immediately visible, utilitarian and inherently meaningful because it satisfies physiological needs and is interpretable with everyday experience within the visible world

Like any socio-cultural complex, shrine activities (a) and the ecological process (b) have a formal, if you like, symbolic, structure of their own: the integrated configuration of concepts, objects and activities by which such a complex can be defined, recognized, understood and reproduced, either by the participants or (analytically) by the observer. Table 3.1 summarizes the bare outlines of the formal structure of (a) and (b) on the analytical level. Thus it brings out a very crucial point in the relations between shrine activities and everyday ecological activities: their respective formal structures are largely symmetrical and complement one another as if forming one whole. Table 3.1 suggests that the ecological shrine forms a unique complement – an actional, symbolic and spatial counterpoint – to the everyday ecological activities. The ecological shrine is not a more or less accidental epiphenomenon, grown upon the utilitarian ecological process. A much more intimate bond exists between the two: one is the mirror-image of the other.

One might suggest that the unity of these two formal structures (clad with all sorts of local cultural idiosyncrasies, in .matters such as the specific construction of the shrine, the specific ritual, or the specific ecological activities) contains the clue for the almost universal distribution, not just in Central Africa, but on a worldwide basis, of man-made ecological shrines in societies with subsistence economies. For such societies depend on primary ecological processes. Therefore, if it can be made plausible that ritual focusing around man-made ecological shrines forms an obvious, intrinsic counterpart to these ecological processes, then we have advanced a little towards understanding the ubiquity of such ritual. But unfortunately, the only way to arrive at some plausible explanation here is through an abstract thought experiment, far removed from the explicitly conscious notions of any participants, and along the weak methodology of 'phenomenological' interpretation.

Man's everyday ecological activities in subsistence economies have, among others, the following characteristics: they are inherently meaningful to the participant, for they relate to his immediate physiological needs; they involve a large amount of chance; and they are directed toward rather extensive parts of the landscape, such as a garden plot or a hunting area. But ritual needs a somewhat more defined and more localized focus than a plot or a hunting area. One solution is the adoption of movable ritual objects (such as amulets, medicine, or a royal bracelet), while another is the adoption of invisible entities with whom man can in principle communicate anywhere; but even so, a material focus would be convenient. Since everyday ecological activity is concentrated upon the landscape, the most obvious solution is to create a concentrated spot where ritual will have an effect upon the total ecological system involved.

The basic philosophy unconsciously underlying the ecological shrine might then perhaps be reconstructed as follows: 'If there is a high chance (i.e., uncertainty, failure) element in the extended landscape, let us isolate one small part of that very landscape, and perform some ritual operations upon this small part which – through a process of transfer – will influence the utilitarian operations in the wider land-scape so as to transform chance into fortune.'

This tentative formula sums up the very close intimacy between ecological process and shrine cult. First, the construction of the man-made shrine is a quasi-ecological process in itself. Elements are selected from nature (such as a spot, poles, grass or bark), transformed and arranged so as to meet a human purpose; the whole 'idiom' of the under-taking is ecological, except that the result (the finished shrine) has no immediately utilitarian reward in terms of physiological needs fulfilled. For instance, although in Zambia the most common hut-like type of shrine is a model of the ordinary human dwelling, the shrine hut does not primarily serve such utilitarian purposes as shelter and storage. The shrine derives its significance from this dialectical combination of identity and difference *vis-à-vis* its non-ritual counterparts. Furthermore, once the ecological shrine has been constructed the ritual activities there can be viewed as a formal rhyme to everyday ecological activities, in that a part of the visible world is manipulated with ultimate reference to man's physiological needs. But again, the ritual is only pseudo-ecological: con-trary to ecological activities which require material objects such as tools, the means in ritual are immaterial (words, songs) or sham tools (like the miniature wooden hoe and axe used in ritual in western and north-western Zambia), and the ritual has no perceptible, concrete, immediate result.

The ecological shrine is a model of the world-as-being-humanized, a microcosm in which essentially the same entities which move the ecological macrocosm can be approached through a ritual reminiscent of, but different from, everyday ecological activities, and thus (in ways that would not work outside the shrine situation) can be made to render the ecological conditions outside the shrine favourable to man.

This formal analysis is abstracted from actual social and historical forms. The concrete shape of the ritual around ecological shrines can add a lot more colour to our picture; a multitude of invisible entities elbow to catch our attention, and beautiful, archaic and wise rituals take our breath. If there is some general, formal structure underlying this colourful surface (and the ubiquity of ecological shrine cults strongly suggests that there is such a fairly uniform structure), then we have to try to discern its principles – even if blundering.[37]

The village shrine and its dual nature

The speculations developed so far may make the principle of a man-made ecological shrine plausible, but they need elaboration before they

112

can hope to account for entire ecological shrine cults, involving not just one individual hunter or ironworker, but an entire human community.

We may generalize that people forming a small-scale community (a village) in a subsistence economy are knit together by common interests and activities which have a primarily, though by no means exclusively, ecological reference. In the same way primarily ecological factors (in Zambia especially the level of minimal annual water supply)[38] seem to lead to the breaking up of such units and the subsequent founding of new units; although these factors often also manifest themselves on the social plane in local political conflict or witchcraft accusations. Dependent upon each other through the use of the same ecological field, confined by the force of distance and by the claims of surrounding communities, and through a division of labour where specialists and non-specialist members of the small community exchange the fruits of their activities in this field (such as food, tools or medicine), the villagers are primarily linked by a common concern with their environment. If, on the basis of more general principles I have attempted to gauge, ecological concern tends to express itself in the erection of ecological shrines, then the creation of ecological village shrines seems a logical step. One reason why village shrines are so widespread and prominent in Central Africa is probably that the ecological pressure is most keenly felt on the village level; again, Richards's pioneer study offers an excellent example of this state of affairs.

But let us guard against economic or ecological determinism. The Central African village is an 'ecological' unit, but it is more. One of the crucial insights of the social sciences battling against various forms of reductionism[39] has been that 'the social' creates forms of interaction and of symbolism which must be studied in their own right. Specifically, the village, however ephemeral and prone to disruption, generates a sense of identity which is not just the sum of its internal economic activities and division of labour, and which seeks a charter and a symbol in the social and ritual field, rather than in the ecological. The village shrine can and does serve as such a symbol. It thus performs the dual function of being, at the same time, a focus in the ecological process and a communal rallying point (both socially and ideologically) for the village members.

From the ecological viewpoint, the obvious invisible entities to be associated with a village shrine should be such general beings as collective anonymous land spirits, culture heroes, and the High God; from the communal point of view, however, the obvious association is with humans who have a direct and specific historical significance for the local community: the village founder,[40] some other deceased local celebrity, or lineage spirits in general.

This essentially dual nature of the village (or neighbourhood) shrine has not been sufficiently analysed in Colson's studies, which nevertheless provide the best material on shrine cults so far available for Zambia. Colson has presented the shrines as primarily communal, elaborating on their functions in local and inter-local social relations but largely ignoring their ecological significance. Thus she leaves us in the dark as to why precisely *rain* shrines should perform these functions in Tonga society.[41]

Meanwhile, it should be borne in mind that the village shrine is not the only possible way to focus communal feelings and actions at the village level. In a large part of Zambia a village is characterized by the men's shelter at its centre, where most male social and communal activities apart from economic ones are concentrated.[42] Often the shelter is located only a few metres from the village shrine.[43] Although in the unifying and rallying functions of the shelter the secular aspect dominates, it reminds us of a shrine in that access to it is restricted (women and children should not enter the shelter), and in that it is a place for libation, since beer is served here. Thus, though the communal and ecological referents of shrine and shelter merge to some extent, their double presence in a village can be viewed as a far from strict dissociation between these two aspects, the shrine being primarily ecological, the shelter primarily communal.

Inter-local shrines

On the inter-local level the shrine becomes the symbol of the effective political group, and particularly of its leadership (headman, chief). From this viewpoint, irrespective even of ecological implications, the erection of a communal shrine is a claim to autonomy as a social and political unit.[44] Along the same lines, displacement of a shrine is a manifestation of migration; the decline of certain shrines and the rise of other shrines within the same geographical area is a manifestation of shifts in group composition and political alignment;[45] maintenance of relations with a distant shrine is an admission of imperfect autonomy *vis-à-vis* the distant group associated with that shrine;[46] while for immigrants and invaders the destruction of pre-existing shrines is a meaningful way to destroy local religious power structures and to assert themselves as a new, socially and religiously superior group.[47]

If shrines perform these essentially political functions, then we expect political leaders (clan heads, headmen, chiefs) to associate themselves with shrines as visible symbols of their political autonomy and of their legitimacy. Again, this association does not necessarily imply an ecological function for these 'chiefly' shrines; the duality between communal and ecological function, so manifest at the village level, could at the higher inter-local levels very well be dissociated to such an extent that different types of shrine specialize in either the ecological or the communal-political function. Though in some Zambian cases (particularly the Bemba) royal shrines claim the monopoly of both political and ecological power, chiefly shrines without elaborate ecological functions are more the general rule (Map 2). In the latter case the chiefly shrines provide political legitimacy and the focus for royal ritual, particularly on the occasion of accession to office, since they contain royal attributes or the remains of deceased rulers. Ecological functions are then primarily fulfilled by other shrine systems: shrines associated with priests in an inter-local cult; village shrines; and shrines associated with individual specialists. Yet, if the ecological functions of chiefly shrines are usually not elaborate, few if any totally lack ecological connotations. Chiefly cults tend to supplement, as a last resort, the regular non-chiefly ecological cults in times of great crisis. Ritual control over the land (exercised directly, or through supervision of inter-local ecological priests and ritual leaders) seems to provide the most adequate legitimation of political power as exercised by chiefs. Thus the dual nature of the domestic shrine tends to have a counterpart in the communal-political and, at the same time, ecological functions of the chiefly shrine at the highest inter-local levels.

We could leave it at this, and simply view the variety of chiefly, priestly, and village shrine cults with communal, ecological or combined emphasis, as the timeless manifestations of the fundamental duality of the shrine above the individual level. There is, however, a much more attractive though ill-documented alternative on which I shall elaborate now: the interpretation of the variety of shrine cults as the outcome of a historical process, in which shrines and the ecological claims associated with them have been manipulated in a prolonged contest over power and legitimacy – a contest between secular immigrant rulers and earlier territorial priests.

Chiefs and shrines in Zambia's history

Zambian societies before the Luba expansion

Zambia's early history is still very dim. Oral traditions do not normally penetrate deeper than the sixteenth or seventeenth century; in the Tonga case they are said to reach only to the early nineteenth century. Moreover, despite its tremendous achievements in recent years, Zambian archeology is by no means capable yet of depicting in some detail the political and religious features of the Zambian societies before the Luba expansion.

Yet a speculative model can be drawn. By extrapolation of recent work on early Malawi and southern Tanzania,[48] we can postulate that some form of a shrine cult existed in eastern and northern Zambia at least half a millennium ago. Some traditional evidence even suggests that aspects of the Central African territorial cults have a pre-Bantu origin.[49] Moreover, there is some evidence[50] that peoples not unlike the Tonga and Ila (among whom shrine cults are still prominent) have occupied much of eastern, central and southern Zambia since the first centuries of the present millennium. Finally, there are indications that the chieftainships which, as part of the Luba expansion since about 1500, were established in Zambia, were generally imposed upon peoples who had already been settled in their areas for some time, and who had no centralized political system involving chiefs, but instead a little-developed segmentary system of mutually feuding clans or clan segments.[51]

This hints at a type of society consisting of small units of gatherers, husbandmen or shifting cultivators, with only an informal type of secular leadership presumably based not so much on ascription as on the skilful manipulation of immediate economic and kinship relationships as built up during one's lifetime. Such political leadership is in itself hardly capable of checking the structural tendency towards small-scale warfare over ecological resources, women and honour; on the contrary, it can be said to need violent conflict since this provides a setting in which the leader's service is most valuable.

Much of social anthropology from the 1930s to the 1950s was concerned with this type of society.[52] The concepts of segmentation and unilineal descent groups were primarily conceived and tested in the analysis of such societies as the Nuer, Tallensi, Alur and Somali; descriptions of these peoples have become anthropological classics. In retrospect much of this work remained too faithful to neat armchair models and diagrams. Deeper insights into the actual complex mechanisms of feuding, complementary opposition, reconciliation, and in the acephalous political order in general, were mainly obtained from those areas where the classical segmentation model, after initial trials, turned out not to fit properly. Such areas are North Africa,[53] Papua New Guinea,[54] and particularly Central Africa, where the absence of real segmentary lineages was realized many years ago[55] and where some of the most brilliant work of the Rhodes-Livingstone Institute researchers (even when conducted in societies with formal chieftainship) provided new models for the interpretation of this type of society.[56]

In the older studies the essential process of arbitration in acephalous societies was mainly presented as lying in the hands of informal secular authorities. It is only recently that North African studies have begun to yield a new, probably widely applicable, model of the way in which religious authorities within a shrine cult can become a central element of social control in an acephalous society. In rural North Africa, pacifist priestly lineages administered widely dispersed shrines amid secular groups engaged in constant feuding. By virtue of their religious status, the supernatural sanctions surrounding them, the backing they received from secular groups, and the general recognition of their indispensability to all the feuding parties involved, these shrine-keepers ('saints') could successfully operate as judges and arbiters in feuds, meanwhile accumulating impressive wealth from donations and their protection of trade.[57]

In the absence of concrete data I cannot suggest that shrine cults in pre-Luba Zambia have performed a similar function. Yet if the latter-day forms of the Tonga and Ila social systems can to some extent be extrapolated back into time, some very interesting patterns emerge.

The closest resemblance to the North African model is found among the Ila,[58] where priestly custodians of the shrines (groves) of such major land spirits as Shimunenga and Munyama are reported to receive compensation in cattle in case of murder in the local community. Moreover, these groves served as neutral meeting grounds where emissaries from other areas could solicit the local community's assistance in war.[59] Compensatory payments to the shrine's ritual leader existed also among the Gwembe Tonga[60] and remained effective up to the first decades of this century. Colson feels compelled to deny the ritual leaders all political and judicial significance, and mentions the territorial cult only once in her famous work on Tonga social control.[61] Yet she claims in her study of Tonga rain shrines that the cult is 'still the fundamental element in Tonga social structure'[62] and that it creates a small community within which the rudiments of community law can be discerned, forcing its members to remember occasionally that they belong to a wider unit than the village or kin-group.[63] Similarly, mediums among the neighbouring Valley Korekore are described by Garbett[64] as playing a major role in the settlement of disputes, both at the domestic village level and in chiefly succession.

Thus in the recent Zambian context the territorial cult could form a major source of social control. This potential is given in the dual, dialectical nature of the shrine. It is a symbol of the local group, and as such it is charged, much in the vein of the classic analysis of Durkheim,[65] with the authority that the group exercises over its members as basis and source of legitimacy for the normative system. At the same time the shrine is a symbol of the ecological processes upon which depends the very life of the community and of its individual members – processes which are supposed to be negatively influenced, again, if the members misbehave with regard to the natural order (disrespectful use of natural resources), the social order (murder, incest, sorcery) or the shrine itself. An additional factor might be that the social positions (priest, medium) in which the territorial cult invests authority, often devolve on people who, through birth or way of life, tend to be outsiders (and therefore potential arbiters) to the general process of secular social life; however, evidence on this point is scanty and contradictory.[66]

The Tonga, Ila and Korekore territorial cults promote social control in contemporary societies that have diffuse and limited political leadership. Thus the territorial cult in general may form an alternative to highly developed chieftainship; where chieftainship is limited or incipient, it can be supplemented or antagonized by the political functions of the territorial cult. We can even postulate that the territorial cult is capable of creating a rudimentary form of social control in situations where specialized secular political organization is altogether absent.

If we accept that the Zambian societies before the Luba expansion were either acephalous or had only limited and incipient forms of chieftainship, then we can assume that priestly territorial cults played an important role in the maintenance of some social and political order beyond the village level.

From about 1500 onward, this type of society was exposed to bands of immigrants who brought different conceptions of social control: a new political culture, focusing on the exalted position of the chief or king.[67] Hithertho this political revolution in Zambia has been presented in two versions: as the imposition (through force, but equally through persuasion) of a political order where previously there had been virtually none,[68] or as the replacement of a rudimentary secular political order by a more developed and centralized one.[69] Both views ignore the possibility of a pre-existing politico-religious order based on the territorial cult. A third view emerges which presents the Luba expansion as, among other aspects, a battle against the religiously-anchored political power vested in the territorial cult.

If there is some truth in this hypothesis, it should enable us to reinterpret this political expansion process in Zambia, and moreover to throw some light on evidence not yet explicitly accounted for in the literature. This will be the theme of the remainder of this chapter.

The confrontation between immigrant chiefs and earlier territorial cults in Bemba history

Let us first consider the evidence for a religious dimension to Luba expansion in the case of one Zambian kingdom: the Bemba. Some mythical evidence is contained in the tradition about the filial conflict which drove Nkole and Chiti away from their homeland to establish the Bemba kingdom:[70]

> As a result of some project[71] of Chiti and Nkole, people were killed and Mukulumpe made his sons do menial punishments, such as sweeping the royal yard. When further tasks of *cleaning the shrines* were given, Chiti refused and his men killed the men his father sent to beat him. They and their people then left . . .

The mythical accounts of the brothers' further exploits contain at least two other hints at what could have been a religious dimension: their repeated encounters with the friendly white-skinned *nganga*, Luchele, on whose intervention and favourable divination their entry into Bembaland ultimately depended, and the hitting of a tree with a spear when finally taking possession of the territory.

It is important that the latter two mythical themes are not confined to Bemba tradition but have a wide distribution among the Luba-ized peoples of Central Africa.[72] This means that if these themes can be taken as manifestations of the hypothetical conflict between immigrating chiefs and the earlier territorial cult, this conflict might be postulated among these other peoples, although of course we have to consider the possibility of myths being diffused irrespective of the historical events to which the myths originally referred.

Interpretation of the three themes in terms of my hypothesis does not seem too far-fetched. The religious content is clearest in the shrine-cleaning episode. The myth contains evidence of some religious conflict in the very beginning of Bemba expansion, although it might be argued that the myth in the version given here should be interpreted as an attempt to assert politico-religious independence by rejection of the parental groups' shrines, rather than as evidence of conflict between the royal immigrants and a local shrine cult in Bembaland. The tree, in the second theme, is the very prototype of a natural shrine in Zambia, and hitting a tree shrine with a spear is a very audacious challenge; hence this theme could be interpreted as memorizing a spectacular challenge to earlier territorial cults by the immigrants. Although the character of Luchele remains dim, as a specialist in religious matters he has unmistakably 'ecological' connotations, such as divining by producing a fish in a basket – in an area where much of the ecological ritual is in fact concerned with fishing.[73] He may be considered a symbol of the 'ecological' powers (and of the territorial cult that deals with them) upon whose agreement and co-operation political success depends.[74]

These general mythical themes therefore provide some slight evidence for my hypothesis. Fortunately the religious aspects of early Bemba history have recently been subjected to careful study by Werner.[75] On the basis of other evidence he arrives at conclusions rather similar to mine.

Mainly in view of the occurrence of priest-councillors from clans that otherwise have no political significance in the Bemba political structure,[76] Werner postulates that when the *bena ngandu* royal clan of the Bemba developed its ancestral cult into a national chiefly cult, it had to accommodate earlier chiefs within its religious structure. These chiefs, Werner claims on Roberts's authority,[77] did not belong to the royal clan but they largely shared the general Bemba culture. They are said to represent an immigrant majority that reached Bembaland not long before the *bena ngandu* themselves.[78]

> The religious powers which these men exerted as the ritual leaders of their small territories were . . . incorporated into a much larger system in which the ancestral spirit of the *bena ngandu* chief became the ritual focus of the territory. . . . Religious powers of earlier chiefs were eclipsed . . . . The ancestors of previous chiefs were forgotten. . . . It would appear that as earlier chiefs were assimilated by the Chitimukulu dynasty, the political leadership which preceded

bena ngandu rule . . . was undermined and the ritual powers held
by the previous chiefs were transferred from their own group affiliations to those of the *bena ngandu.*

Werner clearly recognized that the Luba expansion had religious
aspects in addition to the salient political aspects; in order to consolidate
and legitimize the immigrant dynasty, a royal cult had to be developed
that could compete with, encapsulate, and so accommodate earlier
politico-religious authorities. Yet there are gaps in Werner's argument,
particularly when it comes to identifying these earlier authorities. If the
'chiefs' who were to be caught in the *bena ngandu* political and ritual
structure were essentially newcomers, still trying to consolidate themselves politically, how could they already claim the inter-local ritual
control over the land that is the prerogative of 'original' inhabitants?
What real evidence is there that these earlier chiefs in fact combined
secular-political and religious functions? And, supposing they combined
functions, why should they have entered the *bena ngandu* structure as
priest-councillors, rather than as tributary *secular* chiefs – in other
words, why should they have been deprived of their secular rather
than of their ritual connotations? Werner would probably agree that the
creation of a unitary ritual system controlled by the *bena ngandu* was
as essential a concern of the immigrant dynasty as the creation of a
unitary political system; depriving politico-religious authorities of their
ritual connotations could be one way to achieve such a unitary ritual
system.

It seems that Werner's argument stagnates in his use of an ill-defined
and ill-analysed concept of 'chief'. We cannot blame him, since 'chief'
is perhaps the most frequently used concept in African history and
political sociology. Yet if we continue to apply this word to any type
of historical authority without analysing in as much detail as possible
the political, religious and economic components of this authority – if
we continue to assume that these components, throughout Zambian
history, always tend to coincide – then we cannot hope for progress
in our analysis and understanding. Therefore, what is a chief?

Linguistic evidence does not help us very much here. The Bemba
word *mfumu* has the following equivalents in English: political authorities ranging from 'king', via 'senior chief', 'senior headman' to the
lowest level of 'village headman'; 'owners of the land' or 'land priests'
with ritual rather than political connotations; and finally, invisible
entities associated with shrines and territorial ritual,[79] entities that may
be traceable in local tradition as spirits of deceased political authorities,

but that often lack such historical political connotations and then are better described as 'anonymous land spirits' or perhaps 'saints'. This only suggests that, on the participants' level, there is evidence of a general conceptual system in which little differentiation is made between spiritual authority, secular authority, and manifestations of invisible entities with ecological connotations. Such an insight is important for us, but it is not enough. We are not only interested in how the participants see their society: their views form only one of the entries through which we hope to approach the historical and sociological reality, including its more objective aspects. In the last analysis we have to forge and define our own scientific terms with greater precision than the participants need or can even afford.

It is remarkable that the only serious criticism of the indiscriminate use of the concept of 'chief' for academic and administrative purposes in relation to Zambia came as late as 1960;[80] and that Apthorpe, with his attack on what he called 'mythical political structures', met with so little response. His own argument lacks some consistency. On the one hand he claimed (with particular reference to the Zambian chiefs outside the great dynasties of Lozi, Bemba, Ngoni, Undi and Kazembe) that[81]

in much of Northern Rhodesia, the present state of social anthropological knowledge suggests that perhaps there never has been a ritual spiritual life surrounding chieftainship and related institutions to the same great extent which was . . . characteristic of some other parts of Bantu-speaking Africa.

On the other hand, he largely failed to give concrete evidence as to the relative absence of a ritual role for the minor chiefs. Moreover, his own study of the Nsenga[82] elaborates precisely on the spiritual basis of Nsenga chieftainship: the chief's relic shrine.

Yet Apthorpe points out a very weak spot in Central African studies. The variety of types of authority should not be concealed by calling them all 'chiefs', and assuming that under this general label the different types will automatically merge. I shrink from developing here all the permutations of formal authority in historical Zambian societies; and in fact, the term 'chief' is so inveterate that trying to avoid it altogether would amount to spasmodic artificiality. Let me merely suggest that we need at least three crude basic categories:

1 The ruler, who specializes in politics: the manipulation of power relationships in the process of the social allocation of scarce goods (land, labour, food, trade commodities and women).

2 The priest, who specializes in religion: the manipulation of relation-ships with invisible entities, as relevant to such matters as ecology and legitimation of political structures.

3 The ruler-priest, who more or less equally combines the above specialities and who may well be as rare, on the Zambian scene, as Apthorpe suggests.

These tentative definitions do not imply the absence of secondary ritual functions for the ruler or of secondary political functions (such as arbitration) for the priest. They only claim that it is useful to distin-guish between two institutional frameworks that are analytically (though perhaps not in the perception of the participants) separate and not mutually reducible. Let me finally emphasize that the defini-tions do not specify a level or scale for the authority that is exercised: in principle, they apply to the domestic as well as to the inter-tribal level.

We can now go back to Werner's reconstruction of early Bemba history. The crucial question is: to what type of pre-*bena ngandu* historical authority (if any) does the institution of non-royal Bemba authorities refer? If Werner's answer is somehow unsatisfactory for the reasons outlined above, what tentative alternative can we offer?

The *bena ngandu* came late in the process of Luba expansion. The society upon which they tried to impose their domination mainly consisted of similar groups of earlier Luba immigrants, and these had already been involved for some time in a process of religious and political accommodation *vis-à-vis* the 'original' pre-Luba population. Above I postulated that pre-Luba society did have priests, but probably lacked formal rulers; political functions may have been exerted by informal, non-ascriptive leaders on the clan or sub-clan level, or, failing even these, may have been in the hands of priestly arbitrators – without these priests being 'ruler-priests' exercising genuine political control. There is some fragmentary traditional evidence of a pre-Bemba priest-hood, associated with such prominent natural shrines as the Chisimba Falls near Kasama.[83] The earlier Luba immigrants, preceding the *bena ngandu*, began to build up ruler status; but they could not effectively claim ritual power over the land, and thus had no easy access, for the time being, to priestly status. Yet, in accordance with my general hypothesis, they may have started already to boost their ancestral rituals in rivalry with the pre-Luba territorial cult. Pre-Luba priests, perhaps deprived of their political functions of arbitration, would con-tinue to act as territorial priests. Those previously eligible for the rudimentary pre-Luba secular political leadership (if it existed at all) could now try to penetrate the Luba ranks, or alternatively could play off their status of original inhabitants and seek an outlet in the assumption of priestly functions as well.

While still in a nascent state, this Luba-izing political system was then invaded by the *bena ngandu*. What interests would the latter have had in ritually formalizing their relationship with the earlier Luba immigrants, their kinsmen, by making the latter priest-councillors? The similarity in culture and origin and the relatively short stay of the earlier immigrants in the area did not justify such a move. The interests of the *bena ngandu* were clearly with the pre-Luba priests, for these possessed the key to ultimate legitimacy: ritual control over extended land areas. If the existence of non-royal Bemba authorities is the precipitation of an early conflict in *bena ngandu* history, my argument suggests that this conflict consisted in the encapsulation of pre-Luba territorial priests into the *bena ngandu* system. Presumably the priest-councillors were not 'chiefs' (that is, rulers or at most ruler-priests) deprived of their political functions, but priests whose religious frame of reference was successfully redefined by the immigrants, and politicized.

A significant demonstration of the same, as yet hypothetical, principle is the case of Shimwalule, the most senior non-royal Bemba authority, who buries the Chitimukulu and who has important ecological functions. There are indications that the Mwalule burial grove was a territorial cult centre before the *bena ngandu* came to be buried there, and tradition claims that it was again Luchele who arranged the relationship between the *bena ngandu* and the Bisa priests of this shrine.[84]

What we gain from this argument is not only a modification of Werner's reconstruction, but also an insight that may have more general applicability to the Luba expansion into Zambia: the hypothesis that original owners of the land, made subservient to latterday chiefly dynasties, may not only or primarily have been defeated earlier 'chiefs', but also encapsulated earlier territorial priests.

A comparative overview of the confrontation between rulers and territorial cults in Zambian history

We can now try to generalize the insights derived from our review of early Bemba history. From the sixteenth century onward, Zambian societies were invaded by groups aspiring to establish themselves as rulers. The immigrants found themselves in a situation where they did not command legitimate authority. Their conception of politics, however, required that their leadership, won as it might have been through small-scale conquest or opportunist submission by local people, become supported as soon as possible by a structure of political relations, and political-mythical concepts and ritual, which would have legitimacy in the eyes of their newly acquired subjects. This attempt at legitimation brought them into conflict with pre-existing foci of legitimated social control: the priestly territorial cults in their political functions of arbitration and inter-local communication.

Within the social and ecological framework explored above, the most obvious source of legitimacy must have consisted of ritual relations with the extended land territory and with the ecological process – a form of religious power newcomers could not automatically claim. So the best strategy for the immigrants was to claim ecological powers rivalling those of the priests but deriving from a new principle. One way to achieve this appears to have been the claim by the immigrants of having their own direct access to what is the principal concern of the territorial cults: rain. Descent from 'Rain', or from the High God mainly associated with rain, is claimed by, for example, the royal lineages of the Lozi, Luchazi and Nkoya.[85] The general solution for the immigrants was to create a type of shrine which, while associated with chieftainship (chiefly relics and graves) and effectively controlled by the chiefly group, yet could claim to have an ecological impact comparable to that of the earlier priestly cult.

It should be noted that such a strategy, whether adopted deliberately or followed unconsciously by the actors, need not have been so revolutionary as may be suggested by my presentation here. In view of the universality of village shrines in Central Africa, we can safely claim that on the domestic level all aspiring rulers were in fact associated from the very beginning with communal shrines that, by virtue of their dual nature, had ecological connotations – but on a very small geographical scale. The religious rivalry with earlier inter-local territorial cults simply required an enlargement of scale of these domestic shrine cults associated with the aspiring rulers, rather than the invention of a completely new type of inter-local ecological royal shrine. As was suggested by Werner for the *bena ngandu*, the development of royal territorial cults lay within the potential of the general domestic territorial cult.

If the confrontation between immigrant chiefs and earlier inter-local territorial cults did in fact take the course suggested above, then the typology and distribution of types of shrine cults as discussed in the first sections of this chapter must be interpretable in terms of this confrontation. I shall now attempt such an interpretation.

125

Further research will have to reveal to what extent chiefly shrines formed a local adaptation of the immigrants facing the challenge of an indigenous territorial cult, or rather reflected the diffusion of a trait already existing in the Luba and Lunda homelands. There is no doubt that the notion of the chief or king having supernatural powers over the land belonged to the original Lunda political culture, but these powers seem to have been invested in movable attributes (particularly the royal bracelet of human penises) rather than in shrines.[86]

In this light it is significant that the chiefs of the north-western part of Zambia have retained the original attributes. As we have seen, this part of Zambia is exceptional in that no evidence of a non-chiefly territorial cult above the individual and village level has been recorded.[87] If we extrapolate that in effect no inter-local territorial cult of the type postulated for pre-Lunda Zambian societies existed in the north-west, then the strong suggestion emerges that a chiefly territorial cult was particularly developed in those parts of Zambia where the immigrants met with a strong challenge from a pre-existing priestly cult. If pre-Lunda north-western Zambia lacked both rulers and inter-local territorial cults, there would have existed a need for an outsider arbitrating institution; and the literature emphasizes that the Lunda immigrants could establish themselves precisely because they could satisfy this need.[88]

Whatever the intricacies of the religious history of north-western Zambia, it is a firm fact that elsewhere in Zambia most immigrant chiefs have developed some form of a royal shrine cult with (though in general only secondary) ecological connotations. No doubt the Bemba formed the most successful case. Here the cult of royal relic shrines, deceased chiefs' capitals and chiefs' burial groves, administered by hereditary priests under control of the royal clan, attained a high complexity and effectively claimed major ecological significance.[89] In the Bemba case the distinction, so characteristic of Zambian pre-colonial political systems, between original owners of the land and later chiefly immigrants has been largely obliterated: the royal clan became the owner of the land. Yet the continued existence of territorial shrines outside direct chiefly control, the occurrence of non-Bemba priests (of Lungu and Bisa extraction, and including Shimwalule),[90] and spirit possession attributed to presumably pre-Luba culture heroes and anonymous collective land spirits – the 'people's religion' in this strongly hierarchical society – all this suggests that even among the Bemba the chiefs' hold on religious power was uneasy and likely to be shaken by severe crises like those that occurred in this century and the last.[91]

Considerably less monolithic was the result in two other, not dissimilar great kingdoms: Undi's and that of the Lozi. In both cases the immigrant royal lineages established themselves as the unchallenged owners of the land, and a cult of royal graves was developed which included claims of ecological power. Yet in both cases the ecological functions of the paramount were limited. Significantly, these functions were associated with royal burial and succession, i.e. situations in which chiefly shrines as foci of political legitimation are particularly relevant. And these ecological functions were actually discharged by groups which (though official ideology tended to underplay or ignore this fact) could be regarded as previous owners of the land: in the Lozi case the commoner (predominantly Mbunda?) priests, in the Chewa case the Banda clan that administered the priestly territorial cult headed by Makewana.[92]

The Lozi-Undi pattern is further developed to a unique form in the eastern Lunda kingdom of Kazembe. Here the relationship between pre-Lunda owners of the land and the Lunda immigrants is explicitly recognized and forms the very basis of much of the political, ecological and religious system. Cunnison describes this in terms that again fit my general hypothesis (of a confrontation between chiefs and earlier territorial priests) remarkably well:[93]

> The ancestral ritual of the Owners of the Land is generally spoken
> of as having been the most important ritual in the old days. When
> the Lunda came, prayer to dead Kazembes was also made, not
> regularly but in case of drought or special hardship. In addition . . .
> on such occasions Kazembe would call the Owners of the Land to
> his capital and tell them that since the country was in a bad way
> it was fitting that they should all go to their homes and pray to their
> ancestors on a certain day. Kazembe would also order other sorts of
> ritual to be carried out generally, for the good of the country.

But on the latter occasions he would work through the village headmen and not rely on any supernatural power he or his ancestors themselves might claim. In addition to honouring the owners of the land, Kazembe would keep up a respectful contact with three important ecological shrines controlled by priests, one of whom, Mwepya, was recognized as an owner of the land. The most important of these shrines was the Aushi shrine, Makumba, that was originally destroyed by the Lunda invaders but later restored.[94] Though Kazembe could theoretically assert himself as the ultimate owner of the land since he defeated the previous 'owners', the legitimacy of his kingship derived

127

not from a direct ritual relationship between king and land but rather from a symbiosis between king and owners of the land, in which the latter enjoyed prestige and protection while paying tribute in recognition of the exalted political status of the king and his representatives. Kazembe's is a rich country which became the most prosperous and powerful of the Luba-Lunda empires. Management of these natural resources required a balanced, harmonious relationship between king and owners of the land. The initial conflict between Lunda invaders and local territorial cults (manifest in the Makumba tradition) dissolved into a situation where Lunda political supremacy was unchallenged, while the Lunda on their part acknowledged the religious supremacy of the older territorial cults.

On a smaller scale, outside the major kingdoms, chiefly relic shrines and graves with ecological connotations can be found in most of central Zambia (Map 2). We can agree with Apthorpe that in most cases these minor chiefs' role in ecological ritual is modest, and below I shall present a tentative historical explanation of this fact. My Nkoya material reveals an analytical difficulty in the case of these minor rulers. Among other functions, their status is that of headman of the chiefly village and neighbourhood; the village or neighbourhood shrine, possessing ecological connotations, coincides with the chiefly relic shrine or chiefly graves. When officiating at this chiefly village shrine, does the minor ruler engage in religious activities that are merely a slightly glorified territorial cult at the domestic level, or must we interpret them as a chiefly ecological cult? Much will depend on the degree of participation of representatives from other parts of the minor ruler's territory, but even so the distinction seems artificial.

In general, the relations between priestly inter-local cults and rulers outside the few great royal dynasties remain a point for further study. Detailed information on this topic is available only for the extreme north[95] and for the Lake Bangweulu area.[96] It is perhaps significant that in both cases an inter-tribal priestly territorial cult was revealed, which maintained a relative independence *vis-à-vis* the local political leadership.

The no-man's-land situation and the Tonga-Ila case

Vansina has identified a factor that might be of primary significance for our understanding of the central Zambian territorial cults. 'Kingdoms of the savanna' were not bureaucratically centralized, but each imposed upon an extended geographical area a network of ideological identification with the rulers, as well as a flow of people, goods and services.

Tribute relationships, trade, emissaries and military operations became less and less dense towards the periphery, so that between adjacent kingdoms large areas of relative no-man's-land would remain.[97] In these marches, successful large kingdoms could only rise if the distance, both geographically and interactionally, to any already existing kingdom was sufficiently large (the case of Kazembe of the Lualaba),[98] or if any existing kingdom collapsed so that its place could be taken. In the centuries immediately preceding the colonial era most of central Zambia, with extensions towards the north-west, south and north, exhibited this ambivalent state of affairs: being too far away to be firmly controlled by the great kingdoms (Lozi, Mwaat Yaav, Kazembe, Bemba, Undi, Mutapa, Rozwi), but lying too near to produce locally another kingdom of similar dimensions out of the exploits of a large number of immigrant minor rulers. The external check on these minor rulers' powers must have had repercussions upon their dealings with the territorial cult complex wherever it existed. While unable to expand maximally on the political plane, these rulers tended to adopt, or at least further develop, a religious consolidation (on the lines of a chiefly shrine cult), but they were never able to claim such ritual power over the land as did the great kings, particularly in the Bemba case. Brelsford's statement on the Bemba chiefs seems to be more generally applicable:[99]

> Association [between rulers and ecological powers] was only permanent when it was backed by political control of the land.

Though illuminating, the notion of the relative no-man's-land is insufficient to explain the complex case of territorial cults, chieftainship and absence of Luba-ization among the Ila and Tonga. One element in our predicament here is the almost complete lack of data on the western Tonga groups that have of old belonged to the Lozi kingdom. Another element is the nature of the writings of the main student of Tonga society, Elizabeth Colson, whose a-historical emphasis on contemporary social structure has so far failed to present a convincing picture of Tonga chieftainship – beyond the hardly substantiated assertion that in the past the Tonga had no chiefs.[100] A thorough historical study of Tonga society is urgently needed. In view of the large amount of research into Tonga history currently being undertaken by a number of scholars, it can be expected that before long we shall be able to base a discussion of pre-colonial Tonga history on sound data. Meanwhile we have to limit ourselves to speculation based on very fragmentary evidence.

In the last century Tonga society was decimated and brought to political collapse by the effects of Ndebele and Kololo raids, which even seem to have wiped out much of the oral tradition of the area. Absence of Tonga rulers at this stage would not prove anything about previous periods. But is it at all true that Tonga rulers did not exist in the nineteenth century? The evidence of David Livingstone on Monze and other Tonga (or Toka) chiefs,[101] the impressive funerary customs reserved for those whom early twentieth-century writers chose to call chiefs,[102] and the fact that Tonga use the term 'chief' for many of the land spirits associated with their territorial shrines,[103] strongly suggest that Colson's view of Tonga chieftainship as a colonial creation is untenable. She herself reports, for the Upper River Tonga, modern chiefly families that are known by the ancient term of *bana kokalia* ('nobles' or 'people of the shrine'), which could hardly be a colonial innovation.[104]

Tonga colonial chieftainship appears, therefore, a restoration and partial re-interpretation of a much earlier pattern. That yet the Tonga as described by Colson display a normative system that, with its emphasis on diffuse leadership and achieved status, seems particularly appropriate for a chief-less society, need not surprise us. Rather than assuming that this normative system is of entirely modern origin (which Colson does not suggest), we could link it meaningfully to a particular type of historical political system: one where the ruler, though exercising political functions, is considered a *primus inter pares*, not ritually separated from his subjects, and recruited not according to fixed kinship rules (which could safeguard the political monopoly of a particular lineage, clan or estate) but instead collectively chosen from a rather large pool of candidates. This is exactly the kind of political leadership described for the neighbouring Ila,[105] who are very similar to the Tonga in language, economy, and general cultural orientation, including religion. The presumably recent difference in political organization between Ila and Tonga seems then to be due mainly to differences in local experiences, precipitating different responses in a basically similar political system during the upheaval in the nineteenth century.

I shall now explore the implications of such a view for the theme of this section: the confrontation between immigrant rulers and territorial cults in the process of Luba expansion. Luba influence did not successfully penetrate into the Tonga-Ila area. The chieftaincies in southern Zambia have no recorded tradition of immigration from the north and also lack the material attributes (ceremonial ironware: gongs, axes, bow-stands) generally associated with northern chiefly origins.[106]

The particular type of chieftainship postulated here for the entire Tonga-Ila group was very different from the Luba political culture, since it denied the ruler a socially and ritually exalted position. Moreover, among the Ila and the Tonga, inter-local territorial cults under priestly control have been very prominent and have fulfilled major functions of social control and inter-local interaction; we have identified these functions as an alternative to well-developed chieftainship along Luba lines. While southern Zambia has been overtaken by most other parts of the territory as far as material culture is concerned (pottery, iron technology),[107] it has a relatively high agricultural potential.[108] The area has remained occupied by the same civilization since the beginning of the present millennium.[109] It was the first part of Zambia to develop long-distance trade;[110] and this trade, not monopolized by chiefs as was the case in many other parts of Zambia, was of remarkable dimensions even in the turbulent nineteenth century.[111]

The obvious question is: what kept the northern immigrants out of this attractive area? Distance cannot have been a factor, since some effectively Luba-ized parts of Zambia, such as the lands of the Nkoya, Lenje and Soli, are hardly less distant from the northern homelands. In fact, one Luba ruler managed to establish himself at the southern periphery of the area: Mukuni of the Leya, east of the town of Livingstone.[112] Doubtless there have been many other immigrant groups, but they were either assimilated without retaining their own identity let alone assuming hereditary ruler status,[113] or they were violently repelled, as tradition has it for one branch of the Kaonde venturing south of the Kafue.[114]

Traditions surrounding the origins of the major land spirits of the Ila may give us the key to an answer.[115] Among the Ila each chief's area has its sacred grove, where a major land spirit is venerated. There is some hierarchy of these major land spirits: those at the bottom being only venerated in one particular area, whereas those at the very top of the scale (Shimunenga, Munyama and especially Malumbe) are each venerated in the groves of a number of neighbouring areas. In fact, the three spirits named here are the main powers in the Ila pantheon after the High God and the Earth Spirit, Bulongo. Tradition presents these three land spirits as historical human beings who arrived in Ilaland as great chiefs and magicians. Munyama is explicitly remembered as leading a Lunda expedition into the area, whereas Malumbe is said to have come from the distant east. Although these immigrant rulers may have made some impact on the Ila political structure (Smith and Dale[116] suggest that the areas they conquered coincide with the

131

areas in which they are now venerated), they were not able to found chiefly dynasties alien to the flexible, open and non-ascriptive nature of Ila chieftainship. In other words, though impressive enough in their time, they failed to Luba-ize the Ila but instead were Ila-ized: they were accommodated within the already existing politico-religious structure which encapsulated them and turned them into major local divinities.

Here we find the exact opposite of what happened in the Bemba case; among the Ila the struggle between, on the one hand, the immigrant rulers and, on the other, the priests in association with non-ascriptive rulers without religious connotations, ended in an absolute victory on the home side. The immigrants were redefined in a way that was harmless for the earlier political system and that could only boost the earlier religious system. The ironical fate of the immigrant chiefs in Ilaland is rather reminiscent of the fate of the agents of formal Islam who have spread over rural North Africa since the twelfth century: going out to propagate their particular version of the true Islamic doctrine (cf. the Luba political culture), they rapidly became encapsulated in the earlier rural religious system and ended up as local saints, the very cornerstones of the peasants' popular religion which they had tried to alter.[117]

Thus one is brought to assume that northern rulers, so successful in most of Zambia, failed to establish themselves in the southern part largely because the political and religious organization of some Ila-Tonga groups before the nineteenth century was in certain aspects superior to, and had a greater survival power than, that found elsewhere in the territory. With our present data it can only be speculated what these superior aspects were: a more developed yet flexible system of non-ascriptive secular rulers, supported not only by small-scale warfare (which may have been general throughout pre-Lunda Zambia) but also by long-distance trade and by the specific nature of a cattle economy (which offers the unique possibility of accumulating wealth in a subsistence economy), and a balanced relationship between these rulers and an inter-local territorial cult system that, while providing additional political integration and arbitration, was perhaps more highly developed than anywhere else in Zambia because of the uncommonly unpredictable nature of the southern Zambian climate.[118]

Conclusion

I have suggested that the Luba-Lunda revolution represents one major theme in the historical study of territorial cults in Zambia. Certainly another such theme concerns the changes territorial cults have undergone in the general process of rapid social change that has characterized Central Africa since the first half of the last century; aspects of this theme I shall pursue in the chapters that follow.

The main purpose of this chapter has been to develop a number of hypotheses, which, though as yet untested, seem to meet the fragmentary and shallow factual data that we have on the sociology and history of territorial cults in Zambia, and to collate these hypotheses tentatively into a plausible but conjectural historical process. It could be argued that a similar methodology is followed in most, if not all, sociological and historical interpretation; however, in the present case the imbalance between speculation and data is exceptionally great.

The only justification I can offer derives from an observation which I share with many of my colleagues in the field of African anthropology and history. Generally there is no dearth of empirical data, and ever more is being collected by African universities and international research institutions. In view of the enormous expansion of our historical knowledge of Central Africa during the last fifteen years I am confident that within a few years the major factual gaps in this study of territorial cults in Zambia can be filled. However, in order to achieve this it is absolutely necessary that we formulate our research priorities, in the form of testable hypotheses which clearly bring out what we presently take to be crucial aspects of our subject matter, and which can be substantiated or refuted in the light of subsequent data collection precisely guided by these hypotheses. The point is that, against the abundance of data, there is a lack of sophisticated interpretative hypotheses in much of the study of African society and history.

I believe that a greater insight into the history and sociology of territorial cults in Zambia can be gained by further testing, expansion or refutation of the main hypotheses employed in the present chapter: the hypothesis of the shrine cult as a systematic, formal complement of the process of everyday ecological transformations in societies with a subsistence economy; the hypothesis of pre-Luba Zambian societies as composed of feuding clan segments with little-developed secular leadership, and with priestly territorial cults maintaining a minimum of interlocal social and political order; and finally, the hypothesis of Luba and Lunda expansion as, among other aspects, a struggle for legitimacy and power between immigrating chiefs and pre-existing priestly cults – the latterday varieties of the Zambian shrine cults being interpretable as the differential outcome of this struggle.

Chapter 4

Religious change and the problem of evil in western Zambia

For Professor H. Jack Simons, upon his retirement

Introduction[1]

Witchcraft and sorcery, the political institutions concerned with their control and the mass movements striving towards their eradication, have attracted much attention in the literature on religious change in Central Africa during the late nineteenth and the twentieth centuries. It would appear as if these themes (along perhaps with the establishment of Christianity) constitute the main aspects of (rural) religion in this period.

Witchcraft does not exist in isolation: it is one out of several ways in which members of Central African and other societies have interpreted and manipulated human suffering, against the background of a total cosmological and societal order.

The present chapter does seek to contribute specifically to the literature on Central African witchcraft, but has a more important aim; it tries to define the general religious themes and processes of change which, I believe, are essential for a balanced assessment of the 'problem of evil' in this part of the modern world.

I shall concentrate on a relatively small area: central western Zambia,[2] the immediate vicinity of what is at present the Kafue National Park. For this region I shall reconstruct the religious situation in the nineteenth century, and describe the major religious innovations that have appeared during the twentieth century. The central part of the chapter consists of an attempt towards a synthesis which embraces these various innovations, and the pre-colonial religious change of which they are largely the continuation. This synthesis will identify the major, inter-related themes of religious change in the region as manifested throughout these innovations; and it will relate these themes systematically to the tensions which were generated in the social structure and the religious system of central western Zambia by socio-economic and political change in both the pre-colonial and the colonial periods. The chapter concludes with a tentative sociological model of religious innovation in Central Africa and an assessment of the implications of the present argument for the general topic of witch-craft and its eradication.

On a comprehensive and detailed empirical basis, I shall propound an integrated, but greatly simplified and extremely tentative model of religious change in a very small part of Africa. I suggest that this model, with all its deficiencies, is the best-fitting one in view of our present limitations in knowledge and insight. This leaves us with two tasks: to account explicitly for, and to improve, the rather preposterous methodology and theory underlying the present attempt (something I have attempted to do in the introductory chapter of the present volume); and to test out, and accordingly improve, the model against such other data as are already available or as may be collected in future for this specific purpose. I repeat my contention that the study of African religious history at its present stage needs explicit, complex, testable models perhaps more than it needs fresh descriptive data. But such models are meant to be research tools, of productive and heuristic value; least of all are they instalments of historical truth – despite my concern to bring to bear on the argument most published, archival, oral-historical and participatory field-work data yet available.

Dominant aspects of village religion in the nineteenth century

Central western Zambia

Central western Zambia is a contact area between Tonga-speaking groups in the south-west, south and east (Totela, Subiya, Tonga, Ila, Sala, Lumbu, Lenje) and Luba-speaking groups (Kwangwa, Nkoya, Mashasha, Mbwera, Kaonde, Luba, Tema, Lamba) who for several centuries have expanded into the region from the north and west.[3] Sometimes the incoming Luba-speaking groups were assimilated into the Tonga-speaking groups, swelling the ranks of the latter. Yet in the course of centuries the Luba-speaking groups took possession of the bigger part of the region, while retaining such distinctive features as language, a particular style of political organization and certain aspects of material culture (e.g., musical instruments, fishing and hunting devices). The prolonged historical confrontation between the two major ethnic clusters in the region found an expression in standardized joking relations between groups across the Luba/Tonga ethnic boundary.[4] Despite the retention of the distinctive ethnic features mentioned, a striking social-structural and cultural homogeneity was produced by the Luba-Tonga cultural exchange and assimilation, on the basis of a common Central Bantu cultural substratum. An additional factor was the common natural environment,[5] conducive to shifting cultivation, hunting and gathering, and small-scale animal husbandry, with as local variations the tsetse-fly area in the centre of the region (vastly expanded by the creation of a game reserve in the present century),[6] where stock-raising is impossible, and the rich cattle area of the Kafue flats with extensions into the eastern periphery of the region.

This regional homogeneity applies particularly in the field of the village religion,[7] despite the fact that, at a level surpassing the single village, the Tonga-speaking groups in the region (particularly Ila and Lenje[8]) possess elaborate inter-local shrine cults for major land spirits, which are much less developed, or altogether absent, in the greater part of the region. However, rather than being a distinctive feature of the Tonga-speaking groups in this specific region, these inter-local cults can be considered as variants of a general ecological cult complex existing throughout the region and far beyond, as we have seen in the previous chapter.

Setting the base-line

Defining the initial situation is a major problem in the study of change in Africa. Because of the paucity of oral or archeological data, we can do little more than sketch an ideal-type, based on the intuitive extrapolation of conditions recorded in better-known periods, particularly the present. By tracing back the major historical processes that occurred in the region from the seventeenth century AD onwards (enlargement of political scale and of the social horizon in general, through growth of trade, tribute and chieftainship), and deducting their apparent effects from the latterday religious system, one arrives at a tentative ideal-type of the primordial religion of the western Zambian village society. Revolving around the twin concerns of ecology and human suffering, this ideal-type of religious system identified the local dead (and not, for example, the otiose High God) as largely controlling man's access to nature. This religious system stipulated collective ritual to communicate with the dead, and emphasized individual suffering as a communal concern. It further reflected on the moral relation between the individual and the community: by invoking supernatural sanctions over the individual who neglected his kinship obligations; and by associating high status, based mainly on individual achievement (hunter, doctor, entrepreneur, chief), with medicine procured through sorcery.

This religious system had a strong communal emphasis, not so much because sacred ties of reciprocity and solidarity were all that effective in the actual social process, but rather because other collectivist norms formed an imperfect mechanism to keep the inevitable conflicts (over limited ecological resources and authority, against the background of individual achievement aspirations) from becoming immediately disruptive to the village community.

Much of this ideal-type, which below I shall sketch in greater detail, has persisted in the local religion until today. The religious innovations of the last few centuries were superimposed upon this old base (whose immutability I assume for the sake of the present argument only) rather than eradicating it. The contemporary religious system therefore appears as a composite of several historical layers. This chapter seeks to describe and explain the appearance in time of the successive innovations. The equally complex problem of the contemporary coexistence of the resulting 'layers' within one community falls outside our present scope.[9]

Ecology

In chapter 3 I explored the forms and significance of the 'ecologico-religious complex' throughout the societies of Zambia. People who are tied together by common economic interests (agriculture, husbandry, hunting and collecting) in the same, limited, surrounding land area, tend to take ritual care of these interests through shrine cults. We can distinguish between communal shrines and specialist shrines. In the region both types usually consist of wooden poles (typically forked), or shrubs. Communal shrines are mainly found in the centre of the village; they link all living members to the totality of the deceased from whom the living members supposedly descended and/or whose previous habitat they inhabit. Communal shrines are erected at the occupation of a new village site. Once the village has been established, the predominantly collective shrine ritual (implorations, and offerings of beer, meal, meat stock and white beads) is practised to underline the cycle of everyday non-specialist ecological undertakings over which the dead are held to have great powers. Specialist shrines, owned and administered by individuals and associated with deceased kinsmen who pursued the same speciality as their living descendant, are typically situated away from the village, in the forest; their main form is the hunting shrine, while also fishing, honey-collecting, ironworking and witch-doctoring shrines exist.

The shrine religion is much more than a simple ritual mechanism to enhance ecological success. It is a comprehensive world-view, a cosmological as well as a moral system, and as such it underpins the total social order. It is the central source of existential meaning in the culture of the region.

Through ecological processes man transforms nature so as to carve out a human and social existence, selecting and using the raw materials of the forest, the animals and other natural resources. For these transformations technical knowledge, physical power and human organization are indispensable; but to make them ultimately meaningful they have to be embedded in a cosmological system of classifications, relations and ritual activities which constitute the religion. Cosmogonic myths[10] relate nature in its present state to primordial times when man stayed with the supernatural beings in the sky, when everything man needs was created, and when, at the disruption of the heavenly society at the invention of sorcery, man and nature were expelled from the sky by an angry God. In historical times this God is hardly directly approached through ritual.[11] But man is obliged to make the full and proper use of the amenities that were created for him, and thus ecological activities border on worship. They implicitly express man's place in the total world order, and man's recognition of his primordial dependence on God. Therefore ecological activities are considered as wholesome and worth engaging in – even beyond their economic necessity.

These religious connotations underlying ecological activities are very rarely verbalized in everyday life. They come closer to the level of consciousness at ecological highlights: the preparation of the gardens when the first rains fall; harvesting and eating of the year's new crops; the festival associated with the killing of an elephant. Probably the intimate association between man, nature and God is most keenly felt by hunters, whose speciality (combining high social status, frequent exposure to great danger, and solitary wanderings – often for many days – through the deepest parts of the forest) sets favourable conditions for the development of mysticism.[12] While in principle every aspect of the natural world is considered to be associated with God, this is particularly so for the forest.

Man's relation with God is channelled through nature, and is almost exclusively pursued through ecological activities. Prayers, songs, and oaths rarely mention God's names. Ecological ritual is propitiation, not so much of God but of the dead, who, through ties of kinship or locality, are considered to have both an interest in the living and power over the natural conditions in the area they inhabit. In general the dead are considered to act autonomously; the model according to which the living explicitly ask the dead to intervene with God on their behalf is seldom employed in the region – and when it is this may be due to Christian influences. The dead may interfere with the ecology when asked to do so by the living. But they can also frustrate ecological efforts when the living fail to live up to their kinship obligations *vis-à-vis* one another or show insufficient respect with regard to the dead.

Thus the shrine religion functions as a moral system, with considerable supernatural sanctions. Moreover, the village shrine constitutes a charter and a symbol of the village as an effective social group, and provides a communal rallying point (both reciprocally and ideologically) for the village members.[13] It is at the village shrine that new-born or returned members of the village are incorporated into the group. It is also here that living individuals receive the names of deceased ancestors, and thence their social position and inheritance, including titles of headmanship or chieftainship as the case may be.[14] Final reconciliation after intra-group conflict also takes place at the shrine.[15] The shrine religion is a major factor in the maintaining of whatever stability and continuity exists in the region's social organization, in which conflict and fission play such dominant parts.

Human suffering

The other major theme in the religion of the region revolves around human suffering: illness and death. This theme is closely related to the ecological one, not only because ecological failure is one of the factors producing suffering, but particularly since both themes find expression through the same religious institutions.

Suffering becomes part of a religious system whenever a culture identifies and classifies the conditions, causes and agents responsible for suffering, and stipulates ritual ways in which this set-up can be manipulated by man. In the aetiology of the region, two main causes of illness and death are recognized; these clinically tend to correspond with specific types of symptom patterns; in addition there are several residual categories. Dreaming, and divination by a specialist, have to identify in each case which type is involved before any attempt at treatment (in the case of illness) or retaliation (the most common reaction in the case of death) can be made.

The first aetiological type is considered to be caused by personal supernatural beings: God or an ancestor. The typical symptom pattern here is that of a slowly deteriorating or chronic disease (e.g., leprosy, tuberculosis) which leaves the patient ample time to sort out the cause and seek treatment. Identification of God as the cause is very rare: this is resorted to when the diviner fails to indicate moral shortcomings and intra-group conflict at the root of the disease (or when he shuns doing so in view of his own relation with the patient and with the latter's opponents). If God is divined as causing the illness, there is no recognized healing ritual, although (on the more strictly technical-medical level) herbal medicine may be administered.

Much more often this type of disease is attributed to an irate ancestor, and treatment will involve both specific medicine (procured from the forest) and the removal of the causes of the ancestor's wrath as divined. Failure to honour the illness-causing ancestor after his death is made up for by the erection of a shrine and by giving his name to a living kinsman in the course of collective ritual at the shrine. Failure to maintain ideal kinship relations amongst the living is corrected through discussion, reconciliation and collective ritual of redress at the village shrine. Not always is the ancestor-inflicted disease just a warning: the death of a particularly troublesome individual is often interpreted as the result of purgative action from the part of an ancestor, who would rather sacrifice one member of the community than bear the annihilation of the entire village through conflict.

A transition towards the second category forms 'post-mortal sorcery', where a deceased person (particularly when of high social status), by virtue of medicine taken before his death, is considered to harm the living without any offences being committed by the living.

The second aetiological category is considered to be the result of human malice. The characteristic symptom pattern is violent and rapidly deteriorating disease with swift fatality; although, once again, virtually any pattern of symptoms may be attributed to human malice, including those patterns more typically associated with the High God or ancestral wrath.[16] One distinguishes between three alleged motives. Divination commonly points out, as the major motive, someone's desire to inflict suffering and even death upon a rival individual or faction, as one particular phase in social and political conflict. For both other motives any personal conflict relation between the attacker and the victim is immaterial: the attack is then considered to aim at the procurement of fresh human carrion upon which one might secretly feast during nocturnal visits to the graveyard (in what is perhaps best described as a 'cult of evil'), or to prepare extremely powerful medicine out of the corpses (directly, or by having the flesh eaten by familiars).[17]

For the comparative and historical study of the 'problem of evil' it is of great importance to distinguish between those attacks (real or alleged) which consciously and concretely express social conflict in the specific social situation of a particular individual or faction (the first motive) and those attacks that are impersonal and that at most reflect deep, structural oppositions and tensions within the society and the culture as a whole (the other two motives). Both forms of attack represent 'evil'. The former, however, has to do with evil 'with a human face': on a largely predictable and almost justifiable scale, it is an evil act with which most members of the society (as long as they are not the victims) can identify, and which many of them may at one time or another seek to employ themselves, either directly or through the services of specialists. The latter form of impersonal evil (in which allegedly only a small minority of the population engages, and which may well have no existence in objective reality at all) lacks these human characteristics and therefore forms the most abhorred, diabolical incarnation of evil conceived of in the region.

It is highly significant that medicine prepared out of human remains, so central in impersonal sorcery, is considered to be essential for the attainment and maintaining of precisely the few elevated statuses existing in the society of central western Zambia: the hunter, the doctor (*nganga*), the commercial entrepreneur, and especially the chief.[18]

Both archeological evidence[19] and historical traditions[20] suggest that an institution of chieftainship has existed in the region for centuries. Such chieftainship derived its limited political power largely from economic manipulation:[21] control over production and (initially only local, later increasingly long-distance) distribution of such commodities as game meat, fish, cattle, tusks, skins, copper, iron, implements and slaves. The chief was a *primus inter pares*; there was little, if any, ritual separation between chief and followers, and little in the way of chiefly paraphernalia, prerogatives or ritual; accession to chiefly titles was widely and openly competed for. The Tonga-speaking groups have retained much of this pattern right into the colonial era.[22] Perhaps from the sixteenth century onwards the region experienced attempts to superimpose upon this older structure Lunda-type notions of exalted chieftainship with elaborate ritual and paraphernalia (ceremonial weapons and musical instruments). While largely abortive among the Ila (where they only gave rise to the cult of major land spirits[23]), these attempts led to the Beni Mukuni dynasty among the Lenje in the seventeenth century[24] and to various dynasties among the Sala,[25] the Kaonde[26] and the Nkoya[27] in the late eighteenth and early nineteenth centuries.

This recent introduction of more hierarchical political notions has not given rise to an effective aristocratic class. And although slavery was common, the status of slave was largely an individual legal position which apparently was not automatically transmitted to a slave's off-spring, and which occasionally did not even prevent the slave himself from attaining high social status.[28] There appears to be little reason why we should not project the following structural characteristics of contemporary social life of the region back into the nineteenth century. Inheritance and succession are fairly open, and every member of society is free to engage in contracts of marriage or friendship with anyone else. The main social distinctions are based on age and sex. Ascribed status hardly exists: individuals are not once for all born into high statuses, they achieve them during their life-time and, while doing so, they attract the deep resentment of those who for the time being are less successful. The societies of the region are deeply egalitarian. A member of such a society can hardly explain away the greater success of his neighbour by reference to factors beyond direct human control: noble birth, better opportunities, etc. There is no fundamental excuse why an essential equal should do better. The pangs of personal envy are lessened neither by the excuse that an ideology of fundamental inequality could have provided, nor by internalized values: the existing local values, while suppressing the overt expressions of envy, actually generate envy by emphasizing individual honour and self-esteem against a background of fundamental equality.

So if high-status individuals are to survive for some time in a society where the envy and rivalry they attract are settled in rather drastic ways, they indeed need powerful medicine. Whether or not they actually resort to murder in order to procure this medicine, it is surroun-ded with all the terror that the reckless manipulation of human material for purposes of individual power and status can inspire. Impersonal sorcery is a cult of manipulative power taken to its ultimate implication (cf. note 39). And the successful do pay the price, not only in valuables but particularly in seeing the basis of their achievement popularly exposed as deriving not so much from supernatural benevolence as from utter wickedness.[29] On the other hand, the terror thus surrounding high status is bound to consolidate the structural *status quo* as long as the concept and the practice of sorcery, as well as the socio-economic and political system on which it is based, are not fundamentally challenged.

In addition, to the two major categories of suffering discussed above, there are several residual categories. Some refer to unmanipulated human remains, particularly those in old, forgotten and overgrown graveyards once belonging to village sites which have since long been abandoned. The violation of taboos (e.g., such as relate to menstruation, miscarriage and a man's sexual activities while his wife is pregnant or nursing), and the effect of a curse in inter-generational conflict, are further residual explanations for suffering.

Also important are entities supposed to have resided since times untold in the deep forest: mythical beings, often conceived as of huge shape and with a snake-like appearance, but normally invisible.[30] In this region it is believed that occasionally one hits upon these beings during hunting or gathering trips, or that they venture near the villages in search of game and birds upon which they feed; such a confrontation normally leads to possession and disease, but can – on this basis – also initiate a secret, personal bond where the forest-being allegedly bestows upon a man or woman great riches, unknown medicine and healing powers, and general success. Related concepts are reported for neighbouring peoples whose cosmology and ecology are similar to those of central western Zambia.[31] Apparently this is a very archaic part of the religious system. The more recent appearance, in the region, of the related concept of *muba* (one of the earlier cults of affliction to be introduced into the region in the late nineteenth century, and now associated with the forest-being *Mwendanjangula*) suggests that these forest-orientated disease concepts, with their ambivalent connotations of suffering, healing and success, contributed prototypes towards the later, modern cults of affliction.

Specialist religious roles

The religious system discussed here defines four main specialist religious roles: the diviner, the officiant at the communal shrine, the doctor and the prophet. While divination may be included in any of the latter three roles, a diviner is often an inconspicuous part-timer, who identifies causes of trouble without entering into the specialist action of removing them. Officiating at the shrine is usually implied in the role of senior members of the local community, but in the hands of senior officials in the case of the Ila and Lenje cults of major land spirits. Throughout the region the most prominent religious specialist is the doctor, who intervenes between the living and the dead, detects and eliminates troubling ancestral spirits, forest-beings as well as sorcerers and their familiars, and provides medicine.[32]

For several reasons the role of the prophet is least documented. First, there is the problem of definition, since in the description of Central African religion the word 'prophet' tends to be used for almost any specialist role, ranging from spirit medium, via diviner, shrine priest and doctor, to senior adept in a cult of affliction. We could decide to reserve the term 'prophet' for an individual who has had particularly original and direct experiences attributed to the supernatural and who, on that basis, attempts to persuade society to adopt his particular interpretation of the contemporary situation and to embark on new or exceptional practices.

The second problem then is that such prophets are by definition rare. They constitute a latent institution which only occasionally will have actual incumbents, and therefore they may easily pass out of oral traditions or ethnographic descriptions. As it is, no oral records on pre-colonial prophets are available for central western Zambia, and written sources only mention nineteenth-century prophets outside the region: Tlapano among the Kololo, Mwana Lesa in what is now the Lusaka area, and Bwembya among the Bemba.[33] These prophets were probably not attached to shrines; they claimed to derive their messages directly from God (the former two) or from a deceased king (Bwembya). In an ethnographic present, but without any suggestion of a particularly recent phenomenon, prophets concerned with ecological conditions and morality have been recorded among the Tonga, Lamba, Soli and the Luapula peoples.[34] These data, and the appearance in the early decades of the twentieth century of a series of prophets among the Ila and Sala who encountered an eager response,[35] suggest that prophetism was an integral part of the region's religious system in pre-colonial times.

The nineteenth-century religious system as described in this section was intimately related to the general socio-economical and political structure of the society in which it occurred. Changes in this overall structure therefore produced tensions calling for religious innovation. I shall first outline the main religious innovations occurring in the region over the last few centuries; then identify five main dimensions in these

145

innovations and link them to economic and political change; and finally, show how all these innovations can be meaningfully placed in one overall historical framework.

Descriptive overview of modern religious innovations

The above reconstruction of the main features of the nineteenth-century village religion of central western Zambia will form the basis for a description and interpretation of twentieth-century religious innovations.

I shall claim that these innovations were at least as much a continuation of trends of pre-colonial change as a response to the new socio-economic and political situation brought about by colonial rule. Particularly the colonial-protest element in most of these innovations would appear very slight or non-existent to the unbiased observer, and, while a dominant aspect of certain innovatory movements (e.g., Watchtower), it does not provide the central explanation for the massive popularity of modern religious innovations in general.[36]

This is exemplified by the Ila prophets. They operated in a society that was heavily, and negatively, affected by the imposition of colonial rule. From about 1900 onwards, the Ila saw their unequalled wealth (largely in the form of cattle), which they had managed to maintain and expand despite Lozi, Ndebele and Yeke raids throughout the nineteenth century, threatened by the creation of hut tax and the encroachment of Lozi representative Indunas.[37] An end was put to the raiding of neighbouring groups for cattle and slaves, which had been the main mechanism to consolidate and expand Ila wealth and to maintain their unstable demographic balance.[38] Strong anti-white feelings existed in the Ila area during the early colonial period, as is shown by the expulsion and murders of white traders and the strong racial tensions in the early years of mining in the Mumbwa area.[39] The Primitive Methodists had founded two missions south of the Kafue Hook (Nkala, 1893, and Nanzela, 1895), but had met with an extremely discouraging response from the population.[40] The Ila were very reluctant to adopt such new ways as labour migration and western clothing.[41] They openly opposed hut tax in 1907.[42]

Yet very little of this found a perceptible expression in the messages of the early Ila prophets. These prophets betrayed their allegiance to an older religious institution by their strong emphasis on ecological conditions (fish, game, crop pests, rain). Around this common theme, however, they each adopted innovatory elements: one denounced praying to God as nonsense, others claimed themselves to be God or God's son. Only Chilenga, failing in his ecological endeavours, subsequently tried his hand on eschatological messages involving a prolonged darkness, destruction of the new railway and of the Kafue railway bridge, the departure of the Europeans, and the killing of the few heads of cattle that the Batwa minority, peripheral to Ila society, had managed to scrape together.

Thus Chilenga is the only Ila prophet in the early twentieth century known to have incorporated, on second thoughts, colonial protest in his message.[43] Mupumani, no doubt the greatest and most successful of these prophets, refrained from such protest altogether. Let us discuss Mupumani's prophetic career in some detail.

An early prophet: Mupumani [44]

Mupumani started his prophetic career in 1913 in a village only six kilometres from Nanzela mission. He followed what appears to be the standard biographical pattern for Central African religious innovators: a chronic disease or handicap (he was a leper), culminating in an allegedly fatal crisis; a short 'death' during which the prophet visits God in the sky and receives his message; resurrection, immediately followed by the now recovered patient revealing himself as a prophet and beginning to divulge the message.[45]

Mupumani's message was claimed to derive from God himself, preferably referred to by the names of Shakapanga (Creator) and Mulengachika (Creator of Pestilence). Crucial issues in the message were the following. Mourning, and particularly the killing of cattle at funerals, was denounced as ridiculous in the eyes of God, who holds absolute sway over life and death, 'took men from earth and caused men to be reborn',[46] without paying attention to human emotions. Witchcraft was also denounced, although the sources do not disclose in what terms. And finally Mupumani introduced new ritual: the erection of white poles (tree-trunks stripped of bark) in the centre of villages, where God was to be prayed to, using the formula 'We are humble to the Creator of Pestilence'.[47] The poles are, on a magnified scale, identical to the ordinary village shrines which are erected for the ancestors throughout the region; and the prayer formula 'we are humble' was standard in such pre-existing cults as those of the Ila major land spirits, and Nkoya ancestral cults. Alongside these older formal elements, Mupumani's major innovation consists of explicitly making God (to-

147

wards whom little or no ritual used to be directed) the immediate and exclusive focus of a new ritual and theology.[48]

Very interesting is the interplay between the prophet and two other religious institutions in the area: the Primitive Methodist mission and the cult of the major land spirit Shimunenga.[49] Whereas Mupumani was not a Christian, he was to some extent aware of the teachings of the local missionary; he recognized the missionary as representing the same God as the one whose prophet he was himself.

When pilgrims began to flock to Mupumani, he would send them on to the mission. The missionary reciprocated by interviewing Mupumani and taking his photograph. A month later the Shimunenga medium volunteered a favourable message on both the prophet and the mission, and reproached the people for ignoring these two representatives of God. This exhortation may have contributed to the expansion of Mupumani's movement, and it certainly inspired the population to an enthusiastic, if short-lived, interest in the mission; moreover, it reinforced the popular conception (to exist still for many years afterwards) of the missionaries as representing a new ecological cult not too dissimilar from Shimunenga's.[50] Further research is required before this fascinating episode can be properly understood.

Meanwhile Mupumani met with a phenomenal response, not so much among the Ila but especially in other parts of central western Zambia and far beyond. Within months of his first appearance as a prophet, people from as far away as Angola, Mwinilunga and Serenje would come to visit him, and on their return home they would erect the white pole and pray to God.

Various factors contributed to this rapid spread over an enormously vast area. Mupumani's message was hardly specifically Ila. The prophet lived in the Luchena area west of the rich cattle belt,[51] where the population at that time was for a considerable proportion Lozi.[52] As a leper from an area with few cattle, Mupumani was most probably a poor man at the outset of his prophetic career, debarred from successful entrepreneurship around which the dominant Ila value system revolved.[53] Against this background Mupumani's denouncing of the slaughter of cattle at funerals (which was a pivotal element in the Ila socio-economic system[54]) may have reflected a personal rejection of Ila values by one who was denied the economic achievement stipulated by those values. And as such the prophet may even be taken as repre-senting a large group of individuals who, living outside the rich cattle belt, saw themselves unable to comply with the achievement- and aggression-centred Ila culture, and who in fact were its most immediate victims through raids. From this starting-point a transfer becomes possible to other parts of central western Zambia and adjacent regions, where a very similar culture prevailed and where cattle were likewise scarce or absent. Mupumani's explicit rejection of the killing of cattle rendered his vision just as applicable to the cattle-owning Ila as to others lacking cattle.

The spread of Mupumani's movement was facilitated because of the fact that the main other cultural elements it incorporated and transformed (the tree shrine, the High God, witchcraft) were, far from being specifically Ila, common throughout Central Africa. So much for the cultural substratum. In addition to the existing rural social networks of wide geographical extension,[55] labour migration (which outside the Ila area had expanded rapidly) provided the major vehicle for the actual spread of Mupumani's prophetic movement: non-Ila came in contact with the movement while working along the line of rail, or while travelling between their homes and the mines and farms in the south. Yet, after the initial stage of the movement, pilgrims may have started from their village homes specifically to see the prophet irrespective of their search for work. Finally, Mupumani himself seems to have travelled extensively in order to divulge his message: his prophetic career came to an end in 1914 in Mumbwa, where the Native Commissioner, worried by the prophet's activities and the massive response, had him imprisoned on a charge of vagrancy and false pretensions.[56]

While thus ample conditions for spread existed, the actual process by which the movement took shape was far from mechanical. A dialectical relation developed between Mupumani's vision and the popular response. With our present, limited knowledge the details of this dialectic are hard to reconstruct, but the available data strongly suggest the following pattern.[57] As Mupumani's message spread, his original mystical experience gave way to eschatological or millenarian ideas which, paradoxically, were more directly geared to the day-to-day life of his followers. His idea of the futility of mourning in the light of God's arbitrary power of life and death (the central theme of his heavenly vision) was popularly transformed into the enthusiastic belief that mythical, primordial times were about to return: plenty of game meat, prodigious harvests, the denial of death (and the return of those already dead), and the absence of witchcraft. As in the primordial village in the sky, God would once again care directly for his creatures, who could now ignore the powers of the village dead – in line with Mupumani's attack on funerary custom.[58] Apparently no active eradication of

149

witchcraft did occur in the movement. Instead, the idiom of the popular response took an entirely ecological form. Those who had visited the prophet returned to their villages, erected the white pole and organized communal prayer where the 'Creator of Pestilence' - far from being acknowledged and emphasized in precisely this hideous capacity full of connotations of illness and death - would be implored to intervene with regard to hunting, women (i.e. their fertility), and agriculture. 'It was accepted with great exultation and ecstasy that everybody would become . . . a good hunter'.[59] The people expected the prophet to provide hunting and crop medicine which was to bring about this golden age. Mupumani 'had to yield to their requirements. He gave them drugs and they gave him money, cloth and beads in return'.[60] The medicines thus obtained would be stored in small huts erected along with the white poles.

Thus the widespread movement triggered by Mupumani's appearance largely followed the principles and concrete cultural forms (e.g., the prayer formula, the shrines shaped as poles and huts[61]) inherent in the older ecologico-religious system prevalent throughout Central Africa, as discussed in the previous chapter. While the movement swept on Mupumani saw himself forced to compromise to popular demands along these lines, in order to retain his newly-won, exalted status.

The expectations contained in the popular movement met with a quick disillusion. The primordial times were evidently not restored, the prophet's medicine turned out to be useless,[62] his supernatural powers were ineffective against those of the district officer who committed him to prison; and the movement died out as quickly as it had arisen. Funerary procedures were resumed. The dead became once again a power to be reckoned with. Nor had the witches been permanently evicted from the scene of popular religion in the region, as is borne out by the later occurrence of witchfinding and witchcraft eradication[63] (see pp. 152-3, 162-7).

> And it seems that the only result of his visions is the inauguration
> of a new kind of salutation. He . . . taught them to raise their hands
> high over their heads and reply 'Twakabomba' (we are humble).

This suggests that something survived of Mupumani's attempt to formalize and consolidate the rise of the High God to unique prominence in the religious outlook of the region.

This account of an early prophetic movement has introduced some major themes that we shall continue to pursue with regard to the later religious innovations in the region.

Other religious innovations in the early twentieth century

Although no single later prophet was able to instigate a religious movement on the same geographical scale as Mupumani, in the decades
following his appearance central western Zambia, much as the rest of
Central Africa, continued to seethe with religious innovation.

The Christian missions were further expanded, in co-operation with
the colonial government. The latter looked upon this familiar and
European-controlled brand of Christianity as an important factor for
order and well-contained progress, utilized the secular skills which
the African converts had acquired in their association with the missions
(literacy, trades), and let the missions provide the bulk of what little
medical care existed for the African population.

An altogether different basis underlay the cults of affliction,[64] which
offered a new interpretation[65] of physical and mental disorders: these
were no longer ascribed to the actions of dead or living members of the
village community, but to abstract general disease principles, such as
viyaya, kayongo, muba, mayimbwe, bindele, kasheba, etc. An idea
common to all these cults is that one would contract such a disease
from strangers, particularly in situations of trade, slavery, and labour
migration. Cults would serve the diagnosis and treatment of these new
diseases, in such a way that patients in the course of their treatment
became adepts of the cult named after their particular disease, and
could then start to diagnose and heal others, thus spreading the cult
without any centralized organization being required.

For the prototypes out of which the modern cults of affliction were
to develop, at least two clearly distinct sources are suggested by the
data. Among the Tonga-speaking groups to the east and south of
central western Zambia (and shading over into the Shona-speaking
groups), cults of affliction associated with abstract, impersonal principles
seem to have developed, during the last few centuries, out of the mediumistic tradition of the elaborate ritual surrounding major land spirits, generally identified with deceased chiefs.[66] It is not impossible that the chiefly
spirits in this area in themselves were partly redefinitions of older forest-
beings; such a line of development may be suggested by the co-existence
of the *muba* and *ngulu* cults alongside mediumistic chiefly cults in central
and northern Zambia. To the north-west of our region inter-local ecological cults are absent;[67] there cults of affliction seem to have developed
more directly out of the doctors' tradition of medicine and healing, which
is more obviously related to the ancient cult of forest-beings, as it still exists on the periphery of the religious system.[68] Confined to a limited area,
such prototypes may have existed for an indefinite period, but it is only in

151

the late nineteenth and particularly in the early twentieth century that these cults proliferate both in number and in ritual elaboration, and start their phenomenal geographical expansion, in a way reminiscent of the spread of fashions or epidemics. Their spread depends on senior adepts who introduce the new interpretation of disease further afield; these new-style doctors are then generally regarded by the people as agents of a cult which already exists elsewhere, rather than as creators of a new cult.

Once these cults of affliction were firmly established, secondary interpretations began to appear. The doctors' routine was challenged; and prophets, claiming a fresh supernatural inspiration, would in their turn create new ritual and a new organization (typically much more centralized than the previous one) to deal with these afflictions. For western Zambia several of such 'prophetic cults of affliction' have so far been described: Kamanga's *Twelve Society*, which is identical to Chief Katota's *Nzila* (both dealing with *bindele*); Simbinga's *Bituma*; Moya's *Moya* cult.[69] The phenomenon, however, has a much wider distribution; examples from other parts of Zambia include: the Church of the Spirits in the Chipata area,[70] the influence of the *ngulu* cult upon Alice Lenshina and her Lumpa Church;[71] and the central part which 'possession by evil spirits' (sometimes identified with, sometimes held to be counteracted by, the Holy Spirit) plays in many Zambian churches of the Apostolic and Pentecostal types.[72]

The distinction between diffusing agents and local prophets is analytically useful, but we have to realize that it is rather arbitrary, based as it is on our reconstruction of how these innovators were subjectively perceived by themselves and their followers. Selecting, collating and transmitting the same limited set of religious themes propounded by cults of affliction (the many cults are strikingly similar to each other over a large area), some agents will have actively reshaped the cultic material they were spreading. Alternatively, the great similarities between the affliction prophets mentioned here (for instance, all followed what I called 'the standard biographical pattern') suggests less originality than they and their followers claimed (cf. note 95).

Different themes again were propounded by representatives of yet another, composite movement which penetrated central western Zambia in the 1920s and particularly the early 1930s. These innovators concentrated not on physical and mental suffering as such but on eschatological views of a total cleansing and radical transformation of the community, as a prerequisite for the new society which was allegedly imminent. Dipping (ritual total immersion in water), the exposure and removal of witches, and the singing of hymns were their main ritual activities. While pursuing these common themes, many explicitly claimed to be agents of Watchtower (*Chitawala*). Others worked more independently, and appeared more as original prophets. Many expressed adverse views with regard to the colonial government, the whites in general and (in Barotseland) the Lozi Paramount Chief and his indigenous administration.[73]

By that time Central African colonial governments had for several years been in a constant state of alarm, if not panic, about what they classified, somewhat too schematically, as either 'Watchtower' or *'mchape'* (cleansing). In central western Zambia as elsewhere, trials would ensue whenever there was evidence of witchcraft accusations and anti-white statements having been made. When these legal grounds were found not to apply, the administration would prosecute the dippers and preachers under such pretexts as the Vagrancy Act – as had happened already to Mupumani.[74] The Lozi administration, recently disgraced by the scandals surrounding alleged ritual murders at the court,[75] and struggling to retain and consolidate its powers in the outlying districts of Mankoya and Balovale,[76] could not afford to take any challenge lightly; having acquired the authority to deal with the preachers throughout Barotseland (much of the western part of the region under study), the Lozi *khotlas* (councils) punished them severely and expelled them from the Province. Moreover, the administration tried to smother the effects of the preachers' teachings by threatening sympathizing chiefs with demotion.[77] The political overtones of the movement died away after some years, the administration's vigilance was relaxed, and the Watchtower excitement was to crystallize into a number of regular congregations which, with relatively little controversy, were to survive until today.[78]

This movement temporarily intensified eschatological notions and gave them a new ritual expression; but the expectation of a radically new, final society about to be established had already existed in central western Zambia at least since Mupumani's movement. Later movements not unlike Mupumani's have been recorded for other parts of western Zambia before the preachers and dippers gained a massive response. Prophets arose claiming that they had visited heaven and had been sent back to prepare for the imminent changes. A central feature in their messages was the imposition of new taboos on certain crops and domestic animals (black sheep and goats). These ideas, and the distorted rumours that would proliferate about them, spread again quickly and gained sufficient momentum to worry district officers on the look-out for subversive 'Watchtower' activities. It was soon realized that this was a different affair, not likely to threaten the *status quo*, and without much further interference the administration allowed these eschatological prophetic movements to subside.[79]

There are other indications of the local growth of eschatological awareness prior to the dipping and Watchtower-type preaching. Self-accused witches would seek redress before it would be too late,[80] and the introduction of new Rhodesian money showing effigies of animals and implements familiar to the people was widely interpreted as a sign that the social order was about to change.[81] Upon their arrival the preachers found the soil thus prepared, and eclectically they adopted some of the earlier eschatological expressions: e.g., the new food taboos imposed by the eschatological prophets.[82]

Finally, there was a line of response which was only marginally religious, but which is clearly related to the older ideas concerning 'success' medicine as well as the ambivalent disease/success connotations of the archaic forest-beings. In the first decades of the twentieth century we see the search for formidable medicine (through which an individual would command unequalled longevity,[83] success and wealth) turn into something of a mass movement, with an increased emphasis upon types of medicine other than the usual ones notorious for their sorcery connotations. For obvious reasons European medicine became a highly desirable thing.[84] At the same period we witness the intensive, systematic hunt after the luck-bringing *kambuma*, a small mythological animal supposed to dwell in the forests of the Mankoya and Feira districts; once again labour migration provided the vehicle for the spread of rumours concerning this animal, and hunts to catch it were staged from as far away as Tanganyika and South Africa.[85]

Themes of religious change: towards an interpretative synthesis

Revolving around the twin concerns of ecology and human suffering, the old religious system had identified the dead as largely controlling man's access to nature, had stipulated collective ritual as a means to communicate with the dead, had emphasized suffering as a communal concern, and had further reflected on the relation between the individual and the community by invoking supernatural sanctions over the villager who neglected his kinship obligations, and by associating individual achievement (as hunter, doctor, entrepreneur or chief) with medicine procured through sorcery. This world-view had a strong communal emphasis;

it provided a mechanism to keep the inevitable conflicts (over limited ecological resources and over authority, against a background of aspirations for individual achievement) from becoming immediately disruptive.

This religious system was intimately related to the general socioeconomic and political structure of the society in which it was found. Changes in this overall structure therefore produced strong religious tensions which could only be resolved by religious innovation. In this section I shall outline the major dimensions along which these tensions occurred, explore their relations with secular social change, and show how the various religious innovations discussed in the previous section formed related attempts to resolve these tensions.

Time

Much has been written on the concept of time in relation to religion in Africa, and I do not intend to make an original contribution on this point. However, if we want to study religion as an attempt to come to terms with the universe and the human experience, we have to pay attention to time as a crucial dimension of both.

The annual ecological cycle, and the individual life span between birth and death, provide the invariable non-social input out of which any society can mould (in historical traditions, ritual, socio-economic aspirations and collective expectations for the future) its peculiar perception of time. In Central African village society (which of course is an ideal-type rather than a reality) the dominant perception of time seems to have been that of a cyclical present. Awareness of time did apparently not stretch far back either into the past (unless to a mythical primordial situation) or into the future. Enduring social groups were either of limited operational value to the social process (clans, nations), or if of central relevance, had a maximal time-span of only a few decades (conjugal families, households, villages). Ritual was predominantly ecological, suggestive of an annual *Wiederkehr des Gleichen*. And such ritual concentrated on the village dead, who thus continued to belong to the community and who in fact were considered to return after their deaths, as a younger generation inherited their names and social personalities. Individual careers would largely follow a standard pattern of rise and decline, in line with the biological process.

The closely related phenomena of the growth of chieftainship and long-distance trade modified this situation in two ways. For a limited number of people time would increasingly be perceived as a process of unique individual ascendance in the pursuit of a special entrepreneurial and political career; and as this process produced enduring and exalted positions and titles, legitimation for their persistence and prerogatives would be sought in historical charters. The cyclical present began to give way to a perception of the linear progress of both individual careers and political history. Much more regional and comparative research, and theoretical thinking, will be required before we can understand the factors and the meaning of the appearance of yet another time perception: the eschatological conception of time as drawing to an end in the (typically near) future. The upheaval in nineteenth-century Central Africa caused by the apotheosis of long-distance trade and the military exploits of invading groups (Kololo, Ngoni, Ndebele, Yeke), as well as the economic and political changes brought about by colonial rule, certainly prepared the soil for eschatological expectations; but these facts fail to explain the mechanism by which such expectations germinated and spread.

Eschatological notions play an important, but not a universal role in the religious innovations described in the previous section. They were prevalent amongst, per definition, the eschatological prophets, and moreover amongst the Watchtower-type preachers, in missionary Christianity (where the linear time perspective of individual conversion and salvation leads to the collective eschatology of the Second Coming), and in several prophetic cults of affliction that took on a Christian-inspired idiom and organization. Such notions were completely absent from the medicine hunts, primary cults of affliction, and from the majority of prophetic cults of affliction that did not adopt Christian forms.

Ecology

With the growth of trade and of more complex political systems, an increasing segment of society would become engaged in other economic fields than ecological activities. This trend was to be reinforced by the expansion, much later, of labour migration and the rise of new, European-introduced careers at missions, administrative centres and in modern private enterprise. While the rural population continued to rely on gardens and the forest for most of its food supply, trade goods and (after the imposition of hut tax) the need for cash created a general participation in an economic system external to the village ecology. This led to the decline of ecological concern in the religious system. Such decline can be observed in all the innovations discussed in the previous section. Christian missions may have dabbled in rain and harvest ritual,[86] but in general such attempts appeared rather opportunistic and they would be abandoned for themes more in line with the missionaries' own spirituality (reflecting their European, industrial society of origin), as soon as the mission had attained sufficient local response. In the cults of affliction, the secondary prophetic affliction cults, the eschatological prophetic movements as well as among the Watchtower-type dippers and preachers, we do not encounter the slightest trace of a concern for the land or of claims of power to influence the human ecological transformations. The significance of this radical departure from what had been a central issue in the old religious system cannot be overestimated. If nature enters at all in these new cults, it is as something to be feared and avoided: elements of the natural world (certain crops and animals) are declared taboo.[87] In one case (the Bituma cult) an old first-crop ritual has been adopted in a new form; deprived of all elements of ritual care for the land, it now only serves to protect the participants against harmful powers supposed to reside in the newly-harvested maize.[88]

But while the religious innovations underplay or reverse nature's economic significance, nature (particularly the deep forest) retains or develops strong symbolic qualities: it is the place from which both primary and secondary prophetic cults of affliction procure their vegetal medicine, and where medicine hunters try to trap the *kambuma*; and it is a place of retreat and supernatural inspiration for sufferers from affliction, for prophets, and for leaders of certain independent churches.[89]

Supernatural entities

The supernatural beings recognized in the old religious system, predominantly the village dead, could no longer reasonably be held to control the entire large-scale society to which the village setting was giving way.

Colonial rule gave a new direction and impetus to this increase of scale, through the creation of a formal national and international administrative system along bureaucratic lines, the introduction of labour migration, and the incorporation of the village economy in a worldwide system of production and consumption. Yet increase of secular scale had been a trend in Central African history for perhaps a millennium or more: the emergence and growth of long-distance trade, chieftainship and complex state systems. In line with this secular change we see new cultic forms superimpose new supernatural beings upon the older ecologico-religious system of the village, the village dead, the shrine and the surrounding land area. Cults of deceased chiefs arise and assume both ecological and political functions (of legitimation and integration) often operating across larger areas than would previously be served by one non-chiefly ecological cult.[90] When in the nineteenth century long-distance trade is increasingly mono-polized by such specialized middlemen as the Mambari,[91] Chikunda and Bisa, and concentrates on slaves and guns, the religious reaction is the proliferation and rapid spread of cults of affliction, explicitly associated with foreigner groups and sometimes directly named after them.[92] These cults venerate supernatural entities that are only dimly conceptualized: often they appear as just abstract names conveying nothing more concrete than a sense of alienness (even to the extent of not being personalized or not anthropomorphic), whereas sometimes – when explicitly contrasted with the familiar, local dead – they are suggested to be ancestral spirits of these alien groups.[93] Such more universalist supernatural entities correspond well with the features of high geographical mobility, displacement and increase of scale charac-teristic of the secular aspects of nineteenth-century Central African society.

The political and economic changes brought about by colonial rule affected not only the village and its ecologico-religious system; they also radically redefined chieftainship (almost beyond recognition) and greatly diminished its powers, while replacing the circulation of traders, slaves, guns, other trade-goods, and tribute by a circulation of labour migrants, tax, and European manufactured products. Deceased chiefs and affliction principles – the supernatural entities that arose in response to pre-colonial increase of scale – became capable of substitution by again other supernatural entities.

Even if we allow for an element of historical dependency (missionary teachings having influenced both local prophets and the Watchtower-type innovators), it is most remarkable that (with exception of the medicine hunts) all religious innovations following the primary cults of affliction highlight the conception of the High God. In the case of missionaries and Watchtower-type dippers and preachers the High God element evidently occupies a central place. But also the local, eschato-logical prophets lend credibility to their messages by the claim of a visit to God in the sky (normally during a temporary 'death' within the standard biographical pattern), and the same is true for some prophets of affliction. Several prophetic affliction cults supplant the abstract

158

affliction principles by concepts synonymous with, or closely related to, the High God: the Angel[94] and the Holy Spirit.[95] What is new here is not the conception of the High God itself, but the attempt to endow this conception with so much splendour, power and immediate relevance that it is capable of eclipsing all other religious entities that were previously so conspicuous. Only the High God seems of sufficient calibre to serve as the credible religious counterpart of the political and economic structure of modern Central African society.[96] And along with the propagation of the High God, iconoclastic attempts are made to eradicate the other supernatural entities – primarily the village dead, whose cults and shrines come under attack from mission, Watchtower, eschatological prophets and Mupumani alike.[97]

Communalism

The communal bias in the normative system of Central African village society, and the emphasis on collective ritual, far from producing or reflecting well-integrated and stable communities, served to counteract the perennial tendencies towards fission inherent in the ecology and the authority structure of this society.[98] The life of the village would typically go through the following stages: founding by a dissident individual or faction immigrated from elsewhere; expansion under conditions of ecological plenty and co-operation; mounting of factional and generational opposition under increasing ecological pressure, still checked by collectivist norms and redressive collective ritual; and finally fission. In this cyclical process individualism would be played down as a temporary crisis; the dominant, explicit societal ideology would follow a collectivist idiom.

This ideology and its ritual expression, already counteracted by aspirations of individual ascendance as built into the very structure of this society, would no longer be adequate as a situation developed where an individual would increasingly find himself at a considerable geographical distance from his close relatives, facing a situation different from theirs, and at least temporarily unable or unwilling to claim or to provide support along kinship lines. This again is not a situation newly introduced along with colonial rule. The pre-colonial trader and especially the slave or captive (forcibly displaced and unlikely ever to return) were not in a less individual situation than the later labour migrant, boma messenger, evangelist, store-boy, etc.

Under these conditions one might expect a counter-ideology of individualism to arise, finding expression in alternative ritual forms.

Perhaps we may trace this development back as far as the emergence (possibly in the first millennium AD[99]) of cults of local celebrities: chiefs, diviners, doctors, and ironworkers. A historical sequence is then suggested where the cult of the collective village dead, namelessly represented in the one village shrine, gives way to the 'cult of personality' around particular individuals whose names may be remembered and for whom distinct shrines may be erected. The associated ritual is still largely carried out by the community as a whole, and has strong ecological emphasis, again for the benefit of the entire community.

It is almost certain that such communal cults for individualized celebrities (together with the cults of forest-beings) contributed prototypes to the more recent cults of affliction, which generally revolve around one particular abstract principle after which the cult is named, but in which occasionally deceased celebrities continue to play a part.[100] The concern of these cults of affliction is not the total community, but the afflicted individual. The ritual intends to initiate or reinforce the individual as a member of a cultic group, which is not an operational social group in everyday activities outside the ritual sphere, but instead cuts across existing kinship and residential groups. Communal concern is altogether absent in these cults of affliction. The individual's suffering is not attributed to adverse conditions in his social group (as is the case with suffering interpreted as inflicted by the dead, or as resulting from a breach of taboos or from witchcraft between opponents). The affliction ritual makes no attempt to redress social conditions. Instead the individual is brought to relieve his heart from fears and suspicions in the course of private therapeutic conversations with senior adepts. No moral obligations are conferred upon the individual as a member of the cult, and outside the ritual situation the adepts do not look to each other for assistance in everyday matters. In certain cults the adept is encouraged to have frequent mystical communications with the affliction principle inside him, and to make very high and unusual demands upon his immediate social environment. He will reject certain food, places and undertakings as 'dirty' and as contrary to the wishes of his affliction principle, will instead insist on luxury food (bananas, rice, biscuits, processed mealie-meal, soft drinks, bottled beer) and expensive other articles (white beads and cloth), and expects his relatives to organize ecstatic sessions for him, which are often also very expensive.[101]

Modern cults of affliction are cults of egotism *par excellence.* This central feature partly explains their fashionable appeal, and the creative proliferation of new and extravagant ritual elements (many of which are ridiculed or denounced as immoral by non-adepts).

Most secondary prophetic cults of affliction have retained these egotistic, a-moral and non-communal characteristics. However, when they adopt, and succeed in retaining, churchlike features, their individualism will be mitigated by at least two factors, which apply *a fortiori* to those Christian churches that do not emphasize possession and healing. Like the cults of affliction, these churchlike forms of organized religion disengage the individual from his immediate kinship and residential setting, and make him a member of a cultic group cutting across the community. However, first there is the tendency for such a Christian-type cultic group to become an alternative partial community, taking care also of some other than immediately religious aspects of the members' lives: e.g., marriage, visiting the sick, burial, economic enterprise, recreation. And second, even the churches that concentrate on possession and healing will propound moral teachings such as relegate the believer to other members of society: sometimes only to his fellow-members of the cultic group, but often extending to all his fellow-men (including, but now in a more detached and optional way, the believer's immediate kinsmen and neighbours).

Cults of affliction appeared in Central Africa prior to healing churches and other forms of organized Christianity, and now seem to be losing ground to the latter.[102] This historical sequence suggests that the former's extreme individualism was merely a passing stage in a more general process: *the religious reformulation of the community.* The same reappearance of communal concern can be seen in the eschatological prophets (whose messages of imminent changes and new taboos refer to the total community and not to singled-out individuals), and particularly the Watchtower-type dippers and preachers, who urged a total transformation of the entire community by means of collective baptism and the eradication of witchcraft. However, these two religious movements still accepted the existing, increasingly ineffective rural communities as their frame of reference and point of departure. The eschatological prophetic movements died down soon, not only because their prophecies did not come true immediately,[103] but also because they did not actively undertake the reshaping of the community. The Watchtower-type approach, despite its much richer cultic and conceptual apparatus, proved equally unable to transform the existing communities entirely and lastingly, and was only saved from extinction, it appears, by virtue of a process of separation between persisting converts and renegades. In fact, Watchtower became just another cross-cutting cultic group, which could acquire far-reaching non-religious functions because of the tendency among Watchtower members to concentrate in exclusive villages.[104] Thus at the village level a permanent transformation of community was often achieved – albeit in a routinized and attenuated form, which is only a dim reflexion of the original Watchtower enthusiasm.

Witchcraft and the problem of evil

Above I explored some of the social and economic principles underlying the system of witchcraft in Central African society: insufficient ideological justification of high status; the fact that a person's advancement – based on a redistribution of commodities present within the village community, including people eligible to become spouses or slaves – would often be at the expense of his neighbour; and the propensity to inter-generational and inter-factional conflict as built into the structure of village society, along with the absence of effective judicial means to resolve such conflict.

It has been suggested that witch-beliefs date back to a very early time and form a particularly archaic layer in Central African religion.[105] However this may have been, the growth of long-distance trade and chieftainship is likely to have had a direct bearing on witch-beliefs. Trade provided opportunities for successful entrepreneurs to rise to unprecedented power and wealth, secure local monopolies and establish themselves as chiefs. The development of chiefly paraphernalia and prerogatives, the emergence of strict and formal rules for chiefly succession, and the creation of chiefly cults, were attempts (particularly as inspired by Lunda political ideas) to legitimize and safeguard this exalted status; not only against rivals (who favoured a change of personnel while accepting the structural *status quo* of inequality), but also against popular, egalitarian dissidence. Gluckman's thesis[106] of rebellion by rivals (as opposed to structural revolution) as the characteristic, cyclical crisis of Central and Southern African political systems seems too well taken. Several Central African peoples trace their origins as a distinct group to an episode of upsurge against chiefly arrogance,[107] and similar movements have been recorded for a more recent past.[108] The conception of chieftainship as sustained by basic, unchallenged values effectively internalized throughout the societies of Central Africa increasingly appears to be a myth.[109] The fact that chieftainship often resorted to open, physical violence and cruelty, and surrounded itself with mystical terror,[110] could well be interpreted as a response to continuous and strong popular counter-currents against chiefly legitimacy. One aspect of this was that chiefs took on witchcraft connotations, which they could not shake off even if they went to the extent of attempting to monopolize the right to identify and prosecute witches (e.g., by means of the poison ordeal).

Early trade commodities in central western Zambia were partly procured through hunting (tusks, skins); great hunters would be closely associated with, or identical to, chiefs and would share their witchcraft connotations. When in the last century slaves became a major trade commodity, structural intra-societal conflicts seem to have been intensified both by the opportunity of profitably disposing of opponents, and by the constant fear of being thus disposed of.[111] If sorcery is essentially the reckless manipulation of human material for strictly individual purposes, we can expect that in this period sorcery and slavery (and trade in general) became very closely associated.

Yet about the same time cults of affliction began to develop interpretations of evil which ignore malice and guilt as causes of human suffering and which instead advance the idea of accidental exposure to harmful but propitiable affliction principles. It is a widespread belief in western Zambia that before the advent (remembered as fairly recent) of the many diseases identified as cults of affliction, witchcraft was the main cause of human suffering.[112] One might suggest that the expansion of cults of affliction was mainly a response to the appearance, in the course of the nineteenth-century turmoil, of new epidemics and the spread of venereal disease.[113] It is conceivable that the nineteenth century brought an overall deterioration of health conditions, continuing into the colonial era.[114] However, the most common diseases in the region (malaria, hookworm, tuberculosis, pneumonia) are tied up with constant ecological conditions.[115] We must therefore assume that also the old village society was disease-ridden to a considerable extent, as is borne out by the emphasis on suffering in the religious system. There has probably always been a sufficient amount of disease to warrant disease-oriented cults. Even if the nineteenth-century health conditions were favourable for such cults, they hardly explain the proliferation, rapid spread, and the particular a-moral, a-communal, egotistic idiom of these new cults of affliction. It would be better to treat both the postulated increase of disease, and the emergence of new cults of affliction, as related effects of the same overall process of socio-economic and political change in the nineteenth century.

The pattern of diffusion of these cults and their association with alienness suggests that traders had a direct hand in their proliferation and spread.[116] If this is true then part of their inspiration may have derived from the need of entrepreneurs to adopt and develop such a

163

new conception of suffering as could free them from the evil connotations with which they used to be surrounded.

Doctors seem to form a case different from the other high-status groups so far discussed in this context of witchcraft. Whereas the doctor is the main religious specialist in Central Africa, far too little is known yet, historically and comparatively, about this institution and its political and entrepreneurial aspects. In order to communicate with and to counteract the dead, forest-beings and sorcery, the doctor needed the most powerful medicine (often of human origin), and thus took on sorcery connotations himself. It is uncertain whether the wealth and superior status he acquired in the process in themselves (as contravening the egalitarian ideology) led to sorcery connotations in the doctor: contemporary field evidence suggests that they may often have been redeemed by a recognition of the doctor's rare, superior qualities and of the incomparable services he rendered to the community. Such a position is also in accordance with the fact that chiefs tried to consolidate and legitimize their exalted political and economic status precisely by adopting religious tasks (intervention with the dead for ecological purposes, and exposure of witches) which seem more typically the prerogatives of the doctor.

With the introduction in the colonial period of cash and labour migration, the end of the indigenous long-distance trade, the redistribution of power, and the emergence of new European-defined careers outside the village society, many individuals came to participate directly in a worldwide economic system. Whatever advancement an individual might achieve by his work elsewhere would be largely defined within and derived from this external economy, independent from the limited good of the village, and no longer perceptibly and directly at the expense of his fellow-members of the same rural community. If he had at all injured his neighbours it was not by actively manipulating them for evil, but only negatively, by temporarily withdrawing his labour force and other forms of participation from the village economy and society. The successful migrant who upon his return in the village would refuse to share out his wealth, might be considered an egoist but would structurally not be a witch; however, this would hardly prevent him from being called one, and certainly he would attract sorcery from his less fortunate neighbours.

Anyone pursuing successfully a modern career *within* the rural society would risk being considered a witch, no matter whether he would directly draw from the village economy (shopkeeper, publican), or be paid by an outside agency (messenger, game guard, evangelist, teacher).[117] It was particularly the labour migrants and those who had pursued modern careers who initiated and acted as agents for the witchcraft eradication movements in Central Africa from the 1920s onward.[118]

Thus we find at various stages of socio-economic change a specific, limited category of individuals, endowed with more than average opportunities and resources (chiefs, traders, modern achievers), who have a direct interest in altering witchcraft beliefs, since these beliefs, as associated with individual success, challenge the legitimacy of their newly acquired status and wealth. These achieving individuals propounded alternatives to witchcraft not only because they had so much to fear from witches threatening their position (although this remains a partial explanation, from chiefs abusing the poison ordeal in order to get rid of opponents[119] to modern dynamic young achievers enacting a generation conflict in the idiom of *mchape*[120]), but also and perhaps largely because they risked being considered witches themselves. In their attempts to consolidate their status and to alter witchcraft beliefs, these innovators did not only take on aspects of the doctor's role: as chiefs engaged in ecological ritual and witch-finding, as agents of new affliction cults, as affliction prophets and Watchtower-type witch-cleansers. Significantly, these innovators also staged direct and open attacks upon the old-style doctors. It had been the latters' task to expose witches and thus to preserve the old witchcraft ideas and institutions that were now coming under attack.[121]

Rather than deliberately revising witchcraft beliefs in order to avoid being implicated in them, it is more likely that the predisposition towards innovation along these lines among the achieving individuals sprang from the personal, semi-conscious tension between the incompatible values of, on the one hand, achievement as evil egotism and, on the other, achievement as rendering to life its ultimate meaning and redemption. This indeed is a fundamental and perhaps universal theme. For instance, in an entirely different setting but facing much the same predicament, similar categories of achieving individuals developed the religious systems of Calvinism and urban Islam.

In the case of the modern achievers the predicament was particularly severe. Originating in the village but pursuing new careers as defined in the European-introduced sectors of Central African society, their value conflict was the more acute since they operated at the borderline between the value systems of two vastly different societies. While the village ideology played down individualism and was suspicious of achievement, the value system of modern industrial European society as introduced into Central Africa in the early twentieth century hinged on an atomistic conception of man, and on individual achievement and success as the ultimate goal in life. This value orientation, fundamental for a capitalist economy and an administrative bureaucracy, also pervaded Christianity, in its emphasis on an individual relation with God and on personal salvation. Thus the modern achiever was caught between the values he had internalized in childhood, which made him feel 'bad', and the values both of the small in-group of his emergent African middle class[122] and of the new European-introduced society at large, which made him pursue individual achievement as a dominant, compulsive norm. It was inconvenient to resist the achievement-centred value system that had been introduced from outside. For this achievement-centred system was the basis of the modern achievers' income, and especially of their newly-won prestige and self-esteem. Moreover, this value system had often been internalized religiously, later in life, through a dramatic process of conversion. The logical way out was to attack the old local system, particularly in its conception of achievement and evil, and to induce as many people as possible to pass (religiously, if not yet socio-economically) into the new way of being that the modern achievers had already taken up.

These speculations imply that witchcraft eradication in twentieth-century Central Africa was fundamentally not against individual witches (with whom the modern witch-finders shared, to some extent, a common lot), but against witchcraft as a frame of reference and an institution. This is also suggested by the fact that in most cases the accused were offered a rather simple and harmless method of becoming cleansed – seldom were they killed or severely injured.[123] Witchcraft was still a mental reality. So if (in response to comprehensive socio-economic change) a new community had to come about with new conceptions of suffering and achievement, then the tangible exponents of the old witchcraft idea (the witches, and the old-style witch-finders whose own sorcery connotations now became emphasized) had to be disposed of. One could take their witchcraft away from them, or kill them as witches. Either method does not appear to have been the more authentic, within the movement, although the former was the more frequently used.

But while this may have been the original basis of the movement, in popular practice the eschatological aspects were often eclipsed and the exercise adulterated to become just a set of novel techniques for the age-old handwork of witch-finding; i.e., taking for granted and implicitly reinforcing, instead of eradicating, the conceptions and institutions of witchcraft.

The overall process of religious change

Above I identified five dimensions (time, ecology, supernatural entities, communalism and witchcraft) along which the ideal-typical village religion of central western Zambia (fairly representative for much of Central Africa) was innovated in a series of religious movements. In this section I shall show how these innovations can in effect be considered as the manifestations of one overall process of religious change, and explore the rhythm and some of the direct social mechanisms of this process.

Formal properties of the innovatory movements

The crucial importance of the five dimensions, and the profound inter-relations of the various innovatory movements as manifestations of one overall process of religious change sustained over many centuries, can best be demonstrated by mapping out all these movements in one chart. Table 4.1 represents the result of such an exercise.

For each of the five dimensions of variables, three scale values are specified on the basis of the present argument: the zero state (0) of the village religion, an intermediate state (−) in which alternatives are being formulated, and a final state (+) which represents, within the area and period we are dealing with here, the paroxysm of religious innovation along that dimension. The precise description of these states for each variable is given in the legend to the table. In addition to the village religion, ten innovatory responses are screened as to their scores on the five variables, and as to their approximate first appearance in time.

Nearly all entries are accounted for by the data presented in this chapter. Some, however, need a brief comment. The formulation of alternatives to witchcraft in the interpretation of suffering and achievement, I consider a more advanced state than active witchcraft eradication as exemplified by the Watchtower-type innovators. My reasons for this are largely intuitive, and the opposite view could equally be defended. The scoring of chiefly cults, cults of affliction and medicine hunts as manifesting a mixed cyclical/linear time dimension is based on the consideration that these innovations begin to emphasize an individual

Table 4.1 *Formal properties of innovatory religious movements in central western Zambia*

	Time	Ecology	Supernatural entities	Communalism	Witchcraft	First appearance in time	Index
Village religion	0	0	0	0	0	?	0
Chiefly cults	0/–	0/–	0/–	0	0	1st millennium AD?	1.5
Ila prophets	0/+	0	0/+	0	0?	before twentieth century?	2?
Mupumani (original vision)	0	0/+	+	0	–/+	about 1913	4.5
Mupumani (popular response)	+	0	+	0	–/+?	1913	5.5?
Cults of affliction	0/–	–/+	–	–	+	prototypes:? spread late nineteenth century	6
Eschatological prophets	+	–	+	0	0/+?	1920s?	6?
Medicine hunts	0/–	+	–	–	+	early twentieth century?	6.5
Prophetic cults of affliction	–/+	–/+	–/+	–/+	+	1930s	8
Watchtower-type dippers, preachers	+	–/+	+	+	–	1920s	8.5
Christian missions	–/+	–/+	+	+	–/+	late nineteenth century	8.5

Key: Time: 0 cyclical present; – linear progress (individualism); + eschatological
Ecology: 0 central concern; – negative cult; + eclipsed
Supernatural entities: 0 the village dead central; – alternative offered; + High God central
Communalism: 0 communal emphasis; – individualist emphasis; + transformed community
Witchcraft: 0 its frame of reference accepted; – eradication; + alternative interpretation of suffering and achievement
0 = 0   – = +1   + = +2   ? = information lacking or classification difficult; the total of the numerical values of the row
entries yields the index of innovation

career against the general background of the ideal-typical village system. In medicine hunts an eclipse of ecology is witnessed, since, although the medicine mostly derives from the forest, it is not employed for ecological purposes (rain, harvest, hunting), but for individual entrepreneurial success.

Christian missions represent a negative cult element in their objection to drinking and smoking (except for the Roman Catholic missions in the area, though they imposed fasting on certain days). And while the missions actively undertook the eradication of witchçraft as a belief system, they provided alternatives both in the abstract form of the Christian theology of suffering, and in the concrete form of propagating modern European medicine. Thus for many people in central western Zambia Christianity, in its combination of evangelism and medical work, appears as a new and powerful cult of affliction.[124]

The unmistakable crudity of the classification (typical of exploratory attempts towards systematic and formal analysis), as well as the limited state of our present knowledge, are reflected by the tendency to enter mixed values for many of the scores in the chart. Even so, the approach might be stretched to yield summary numerical indexes of overall innovation for each of the movements considered; the procedure to arrive at these indexes is likewise stipulated in the legend, and the index values are given as right-hand column entries.

The fact that the various religious movements, over many centuries, persistently show systematic tendencies towards innovation along the same few lines, and that the level of such innovations (as very tentatively measured by the numerical index, which emphatically is nothing but a quantification of common-sense impressions) keeps pace beautifully with historical time, strongly suggests that what we witness here is in fact one overall process of religious change, precipitating in a series of distinct innovatory movements.

The rhythm of religious innovation

How did this overall process take place over time? The time scale in Table 4.1 suggests a slow initial evolution towards more advanced stages of innovation, with a marked acceleration from the late nineteenth century onward.

For a more detailed insight into the rhythm of innovation it is instructive to take another look at Mupumani. This prophet appears a more powerful innovator than his predecessors among the Ila, in view of the profoundness of his message (the futility of life and death against the arbitrary power of God), his attention to ritual innovation, and his impact over a very large area. If we may consider the selective popular response to Mupumani as an indication of the stage of religious change that many communities in western Zambia had reached immediately prior to Mupumani's appearance, we must conclude that several of the themes discussed above were still little developed by that time. As a concession to Mupumani's followers, ecological concern was to occupy a central place in the movement, in the form of collective ritual for the benefit of the total community. Mupumani's admonitions against witchcraft apparently failed to get much response.

As it worked out, the movement he triggered was a short-lived attempt to revolutionize, rather than supersede, the old ecologico-religious system. As in some other innovatory movements along the Ila, crucial innovations in Mupumani's movement were the absolute prominence of the High God, and the appearance of strong eschatological expectations. In the latter aspect the popular movement deviated from the prophet's original vision, which did not contain a clear eschatological message but instead concentrated on death and rebirth as universal and perennial conditions of humanity.

But the trends of change rapidly gained momentum. In the mid-1930s the Christian missions of central western Zambia would claim over ten thousand members and adherents.[125] A few years earlier the Watchtower-type activities had found an eager response throughout the area; they led to the creation of congregations still in existence today. New cults of affliction continued to spread and affliction prophets were beginning to appear. Medicine hunts were undertaken, and eschatological prophetic movements swept across western Zambia. Processes of religious change that may have been initiated long before colonial times were now greatly accelerated.

The speed with which religious change precipitated in the period between the two world wars is perhaps best illustrated when we compare Mupumani's movement with the Bituma movement, founded by the affliction prophet Simbinga in the 1930s.[126] Simbinga's movement was considerably more limited, but still made a rapid impact over much of the Mankoya (now Kaoma) district, and was later taken to the urban centres along the line of rail. This massive response again indicates that Bituma actually met innovatory religious demands prevalent in the region at that time.

Bituma offers something of a test-case in that the years immediately preceding Simbinga's appearance were disastrous ecologically (repeated locust outbreaks, violent cattle pests, and the ecological pressure caused by the massive immigration from Angola), medically (epidemics of smallpox and influenza), and macro-economically: the worldwide depression was felt keenly in the region, all recruitment activities for labour migration had ceased, hardly anyone succeeded in finding work on his own initiative, and hut tax arrears reached an all-time high.[127] The times seemed more than suitable for a revival of the communal ecologico-religious complex much in the way of Mupumani's movement twenty years earlier. But nothing of the sort happened. The communal and ecological frame of reference had ceased to be sufficiently relevant; it could no longer dominate any religious expression. Nor did the suffering population of the Mankoya district find lasting solace in eschatological interpretations of their predicament, although Watch-tower-type preachers had received a massive response in the first years of the depression. Even witchcraft (in whose prosecution and eradication people in the region have indulged to the present day[128]) was not for long considered an adequate explanation for the unprecedented amount of misfortune. It appears as if the frustration of individual socio-economic careers was all-important; the hardships were experienced within an extremely individualist frame of reference, and the people adopted Bituma, revolving around God and his Angel, as a means to interpret and to alleviate individual suffering, not on a communal scale but in ephemeral, cross-cutting cultic groups.

While the above refers to the increased speed of innovation, comparison between Mupumani's and Simbinga's movements, and those in between, shows yet another aspect of the rhythm of religious change in central western Zambia: its strikingly dialectical nature. Innovation along the five dimensions would not be accumulated from movement to movement in a simple, one-way fashion: rather than consistently following up the themes that an earlier movement had emphasized, a later movement might show a relapse into a less advanced state of these particular themes and instead emphasize other themes. Yet, through the total series of movements a persistent, sustained process of gradual innovation is perceptible.

Some social mechanisms of religious innovation

Why then does this overall process take the form of so many different movements? What is the concrete social mechanism underlying each distinct movement? What explains, in concrete cases, the rapid decline of some of these movements and the gradual but thorough redefinition of some others? What new data, and especially what theory, do we

171

need to answer these questions? I will conclude this chapter by exploring such answers as the present data suggest, without however any pretensions towards the formulation of a fully-fledged and adequate model.

A simple model of diffusion through increased inter-regional contact would be of little help. No matter where certain new religious elements originated, they were integrated into new religious ideas and ritual within Central African society, by Central Africans. We cannot hope to understand the process and mechanism of innovation just by tracing the supply lines of the raw materials used.

Religious change in central western Zambia has been shown to proceed along five dimensions, which also represent the lines along which tension is generated within the existing religious system. Such tensions are not equally felt by all members of a given society. To invoke certain unequally distributed personality traits which would make certain individuals more sensitive to these tensions than others, would take us back to a 'great man' approach to social change, rightly denounced by modern sociology and history. Instead I have pointed to particular categories of individuals who, occupying an extraordinary position in the process of secular change as compared with other members of the same society, are as it were in the front line of religious change. In their advanced position they are socially predetermined to experience the religious tensions most acutely; and since religion is a source of meaning, evaluation and orientation in any society, they will have immediate personal interests in resolving these tensions which are disrupting their existential situation.

This limited category of individuals (perhaps an emergent social class) is actively in search of religious innovation. It will show a greater tendency than the rest of society to produce articulate and powerful religious innovators in their midst. The messages of these innovators will be likely to be relevant to those sharing their socio-economic position, since they largely derive from the innovators' personal semi- or sub-conscious responses to such religious tensions as are felt, much in the same way, by the other members of the same advanced category. Even so the various new solutions engendered within this category (and possibly other, foreign elements to which those in the front line of change may be exposed), all need testing-out as to their applicability and attractiveness, among the members of the advanced category. This produces a seething of experiment, innovation, spread, acceptance and rejection as is covered by the term 'religious *avant-garde*', in very close analogy with the literary *avant-garde* in complex literate societies.

172

The argument is based on the idea of various segments of a society being 'out of phase' *vis-à-vis* one another in a process of socio-economic change, with the segment in the most advanced phase forming one of the points in society (there may be others) where religious innovation is generated. In this situation no smooth transfer of religious innovation can occur between the *avant-garde* and the less advanced segments. The latter are still in an earlier socio-economic phase where the religious innovations of the former (formally corresponding with the more advanced socio-economic phase) would not yet apply. Therefore, if any such transfer does occur (and after all the various segments are in communication with each other as parts of the same society), its initial result will be that the innovations of the *avant-garde* are altered almost beyond recognition in the popular response, and typically are relegated to earlier, less-advanced religious ideas and rituals.

Of this the present chapter offers some illustrations: the lack of response in the first decades of the Primitive Methodist mission, when the missionaries were mainly regarded as representatives of another territorial cult; the redefinition of Mupumani's original message in the hand of his 'followers' (however, see below); and a similar redefinition of Bituma, which from a prophetic affliction cult centred on God and his Angel (intended to supersede previous primary cults of affliction), gradually became just another cult of affliction hardly distinguishable from the primary ones.[129]

As time and change go on, the less advanced segments gradually move into a socio-economic phase similar to the one previously occupied by the *avant-garde*, and then re-discover, adopt and further develop on a large scale the earlier innovations for which they are now ripe. This was, for instance, the case with the popular expansion of cults of affliction in the late nineteenth and early twentieth centuries. Thus the tensions which have existed in an intensified form among an earlier *avant-garde*, later appear (perhaps in a more diffuse form) among large segments of the society.

Meanwhile the front line of change recedes; small segments (not necessarily the earlier *avant-garde*) move into a new socio-economic phase. A case in point is the emergence of labour migrants, and of pursuers of new European-defined careers at missions and administrative centres and in private enterprise. These people experience new religious tensions which give rise to a new religious *avant-garde* and new religious innovations: Watchtower-type dipping and preaching, prophetic cults of affliction, independent and mission Christianity. Less advanced segments are again barred from these innovations by a phase difference. In this way it could be explained, for instance, that rural women in central

173

western Zambia (as a segment less involved in labour migration and new careers) have continued to adhere to primary cults of affliction, whereas their menfolk (a more advanced segment as a whole) have already largely proceeded to Watchtower and other forms of Christianity.[130]

A closer look at the new above-cited examples of radical redefinition of original content in the case of inter-phase transfer shows the limitations of this approach and forces us to search for additional mechanisms of religious innovation. For many crucial questions remain unanswered. Whence the enthusiasm and rapid extinction of the massive response to Mupumani and Simbinga, in contrast with the weak but persistent response to the mission? Were Mupumani and Simbinga really in an advanced socio-economic phase? Were their followers?

We first have to realize that these innovations were not transferred on to societal segments still in the 'zero phase' of an ideal-typical 'primordial' village religion. On the contrary, the average rural population of central western Zambia had certainly been thoroughly affected by the general socio-economic changes of the period, and some of the religious tensions discussed above were already mounting among them. Yet there was still a considerable phase difference between the European missionaries and the general population, and the lack of response to the mission in the early period of 1890 to 1920 could very well be attributed to this. The persistence, notwithstanding, of the mission is, of course, explained by the fact that this institution was sustained by an input (of personnel and funds) external to the region. Missionary expansion, however slow, in later years derived from two factors. First, the population entered into a phase more similar to that of the missionaries (whose frame of reference was that of North Atlantic industrial society); thus the phase difference between the local population and the missionaries decreased. Second, the mission provided an entry to new, European-defined careers, thus forming a growth-point for a new *avant-garde*.[131]

The initial enthusiasm triggered by Mupumani and Simbinga seems to indicate a closeness of phase between these innovators and their followers. Relevant religious tensions had pervaded large segments of the rural population, and the new movements (which initially appeared as the longed-for solutions) were eagerly adopted. The rapid decline might then be attributed to the fact that these innovations proved either too advanced to apply (Simbinga), or, after redefinition by the followers, too hybrid a blend between crude eschatological expectations and the ecologico-religious elements of an earlier phase (Mupumani).

174

Mupumani's case requires a more convincing answer than this, and we may arrive at one along the following lines. While Simbinga was clearly a modern achiever,[132] there is no indication that Mupumani was. He was debarred from entrepreneurial success along standard Ila lines, and in the modern sphere he was neither associated with the mission nor a labour migrant.[133] It was only through his prophetic career that he could, and reluctantly did, accumulate wealth – which derived primarily from non-Ila. The subsequent popular redefinition of his message superficially suggested Mupumani to be an *avant-garde* innovator; but if he was not a modern achiever, to what *avant-garde* did he belong?

One possible explanation is that the mission created a general heightened religious tension amongst all those living at close proximity, turning them all, including Mupumani, into a potential *avant-garde* as compared with those living at greater distance. Greater exposure to the missionary activities would shake their religious notions and activities, and they would search for innovation. Mupumani's message would then have to be viewed as an, indeed highly original, adaptation of missionary teachings, capable of catalytically reducing the phase difference between mission and general population (the fake exactitude of my index would reveal a reduction from the mission's 8.5 to the movement's 4.5). Such an interpretation is suggested both by the contemporary missionaries and by Fielder; they look upon Mupumani mainly as a translator of missionary ideas.[134] However, the mission's very limited impact in the twenty years preceding Mupumani's appearance hardly suggests any increase of religious tension created by the mission among the surrounding population *in general* (instead of among a small minority of converts and adherents, to which Mupumani did not belong). The popular redefinition of Mupumani's message consisted in a partial substitution of certain advanced features for other ones, the outcome being as a whole slightly *more* (instead of less) advanced than the original vision of the prophet (cf. Table 4.1). This upsets the view of the prophet as bridging the phase gap between mission and population, and points towards a dynamic independent from the mission.

The slightly more advanced phase of the followers can be accounted for by the fact that the movement was initially spread by labour migrants, i.e., people in a more advanced socio-economic phase than the prophet himself. This does not yet enable us to understand the prophet sociologically, that is, as a member of a particular structural category involved in a social process, and not just as a gifted individual. If he was not the exponent of an *avant-garde* of individuals spearheading socio-economic change, what accounts for his prophetic calling?

At least two other *avant-garde* situations conducive to religious innovation become now discernible, both of potential relevance to the interpretation of Mupumani. One is the situation of religious authorities, and offers a mirror-image of our original, achieving *avant-garde*. Confronted with socio-economic change, the existing religious authorities experienced particularly strong tensions between their established religious system and the implications of the new socio-economic conditions (along such dimensions as time, ecology, supernatural entities, communalism, and suffering and achievement). They experienced these tensions, not because they were more than other members of their society in the front line of socio-economic change, but because they were more than others involved in the old religious system. Religious innovation became as imperative for them as it is for those spearheading socio-economic change:[135] they had to find new answers and a new conceptual and ritual idiom, not only to maintain their high social status, but particularly to satisfy their own existential needs of meaningful interpretation of life, society and the universe.

As long as we have no more biographical details on Mupumani, it is impossible to say whether this second *avant-garde* model applies to him. The data on the other Ila prophets suggest that Mupumani had been a rather usual sort of prophet before his highly original visions made him radically depart from existing prophetic institutions, and, for instance, made him temporarily reject the ecological emphasis, as unessential in the light of his more profound and direct mystical experiences. However this may have been, religious authorities in the *avant-garde* situation postulated here did certainly play an innovatory role in other episodes of religious change in western Zambia: e.g., doctors are known to have contributed to eschatological prophetic movements, and to both primary and secondary prophetic cults of affliction.[136]

The other additional *avant-garde* situation concerns the effect of thorough political change upon the relation between dominant and underlying socio-economic segments of a society. When social power is radically redistributed (particularly under the impact of external forces), the dominant segment will, under certain conditions, decline in power, and the underlying segment, perceiving this, will attempt to gain ascendance. The emerging new power structure may be favourable to the latter. Yet initially the former underdogs lack the concrete economic and political resources and skills necessary for direct, open competition with the declining dominant segment. Values, and ideas about non-empirical aspects of life and society (such as constitute the religion) may be manipulated and altered in anticipation of a desired future state of affairs with which the hard facts of political and economic life are still at variance. Thus the emergent aspirations of the formerly underlying group may initially get channelled into the religious field. Here new skills, strategies, goals and forms of organization are developed which subsequently, in the course of a process of consolidation and transfer, may lead to effective economic and political expansion. Perhaps it is stretching the concept of religious *avant-garde* (so far used for relatively small socio-economic and religious categories) too far if we apply it to this situation of a (typically large) underlying segment that is increasingly freed from its dominant counterpart. Yet this is certainly another situation of structural propensity towards religious innovation.

This third type of religious *avant-garde* does apply to Mupumani, although further research will have to establish the extent to which it was actually a major aspect of his prophetic calling. As a leper from an area poor in cattle, Mupumani belonged to an underlying segment, for which a great potential of upward social mobility was released when colonial rule (after the much less successful attacks by Lozi, Ndebele and Yeke in the nineteenth century) rapidly and visibly undermined the political and economic power of the Ila dominant segment.[137]

Besides Mupumani, this third type of *avant-garde* situation is particularly applicable to the Kansanshi episode in 1908 (cf. note 39), and to the political overtones of Watchtower-type activities, challenging indigenous authorities, European administration and European missionaries.[138] In these cases we see an underlying segment of Central African society adopt an initial religious expression not simply because that segment is suppressed, powerless, miserable and desperate (as is suggested by standard analyses in terms of protest and deprivation[139]), but on the contrary because that segment is going through a phase of ascent, in terms both of subjective aspirations and of objective structural power. In the Kansanshi case a small group of African foremen used the idiom of sorcery as a cult of manipulative power, to express not their humiliation but their very great actual power: controlling an African labour force upon which the mining activities were dependent and which outnumbered the white miners 40 to 1. Watchtower reflects the ascendance, not only of the individual modern achievers who became its instigators and leading agents, but also of the entire African population in Central Africa, a population which became increasingly involved, and indispensable, in the economy and administration, while witnessing the erosion of indigenous political structures and the debilitating effects of the depression upon the European presence in the area. The New Heaven preached by religious innovation (even if it is in the infernal version of the Kansanshi sorcerers) is not necessarily based on illusory compensation; it may also be based on quite rational hopes and expectations.

Conclusion

In this chapter I have considered religious change in central western Zambia at two levels. On the more abstract level, it appears as a systematic evolution, sustained over many centuries, of the same set of ideas concerning nature, time, supernatural entities, the individual, suffering and achievement. On the more concrete level it takes the form of a considerable number of distinct movements, greatly overlapping in time, each of which manifests particular innovations in these ideas, as the specific responses to socio-economic and political change, not of the total society viewed as a monolithic whole, but of particular segments in that society which (as achievers, as established religious specialists, as members of an underlying group in the process of emancipation, and possibly other significant categories overlooked in this tentative analysis) occupy a specific *avant-garde* position.

This preliminary model is clearly too schematic and still has to have recourse to *ad hoc* explanations for individual cases. Other weaknesses of the entire approach include its highly speculative nature, the sweeping generalizations about the primordial village religion and pre-colonial change on which it is partly based, and the fact that it ignores the purely instrumental, cynical use of religious innovation as a means for personal gain rather than as existential reconstruction and redemption. Finally, an obvious point for further study is the relation between general socio-economic and religious change in Central Africa. While my argument in this chapter one-sidedly emphasized the impact of the former upon the latter,[140] a process of mutual reinforcement seems more adequate as a model. The religious innovations, with their new conceptions of nature, God, time, the individual and achievement, not only *reflect* the emergent industrial, bureaucratic mass society, but also are equipping more and more individuals with the new world-view and value system without which such a society can hardly be realized.[141]

However, the present approach has some advantages. It is explicit.

It offers a synethic interpretation of religious innovations so far largely studied in isolation. It casts some light on the intricate time sequence of these innovations, by relating them to the specific response of particular segments of society. As an alternative to naïve models of religious genius, or diffusion-through-exposure, the present approach proposes three more complex social mechanisms of religious innovation in Central Africa, and suggests ways in which the substantive themes in these innovations may be related to socio-economic change. It provides a model not only of innovation but also of retention, and thus helps to explain the wealth of older religious forms still to be found among the non-*avant-garde* segments of modern Central African society.

To the specific theme of the 'problem of evil' in Central African society, this chapter has the following contributions to make. It emphasizes the relation between the religious explanation of evil and human suffering on the one hand, and the prevalent socio-economic structure of society on the other. While thus highlighting the place of the dead within the ecologico-religious complex, as well as individual rivalry and achievement aspirations, I have ignored other possibly important themes: witchcraft as an imputed hereditary quality of selected individuals,[142] and the evil connotations of the unknown and the unusual, as embodied in strangers, the old, and the disabled – who, along with achieving individuals, have had their share of witchcraft accusations both in Central Africa and elsewhere. Second, I have presented the problem of evil as just one among several major themes in the changing religious system of central western Zambia, and attempted to outline its place in the total religious system in relation to these other themes. And finally, I have claimed that the processes of religious change characteristic of the colonial period in Central Africa had started, and that their substantive themes first began to emerge, many centuries before colonial rule. The socio-economic and political changes introduced in colonial times, and the implantation of Christianity as from a slightly earlier time, have intensified and accelerated the general process and occasionally rendered it an element of protest, but they did not *cause* the innovations, and determined their course only to a limited degree.

Chapter 5

Regional and non-regional cults of affliction in western Zambia[1]

Introduction

A generic relation holds between two types of cult of affliction in Zambia's Western Province (formerly Barotseland). Cults of one type, the non-regional, form a substratum out of which cults of the other type, the regional, may spring forth under certain conditions, and into which they submerge again under different conditions. To understand this process and the conditions that govern it, I shall first describe the non-regional cults of affliction and then define the general characteristics by which the others set themselves apart from the substratum. Then I shall compare in some detail the development of two regional cults in order to make clear the importance of two series of variables: each distinct cult's characteristics of idiom and internal organizational structure, and the structural characteristics of the geographical area which the cult transforms into a cultic region.

Several working definitions are useful in order to establish the contrast, briefly, between the types of cult within the general class of cults of affliction. The first type covers a few regional cults which have three main characteristics. Each of these regional cults has a specific idiom of its own. This idiom is pursued by a number of local congregations spread over an area of thousands of square kilometres. Third, and most importantly, an inter-local formal organization binds these dispersed congregations through the interactions of the cult's officials. In this way the geographical area over which the cult spreads is transformed into a region. What structures a cult's region is thus the process of inter-local communication, interaction and distribution which the cult gives rise to. By contrast, the second type covers cults which I shall call non-regional. A cult of this type, too, has a specific cult idiom which is

180

pursued by a number of congregations. However, although it may have spread over a vast area, it has not yet transformed the area into a region of its own, or it has ceased to do so and a former region has become merely a non-regional area.

As for the general class of cults of affliction, in terms of cult idiom individual affliction invariably stands out as a major concern. This is central in Turner's classic studies[2] and in the earlier works[3] which he developed. Turner coined the phrase, 'cult of affliction', to denote a cult (religious sub-system) characterized by two elements: (a) the cultural interpretation of misfortune (bodily disorders, bad luck) in terms of exceptionally strong domination by a specific non-human agent; and (b) the attempt to remove the misfortune by having the afflicted join the cult venerating that specific agent. The major ritual forms of this class of cult consist of divinatory ritual in order to identify the agent, and initiation ritual through which the agent's domination of the afflicted is emphatically recognized before an audience. In the standard local interpretation, the invisible agent inflicts misfortune as a manifest sign of his hitherto hidden relationship with the afflicted. The purpose of the ritual is to acknowledge the agent's presence and to pay him formal respect (by such conventional means as drumming, singing, clapping of hands, offering of beer, beads, white cloth and money). After this the misfortune is supposed to cease. The afflicted lives on as a member of that agent's specific cult; he participates in cult sessions in order to reinforce his good relations with the agent and to assist others, similarly afflicted, to be initiated into the same cult.

Cults of affliction represent a dominant class of cults in present-day western Zambia. In addition there are ancestral cults, individual specialists' cults, chiefly cults and various types of Christian cults.[4] Of these, Christian cults and the major chiefly cults are regional.[5]

Non-regional cults of affliction

Main characteristics

Non-regional cults of affliction occur in scores of versions throughout western Zambia and surrounding areas.[6] These various cults have much in common. They differ from each other mainly in the following respects: the associated paraphernalia (e.g., type of adept's shrine, musical instruments, vegetal medicine, ritual objects and bodily adornment used); the specific misfortunes for which each cult caters; and the name and alleged nature of the invisible agent venerated in each cult. Each cult is locally known by the name of this specific agent. Some particularly successful cults are encountered over large areas and are mentioned repeatedly in the literature; these include such cults as *mayimbwe*, *muba*, *songo*, *viyaya*, *liyala* and *bindele*.

We are indebted to Turner for his masterly description and analysis of some cults of affliction among the Ndembu. He shows the role of these cults in the succession of 'social dramas' that make up the micro-history of villages over a time-span of several decades. However, he does not analyse the historical dimension of these cults themselves.[7] In Turner's work these cults are viewed as given institutions that are manipulated within the local social process, rather than as the dynamic outcomes of a process of religious change that in itself needs elucidation.

White[8] was the first to explore the cults' historical dimension. He pointed to a major conceptual shift that has affected cults of affliction in Luvale country since the 1930s. The shift was away from cults that claimed local ancestors (particularly diviners and hunters) as their afflicting agents. It was towards new cults that attributed affliction to abstract, scarcely personalized agents whose names were reminiscent of contacts with distant alien groups, African and European. Some of these new cults were *songo* (after the Songo people of Angola), *ndeke* (airplane), or *bindele* (white people or people clad in white: either Europeans or alien African traders). Turner's[9] and my own field-work suggests that the conceptual shift was accompanied by a shift in the recruitment pattern of the cults' congregations. This structural shift was from a ritual congregation that was rather co-terminous with the local community and that focused on communal symbols (village shrine, ancestors), to a congregation whose members, individually drawn from a series of adjacent local communities, would associate for *ad hoc* ritual purposes in a pattern that cuts across, rather than reinforces, the structure of distinct local communities. However, as I shall show, in contrast to Turner's observations, my data point to the significance of local factors in the cults (see pp. 187 ff, 208 ff).

White suggested that the conceptual shift may be attributed to a complex of inter-related changes. These included increased inter-local contacts (through nineteenth-century long-distance trade and twentieth-century labour migration), the breakdown of the village community, and the emergence of new causal models for the interpretation of misfortune. White interpreted these new models (featuring new, impersonal, non-ancestral affliction agents) as the conceptual response to the widening of the social horizon beyond the area where the ancestors could be thought to hold sway.

In the preceding chapters I have developed White's stimulating ideas in the light of more comprehensive data on religious change in this part of Central Africa.[10] There I argue that the emergence of these non-regional cults of affliction represents just one specific outcome in an overall process of religious transformation. This process has extended over centuries and, as other outcomes, has produced such religious forms as chiefly cults, prophetism concentrating on 'ecological' concern for the land and its produce, eschatological prophetism, and sorcery-eradication movements. Throughout a succession of emerging religious forms, the overall process produced systematic changes in religious idiom. These changes can be conveniently mapped along five dimensions: the perception of time; the degree of ecological concern; conceptions concerning the nature of supernatural beings; the degree of individual-centredness; and the interpretation of evil. Ultimately, major political and economic changes can be seen as the motor behind the overall religious transformation. In this context I am thinking primarily of the increase of inter-local structures of political and economic power, distribution, and movement of people due to pre-colonial and colonial state-formation, raiding, long distance trade, and labour migration. These extra-religious changes called for new religious forms (including non-regional cults of affliction) that were capable of legitimating the new structures and that could meet the existential and interpretative needs of the people involved.

My field data mainly derive from the Nkoya, an ethnic group inhabiting the wooded plateau of central western Zambia.[11] Among the Nkoya, ancestral cults of affliction have continued to exist until today, but the great majority of affliction cases is now treated within the more recent, non-ancestral cults, particularly those of the non-regional type to which the present section is devoted. People recognize the recent nature of these cults, and can state the period in which a particular cult first reached their area. The non-ancestral, non-regional cults of affliction spread like fashions or epidemics. For many cults occurring in any particular area it is known from which direction they arrived; they became locally associated with ethnic groups living in that direction, and are sometimes held, incorrectly, to represent those groups' ancestral ritual.[12] Intervals of a few years would pass between a new cult's arrival and its being forced out of fashion by the arrival of yet another one. As an area is hit by a succession of cult fashions, many people come to be initiated into more than one cult. As a fashion wears out, the ritual for that cult will be staged less frequently and fresh cases of affliction will be attributed mainly to more recently arrived cults. However, cult leaders keep staging the rituals of non-ancestral cults of somewhat older vintage. In this way they revive their ritual links with adepts whom they initiated some years before and who may since have taken not only to other cults but also to other leaders.

The spread and contemporary distribution of non-ancestral non-regional cults of affliction show that Central African ethnic groups ('tribes') are not rigidly bounded either geographically or culturally. The cults spread easily from one ethnic group to another, despite such great language differences as between Luvale and Lenje, Tonga and Lozi. Moreover, immigrant adepts from a distant ethnic group often proved acceptable as local cult leaders (a point emphasized by Symon[13]). Cult songs have sometimes been translated into a local language, but have often been retained in the original language of the ethnic group from which this cult was borrowed locally. Sometimes the original ethnic group even gave its name to the cult (*songo, chimbandu*). All this bears out the fact that, among other aspects, the non-ancestral cults of affliction represent an attempt to come to terms (both conceptually and inter-actionally) with the reality of extensive, inter-ethnic, inter-local contacts.

Ritual

Usually the differences between the non-regional, non-ancestral cults of affliction which occur in one area are slight. There is somewhat of a tendency – it is not invariable – to associate certain paraphernalia (a peculiar type of headdress or scapular, miniature axes and hoes, fly-switches, etc.) and certain bodily movements with particular cults. The main way, however, to tell one cult from another is from the contents of the songs that are chanted during the sessions. Below are some typical song texts:

1

Bakesheba iyale yomama	From *kasheba,* really, mother,
yowelile mama	I am ill, mother
bamikupe iyale yomama	from *bamikupe,* really mother,
iyale yomama	I am ill, mother
ba mushelu iyale yomama	from *mushelu*, really mother,
yowelile mama	I am ill, mother
iyiyo mama yowelile	o mother, I am ill

(text used alternatively for *kasheba, bamikupe* and *mushelu*)

2

Tu ba kombele	We pay formal respect
biyaya bi neza	for *biyaya* has come
tu ba kombele	we pay formal respect
biyaya mama	to *biyaya*, mother

(text for *biyaya*)

3

Ba ka lenda mawulu mu pange	For this foot disease, treat me
mu ni yoyise	to make me alive
lelo moyo	today the life
mu pange mu ni yoyise	treat me to make me alive
bi nakunisisayela lelo moyo	they don't restore my life today
by nganga na ba nganga	these cult leaders or those cult leaders
kumpanga bafako	they don't treat me

(text for *kalenda-mawulu*)

These songs are sung by a small chorus of adepts, instructed and led by a cult's local leader, usually a woman. The adepts (usually women) stand in a semi-circle which is closed by a row of (male) musicians. Within this enclosure the cult leader and one or more novices dance, and enter into a trance. Before the session starts the leader has undertaken to treat the novices. She exhorts the latter, the chorus and the musicians so that the novices' movements may catch up and gradually harmonize with the music. Thus the novices may reach ecstasy. In the course of most sessions vegetal medicine is prepared from a selection of plant species which varies with each cult. Although each session tends to be dominated by the songs and ritual for one particular cult (the one in which the leader excels), often elements of other cults are used in abundance. This is particularly the case when a patient cannot be brought to respond properly to a session's main cult. Then one cult after another has to be tried in order to arrive at the correct diagnosis and treatment. Sessions last through the night and end at dawn with the final distribution of medicine to novices and adepts and occasionally to non-participant on-lookers. For in contrast with the situation in the extreme north-west of Zambia, as described by Turner, in this area an audience of non-adepts is present at every session, to share in the beer, to help out with the music, and to witness the patients' struggle for healing.

Morality

Part of the night's proceedings is private: the therapeutic conversations which the leader and some senior adepts have with each novice. Their aim is to ascertain the specific personal conditions under which the affliction, dormant until then, has become manifest. Such conditions may include a recent death, ill-will and suspected sorcery in the patient's environment, or the occurrence of a major healer, diviner or hunter among the patient's deceased kin.

The information obtained in the 'anamnesis',[14] however, is not fed into the patient's social environment. The information only serves to identify to the officiants' satisfaction the occasion at which the affliction agent chose to manifest itself. This occasion may highlight inter-personal conflict and illicit aggression (in the way of sorcery); yet moral redress, rehabilitation or prosecution never become the cult's concern. Once the diagnosis in terms of the cult's aetiology has been pronounced, the cult tries to curb the invisible agent's harmful effects, but does not try to take away any group-dynamical causes of the misfortune. The non-ancestral, non-regional cults of affliction aim at individual readjustment. They fight symptoms of maladjustment but do not try to expose or resolve any underlying social tension. Nor are they meant to do so. These cults are concerned with suffering, and not with morality. Their frame of reference features patients afflicted by essentially unpredictable, non-human agents, and not victims injured by human evil-doers or by the effects (through ancestral revenge) of their own sins.

The non-ancestral non-regional cults exist side by side with rival and alternative approaches to misfortune which do emphasize morality and guilt, reparation and retaliation. Among the contemporary Nkoya, these rival approaches are frequently applied. They include: divinatory and redressive ritual in the idiom of ancestral intervention; similar ritual in the idiom of sorcery and counter-sorcery; litigation in more or less formal courts of law;[15] and regional cults of affliction, whose relation to non-regional cults with regard to morality I shall discuss below.

A number of venues for redress are thus open to an individual facing misfortune. The choice is largely his own. He may apply to a diviner/healer known for diagnosis in terms of a cult of affliction, rather than to one who habitually propounds interpretations in terms of ancestors or sorcery; or he may apply to a court. The actor's underlying decision model is complex and can only be analysed on the basis of detailed description of the various institutions involved, and of specific extended cases. However, if one pursues the option of cults of affliction, this can be safely said to indicate one's reluctance to present one's misfortune publicly as caused by human conflict (sorcery, court) or guilty neglect in one's dealings with kin (ancestors). Such reluctance usually reflects lack of power, material resources and social support; the victim can neither answer a challenge through counter-sorcery and litigation, nor face such public disapproval as offences punished by ancestors inspire. Non-ancestral cults of affliction, however, interpret misfortune as an entirely individual condition which (in contrast with sorcery, ancestral intervention, or litigation) is not primarily determined by the victim's interaction with other people – although such interaction may form the occasion for the hidden affliction to manifest itself for the first time. Amongst the institutions dealing with misfortune, these cults have, therefore, a marked competitive advantage for certain people: those who are dependent, relatively powerless, and short of social credit. Little wonder, then, that most of the patients in the non-ancestral cults of affliction are women and youths. Mature and elderly men, as a rule, pursue other venues for redress. And if they involve themselves at all in such cults of affliction, it is not as patients, but (occasionally) as cult leaders, as musicians, and particularly as sponsors for their womenfolk.

This implies that at least for women, as patients, the cults of affliction do not provide an idiom of internationalized powerlessness, but rather an alternative way to demand, and receive, male support – albeit outside the arenas where mature men compete with each other. This, of course, does not preclude such competition between leaders and sponsors.[16]

Roles, personnel and organization

For a successful session all the following conditions have to be met. The cult leader must be generally recognized and accomplished. The chorus (of minimal size of four or five adepts) must know the basic song texts and must be prepared to assist in the proceedings. Musicians are needed who know or can quickly pick up the music peculiar to the various cults, and who are prepared to follow the directions of the leader. Musical instruments, beer and firewood are required. And somebody has to organize the session and meet its expenses.

In a rural society where firewood is becoming less abundant, where beer has become a marketable commodity, and where drums and other instruments are scarce and privately owned, the logistics of the sessions often turn out to be complicated and problematic. Each session necessarily involves the sponsor, and the other participants in the session, in a network of transactions and obligations that both reflect and bear upon the extra-religious social process in the community. Good musicians cannot always be recruited from amongst a sponsor's close kin, and even if they can, they often demand a payment roughly equivalent to a day's wages. The adepts who constitute the chorus do not receive any remuneration beyond a share in the beer that the sponsor furnishes for the cult leader. Besides this beer, and occasional gifts of white cloth, bottled fizzy drinks, bottled beer and other luxuries, the leader receives a small sum of money for the diagnosis and treatment during the session. This sum is again equivalent to a day's wages. Even more important, the leader establishes a firm claim (actionable in court) against a much larger sum, easily a month's wages. This large fee is payable any time after the patient has made significant improvement, no matter what additional treatments are pursued elsewhere.

From the sponsor's side, therefore, the session involves immediate costs that are considerable, both in social and financial terms and, if the treatment is successful, heavy debts in the future. For the leader, the session means a significant gain immediately, and very likely a large financial claim in the future. At the same time, it also means a public test both of ritual skill and of such management power as is required for the mobilization of the chorus in the first place (it is the sponsor's responsibility to recruit the musicians), and for the leader's control over adepts and musicians during the many hours of the session. The adepts in the chorus clearly hold a key position. They are indispensable to the leader's success but hardly share in the latter's benefits.

The basic organizational form of non-regional cults of affliction is a small faction of loyal adepts around a leader, all living within walking or cycling distance from each other: within a radius not exceeding 10 kilometres, and usually much less. The leader can effectively control the chorus's adepts in two cases, which often coincide: when the adepts are themselves still under a course of treatment with the same leader (and treatment may, partly for this reason, be extended over a period of years); and when the adepts are very close kin of the leader. Kinship ties among the Nkoya are, however, not automatically effective in bringing about and maintaining solidary social relationships. In order to be effective they need to be backed up by frequent interaction, e.g., through co-residence. Attachments between kin are readily disrupted as people change their residence in order to seek their economic and local-political fortune elsewhere, among a different set of real or putative kin. Such individual intra-rural geographical mobility is extremely frequent and, in fact, constitutes a major structural theme in Nkoya society. Likewise, the curative link between leader and adept is often threatened, both by rival leaders who compete for adepts (as well as for new patients) and by the senior adept's own aspiration to set up as a leader herself. Therefore, within (and between) the cultic factions tensions and conflicts are rife; and these tend to come to the fore during sessions, when the leader is most dependent upon the adepts. I have never attended a session that was not repeatedly interrupted by heated argument between the officiants. After a session there tend to be shifts in the faction's internal structure of relationships, and even in its membership.

The leader's status is rather insecure. Non-regional cults of affliction define the roles of leader, adept and novice, but they do not stipulate in detail the requirements by which one gets access to these statuses. These cults do not have a formal organization with fixed rules of eligibility to office. Instead, recognized ritual leadership is a matter of public opinion. Whoever can persuade others to let themselves be treated by her, and can mobilize the necessary assistance, is a cult leader. On the other hand, a leader whose curative effectiveness begins to be doubted by many (partly as a result of her being forced out of competition by rivals) loses her patients and adepts.

How does one get launched as a leader? Long-term apprenticeship as an adept of an established leader is one way. In the take-off period as a leader, other standard methods to woo public opinion include self-appointed curative capabilities which are claimed to derive from dreams, from accession to the name of a deceased relative who was a well-known healer, or from a serious psycho-physical disturbance finally overcome by a recovery, so that one has become acquainted, better than most people, with the experience of illness and death. Gradually, new songs (often featuring the name of the leader herself), an original choice of paraphernalia, a notebook in which the names of treated patients may be recorded, fake or real licences issued by local authorities, can all help to lend credibility and identity to the new leader. In this search for a personal 'trademark' considerable expense and creativity is invested, even though the result is usually a permutation of the same limited set of elements used by all leaders and all non-regional cults of affliction throughout western Zambia.

The main condition, however, to make the grade as a cult leader is the construction of a local network of loyal adepts who can assist in the treatment of new patients. My use of the term 'faction' for the basic local unit of officiants has suggested the problematic internal dynamics and shifting membership of these units, and (as a major cause of this) the intense competition between units. In the immediate social environment of each afflicted individual, a number of leaders with their temporarily loyal adepts are active. Leaders are in competition with each other both for the senior adepts on whom their practice is dependent, and for new novices who will boost the leader's public status and bring in large fees.

The fees enhance a leader's power in two ways. Once received, this wealth is largely redistributed in non-ritual transactions with kin and neighbours. But since most fees cannot be paid immediately, they also tie the patients to the leader with heavy debts. Both ways, the leader's power must have considerable effect on the extra-religious social process. The fees are so high and cash is so scarce in the villages that the modern cults can be properly said to constitute a major redistributive economic institution. This holds true not only between villages, but also between village and town. Rural-based leaders treat afflicted urban migrants either by receiving them on short visits in the rural area, or by travelling to town at irregular intervals.

Both within and outside the religious domain, leaders hold enviable positions, which they are constantly defending against the encroachment of others. As adepts and leaders have usually been initiated into more than one non-regional cult of affliction, and as the basic idiom of these cults is constant and well-known, an adept's shift from one leader to another (which often means: from one cult to another) presents no great difficulties in terms of knowledge and skills. Leaders greatly resent it when such a shift diminishes their effective following. For this reason, leaders tend to avoid each other and, when they operate within the same social field, are often at daggers drawn because of having snatched each other's followers in the past.

Sometimes leaders combine locally, stage sessions together and visit each other's sessions as guests of honour. On such occasions, emphasis is on manifestations of mutual professional respect, symbolized by the ostentatious furnishing of a chair for each leader.[17] But even then each leader is on her guard lest her colleagues make too favourable an impression on the audience, or attempt to lure adepts and patients away. Only in the very rare cases that such professional contacts are backed up by residence in each other's proximity along with close kinship ties and good extra-religious relationships in general, can they be seen to develop into stable, prolonged co-operation. In such a case leaders are no longer afraid of mutual poaching; they share patients and adepts.

These local ritual factions with their occasional co-operation between leaders, constitute all the rudimentary organizational structure that the non-regional cults of affliction possess. Leaders are predominantly ritual entrepreneurs, who exploit a local market on the basis of the population's general adherence to the cult of affliction model. Even between leaders in different localities who profess that they specialize in the same named cult (e.g., *viyaya*) there is normally no contact – and often downright avoidance. Each may have learned this cult's ritual in a different place, may have added her own innovations, and would have her own local clientele to consider. The differences between the ritual performances of two such leaders of the same cult may be greater than those between leaders who avowedly specialize in different cults. Each elaborates on the general idiom of the cults of affliction in her own personal way, without any inter-local formal organization binding local leaders or dictating any orthodoxy.

Public opinion is prepared to accept a leader's reputation and the size of her following as proofs of expertise, and it favours any innovation that does not greatly run counter to local canons of decency. But such public opinion concerning the cults is in itself mainly a response to the actions and pronouncements of the cult leaders. Thus it is by virtue of a widespread cultural model that each non-regional cult of affliction exists: each cult has its unstructured series of small factions which are disconnected, local and rather ephemeral. The widespread cultural model is continuously reinforced, at the grass-root level, by the unco-ordinated activities of hundreds of leaders in search of wealth, power, ritual prestige, and self-expression.

Ritual leadership as a calling

While exploring the political and economic dimensions of the non-regional cults of affliction, we should avoid reducing them to these and nothing more. Leaders, adepts, patients and outsiders are keenly aware of the economic and local-political aspects of the cults. Yet all of them consider the cults' healing efficacy their over-riding justification.

The leaders, mainly elderly women, are not cynical operators and no more. They are gifted and passionate manipulators of symbols: song texts, paraphernalia, dramatic effects – and cash. Through an existential crisis earlier in life they have paid the price (not just financially) towards becoming specialists in human suffering and some of its remedies. Their life-histories tell of prolonged illness, periods of insanity, ridicule by fellow-villagers confronted with the aspiring leader's first, clumsy attempts at being a healer, and more recently the treachery of once loyal patients who have at last set up as leaders themselves and no longer pay respect to one who, in her own view, fought for their very lives. A leader's strikingly intense and agile performance during the long nocturnal sessions may be partly motivated by a drive for money and power. But it has as much to do with art, while the prime concern is to heal a fellow man. If the ritual does not appear to succeed, it is not only a threat to professional prestige, but also compassion, that forces the leader to exert herself for hours at a stretch finally to bring the patient to join in the rhythm, thus making recovery possible.

Better than anyone else, the leader understands and believes in the idiom of the cults of affliction. She is the mediator of a conceptual system which is commensurate with the changing social order in which she and her patients find themselves. Offering deliverance from suffering is a professional calling for which the easy life, food, marriage, may all have to be sacrificed. The leader Kashikashika vividly describes how her calling affects her life:

> At home I have no time to eat. I eat with one hand, keeping one hand on the head of a patient. [Laying-on of hands is a minor form of treatment in the cults in which she specializes.] I have no time to dress, but instead walk about in my short petticoats. I have no time to sleep. In the middle of the night people come and knock at my door for treatment.

> Years ago, a man fell in love with me and wanted marriage. I told him: 'Before I go and live with you, realize how my calling affects my life. I shall often have to go out in the night. Sometimes I shall have to stay away from you for three months at a stretch, to attend to my patients!' But he did not want to listen and went ahead with the marriage. After a month he started complaining, and we soon divorced. Now I am married again, with one of my patients. He says: 'Look, she has cured me. Should I complain when she goes out and stays away to cure others like me?'

> [The husband is present and amply confirms that this is indeed his view of the matter.]

Underneath this testimony of professional sacrifice there is, unmistakably, a note of pride and female power quite characteristic of elderly Nkoya women, and of cult leaders *a fortiori*. But at any rate, calling obliges; and many leaders have strict personal standards as to the size of fees, the requirements for proper diagnosis, and the ethics of dealing with unco-operative debtors amongst their patients.[18] Without exception, leaders have themselves suffered in the past from the afflictions they treat, and usually they are still in frequent silent communication with their own affliction agent, inside. Allegedly, the agent advises on the leader's well-being, but he does not take mockery and is sure to punish a cheating leader of his cult. Adepts and patients are aware of this security device too, and as a rule expect fair play from the cult leaders they deal with.

The high revenues and other benefits in terms of power and prestige associated with cult leadership can hardly fail to appeal to the ambitious and calculating sides of the incumbents' character. Yet I would maintain that the requirements in terms of artistic and emotional dedication, and in terms of self-confidence *vis-à-vis* the symbols manipulated in the cults, are such as to make the sham leader, who stages for money's sake a ritual whose efficacy she secretly denies, a rare occurrence.

Regional cults of affliction in western Zambia: general characteristics

Due to a succession of non-regional cults of affliction that had been spreading over western Zambia for several decades, the general idiom of such cults had become established by the 1930s. By this time the new type of *regional* cult of affliction emerged. So far, three cults of this type have been studied: Nzila (also known as the *Twelve Society*), Bituma and Moya. It is likely, however, that western Zambia has witnessed the rise of several more, which subsequent research may throw light upon. The first description of Nzila is by Reynolds,[19] on the basis of an administrative report by I. H. Whethey in 1957.[20] In 1972 Muntemba carried out research into this cult, mainly in the Livingstone area;[21] I am greatly indebted to her for the lengthy conversations we have had on the subject. The Bituma cult played a major role in my Nkoya fieldwork.[22] Ranger[23] gives lengthy excerpts from both Muntemba's and my own descriptions. The Moya cult is briefly discussed by Ikacana;[24] although this author mentions the healer Liminanganga as this cult's main leader in Kaoma (then Mankoya) district, thus suggesting a certain centralization that is characteristic of a regional cult, his further discussion gives the impression that by the 1940s Moya was a non-regional cult. During my field work in the early 1970s a regional cult of the same name was active in the eastern part of the district, where, headed by a prophet called Moya after his cult, it had penetrated only a few years previously – but perhaps not for the first time. My limited data on this cult do not enable me to decide whether it became a regional cult only recently, or was already one in Ikacana's time.

Like the factional, non-regional cults described above, these three regional cults are cults of affliction. They interpret disease and misfortune by reference to a non-human agent, and attempt to redress the disorder through divination and subsequent initiation into the cult. As cults of affliction deriving from the same cultural area, the regional and non-regional cults have on the surface much in common. However, there are very significant differences between the two types.

The most striking aspect of Nzila, Bituma and Moya is their regional organization. These cults each have a central place, which is the seat of the cult's supreme leader. Cult officers appointed by the leader are responsible for sections of the total area over which the cult has spread. They communicate regularly between local cult congregations and headquarters. In close co-operation with the supreme leader, they recruit new local adepts and leaders, enforce observance of the cult's regulations (e.g., concerning the size of fees for treatment, and the forwarding of a portion of the fees to headquarters), supervise the ritual locally, and guard against undue autonomy and ritual deviation of local leaders. In contrast with the non-regional cults, effective leadership of a local congregation depends not so much on the manipulation of public opinion and the control of a loyal local ritual following, but primarily on admission and promotion within the cult's hierarchy, subject to approval from headquarters. Literacy, in its simplest forms, plays a role; one may keep a record of the number of patients healed, of their names, and of the fixed fees for each type of treatment. The regional cults are more or less formal organizations that enforce, among local cult leaders, ritual conformity, compliance with the cult's authority structure, and the forwarding of funds, over areas of many thousand square kilometres.

We have seen how leaders in non-regional cults of affliction tend to make considerable innovations upon the cultic material they use. Also, these leaders have usually gone through deep personal crises before establishing themselves as cult leaders. In these respects they have much in common with the founders of Nzila, Bituma and Moya. However, in the case of the non-regional cults a leader's specific innovations and personal history are played down as irrelevant. The leader is viewed not as the inventor but as the mere transmitter of cultic forms which, allegedly, have already existed elsewhere and which could have been made available locally by any other leader. The regional cults, by contrast, are quite sharply considered to be founded by a particular prophet, whose name, visions, life history, the process in the course of which he shaped his cult, are all held to be very important and are often known even among non-adepts.

In contrast with the leaders of non-regional cults of affliction, Chana (founder of Nzila), Simbinga (founder of Bituma), and Moya (founder of the Moya cult) all started out as charismatic leaders in the Weberian sense.[25] Each displayed what I have earlier[26] called the 'standard biographical pattern for central African religious innovators'. Each reached prophethood through the same stages. Falling victim to a chronic disease or defect is a first stage. Chana was a leper and suffered from the *bindele* affliction, which the non-regional *bindele* cult proved unable to cure. (Later the difference between Chana's affliction and *bindele* was acknowledged by renaming the former *Nzila*: 'path'.) Simbinga and Moya likewise suffered from afflictions which could not be accommodated within the non-regional cults of affliction then in existence. In the next biographical stage the affliction would develop to a crisis. In the case of Simbinga and Moya this allegedly involved temporary death. Simbinga was buried and rose from the grave; Moya allegedly came back to life in the mortuary of a rural hospital. In these crises the prophets allegedly received very specific messages and directions from the supernatural agent claiming responsibility for the affliction. Following the indications received in the messages, the prophet would be able to recover. He would then have the power and the calling to apply his new insights to those in his social environment who were similarly afflicted. These first patients (twelve in Chana's case, seven in Simbinga's) would form the original core of the cult, soon to be augmented through the combined efforts of prophet and initial followers.

The regional cults do not merely share the affliction-cult idiom with the non-regional cults. The former actually emerged upon the substratum of these earlier, non-regional cults. All three started as an individual's response to an affliction that might have been cured within the established non-regional cults of affliction. Instead, the three patients devised their own cults.

Now why did these three prospective prophets fail to get healed within the existing non-regional cults of affliction? For all three, contemporary informants claim that they had tried such treatment; in

Chana's and Moya's case, modern medical services were consulted as well. The standard course of their crises suggests that, in addition to any bodily disorders, a profound mental struggle was involved, bearing on existential problems such as the meaning of suffering and the interpretation of the universe. The then current, non-regional cults revolved around affliction-causing agents of an abstract and hardly personalized nature, mainly conveying associations with alienness and neighbouring ethnic groups. The solutions the three prospective prophets were seeking were to be – to judge from what they came up with – of a less particularistic and human scope. In the accounts of the founders' original visions and in their current interpretations of affliction cases and their treatment, the three regional cults propound strikingly similar, new conceptions concerning the nature of the supernatural agents involved in affliction.

Chana, Simbinga and Moya attributed their visions, their miraculous recovery and their subsequent healing power to entities closely associated with, or identical to, the High God. In Chana's case this was a spirit who in dreams and visions manifested itself as a white being, exhorting him to acknowledge God, to invoke God's help, and to preach about God to his patients. Simbinga had similar visions, which he interpreted in terms of an Angel (*Angelo*) from God. Moya's interpretations concentrate on the Life-Spirit (*Moya*), source of life and capable of dispensing health and illness at will; in western Zambia, Moya is also the name by which Christians refer to the concept of the Holy Ghost. These are concepts of a much greater universality and with much more specifically theistic connotations than the affliction-causing principles of the non-regional cults.

But while this conceptual shift may have primarily sprung from the specific existential problems of the three prophets, the prophets were at the same time yielding to a general tendency which since the beginning of this century has been encountered in quite a number of religious innovations in western Zambia. Most of those other movements had no specific concern with healing. They include a number of Ila prophets, amongst whom is the great prophet, Mupumani (1913), whose movement had an impact throughout western Zambia and the surrounding countries; minor eschatological prophets in Namwala, Kalabo and Mwinilunga; the numerous Watchtower preachers and dippers moving through the area in the late 1920s and the 1930s; and even the Christian missionaries. All these religious innovators displayed the same conceptual shift towards ever greater prominence of the High God.[27]

A final major difference between the regional and the non-regional cults of affliction is that the former do display a moral element which, as we have seen, is lacking in the latter. Chana was instructed by the Spirit 'to teach the people what to do and what not'.[28] He was given[29]

> rules and instructions he was to teach his people at the Sunday afternoon gatherings. . . . [T] he rules centre around purity of mind and spirit as the key to a healthy body. At the Livingstone branch service about one hour and thirty minutes are given to instructing the people, in the form of question and answer, in how to attain purity. . . . Members are exhorted to keep clean thoughts and clean minds by not bearing malice against their husband or wife, their brothers, sisters, in-laws and neighbours but instead to love. They are warned against bearing false witness, to avoid quarrelling and drink, drink which often leads to quarrels and other irresponsible acts. They are admonished against eating certain foods . . . which are considered unclean and which would therefore foul the body and soul of man.

Reynolds gives a similar picture and emphasizes the patients' surrender of sorcery apparatus in this context.[30]

In the teachings of Simbinga and Moya the same emphasis on purity versus pollution is encountered. For them, the whole range of local medicine represents evil and pollution in its fundamental form. When Simbinga was called to prophethood in the early 1930s, he immediately launched a fierce attack on local herbalists, diviners, and leaders of non-regional cults of affliction. He wanted them to give up their manipulations of material apparatuses, paraphernalia and medicine, and instead accept his own interpretation of misfortune (which by this time was still blurred and inconsistent), and his treatment by means of laying-on of hands, prayer and dancing.

This is a moral issue for various reasons. First, much local medicine was (and is) locally applied for purposes which, however common in the local society, were considered immoral acts of sorcery: to attain excessive power and success; to harm or kill rivals and enemies. Especially, the most powerful medicine derived from sinful manipulations of human bodies that were killed or (when already dead and buried) desecrated for the purpose. And finally, on the basis of his visions, Simbinga, like the two other prophets, presented an alternative aetiological theory of affliction, a theory whose universalist and theistic overtones implied a moral rejection of previous, medicine-centred interpretations.

Simbinga was at first unsuccessful in his attack. The local practitioners proved disinclined to accept his views. They mobilized public opinion against Simbinga and after a relapse of his affliction he had to leave his area. He travelled to the north-west (to the Balovale – now Zambezi – area). After a few years he returned with a revised version of his cult. This time material paraphernalia, divining apparatus, and vegetal medicine had been given a prominent place in the Bituma idiom. However, the cult has retained its abhorrence of all other forms of medicine and material apparatus, and still considers envy, rivalry and sorcery the main occasions upsetting the harmony between a man and his Angel – interpreting the Bituma affliction as the manifestation of such disruption.

The Moya cult has adopted a rather similar position. But whereas Bituma, though conscious of the dangers involved, does not absolutely forbid its adepts the possession and manipulation of medicine, Moya does, including hunting or fishing medicine, or products from modern dispensaries. In both cults, adepts and particularly leaders are continually aware of the dangers of pollution that threaten them everywhere. For this reason they may avoid certain persons and activities. However, beyond the reluctance to apply sorcery medicine to further their own interests, the purity-orientated personal morality as derived from the regional cults appears to have little impact on everyday life.

For even if the regional cults differ from the non-regional ones with regard to moral connotations, they are quite similar in a more fundamental respect. Both types of cults are based on an individual-centred interpretation of misfortune: misfortune is considered solely a matter of the relationship between the victim and an unpredictable supernatural agent. These cults do not link misfortune to the small-scale social processes in which the victims are involved, and therefore cannot have a direct impact on such processes.

There is an intimate relation between these three outstanding features of the regional cult: their founders' charisma, the appeal to more universal, theistic supernatural agents, and the introduction of a moral element. In the idiom of spirit possession, association with alien or neighbouring ethnic groups (as stressed in the non-regional cults) might well provide a basis for personal charisma: it makes the person having such association stand out among his local fellow-men. But somehow this may have lost much of its initial aura in a society where through inter-local contacts across ethnic boundaries, such association has become commonplace over the past century, and where a considerable variety of religious innovatory movements have already affected an overall tendency towards greater prominence of the High God. Under these conditions, visionary experiences involving supernatural entities of a much wider scope are more likely to endow exceptional individuals with the charismatic qualities that could lead to effective mobilization over a vast area. In other words, I suggest that the founders' charisma, and their propounding of universalist, theistic supernatural agents, imply each other.

Although universalist, theistic concepts were circulating in the area well outside the sphere of missionary Christianity, the three prophets started out under the latter's direct influence. Prior to their appearance as prophets, both Chana and Simbinga had been thoroughly exposed to missionary Christianity. Chana's parents had been converts of the Seventh Day Adventist Church, and Chana belonged to this Church before his prophetic calling. He even continued to adhere to this Church while heading the Nzila cult.[31] Simbinga was among the first evangelists of the fundamentalist South Africa General Mission at Luampa, and appears to have received further Christian teaching as a labour migrant in South Africa. Although very little is known yet of Moya's biography, the preponderance of Christian elements in the ritual of his cult (Bible copies, church bells, and a supernatural entity whose name is the current local translation of the Christian concept of the Holy Ghost) reveals a similar background.

If the universalist, theistic elements endowed the prophets with just the amount of charisma they required to set up regional cults, their propounding of moral elements fits well into the same picture. As Weber[32] wrote,

> From a substantive point of view, every charismatic authority would
> have to subscribe to the proposition, 'It is written . . ., but I say unto
> you . . .' The genuine prophet, like the genuine military leader
> and every true leader in this sense, preaches, creates, or demands
> new obligations.

However, the development of a regional cult organization is an aspect not of charismatic leadership itself, but of its subsequent routinization.[33] Given the charisma, universalist and theistic agents, and moral emphasis by which the regional cults differ from the substratum of non-regional cults of affliction from which they sprang, the development of more or less formal inter-local organization by no means follows automatically. Instead, such development represents a major analytical problem. Apart from the ill-documented Moya cult, we are fortunate in having, in the Nzila and Bituma cults, two reasonably well-known cases whose development into regional cults displays such divergence that a detailed comparison is likely to yield some insights in the general dynamics of regional cults.

The development of Nzila and Bituma as regional cults

Nzila

After a spell of labour migration in Zimbabwe, Chana returned to his village in Kalabo district. He developed his affliction, cured himself through the methods shown to him in his visions, and appeared as a prophet in the early 1940s.[34] His methods involved the erection of a shrine, daily ablutions in this shrine with water medicated by selected herbs, and nocturnal ritual dances. Having recovered, Chana successfully applied this method to his first twelve patients, thus obtaining his first followers: the twelve first Nzila 'doctors'. Subsequent visions instructed him to put faith in God, to organize weekly services for Him on Saturday afternoons and to extend his activities to moral teachings. Thus a formal ritual routine was worked out, quite reminiscent of a Christian church service; the influence, in particular, of the Seventh Day Adventist Church is unmistakable.[35] Assisted by his doctors, Chana treated a rapidly increasing number of patients in the Kalabo, Mongu, Senanga and Kaoma districts. A cult centre was erected near Mongu, the capital of the then Barotse Province (now Western Province). The growth of the cult was such that already in 1952 a larger building had to be constructed.

At the cult centre Chana would personally diagnose the patient's affliction as being similar to his own. After the diagnosis, the patient would return to his place of residence, where under the guidance of one of the doctors he would construct a windbreak in which he was to wash every morning, using medicated water. This would be continued until the patient appeared to be cured – which could take up to five months. Patient and attending doctor would then apply again to the cult centre, where Chana would subject the patient to a series of tests in order to ascertain if he was truly cured. Some of these tests would be public and within sight of the weekly gatherings at the centre, whereas the final test would take place in Chana's sacred enclosure.[36] This finished, the patient would be told what he had to pay:[37]

Payment is normally in the form of livestock; a cow, a few pigs or goats, but frequently a fairly substantial sum of money has to be paid. He must also bring a beast to slaughter for the feast that night.

During this feast the cured patient would be installed as a new doctor of the Nzila cult. This gave him the right to build his own sacred enclosure at his own residence. He would have authority to attend to new patients during their months of ritual washing, but could not use his own sacred enclosure to diagnose or pronounce final recovery: this would have to be carried out at the cult centre, by Chana personally.

In the mid-1950s the Mongu centre under Chana's direct leadership catered for the Mongu, Kalabo, and Kaoma district; a subsidiary branch, led by one of the twelve doctors, was then already in operation in the Senanga district. Branches soon began to proliferate. Muntemba[38] reports that

> By the late 1950s it [the cult] had spread to most areas in Zambia that had strong Western Province influences and also to Bulawayo and parts of Botswana. In the 1960s branches were started in most towns along the line of rail including the Copperbelt. . . . People not only from Western Province but from other societies became Nzila members as well. The movement was registered as the Zambia Nzila Sect in 1966. Its membership stood at 80,000 people then. On 30th March 1972, the membership figure stood at 96,872.

Thus in a quarter of a century the Nzila cult developed from a core of a handful of followers around a charismatic leader into a fully-fledged inter-local formal organization with government recognition, branches and property (in the form of buildings for worship) in most major towns of Zambia. The supreme leader's personal control over the crucial stages in the healing of each patient became, of course, no longer practicable. Branches and their leaders now enjoy a certain autonomy, which is effectively checked by an inter-local organizational structure ensuring overall conformity of both relief and ritual, central administration of membership figures, and centralized control over the recruitment and performance of officers. This control is effected by the Annual Convention at the cult's headquarters, by the distribution of essential paraphernalia,[39] and by formal examinations concerning the cult's beliefs and regulations.

Here a creative process must be appreciated in order to see the general significance of this development of a regional organization in the Nzila cult. Imitation is not the crux of this development; Nzila is far

201

more than a mere copy of the model of a Christian church. A failure to appreciate this leads Wilson[40] to a radical mis-reading of the cult, and a wrong generalization about the primacy of imitation in the organizational development of sects. From Reynolds's account of Nzila, Wilson[41] wrongly infers that Nzila developed no other congregations than the Mongu one over which Chana presided. Wilson goes on to speculate[42] that

> The abilities and facilities necessary for a more elaborate structure, however, were probably not yet available in Barotseland. Only where an organizational model of another type of movement can be imitated should we expect thaumaturgical responses [such as witchcraft-eradication movements and cults of affliction – WvB] to take on these structural characteristics which we associate with sects in advanced society. Such imitation, combining central direction with branch churches over a wide area, first occurred in this region in the *Lumpa church.*

Applied to the Lumpa Church of Alice Lenshina, the explanation in terms of an imitation of the mission as organizational model[43] is gross and superficial, particularly in the light of Roberts's authoritative statement[44] that

> There is very little information of any kind on the internal organi-zation of the Lumpa church – a most important subject which perhaps will never properly be elucidated.

Wilson's errors are plain. Nzila did evolve branches over a very wide area, and even Reynolds mentions the early Senanga branch. Therefore, the structural requirements for a regional organization were obviously met in Barotseland in the 1940s. The Bituma and Moya cults, as I will discuss below, show that Nzila was not even the only cult to develop such regional organization. Admittedly, all three cults borrowed part of their idiom from Christian churches (this is clearly what Wilson means by 'another type of movement'). The fact that Nzila was embedded in a social environment dominated by formal, bureaucratic organizations (including Christian churches) appears to have favoured Nzila's expan-sion (see below). Nevertheless, it is a gross error to explain the develop-ment of regional organization as merely an imitation of the Christian church model. Such an explanation wholly ignores the creative process by which new organizational solutions have been gradually worked out in Nzila and similar cults. These solutions were primarily determined not by the desire to imitate an outside organizational model, but, as I demonstrate in the following discussion, by the founders' personalities, their relations with their early followers and the structural characteristics of the cults' regions.

Bituma

The development of Bituma is much less of a success story. Simbinga's first attempt to found a cult failed. Public opinion rejected his claims to prophethood. His first activities (which included the propagation of unusual healing methods and the free distribution of his herd of cattle) were considered the acts of a madman. His early attack on what he considered the impurity of established healers and diviners, including his cousin Kapata, contributed to his public rejection. He left the area. When he returned in the late 1930s he was in possession of an elaborate collection of paraphernalia[45] and much more developed views concerning the nature of the affliction-causing Angel. The affliction henceforth became known as Bituma ('sent him') or Chituma ('message'), referring to Simbinga's prophetic commission or (according to other present-day informants) to the Angel, who sends affliction and is himself sent by the High God. Simbinga shifted the area of his activities towards the east: the central and eastern parts of Kaoma district. There he treated his first seven patients, including Kapata. Kapata, and several others among these first followers, only joined Bituma after a career of intense personal crises involving previous initiation into such non-regional cults of affliction as *kayongo* and *mayimbwe*. In this respect they were Simbinga's junior colleagues, rather than his disciples; they had access to experiences similar to those on which Simbinga's charisma was based.

Simbinga built for himself a small, hut-like shrine (called *kreki,* 'church') and made his initial followers do the same at their own places of residence. At these shrines healing sessions would be held at irregular intervals, according to the demand from patients. The session would start and conclude with prayer, and be structured around songs featuring Simbinga and crucial signs of his prophetic calling: his communication with heaven, and his rising from death:

1
| Tukuyako, tukuyako | We are going, we are going |
| Ku ngonda, ku ngonda | To the moon, to the moon |

(allegedly the first song Simbinga composed when he rose from death, claiming that he had been at the moon).

2

Thangwe ngoma	Start beating the drum
Ngwa Shimbinga	Here comes Simbinga

(a song Simbinga used during ritual dances in the first years).

3

Kombelele nganga	Pay formal respect to the cult leader
Waya mu kalunga	You descended into the grave, Great
Shimbanda-mwane	Healer
Nganga yetu yele	Our cult leader, indeed
Kombelele nganga	Pay formal respect to the cult leader
Waya mu kalunga	You descended into the grave, Great
Shimbanda-mwane	Healer
Shimbinga-mwane	We have always paid formal respect
kombelelelanga	To Simbinga the Great
Waya mu kalunga mwane	Great One, you descended into the grave
Kapata yele kombelele	Kapata indeed, we pay formal respect
nganga	To the cult leader
Waya mu kalunga mwane	Great One, you descended into the grave

(a major song of the later period).

Despite such distinctive elements as the regional organization centring around a charismatic leader, the theistic interpretation of affliction, and the purity-centred morality, the Bituma sessions in themselves remained, in their outside appearance, very close to the general idiom of the non-regional cults of affliction described above.

The cult took on well in Kaoma district, where in the 1940s to the 1960s a few thousand people were initiated. A more precise number cannot be given since in contrast with the Nzila cult no central records of membership were kept.[46]

In addition to the seven initial followers, about a dozen more leaders were appointed during Simbinga's life-time. These leaders would meet each New Year's Day at the cult's Annual Convention around Simbinga's shrine, where they would hand over part of their patients' fees and would enjoy a collective meal of white chickens.

In the 1950s several leaders settled in Lusaka and other line-of-rail towns, where they held sessions for urban migrants from Kaoma district.

Meanwhile, old tensions between Simbinga and Kapata (going back to the time of Simbinga's first appearance as a prophet) became manifest again. They concentrated on the cult's leadership and on the use of the cult's funds. Simbinga had married a woman from the eastern part of Kaoma district and enjoyed the loyalty of the Bituma leaders there, several of whom were his close affines. Kapata had settled in the central part of the district, and other Bituma leaders there sided with him. In 1960 Simbinga died suddenly and under suspicious circumstances, in the course of a hunting party. This was the occasion for the cult to fall apart. The leaders around Kapata (including those in town who hailed from the central part of the district) accepted his succession to the cult's leadership. They continued to visit the Annual Convention, now at Kapata's shrine, and to forward part of their fees to him.

Those in the eastern part of the district (and urban leaders hailing from there) have severed their connection with the cult's organization and have since practised the Bituma ritual as independent, individual cult leaders, without any organization being maintained between them. For them and their patients, Bituma has lost its regional character and has become merely another non-regional cult of affliction among the many prevailing locally. These eastern leaders retain a reminiscence of Simbinga's original theistic and universal visions. However, for those of their patients that have been initiated only recently, these associations are virtually lost. Surviving only in the central part of the district and among a few urban leaders, Bituma has elsewhere returned to the substratum of the factional, non-regional cults from which it sprang.

Thus the development of Nzila and Bituma has been very different indeed. We shall presently try to identify some of the factors responsible for this difference.

Bituma and Nzila compared from within

Let us first look at both cults from within: their internal structure and specific idiom.

As Reynolds rightly observed,[47] during the first two decades of Nzila Chana succeeded in maintaining control over crucial phases of the ritual. He kept most of his doctors in the position of mere assistants, without autonomous ritual powers. Only Chana's heir (nominated by Chana himself), and presumably his Senanga deputy, were allowed to exercise ritual powers on their own behalf. As the cult spread further, effective devices were worked out to safeguard the cult's unity and perpetuation even when it ramified into a number of geographically distant branches. A body of centralized administration, the Annual Convention, explicit regulations, indispensable paraphernalia whose distribution was strictly controlled, all in combination constituted an adequate structure through which the founder's charisma could be routinized and channelled without becoming dissipated or usurped. These devices constitute clearly recognized principles of legitimation, controlled from headquarters, outside which no cult leader pursuing the Nzila idiom could claim ritual efficacy. The gradual adoption of these devices rendered an ever-increasing specific identity to the Nzila cult. It more and more diverted from the substratum of non-regional cults. Nzila's interpretational idiom and cultic procedures became so specific that a relapse into the non-regional substratum became increasingly unlikely.

This may have been due not only to the cult's internal authority structure. Through the very large number of adepts and the participation of non-adepts in the mass services[48] the Nzila cult must have become something of a generally recognized social institution in the society of western Zambia. Nzila's definition and perpetuation came to be based not just on concepts and actions of leaders and adepts within the cult, but also on public opinion. The latter's influence is suggested by the one case of a breakaway from Nzila cited by Muntemba. There the protagonist had to adopt an idiom explicitly different from Nzila; and even so, Nzila turned out to be so well established that after a temporary decline the population again made a mass demand on its services:[49]

> Two years ago Nzila was thought to be on the decline in the
> Mulobezi area when a former Nzila healer decided to leave the sect
> to concentrate on pure faith healing which he thought (and Christian
> leaders accepted) was more Christian. People went to him from all
> over Livingstone area and his activities met their needs. Yet now
> this man's authority is on the decline as more people turn back to
> Nzila.

A very specific ideology and ritual, and a well-defined structure of organization and authority, externally supported by expectations among the general population, produced for Nzila effective checks against the threat of fragmentation and kept the cult from returning to the non-regional phase.

By contrast, Simbinga failed to assert himself as a continually indispensable source of charisma *vis-à-vis* the other Bituma leaders. Once initiated, the latter could all act independently. Moreover, at least some of them had had experiences similar to those from which Simbinga derived his charisma. Simbinga's personal status in Bituma was far less exalted than Chana's in Nzila. The great benefits in terms of prestige, power and income attached to independent leadership along the non-regional model produced a strong tendency towards fragmentation. Little could counteract this tendency but the leaders' personal emotional attachment to Simbinga, which ceased to have organizational relevance when he died.

In order to possess ritual efficacy in the eyes of adepts and of the general population, Bituma leaders were by no means dependent on paraphernalia that could only be obtained from the cult's headquarters and that, once obtained, would only be regarded as legitimating leadership as long as their owner continued to belong to the cult's organization. Instead, Bituma leaders freely obtained and augmented their paraphernalia, which were similar not only to Simbinga's but also to those in use in the non-regional cults of affliction: white clothes, scapulars, fly-switches, bells, etc. And although the cult certainly became an established institution in Kaoma district, in its public manifestations it remained so close to the equally well established non-regional cults of affliction, that any external check (in the way of expectations from the general population, concerning ritual and organization) against relapse in the direction of these non-regional cults, could not have been strong. In other words, the Bituma idiom was not specific enough.

As a regional cult, Bituma was far less powerfully designed than Nzila. Not so much Bituma's decline, but its part survival around Kapata seems to pose a problem. Personal ties based on past treatment supported the relationship between Kapata and his loyal leaders after Simbinga's death. In addition there appear to be more systematic reasons for the survival of Bituma in the central part of Kaoma district, which will become clear as we now turn to a discussion of the structural characteristics of the regions of Bituma and Nzila.

Let us sum up the position. Nzila and Bituma sprang from the same substratum of non-regional cults of affliction, and both were triggered by very similar personal experiences of their founders. What then explains their very different development? Part of an answer lies in personality differences: Chana was clearly a more creative innovator and organizer than Simbinga. Another part lies in the nature of social relationships between the leaders and their initial followers: in contrast with Chana's self-confident and unchallenged control, Simbinga was much more of a *primus inter pares* and had to compromise with the cultic backgrounds and ambitions of his initial followers. The differences between the cults' organizational structures and ritual idioms as they gradually worked out provide, as a third part of an answer, such explanations as I have just attempted to give that these organizational differences in themselves largely derived from the differences in structural characteristics between the Bituma and Nzila regions.

Nzila's and Bituma's regions compared

Although the regions of both cults extend into towns outside western Zambia, the processes that have shaped the cults in the first two decades after the founders' first appearance as prophets have taken place within western Zambia. I feel therefore justified in concentrating on that area, and I refrain from discussing the cults' wider ramifications. The latter will be the subject of chapter 6 and especially chapter 7 of this volume.

Map 3 outlines the geographical location of the regions of both cults in this area, and indicates the main direction of spread. When we compare Map 3 with Map 1 and with the geographical material contained in Davies's collection *Zambia in Maps*,[50] a number of striking differences between these two regions can be observed.

Demographically the differences are considerable.[51] The Nzila region has, by and large, a higher density of population. In addition to small administrative centres at Kalabo, Senanga and Sesheke (which are perfectly comparable to Kaoma in the centre of the Bituma region), the Nzila region includes the only two significant towns in this area: Mongu and Livingstone.[52] Nzila's headquarters are near Mongu, whilst the Livingstone area (extending into the commercial timber concessions around Mulobezi) appears in Muntemba's description as a major growth area of Nzila. By contrast Bituma has been a rural affair, whose present headquarters are located at about 25 kilometres from Kaoma. Admittedly, Bituma does have a few hundred urban adepts: but these are almost exclusively lower-class migrants from Kaoma district who, unable to become stabilized urbanites, keep circulating between town and village, and in many cases go through the Bituma ritual not in town but in the village. The occurrence, in the Mongu and Livingstone-Mulobezi area, of male/female sex ratios of more than 100 (as compared to under 70 in the Bituma region) further bears out the demographic difference.[53]

The demographic situation has important implications for the regional cults. Where population density is low (in the eastern part of Kaoma district it drops under seven inhabitants per square kilometre), the creation of local congregations and the maintenance of inter-local ties between them poses serious problems in terms of the number of people available, transport and communications in general.

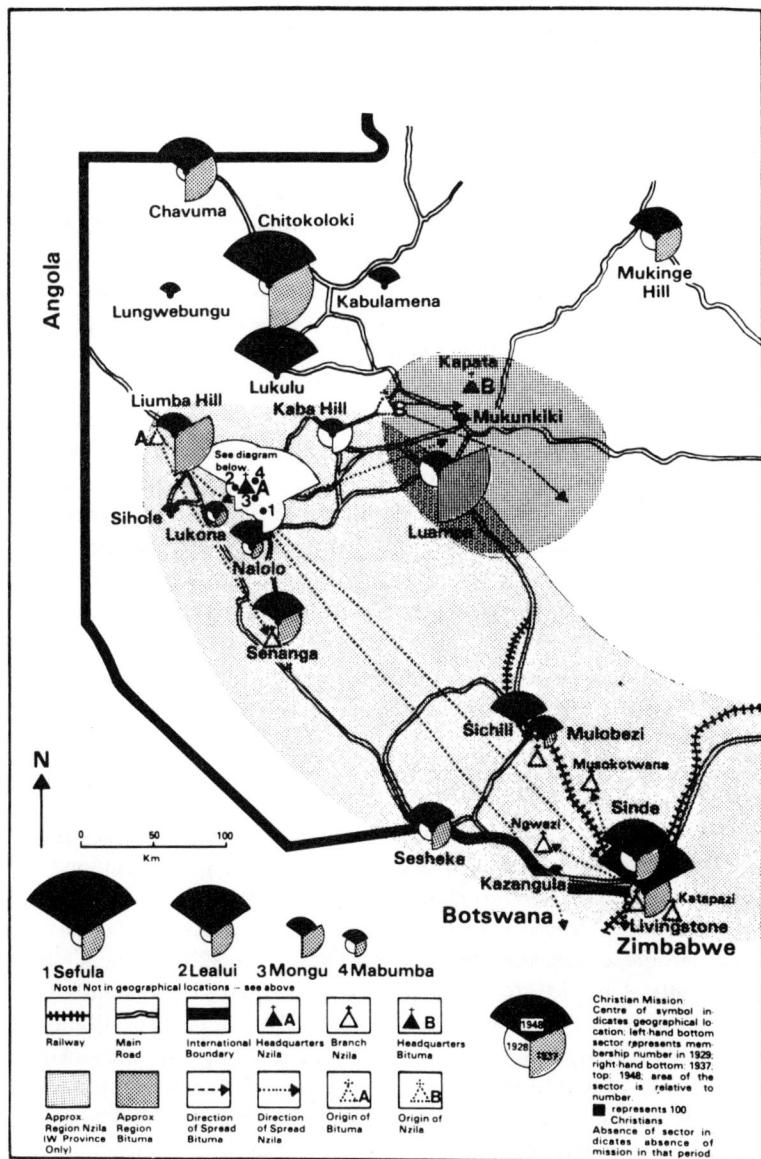

Map 3 Origin and spread of the Nzila and Bituma regional cults

The factional nature of the non-regional cults of affliction is partly explicable in this light. Similar problems play a much smaller role in densely populated areas.

More important perhaps, the demographic differences reveal a social-structural difference between the situation of the typical Bituma adept in comparison with the typical Nzila adept. Bituma caters for a stagnated peasantry whose experience with urban living may be considerable (due to labour migration), but whose prime identification and source of economic and social security is the village. Modern institutions, and particularly formal, bureaucratic organizations in the political and economic sphere, do penetrate from the metropolitan and national centres into the peripheral village scene, and determine the villagers' lives to an ever-increasing extent. But these institutions and organizations, with physical outlets at the district centres mainly, are seldom visible at the village scene. Their impact on rural life does not imply that the villagers frequently participate in them or identify with them – quite the contrary. Debarred from substantial economic and political participation in the wider national context, the people in the Bituma region see themselves primarily as part of an economic and political order whose major concerns and transactions refer to local, largely pre-capitalist, historical structures. Bureaucratic organizations set, from a distance, the narrow confines for the local social process but do not play a prominent role in the participant's subjective life-world.

The social-structural situation that is typical of the Bituma region does obtain in parts of the Nzila region as well. But in the latter's centres of gravity (Mongu, Livingstone-Mulobezi) the structural context is very different. Here people live in an urban or peri-urban environment, where their lives to a large extent consist of participation in economic and political formal, bureaucratic organizations: civil service, industrial and commercial enterprises, schools, medical services, churches, political parties, recreational associations, etc. Understanding of, and identification with, complex patterns of formal task-definition and bureaucratically-legitimated authority based on legal rules are essential for both psychological comfort and for economic survival in town and in the peri-urban and rural extensions of urban-based formal organizations. Parkin[54] has emphasized the potential of urban voluntary organizations to become mechanisms of adaption to the organizational structure of modern urban life. Nzila is likely to play a role in this respect. But what seems more important in the context of the present argument, is that Nzila's being embedded, from the 1940s on, in a

general urban organizational environment, did provide, in the perception of Nzila's potential patients and adepts, obvious organizational
models and patterns of bureaucratic legitimation by reference to which
this cult could successfully make the transition from direct to routinized charisma. Whilst no doubt providing a solution for some of the
problems engendered in its adepts by their confrontation with modern
urban organizational structures, Nzila adopted an organizational model
derived from this very structure (and therefore recognizable and acceptable to its adepts). This appears to have been an important factor in
Nzila's development into a successful regional cult.

The knowledge of such models and patterns was surely available in
the Bituma region as well. But there such a formal organizational
structure did not correspond with the peasants' subjective reality: the
organizational micro-structure of their rural society. Nzila developed
a regional organizational structure borrowed from and commensurate
with the urban society by which it was surrounded. Bituma, after
attempts towards regional organization, to a large extent lapsed back
into a fragmented, factionalized organizational structure which is not
only typical of the pre-existing non-regional cults of affliction, but
which is also (in ways I cannot elaborate on here[55]) in line with
the fragmented economic and political strucutre of Nkoya village
society.

I am not suggesting, though, that the structure of this rural society
was entirely incompatible with formal, inter-local religious organization.
Christian missions throughout western Zambia demonstrate that such
religious organizations are viable provided they receive ample political
and logistic backing from national and metropolitan centres (a condition obviously not met in the case of Bituma). Missions are important
for an understanding of the development of the regional cults in several
other respects. They were among the few formal, bureaucratic organizations that were visibly present in the rural areas. In this way they introduced the rural population to a pattern of social organization prevailing
in urban contexts. In addition the missions contributed to the ideological
shift towards greater prominence of the High God among the general
population of western Zambia.

Both Simbinga and Chana were exposed to local missions. But
whereas Nzila subsequently spread in an area that was very heavily
missionized, and where Christianity grew rapidly in the 1940s, Bituma
spread in an area where missionary activity was very limited and in fact
declining in the 1940s (Map 3).[56] By consequence, Nzila could benefit
much more than Bituma from the missions' instilling, in the minds of

211

potential adepts, such attitudes and organizational models as are conducive to a regional cult organization.

The relation between Nzila and Christianity was and is extremely tolerant. Muntemba points out[57] that Nzila has developed a considerable degree of symbiosis with Christian churches. Many of the adepts and patients are Christians, even some Nzila leaders are church leaders, and Chana has remained a member of the Seventh Day Adventist Church throughout his life. In the early stages of Bituma, on the contrary, Simbinga denounced membership of Christian churches, claiming that 'now we have our own church'. In later years this antagonism made way for tolerance and at present the cult is indifferent with regard to its patients' and adepts' religious affiliations.

A final point of difference between Nzila and Bituma revolves around the role that ethnicity has played in the development of either cult. Belonging to the Luvale ethnic group, Chana was an Angolan immigrant, one of the many thousands that have moved into the rural areas throughout western Zambia since the 1920s.[58] Chana utilized Luvale ethnic identity to get his cult off the ground in the first instance. Nzila's spread closely followed the penetration of Angolan immigrants in the area. However,[59]

> By the later 1940s the movement had spread to other parts of the Western Province and drew adherents not only from the Luvale . . . but from the Lozi as well as other groups in the Province.

The mono-ethnic element now appears no longer to play a role in Nzila.

By contrast, Simbinga could hardly rely on ethnic support. He belonged to the Mbunda ethnic group and was an Angolan immigrant like Chana. Unable to find recognition and support among his own people, at the time of his first appearance as a prophet, he turned to the Nkoya who have lived in Kaoma district at least since the last century. The majority of Bituma leaders that Simbinga initiated were Nkoya, Kapata being a notable exception. Instead of utilizing the enormous numerical potential of the Angolan immigrants, as Chana did, Simbinga thus concentrated on a relatively small ethnic group tied to a rather small territory that was increasingly encroached upon by Angolan immigrants, and with no substantial portion of stabilized urbanites among their number. Concentration on the Nkoya is likely to have contributed to the lack of expansion of Bituma. On the other hand, this very concentration made the Bituma cult into a distinctive cultural feature, a sign of Nkoya identity especially among Nkoya migrants in town. Before that time, only the *mayimbwe* non-regional cult had played that role to some extent.

Ethnicity, or rather local rivalry in an ethnic disguise, also played a role in the later decline of Bituma as a regional cult. The central and eastern parts of Kaoma district form two sub-divisions ('Nkoya proper' and 'Mashasha') of the Nkoya ethnic group.[60] Despite frequent inter-marriage and intra-rural residential mobility between these two sub-divisions, they display mutual antagonism based on a different political, administrative and mission history. Each sub-division has its own major chief. There are close kin relations between the Mashasha chief and Bituma leaders in the eastern sub-division, and the same is true of the chief in the central sub-division and the Bituma leaders there. The latterday cleavage between Simbinga and Kapata, even though both are non-Nkoya, coincided with one between ethnically-articulated power-blocks in the political structure of the district.

The preceding argument suggests systematic reasons why, with the decline of Bituma, Kapata could yet retain around him some remnants of the cult's regional organization. Density of population is much higher in the central part of Kaoma district (and particularly north-west of Kaoma township, where Kapata's village is situated) than it is in the eastern part. Moreover, the large Mangango mission (created in the early 1950s some 15 kilometres north-west of the earlier Mukunkike site), the annexed hospital, and the secular enterprise it has generated in the way of trading firms and co-operatives, along with the proximity of Kaoma and of Luampa mission, create a structural and ideological milieu more favourable for an inter-local regional cult than exists in the eastern part of the district.

Conclusion

My analysis of two recent Zambian regional cults is based to a large extent on far from complete oral-historical data. Even though I can analyse these data against the background of acquaintance with the area, with the non-regional cults of affliction from which the regional cults in question emerged, and with main trends in the religious history of Central Africa in general, the whole argument remains too tentative to approach a theory of the dynamics of regional cults. However, my argument does lead to a few comparative generalizations.

Every regional cult seems to face a dual problem. On the one hand, it has to develop a distinct, specific cultic idiom (in terms of both

213

ideology and ritual). On the other hand, it requires a formal organizational structure which shares out ritual authority sufficiently widely
among officials to enable them to cover an entire region, whilst retaining these officials within an authority-legitimizing structure of such
effectiveness as to prevent them from either breaking away from the
cult or, within its organization, pursuing too deviant an idiom. The
dialectical process in which solutions for this problem are worked
out with varying success is determined by a number of factors. In
addition to personality traits and inter-personal relationships of the
personnel involved, crucial factors appear to be of two kinds. First,
the specific nature of a cult's organizational devices to a large extent
determines its chances of survival as a regional cult. Second, these
organizational devices are partly determined by the structural characteristics which obtain in the geographical area that the cult is to transform into a region. My argument suggests the importance, among these
structural characteristics of the region, of demographic patterns and of
the occurrence, besides the cult in question, of other religious and
non-religious formal, inter-local organizations. Only application to
more and better data from other parts of the world can throw light on
the validity of these suggestions.

Chapter 6

Ritual, class and urban-rural relations[1]

to the memory of Max Gluckman (1911-75)

Introduction

At the end of the 12th International Africa Seminar on 'Town and Country in East and Central Africa', Lusaka, 1972 - a meeting which had brought out the inadequacy of existing models of urban-rural relations in Africa much more than advancing new alternative models[2] - Max Gluckman was kind enough to discuss with me the first paper[3] coming out of my present research: a preliminary description of the Bituma possession healing cult as practised in Lusaka by urban immigrants hailing from Kaoma district, some 200 kilometres from where Gluckman conducted his famous Barotse research in the 1940s. Naturally, Victor Turner was mentioned: he studied the Ndembu Lunda who are, in language, social organization[4] and ritual, closely akin to the Nkoya I was studying, some 250 kilometres away from the Ndembu. Turner has given us one of the best modern studies of a Central African rural society, and against that background has proceeded to map out and interpret Ndembu ritual in a truly masterly way.[5] Gluckman emphasized how Turner, as early as 1958,[6] had propounded a coherent and systematic theory of ritual symbolism; I was challenged to assess whether this theory could or could not be applied to urban ritual - which both Gluckman and I doubted.

In the subsequent years this challenge has formed the persistent background for my field-research (both in Lusaka and in Kaoma district) and my analyses. Close association with Jaap van Velsen drew my attention to the role of manipulation and economic factors

215

in the emerging picture. Specialists on Central African religious history (primarily Terence Ranger and Matthew Schoffeleers) opened my eyes to the historical dimension of the phenomena I was studying. Meanwhile I derived considerable inspiration from the Marxist approach of another colleague at the University of Zambia, H. Jack Simons.

In the present chapter I offer a tentative formulation of some of the central themes around which my analysis now begins to take shape. As the argument develops it will become clear that its main purpose is not to provide a thorough summary and evaluation of Turner's exceptional work. At any rate, in a short chapter like the present, one could not hope to do justice to the dazzling complexity and inspiring sophistication of Turner's work, nor to the unmistakable development in his theoretical position in the course of his twenty-five years of Ndembu studies. Instead, I shall consider only one limited portion of his work, use it to introduce some of the major theoretical problems which both his and my own work are facing, then move away from Turner's work and proceed to indicate the direction from which a partial solution may be expected in future – particularly if we manage to bring into play, in addition, such profound insights in symbolism and the socio-ritual process as Turner's work obviously has to offer.

Local rural society as the referent of ritual symbolism

Why would Turner's approach to ritual, even in its most generalized and systematic form, not be applicable to the kind of ritual phenomena I was investigating among people whose rural society was so similar to that of the Ndembu? For this, let us consider his 1958 argument.

Turner sees Ndembu ritual as mainly revolving around dominant symbols, which have at the same time two series of referents: an 'ideological, normative pole', and a 'sensory pole'. For instance, a tree secreting white fluid is the central symbol in girls' puberty ritual.[7] On the one hand this symbol is claimed to signify social referents (nurturation, mother/daughter relationship, solidarity of women, the Ndembu ideal of motherhood, all members of Ndembu society, these people's dependence on the normative system of their society, etc.); on the other it is claimed to have the purely physiological referents of human milk, breast-feeding and the female breast itself. The symbol couples a physiological life-necessity (a possible source of the emotions the symbol inspires, Turner suggests) to the structural

216

principles, ideologies, values and norms which constitute society.

This suffices to indicate one main line along which Turner develops his approach. I take the above example as an illustration indicating that on the social side (as opposed to the physiological) Turner is working within a tradition which is very well established in religious anthropology. This is the framework set by Fustel de Coulanges, Robertson Smith, Durkheim and Radcliffe-Brown.[8] The central idea is that ritual expresses, under the disguise of symbols, dominant themes of the social order in general, and makes this order appear so eminently meaningful, absolute, over-whelming, and beyond challenge (*sacred*), that individuals are confirmed as loyal members of their society. Society, ritual, the meaning of life, the internalization of values and norms, isomorphism and correspondence between ritual and social structures, etc., have all found a place within the numerous theoretical versions of this basic approach.

A minimal condition, for this approach to make sense sociologically, is that we have adequate definitions of both ritual and society, which enable us to isolate the two (overlapping) parts of empirical reality whose inter-relations we want to analyse.

For Turner, the ultimate social referent of Ndembu ritual symbols is Ndembu society.[9] This is the society of all Ndembu, who participate in local social and ritual life, speak the Ndembu language, and know and subscribe to Ndembu custom. Like most studies originating in the Manchester School and the Rhodes-Livingstone Institute,[10] Turner's work tends to stick to the model of the relatively self-contained tribal society.

Admittedly, Turner's approach is more sophisticated than that of most other authors working in the dominant tradition of religious analysis. He stresses the cleavages and lack of integration in Ndembu society, and sees as a function of ritual not the *expression* of a *self-evident* unity, but the *creation* of a *fragile* unity upon the disunity of Ndembu economic, kinship, and political organization.

But is this one rural society a viable unit of analysis? Turner's own work, and that of so many other anthropologists who have analysed contemporary African rural societies in a skilful and dedicated manner, certainly shows that along the lines of the tribal model one does arrive at revealing and fascinating results. These results are, however, based on the simplification, so often exposed in recent years,[11] of the tribal society as a more or less isolated unit whose internal functioning, including ritual, can be understood on the basis mainly of internal principles and dynamics of the human groups and individuals of which

217

this unit consists. Such isolated units do not exist any more in Africa, and the wealth of historical information now becoming available (on trade, migration, spread of technological and agricultural innovations, language, political expansion) makes it very clear that the period when such societies may have been typical for the continent lies many centuries back in the past.

When Turner did field-work among the Ndembu in the early 1950s, they were, as the rest of Central Africa since 1900, deeply involved in a much wider society which comprised other rural areas with a slightly different social and ritual organization; rural administrative centres from where central policy reached into the lives of all villagers; and rapidly growing towns where central government, migrancy-based industry, and other modern formal organizations were located. The Ndembu were heavily involved in circulatory labour migration: in 1962 their area is reported to have rates of absenteeism of taxable males ranging from just under 40 per cent to over 60 per cent.[12] I am not at all saying that Turner deliberately tried to conceal these modern, wider involvements in his work. He has been clearly aware of them ever since his earliest Ndembu publications, whereas they constitute a recurrent theme in his later work.[13] But it is one thing to acknowledge the social reality beyond Ndembu society, and to bring it in incidentally for a specific argument; it is another thing to make from this wider social reality, or if you like from the tension between the latter and the local, tribal society under study, the pivotal element in one's analyses. And however impressive Turner's work is, however justifiable his choice of theoretical and thematic priorities – he certainly does not do the latter.

The point I am making is that Turner's explanation of Ndembu ritual mainly (often exclusively) in terms of Ndembu society must leave us dissatisfied, once we realize that his so-called Ndembu society is in fact only a portion, a part-society, of a much wider social unit (not necessarily confined to the then Northern Rhodesia, to Central Africa, or Africa as a whole). If the social sub-system that we can conveniently describe as Ndembu society is only a part of the total society within which Ndembu life takes shape, then it is arbitrary and short-sighted to expect from reference to just this sub-system the major clue for an understanding of contemporary Ndembu ritual. We must at least explain not only the positive and systematic relation between Ndembu ritual and Ndembu society, but also how and to what extent Ndembu society and ritual are shielded off from the wider society of which they form part. This wider society involves, in particular, urban, industrial, formal-organizational elements which can hardly be invoked to explain Ndembu ritual. Or can they?

The Bituma cult in town: what is its referent?

Undoubtedly, the rural part-society where Turner was working more than a decade before Zambia became independent (1964), was shielded from the wider society to at least such an extent as to make a ritual analysis in terms of this part-society alone appear acceptable, inspiring, and revealing, within the established anthropological framework. In the afore-mentioned case of the Nkoya Bituma cult in both village and town the same problem becomes much more acute. The study of urban-rural dynamics represent an arduous test of the theory of religion and culture – at least of my theory. Here we have people operating, within short time intervals, in two or three structurally different and geographically segregated segments of the same, overall society: the village; the network contacts with relatives, neighbours and friends in the urban compounds; and the formal and urban organizations where they work, go for shopping, medical treatment, education, administrative documents, etc. None of these three sub-systems can be reasonably considered to be self-contained in any way. In all of them large-scale political and economic structures and processes penetrate deeply, tying them to what is essentially a worldwide social system. Now if Nkoya perform a ritual in town (e.g., Bituma), must this be interpreted in terms of either of these three part-societies, and which, and why, or must we look at it as reflecting the total social order (Zambia? Central Africa? the modern world?), and how? Pointing to a diffusion of cultural elements between these three part-societies is hardly relevant: we are not looking for raw material and their supply lines, but want to know how these materials are worked upon, and function, within a particular complex structural context.

The case of the Bituma cult may illustrate the complexity of the situation at the descriptive level.[14] This cult is a recent innovation: it was created in the 1930s by the prophet Simbinga, a returning labour migrant and ex-evangelist with the evangelical South Africa General Mission (the earliest mission in Kaoma district, at 100 kilometres from my rural research site). Simbinga combined elements of pre-existing cults of affliction which in themselves were also of rather recent origin locally (late nineteenth century), and rendered to these a theistic flavour. Subsequently the Bituma cult, forced to admit into its ranks established local doctors and diviners of earlier cults, and unable to keep up its original inter-local organization after the death of the founder, lost these prophetic and theistic elements again. The cult now lives on as merely one of the many cults of affliction which circulate in western Zambia and surrounding areas. Moreover, Bituma has taken on, and transformed, elements of an older cult complex revolving around fertility, ecology and shrines.[15] The cult is practised in town and in the village. Leaders and adepts frequently travel up and down between the village and the town, for both ritual and other purposes, over distances of up to 400 kilometres.

The cult presents a setting for the mobilization processes and transactions involving people (in such roles as patient, officiant, sponsor, adept, musician, choir member, onlooker) as well as material resources (cash, beer, firewood, instruments, other paraphernalia). The ritual allows hidden conflicts and resentments to be voiced in private therapeutic conversations, and partly remedies certain types of ancestral and sorcery affliction. In this way, each particular cult session clearly relates to specific, identifiable social-structural issues within the immediate social network of the participants. The session is just another phase in the social process, and far from revolving around mere imponderabilia, provides a major setting for such transactions as also dominate non-ritual social life in this group.[16] But does the cult also, beyond this and on a more general and abstract level, relate to ultimate social values, the culture core, the social order? What is it (if anything) the adepts communicate with, when the drumming and the medicinal vapours they inhale, lead them (though rarely) to paroxysms of ecstatic transport?

The cultural aspect of urban-rural relations

At this juncture I wish to make two observations concerning the 'state of the art'.

The first is that Central African studies of urbanization have not yet yielded a coherent and specific approach to the cultural dimension of urban-rural relations. I have elaborated on this point elsewhere.[17] So the anthropologist tackling ritual or other cultural data in the urban-rural context has nothing to fall back upon – at least not for this part of the world. Gluckman's reason to consider Turner's approach inapplicable to urban situations has apparently much to do with this. Gluckman's published work on urbanization[18] implies the following argument:

Turner's theory of symbolism starts with the model of the one tribal society; the structure of Central African urban society is entirely different from the tribal societies found in the same part of the world, and must primarily be understood by reference to the dominant complex of colonial (and post-colonial) and industrial power relations; in this urban structure rural, tribal elements have no place nor function except when, through a process of transformation whose precise characteristics have not yet been identified, they have been disengaged from their rural function and have become urban.[19] With the underlying structures entirely different, African urban ritual, however much reminiscent of the village, cannot be explained by reference to the rural, tribal structure, even if we still lack the theoretical tools to interpret such urban ritual in terms of the urban colonial-industrial structure.

In other words, not only did Turner not systematically[20] include in his analysis the wider society of which Ndembu society was only a segment; but even if he had wished to do so, the kind of interpretational analysis of Ndembu ritual he was pursuing would have revealed apparent incompatibility and incongruence between the village ritual and the non-ritual structure of that wider society. How can we meaningfully and systematically relate the macro-structure of the colonial society of Northern Rhodesia to a performance of the Nkang'a puberty ritual at the village level? How can we relate both the micro-structure of the rural village and kin network, and the macro-structure of post-colonial Zambian society, to a performance of Bituma both in a Lusaka suburb and in a village in Kaoma district? The latter phrase sums up my own present research problems, and where (as far as I can see) theoretical tools are lacking to interpret cultural continuity in a structurally diverse composite society, no easy solution presents itself.

The dominant orientation in religious studies, and a possible alternative

For the second observation, we shall leave behind Turner and other Central African studies, and turn to nothing less than the whole theoretical orientation of religious studies.

Dominant previous analyses from Durkheim, via Parsons, Geertz, Berger and Luckmann, etc., up to Turner,[21] have emphasized how religion renders social life meaningful and inescapable in what is, for simplicity's sake, represented as one close society. But there have always been rival approaches, which may have lacked the prestige and

221

the ambition of the established anthropological tradition, but which may yet be more capable of coping with the problems of religious thought and action in part-societies. Having been rather entrenched in the dominant, idealistic tradition of the anthropology of religion, I have no clear-cut solutions here, in fact am desperately looking for alternative models to cope with my research problems. But I suspect that a way out may be found along the following lines.

When we retain the view of culture as a repository of social meanings; of religion as a device to elevate these meanings (and the associated values and norms) to a plane where they can no longer be critically discussed and manipulated by the participants but instead are imposed upon them; and of social action as an enaction of meanings, norms and values firmly established in this way - then we need a unified, integrated society as our theoretical model. In a part-society there is, by definition, the existence of alternatives which are, however distorted, known to at least a portion of the participants (by virtue of the inter-action between this part and other segments of the wider society - without such interaction the part-society would be a whole society). Either these alternatives hollow out the absolute character of dominant, religiously-underpinned symbols - and then the latter can no longer perform the allegedly crucial functions of absolute legitimation (although in specific ritual contexts something similar, but much less absolute and overwhelming, might yet be seen to work) - or, religion works altogether in a different way from what the established theory claims.

Is it really from religion that social and individual life receives an ultimate meaning and anchorage? And is it necessary for life to have an ultimate societal meaning for the participants (consciously, or in the idiom of ritual and of altered states of consciousness), in order to be lived? Cannot the undeniable emotions participants betray in the course of ritual be explained otherwise than in terms of ultimate societal meaning and communication with the eminently social? One begins to suspect that the dominant tradition in the anthropology of religion is upholding a rationalistic, volitional philosophical position which the mainstream of western thought has largely rejected since the times of Kierkegaard and Nietzsche. Rather than starting on yet another attempt to turn an observed religious system inside out, in order to fit the latter into the straitjacket of an interpretational model that for more than one reason seems untenable, one would wish to adopt a fresh theoretical position altogether.

One obvious way to overcome the problems of interpretation which the established anthropological theory of religion offers in confrontation with contemporary Central African society and urban-rural relations, is to move religion from the core to the periphery, in our theory of society. If religion is considered a secondary reflexion, an expression, comment, adornment, etc. of whatever other more fundamental and central aspects of society, then we require no longer one tribal society to act as societal referent for ritual symbols, but instead we could mobilize as possible referents, amongst other ones, the whole variety of social groupings at various levels and with various structural characteristics as may exist in a given social context.

If we could thus rid ourselves from the burden of an unworkable conception of religion, we might as well include *culture* in this reassessment. Bohannan[22] argues rightly that the anthropological concept of culture as it is commonly used by professionals today covers the same ground as Durkheim's notions *conscience collective* and *représentation collective,* which were so fundamental in the development of the approach to religion criticized here. The researcher trying to apply the concept of culture to urban-rural relations in Central Africa faces similar problems as I discuss here for, more specifically, religion. Is social behaviour the acting out of values? Or are values (as abstract statements concerning behaviour, explicitly phrased by either the participants themselves or - as is equally often the case - by the researcher when the latter tries to identify the general principle implicit in the participants' behaviour) - are such values only a secondary device engendered by factors outside the sphere of values?

I suspect that there are several recent theoretical and descriptive anthropological studies which have pursued these themes in full, both for religion and for other aspects of culture, but I do not know them. It is reassuring to find at least a few inspiring examples of anthropologists who have tackled similar problems in a field where norms and values (which many anthropologists conceive of as ultimately sanctioned by religion) have for so long formed the standard ultimate explanation: kinship studies. Worsley (whose critical studies of religion[23] show him to be another dissident *vis-à-vis* the Durkheimian tradition of religious anthropology) has argued[24] how it is the economic and micro-political structure of the Tallensi homestead, instead of the religiously-underpinned super-structure of overall kinship values so emphasized by Fortes,[25] which makes Tallensi society tick. And of course the most seminal study along this line is Van Velsen's *The Politics of Kinship,*[26] where it is manipulatory and creative, prolonged social processes at the local level, instead of unassailable, absolute kinship values, that are shown to provide the fundamental structure of Lake-side Tonga society.

Worsley is an outspoken representative of a social-scientific tradition, older yet than the line of Fustel de Coulanges, etc., which has explored the alternative perspective: of religion as secondary, even peripheral, to society. Major early representatives of this tradition are, of course, Marx and Engels.

With little intention to be fashionable, and without reference to specific Marxist studies, I will explore, in the remainder of this chapter, to what extent the theoretical difficulties presented by my data might be overcome by an approach which considers the differential distribution of economic power (class) a dominant structural principle.

Culture among an urban ethnic minority

What does a distinctive culture (including ritual) do for people who find themselves as a numerical minority in a social setting characterized by cultural and structural diversity, such as modern Central African towns?

There is, to my mind, a strong case for the view that the majority of urban migrants who have a Nkoya rural background continue to adhere to the Nkoya ethnic label in town and to pursue Nkoya values and ritual, not so much for the sake of any birth-determined, deeply internalized, once-for-all commitment to Nkoya culture, but primarily because, under trying economic conditions, their self-interest leaves them no choice.[27]

As a low-class ethnic minority, these people have (because of a lack of formal education and other opportunities, and the fact that others before them have occupied strategic openings to the labour market) usually very small chances of a stable job and individual social climbing within the wider society. Apart from the very small minority of those Nkoya who have acquired fixed, permanent jobs in the middle and upper ranks of urban formal organizations, they can only cope with the insecurities and vicissitudes of urban life if they have other people to make effective claims upon whenever necessary. Nkoya culture provides an idiom of kinship, the notion of the indispensability of kin assistance in life-crises, and hideous negative sanctions in the sphere of sorcery, ancestral revenge, ridicule, physical attack, as well as positive sanctions in the sphere of status advancement within a particular system (i.e. among fellow-Nkoya), and financial benefits (for ritual specialists, as well as in the case of dyadic exchanges within the framework of the kinship idiom). This cultural system is capable of regulating satisfactorily the necessary economic transactions between most urban people with a rural Nkoya background (in addition some townsmen with a non-Nkoya background are assimilated). It renders transactions within this network well-defined and predictable, and reduces the risks involved. The greatest risk in the relationships between poor urban immigrants is the risk of a breach of reciprocity: whoever is to show himself generous today (e.g., while he is in paid employment) has to be sure of assistance tomorrow, when he may find himself unemployed and on the verge of destitution. Finally, the Nkoya cultural system provides a standard for evaluation.[28]

But however convenient to most, a minority opt out of this system. These are the people who, accidentally, manage to improve their economic and social status and then cut the links not only with their immediate relatives but also with the urban Nkoya group as a whole, ignoring the very values, rituals and relationships which previously seemed so deeply internalized and sacred.

If this tentative analysis makes sense, it suggests that the main function Nkoya ritual performs in an urban, class-determined context, is: to provide organizational elements (notably situational settings, sanctions, statuses) to pool and share out scarce and fluctuating individual resources. One is reminded of the shared-poverty system which Geertz and Wertheim have identified for overcrowded and economically declining Java, and in which kinship values play a similar role.[29]

In view of the theoretical problems discussed in this chapter, such an approach has a few marked advantages. It provides, at least in the urban setting, one clear proposal (though of course not the complete and final solution) of the problem of how to relate ritual to a social sub-system in a composite society. It goes some way to explain how the ritual system under study, once in existence, persists over time. For by participating in the ritual and verbally supporting it (even if this means, at one level of consciousness or another, merely paying lip-service to it – I mean, irrespective of whether the participants 'believe' or not), one asserts oneself as a member of an effective sub-community, publicly presents oneself as subscribing to the organizational terms of this community, and therefore the costs (materially, and in terms of effort, time, care, etc.) one puts in now can be expected to be repaid by the benefits one will, on this very basis, be able to claim in the future. In other words, the necessity to build up effective claims for assistance, in the sure expectation of future need (unemployment, disease, bereavement, conflict), appears to be the primary motor behind ritual participation among urban Nkoya. The sanctions underpinning such ritual, as well as the sanctions stemming from this ritual but operating in non-ritual settings, seem to derive, not primarily from the normative or conceptual system by which, in some Durkheimian fashion, the total society imposes both meaning and conformity upon its individual members; nor primarily from sub-conscious mental structures referring to early childhood and socialization; but mainly from the economic need to mobilize fellow-members of the group in future.[30] Ritual is one occasion to build up, or lose, such social credit as is necessary for survival. And, finally, *any* ritual seems in principle capable of providing organizational devices for this purpose, irrespective of whether the form and content of such ritual betrays systematic structural relations (symmetry, correspondence, reversal, compensations, etc.) with non-ritual structural aspects.

This may come as a surprise to the modern anthropologist of religion, who habitually looks for such isomorphism: e.g., a notion of glory after death to compensate for deprivation during life; or the symmetry between intra-familial authority patterns on the one hand and notions concerning divine power and its worldly intervention on the other. But in fact, and rather ironically, the arbitrary nature of the sacred, its being superimposed upon sacred things instead of being an innate quality of them, has been one of the guiding principles of Durkheim's theory of religion.[31] For such rituals as Bituma, which, after originating in a village setting, have been introduced into town and there frequently bring together a fair proportion of the urban Nkoya population, this is a very important point. It helps to explain both the effective urban functioning of village-bred ritual action and imagery (with frequent references, e.g., to the ecological complex of hunting which has so little to do with the urban economic structure), and the proliferation, both in the village and in town, of new cults, with new elements of ritual action and symbolic imagery which are very hard to explain in terms of social-structural conditions and changes therein, but instead seem to constitute an element of creative mental association and experiment reminiscent of poetry.

Yet I realize that I am grossly overstating my point here. The observable data of ritual behaviour and of the participants' statements about ritual may be far removed from theoretical constructs in terms of the social order, etc., but (as everyone knows who has done field-work on religion) they are also, though in a different direction, removed from non-ritual interaction. Setting, recruitment of personnel, distribution of roles and statuses, group dynamics, transactions and social-structural issues in general may show a considerable degree of correspondence between the ritual and the non-ritual life – as is very often the case in

226

Central and Southern Africa. Yet symbolism and ritual sanctions do have subjective reality in that they function, often with great directness, at the participants' level – and then precisely because the participant is unaware of the economic background of urban ritual participation as indicated above. In fact, ritual tends to impede the participants' awareness of the non-ritual, economic infrastructure in the minds of the participants; ritual may substitute, in lieu of a more or less objective understanding of the overall social process, the false consciousness (Marx) of a religious symbolic system; and in Geertz's words,[32] such a system consists of 'conceptions of a general order of existence [clothed] with such an aura of factuality that the moods and motivations [inspired by them] seem uniquely realistic.' The analyst, however much inclined towards reductionism, can simply not afford to ignore this capability of religious elements to function, not just as symbols of identifiable non-religious referents (as they clearly do at times), but also, in other contexts, as more or less autonomous foci of social life where the derived, symbolizing aspect has little relevance. A particular concept of spirit, and the ritual venerating that spirit, may from one point of view reflect structural aspects of the participants' kinship and economic relations; but from the participants' perspective such a spirit is primarily an interaction partner, much comparable to human partners, and leading a life of its own.

Similarly, it is not difficult to see how the idiom of sorcery fits in with the socio-economic explanation attempted here. Sorcery supports and regulates power relations, at the same time curbing excessive accumulation of resources in the hands of a few successful individuals.[33] But the truth is that in many situations *fear of death through sorcery attacks* (i.e. the participants' subjective interpretation of a social crisis) functions as a powerful sanction, much more so than the *fear of death through starvation or abandonment,* which would be the objective consequence of a social crisis provided the social processes involved were allowed to develop unchecked by a specific cultural idiom of sanctions and associated concepts, including sorcery.

On the one hand, the presumably ultimate referents of ritual (e.g., effective claims to assistance in future need) become disguised in the ritual process; on the other hand, these disguises, symbols, become a subjective reality for the participants; and this subjective reality begins to pattern their behaviour more or less in its own right. We shall have to account for this intermediate, relatively autonomous level of functioning of ritual symbolism and sanctions, even if ultimately it all boils down to an idiom to discuss, anticipate and ensure future non-ritual

227

transactions. If the analyst ignores this issue, there is little to prefer his theory over those in the line of the established tradition. So even the most determinist and materialist theory of religion will need a sophisticated theory of symbolism, not because the researcher has to believe in symbols as a final explanatory category, but in order to account systematically for the relations between the ritual super-structure and the economic infrastructure. To my knowledge, Marxism has but the rudiments of such a theory yet; but in this respect the more classic, 'bourgeois' anthropology and sociology of religion are hardly in a better position, despite people like Geertz and Turner. Meanwhile I have to admit that the present chapter goes only half way in meeting the challenge of assessing whether Turner's symbol theory can be applied to an urban-rural context; before the journey will be completed, we shall have a lot to learn from those aspects of his, and similar, work, that can be rephrased so as to become capable of transcending the limitations of the tribal model, and that do help us to understand the relatively autonomous functioning of the symbolic order.

So I merely emphasize what numerous other studies have brought out: that ritual is used instrumentally to shape social relations. However, I am tempted to claim that this aspect of religion is, at least in the Nkoya case, not a secondary effect of an institution which has mainly other, more fundamental functions, but that it is the crucial issue itself. If so, and if this statement has some validity for other societies, one could conceive of societies where the function of organizing interaction (a function which ritual seems to perform among the urban Nkoya) is met by institutions which are altogether of a non-religious nature. By contrast, the established, Durkheimian approach would consider a society without religion inconceivable. Whether such societies without religion exist is mainly a question of definition. North Atlantic urban, industrial society (where the blessings of the welfare state are reducing to a minimum the need to mobilize individual fellow-members for future economic need, and where at the same time the decline of organized religion is the subject of much socio-logical debate) offers interesting fields for further exploration along this line.

The argument extended to the rural areas

It will be argued that the uncoupling of ritual, values and meaning, even if observable and understandable in the case of urban Bituma, is essentially an aberration, the result of urbanization, detribalization or anomie. Bituma will be called a bad example since it is a recent innovation, presumably not in line with 'traditional', 'tribal' institutions. In the village, one will claim, a very different picture may obtain: the beautiful alignment of ritual symbolism and non-ritual norms and values, inter-connected in the process of legitimizing and sacralizing the social order – everything one would expect on the basis of the dominant theoretical tradition.

Ritual does flourish in the village, and, while modern possession healing cults such as Bituma dominate the scene, there is a wealth of ancestral, ecological and life-crisis ritual, some of which seems centuries old. As in town, this ritual is frequently performed and brings together a considerable number of rural neighbours and kinsmen. Due to the frequent traffic between Lusaka and the distant village, and the low rate of urban stabilization, we encounter partly the same participants in the village as in the urban rituals.

I am more and more convinced that the emerging picture of Nkoya urban ritual as mainly related to non-ritual transactions of a micro-political and economic nature is equally applicable to the rural setting.

Three-quarters of a century of exposure to the colonial-industrial complex and its post-colonial counterpart, preceded by a century of political subjugation due to Lozi (Barotse) expansion, and a rapid escalation of military raiding and slave trade by both Lozi and non-Lozi groups in the same pre-colonial period, have left the countryside of Kaoma district in a state of destitute stagnation.[34] The scarcity and fluctuations of economic resources are even more severe here than among Nkoya in town, and the overall standard of living is lower. If urban Nkoya can be said to constitute, along with townsmen from other areas but in similar social positions, a *class*, the same is true for the majority of Nkoya villagers: they are representatives of the largest class in Central African society, the peasant farmers. Their land and game have been repeatedly encroached upon by government policy, chiefs' privileges and private enterprise; labour migration has continually absorbed a very substantial portion of the rural labour force without in any way contributing towards its reproduction; and while politicians have been keen to solicit rural support, the rural development they have instigated has been very limited, and very unevenly spread. In terms of standard of living, access to labour markets, consumer markets and cash, effective political power, rates of mortality and morbidity, education, etc., these peasants (at least in Kaoma district) are at the bottom of Zambian society. A usual way to escape from this situation has been migration to the urban, industrial centres of Central and Southern Africa; this opportunity is now largely closed due to the prohibition of migration to the south, and the tightening of the urban Zambian market for other than highly qualified labour. People still migrate to the Zambian towns, but chances of securing a job there, and keeping it, are extremely slim.

Thus the relevant structural ingredients of the Nkoya urban situation are present in the village in an even more pronounced form. And much of what I have said about urban ritual seems to apply to the rural situation.

In the village a large proportion of the adults older than forty are ritual specialists in one matter or another relating to the sphere of illness and death. This makes it possible for non-ritual power relations to be constantly expressed and (since usually several people will strive for power over the same individual) contested, in a ritual idiom. Alignments and conflicts such as continually arise out of everyday social life are constantly commented upon by, and partly take shape in the course of, connected series of rituals. Illness and death provide the major occasion for such ritual, and it is here that senior kinsmen, and members of the senior generation in general, seize upon patients and their close kinsmen, either to assert their claims over the latter (in the prospect of political and material support in future), or to exact very heavy medical fees straight away. The central issues in present-day ritual are not so much abstract, impersonal beliefs and values, but power and competition over social relationships which provide access to rare resources: co-residing junior kinsmen, clients, money earned in town. Ritual interpretations and actions are constantly shifted, new ones are invented and improvised, and the rules of the ritual game are largely determined not by immutable custom, but by the individual specialist (to whom the phrase 'ritual entrepreneur' would often be extremely applicable), and the day-to-day vicissitudes of the socio-political process at the local level.

How little of an explanation beliefs and values offer when considered in isolation becomes particularly clear when we consider the confrontation between ritual (medical) specialists and modern, western medical services, both in the village and in town. To the people living at my rural research site, a small and understocked rural health centre was available at a distance of 30 kilometres, in addition to three hospitals, each at a distance of about 100 kilometres; in town private practitioners, clinics and a regular university hospital were available within walking distance. In independent Zambia all western medical agents except private practitioners provide services entirely free of charge. Major costs involved in the use of these western medical services therefore mainly concern the following items: transportation; loss of productivity through absence of patient and escort; food for the latter; the social costs involved in appealing to kinsmen for assistance as escorts and domestic helping-out; and finally, most important, the social cost of challenging the strong informal social control exercised by senior kinsmen who, in rivalry with modern medical services, are eager to treat their diseased kinsman in order to enhance their own power and income.

With regard to the majority of complaints, including those for which modern possession cults claim to provide a treatment, present-day Nkoya tend to acknowledge the theoretical equality, if not superiority, of western medical services, as compared with treatment by senior kinsmen and other local specialists. Incidental experience with modern medicine within the rural area and in the course of circulatory labour migration has broken down whatever effective barriers Nkoya may ever have had, in the way of internalized values, against such medical alternatives as are offered outside the Nkoya local ritual idiom; psychological costs springing from negative attitudes *vis-à-vis* western medicine scarcely play a role in this context. Yet in the great majority of cases, in town hardly less than in the village, treatment is sought not from western medical agents but from Nkoya specialists, particularly senior kinsmen, even if the latter charge fees in the order of magnitude of an average monthly income amongst these people. One key towards an understanding of this paradoxical situation seems to lie in the fact that modern medicine means an escape from the ritual power complex that ties junior kinsmen to their seniors, and urban migrants to their fellow-tribesmen both in town and in the distant village. Senior kinsmen and senior tribesmen in general constantly militate against this loss of what little access to power and resources is left them: they explicitly persuade patients to refrain from seeking western medical assistance, or to give up a course of western treatment already started, and to pursue such local alternatives as they themselves can provide. (Should specific knowledge and experience fail them, they may even resort to improvising new cures, sometimes with disastrous results.) Thus in the sphere of illness and death, senior Nkoya not only compete with each other for the control of junior people as political followers and providers; they also compete with the outside world.

The confirmation between senior kinsmen as healers, on the one hand, and the western medical services on the other, is all the more interesting since, on the rural side, the class aspect is obvious: high morbidity and mortality (due, in addition to the low standard of living and environmental infestation, to the remoteness and inefficiency of rural medical institutions) is a major component of the peasants' class situation in the wider sense.[35] The choice between local treatment or hospital amounts to one between honouring the demands of people in the same class situation (to whom one is tied by the expectation of future need), and ignoring these claims and enjoying a first instalment of the benefits of upward mobility in the wider society. By consequence, mainly two categories of present-day Nkoya can afford to utilize the western medical sphere to a considerable extent: the elderly; and those who are already on their way up socio-economically and at the same time breaking out of the confines of their kin-group and ethnic group. Only those younger people who feel they can (or, due to disrupted kin relations, *must*) build up economic and status security in the wider society dare ignore the social and religious sanctions the elders may direct towards them; it is these incipient outsiders who may pursue healing outside Nkoya ritual, thus risking a crisis which may well cost them their foothold in the village (where the majority of even long-term urban migrants tend to retire because of their economic insecurity in town).

I do realize that these assertions, like the ones concerning the Nkoya urban situation, in order to be taken seriously, require the detailed presentation of both extended case material and systematic, quantitative data. Such information was collected in abundance during years of field-work among this ethnic group; however, the scope of the present chapter, as well as the amount of detail that would have been necessary for a truly convincing argument, preclude its inclusion here.[36]

The historical dimension

Nowadays manipulation of ritual concerning illness and death seems to provide a major basis for power in the social structure of the village, particularly between members of different generations. Among urban Nkoya, who particularly through ritual are tied both to the village and to their fellow-tribesmen in town, the same situation obtains.

There are indications that, on the rural side, this is largely a modern development. In the period preceding Lozi expansion and colonial rule non-ritual power of chiefs and headmen was very considerable, both in extent and in number of followers; but this political power had only limited ritual implications which could not compare, in most cases, with, e.g., the model of the Sudanic or medieval European kingship.[37] From the late nineteenth century on we witness on the one hand a decline of the effective non-ritual economic and political power of the chiefs, headmen and the senior generation in general (due to political incorporation, labour migration, and the development of urban alternatives); on the other hand (and typically outside the sphere of chieftainship) we witness the emergence of religious innovators who create, or introduce from elsewhere, new cults primarily concerned with healing. Why these cults emerged and had a general appeal is a problem I have considered in the other chapters of this volume;[38] there I make plausible that the emphasis on individual suffering has greatly increased in this region, under the influence of structural changes during the last century or so.

Whatever the origin and historical background of contemporary ritual, when recently the directly economic and political basis of the elders' control was taken away, new bases for power came to be explored. With junior kinsmen increasingly embarking upon an independent career as labour migrants, instead of staying in the village and working as junior clients and prospective sons-in-law, senior kinsmen were anxious to explore new claims to divert these migrants' resources back into the village economy. Payment of bridewealth (which under conditions of labour migration has become a condition for any regular marriage) provided a partial solution; but it was counteracted by such enduring sexual unions as migrants entered into with non-Nkoya women elsewhere.[39] The new cults, and whatever other, older ritual could be employed for this purpose, provide an additional solution. At present ritual seems the most important and effective way to assert and maintain economic and kinship-political claims across the urban-rural gap, in addition to structuring the social process within the rural area itself.

Noteworthy in this respect is the role of women. Like the elderly men, they were and are less involved in migration than younger men; the modern possession cults, whose patients, adepts and leaders are mainly (though not exclusively) female, and which are very popular both in town and in the village, now constitute a device to siphon the resources to which men as migrants and urban workers have greater (if still very limited) access, over to women, in the context of cult sessions where husbands and male consanguineal relatives act as sponsors for their womenfolk, provide beer and firewood, and pay high fees to specialists who are predominantly female.

Conclusion

The situation I describe seems peculiar to one particular Central African ethnic group, at one particular moment of time. While my tentative analysis may have some heuristic and theoretical value, it is yet far from providing anything like an adequate basis for an alternative theory of religion. However, the Nkoya data do demonstrate weak spots in the existing body of established theory, and suggest an alternative approach.

It might appear as if I bluntly suggest that contemporary Nkoya ritual is just a trick of cunning elderly people, and of women irrespective of age, to make money at the expense of hard-working and credulous young men. I would like to take away this naïve impression, but this would necessitate presenting not only a somewhat unusual view of the relation between ritual and social structure, but also a fully-fledged theory of symbolism, i.e., of the internal structure and subjectively almost inescapable reality of ritual. I do not have such a theory ready; let alone the impossibility of presenting it in this short chapter. Meanwhile, there are a few points which I must emphasize.

I may have set out to challenge an established theoretical tradition; but my aim is certainly not to denounce the authenticity of the ideas and actions of my informants. There is, without the slightest doubt, much of profound human experience, tragedy and beauty in any ritual. The stranger who is given the opportunity to share in this experience, however imperfectly and at whatever costs, receives much to be grateful for. He is admitted into a great intimacy, and this imposes obligations upon him as a professional and as a fellow man. Professionally, the main obligation is: to strive passionately for understanding. All I am claiming, perhaps, is that for such an understanding it is unnecessary, in the Nkoya case at least, to reach for those exalted, abstract constructs that feature in the current, dominant theories of religion. Ordinary, trivial everyday life and death are sufficiently dramatic, moving and overwhelming to serve as the ultimate referents par excellence of ritual. For the poor man without many options or hopeful perspectives (and this is not only the typical Nkoya but also the typical subject of anthropological research throughout), the struggle for survival (which primarily means a struggle for close relationships implying effective claims on other people) assumes an absolute reality and relevance which not only (painfully and embarrassingly) contrast with the complacent, abstract rhetorics of modern religious theory, but which may also be capable of accounting for such existential profundity, intensity and occasional redemption as religion and ritual may entail.

On the general, human side the main point appears to be application. Frankly, when returning from the field my main obsession was not to understand Nkoya ritual, but to do something about Nkoya society. In this respect my present analysis has a strategic element which may well make critics suspicious. To bring about planned social change will be difficult, and even suspect, anyway; but if we can point, as the crucial issue in the social and ritual process, to economic and kinship-political power relations which locally reflect traceable economic and political conditions in the wider society, this promises a lot more for the future than. if we concentrate on impersonal values. The anthropologist who points over the heads of the participants to timeless, impersonal values, norms and societal meaning as ultimate referents of ritual and as cornerstones of the existing social order, is likely to reinforce the *status quo*. Popularized, his well-meant analysis can be used to discourage interference, or to legitimize active policies inimical to the interests of his informants (as the South African manipulations of the concept of 'traditional culture' clearly shows in the political context of Apartheid and Bantustans). In cases like that of the contemporary Nkoya, where ritual is so much a matter of life and death in more than one sense, an optimal understanding of the non-ritual basis of ritual may well provide the necessary leverage for positive change.

Chapter 7

Cults of affliction in town, and the articulation of modes of production

Introduction[1]

In this chapter I shall explore the extent to which the Marxist paradigm of the articulation of modes of production sheds light upon one of the topics discussed in the previous chapters: the Bituma cult of affliction, as practised in Zambia's capital city, Lusaka, by immigrants from Kaoma district, a rural area 400 kilometres west of this city.

Why should a section of the urban population, a majority of whose male members earn their livelihood in the offices and workshops of modern economic life, in their weekends stage nocturnal healing dramas whose seemingly ancient idiom shows so little correspondence with the urban environment? And what is the historical status of this healing cult?

Before I attempt to answer these questions with the aid of the modes-of-production approach, I shall describe the cult itself in some detail, and discuss some alternative approaches by which it might be analysed. After showing the potential of the modes-of-production approach, I shall briefly indicate its considerable limitations, and outline problems for further theoretical exploration.

Bituma as a cult of affliction and as an urban cult

Background

Spirit possession forms a widespread, and as is generally agreed a very ancient, part of the religious systems of central Bantu-speaking groups.[2] However, during the last century and the beginning of the present

236

century, a shift in idiom seems to have occurred, as recorded in several parts of Central Africa.[3] Ancestral spirits, deceased rulers, and spirits of the wilds, which until then seem to have formed the dominant agents to whom affliction was attributed, gave way to agents which were much less tied up with local kinship and political structures and with the local natural environment. A long series of new cults of affliction gained ascendance, whose names (which also are the names of the invisible agents considered to cause the new afflictions) refer to neighbouring ethnic groups, to new appearances on the local scene such as African long-distance traders and Europeans, and to objects of material culture associated with the latter.[4] In general, the new afflicting agents carry connotations of impersonality and alienness. These cults would, in succession, sweep rapidly across the Central African countryside, across ethnic and linguistic boundaries. People who were suspected of being afflicted by any one of these new spirits, would submit to diagnosis by a member of that spirit's cult. In case of a positive diagnosis, healing could be found by initiation into the cult, after which the new adept could himself assist in the diagnosis and treatment of others similarly affected. At first the new cults did not develop any form of inter-local organizational structure between healers. Instead, organization would be limited to one healer with a small following of adepts: all that was necessary to stage nocturnal, musical cult sessions. The basic model of these new cults, of which all the distinct cults were specific applications, became one standard way of conceptualizing illness and healing throughout Central Africa. Each of the thousands of cult leaders interpreted this overall model somewhat in his or her own fashion, manipulating the common cultic material (rhythms, songs, conceptions of the afflicting agent, types of shrines, and such paraphernalia as scapulars, bells or beads) so as to impress and attract patients and their sponsors at the expense of other, rival cult leaders.

In a few cases, all of them dating from after 1930, exceptional cult leaders transformed this new cultic model in a number of ways. They redefined the nature of the afflicting agent, replacing the connotations of alienness and impersonality by those of universality and the High God. They redefined their own role, from that of cult leaders merely transmitting a cult idiom everyone knew they had not created themselves, to that of prophets, whose life history, culminating in the foundation of the cult, was taken as a sign of divine calling, and as the ultimate legitimation of their cult's superior claims. On this much more elaborate and exclusive basis they were able to create extensive

237

inter-local cult organizations, linking all adepts, via senior officiants (who were not supposed to act as independent ritual entrepreneurs as under the non-prophetic model) to the cult's central place, and to the founder or his successor.

Along with the Moya cult named after its founder, Nzila (founded by Chana), and Bituma (founded by Simbinga), are major examples of such prophetic cults in late-colonial western Zambia. Nzila retained and developed its initial characteristics, to become a large independent church. Bituma declined after the founder's death (1960), and almost reverted back to the stage of non-prophetic cults. Ideas concerning the High God disappeared, and the inter-local organization collapsed. Once more the Bituma leaders became ritual entrepreneurs, who maintained very little contact amongst themselves, accepted no higher authority above them within the cult, competed for patients and adepts, and blended into their Bituma cult practice at their personal taste (and that of their clientele) elements from any of the non-prophetic cults.

Bituma in the city of Lusaka: ritual and economic aspects

It is in the latter form that Bituma sessions are held in present-day Lusaka. The cult was first introduced there in the 1950s, when several Bituma leaders settled in town in order to conduct sessions for urban immigrants from Kaoma district. By that time these immigrants numbered only a few hundred. Their estimated number rose to over one thousand in the late 1960s, when Zambia had become independent and the border had been closed for the customary labour migration from western Zambia to Zimbabwe and South Africa. There are indications that by the late 1970s their number had somewhat declined again, due to worsening urban conditions and slightly improving opportunities in the rural district.

Although Bituma was founded by an Angolan emigrant of the Mbunda ethnic group, it had soon acquired a predominantly Nkoya membership, for reasons which I have discussed in chapter 5.[5] From the start, urban cult sessions were conducted mainly by Nkoya cult leaders for the benefit of patients, sponsors and an audience that was also predominantly Nkoya. Sessions are also conducted in the open, on urban premises that are seldom fenced, or on public sites between houses. Therefore, neighbours and passers-by have easy access. Normally up to 30 per cent of the audience at a session may consist of non-

Nkoya. These may be towndwellers hailing from any part of Central Africa, but with some over-representation of people from western Zambia. For the latter are entirely familiar with the overall cultic idiom, may themselves belong to very similar cults, and are usually able to communicate with the Nkoya people present at the sessions in some Western Province language instead of Lusaka's lingua franca, Nyanja.[6]

Sessions involve between twenty and fifty people: the cult leader, up to a dozen adepts who form the chorus, male musicians, one or several patients (up to about eight, two or three representing a median figure), and a majority of onlookers who sit at either the men's or the women's fire, chatting, drinking beer, smoking or sleeping. The onlookers only occasionally, if at all, join actively (by singing, clapping of hands or shaking of rattles) in the proceedings that go on at the ritual core of the session, opposite the line of drums, and at the foot of the shrine.[7] Assisted by the adepts and the musicians, the cult leader goes through a long series of dances and songs in order, first, to confirm the original tentative diagnosis and, second, to make the patient pay homage to the Bituma spirit by entering into trance and dancing, thus joining the Bituma cult. A typical song is the following. It commemorates crucial episodes in the cult's history: Simbinga's resurrection from the grave, and his succession by his cousin Kapata:[8]

Kombelele nganga	Pay formal respect to the cult leader
Waya mu kalunga Shimbanda-mwane	You descended into the grave, Great Healer
Nganga yetu yele	Our cult leader, indeed
Kombelele nganga	Pay formal respect to the cult leader
Waya mu kalanga Shimbanda-mwane	You descended into the grave, Great Healer
Shimbinga-mwane kombelelelanga	We have always paid formal respect To Simbinga the Great
Waya mu kalunga mwane	Great One, you descended into the grave
Kapata yele kombelele nganga	Kapata indeed, we pay formal respect To the cult leader
Waya mu kalunga mwane	Great One, you descended into the grave

While at the ritual core of the session an intense healing drama is staged which requires maximum commitment from the cult leader, patients, musicians, and chorus, at the fires an animated social intercourse goes on, which is largely fed by other concerns than the patients' well-being. People exchange news about mutual kinsmen and acquaintances in town or in the distant village; a good deal of inter-clan and inter-ethnic joking goes on; love affairs are being attended to; and comments are passed on the current economic and political conditions in the country. Seating arrangements, greetings, the way in which beer and tobacco are offered and passed around, all reflect existing or incipient relationships among those present, as well as hierarchies based on sex, age, specific kinship relationships, and rank and income within the urban environment. Status differences are also expressed by the quality of everyone's clothing, which escapes no one's attention.

Only at certain moments is the attention of almost the entire audience captured: when, near the paroxysms of trance, the dancing becomes particularly spectacular; when the leader, after hours of dancing, makes public pronouncements concerning the nature of her patients' affliction; and in the early morning, when those present are to line up in order to squeeze fluid medicine on to the bare skin of the patient, out of cold and disintegrating water-lily leaves prepared during the session in a pot at one of the fires. Some of the audience will have left by this time, or will be too tired, intoxicated or preoccupied to bother.

Cult leaders in these sessions are usually mature women, forty years of age or older. They have a long standing in the Bituma cult. Normally they are adepts of some of the other, non-prophetic cults as well, whereas in some cases they are descendants or heirs of well-known healers in the near past. Of six leaders present on the Lusaka Nkoya scene in the early 1970s, the major three were in fact rural residents who (in addition to a rural ritual practice) would make long visits to town for the specific purpose of staging sessions and collecting outstanding fees. Of the others, one was too old to preside over the extremely demanding healing ritual. One, Simbinga's widow, was postponing her actual healing practice until she would have inherited the name of her elder sister, a well-known Bituma leader.[9] And of one, the wife of a well-established Nkoya townsman, it is doubtful whether she ever staged sessions in town. All these leaders were Nkoya. Bituma leaders of other ethnic groups (particularly Mbunda and Luvale, both well represented in Kaoma district) were said to operate in Lusaka, but I have no confirming evidence on this.

The adepts who assist the leader are mainly women who have been initiated into the cult in recent years. Without their co-operation, the leader is unable to stage a session; yet they do not derive financial benefits from the sessions, although they share in the drinks. Leaders compete for adepts, both in the village and in town. Therefore a leader will try to bind adepts to her in several ways: by extending the adept's period of treatment in the cult, by recruiting adepts from among her close kin, by providing free treatment for adepts, and by mystical sanctions and moral claims. This cannot prevent adepts from frequently shifting their allegiance from one leader to another, while some adepts set up as independent cult leaders themselves.

Patients are usually women in their child-bearing age, although occasionally elderly women, small children, and men figure as patients. Nearly all patients are Nkoya. In Lusaka I once witnessed the initiation of a Lenje woman, who subsequently became a prominent adept.[10] In view of the strong entrepreneurial tendencies among Bituma leaders, it is unlikely that they would ever turn away a patient from an ethnic group different from their own. The fact that the cult's leadership has never been exclusively Nkoya points in the same direction. So do the formal pronouncements of leaders and adepts, when questioned on this point. The near-exclusive patronage by Nkoya patients rather seems to derive from the fact that few non-Nkoya patients would be able to convince their sponsors of the advantages of Bituma over cults of affliction with which they have become more familiar in their own home area. Given the considerable cultic activity going on in Lusaka townships, with Tonga staging *mashawe* cults of affliction,[11] Luvale staging *bindele* and similar cults from north-western Zambia,[12] Tumbuka staging *vimbuza*, and so on, Bituma can only command the tiny Nkoya section of the urban cultic market. Moreover, there is always the option for people to return to the village and seek treatment there. Many people, both Nkoya and others, do exactly this.

Treatment in case of illness is the main way to recruit new members to the cult, but not the only way. The complaints associated with the Bituma affliction are explained as the stirrings of the Bituma spirit, which has planted itself by accident in the patient, and which wants formal recognition and public respect from the patient and her social environment. But, in the Bituma aetiology, this spirit may be present without making its host ill yet. At many sessions, there will be one or two non-adepts in the audience who cannot control themselves when hearing the cult songs: they start trembling and dancing in the specific ways peculiar to the cult. This is taken as a sign of their being possessed by the Bituma spirit. They are seized upon by the leaders and adepts and usually their initiation into the cult will take place before a few months have passed.

Sessions are planned several weeks beforehand, and require a major organizatory effort. The Lusaka Nkoya community is very small and spread out over all the main compounds of this vast city. Many hours and considerable expense for public transport alone go into the contacting of musicians and adepts, the purchase of firewood and beer (or beer ingredients), and the finding of instruments.[13] Since the leader leaves the responsibility for the organization of the session largely to the patients' sponsors, sessions are only possible if the patient can mobilize the services of several adult men: her husband, brothers, cousins, brothers-in-law, father or uncles. And in view of the considerable expenses involved, a session can only take place if at least one of these sponsors has a regular monetary income.

As one of the songs sung at the sessions runs:

Ku tangalala kwa nganga	In order for a healer to be happy
Kwikuta	A full stomach is necessary

During the sessions, at intervals between songs, the sponsors must supply the healer with bottled beer or soft drinks. This is only a minor part of a chain of transactions between the patient (that is: his or her sponsors) and the healer. All these transactions involve money. A small amount, in the range of K0.50,[14] is paid when the patient (usually suffering from diffuse, chronic complaints such as headache, nausea, backache, nervous tension, general weakness) is first taken to the healer for an initial diagnosis. In most cases the healer advises that a formal cult session be organized for the patient. At the conclusion of the session the healer is paid K1. But when after a few weeks or months the patient shows signs of definite improvement, the healer claims that this is due to her particular treatment (no matter what other cures may have been pursued in the meantime, involving other healers or doctors). She then claims her full fee of K20 or more, a sum equal to if not exceeding the average monthly income of poorly-educated recent urban immigrants, a category most Nkoya in Lusaka belong to. Other expenses connected with the cult session include: the musician's fee (K1-K2 each, for a minimal number of three); firewood (K5-K10); opaque beer for the whole audience (K10-K20); and public transport in the most usual case that the session is held at or near the premises of the leader (or, if she is a visitor to town, those of the leader's urban kinsmen). Even if musical instruments are not always hired for money, their loan implies future obligations which add to the costs of the session. An elaborate and, in terms of healing, successful session can cost up to K100, while K25 represents a minimal expenditure. For the average participants in these sessions, these are very large sums indeed.

Outside the sessions, leaders and adepts are supposed to observe a certain code of behaviour: to keep clear of 'dirty' things (sorcery; all medicines except the few vegetal substances used within the cult) and to consume white food and luxury items such as fizzy drinks, tea and bananas. This means further expenditure, in addition to those associated with the sessions themselves. Also it means further situations in which typically female Bituma adepts assert themselves against the role expectations of their male kinsmen and partners.

Not all patients suspected to be suffering from the Bituma affliction seek treatment at urban cult sessions. Many travel to the distant home villages, where leaders' fees are about half of those charged in town, and where the availability of musical instruments, kin support, firewood, and ingredients to prepare beer greatly reduces the costs of sessions. The few Nkoya who have joined the urban middle and upper classes, normally avoid their less successful fellow-tribesmen in town and do not attend their massive rallies including cult sessions. But they do maintain ties with their home villages on an individual basis, and often refer there, as a last resort, for treatment from diffuse and chronic complaints such as Bituma normally deals with. Working-class urban Nkoya often alternate between urban and rural treatment, as in the following case:[15]

Mary, born and raised in the village, married Muchati in 1969, and followed him to Lusaka, where he had stayed since 1961. In 1970, when visiting an urban Bituma session as a non-adept, she could not control herself and joined in. Early in 1972, in a context of mounting marital tensions, she returned to the village to undergo Bituma treatment there. After a few weeks, when the tensions were partly relieved because her husband paid the last instalment of the bride-wealth, she returned to town. In May and December 1972 she participated in urban sessions. In March 1973 she returned to the village in connexion with her own health problems as well as those of her son (residing with his parents in Lusaka), and of her father (at home). She participated in another session there. Having returned after a month, she again took part in an urban session in July 1973. Over this four-year period, she twice shifted her allegiance to a different cult leader. Throughout this period her husband remained in Lusaka, where he was employed as a domestic servant. In the next five years the same pattern was maintained, although I cannot give precise dates. In this period, the husband found employment as a general worker. Mary's affliction is generally considered to be very strong, and it is expected that before long she will set up as an independent healer. That Mary and Muchati could afford this long series of expensive rituals was largely due to the application of cost-saving devices: Mary shifted from a healer who was no kinswoman of hers, to kinswomen, thus reducing the healer's fees; and she shifted the scene of her treatment from town to country, thus reducing the material costs of the sessions. But even so her involvement in the cult weighed very heavily on the household budget, and for instance repeatedly drained all of the small business capital with which Muchati tried to enter the fish-trade.

The money needed for women's participation in the sessions and for their observance of the Bituma codes in daily life has to come from male sponsors. For only a negligible number of Nkoya women are in a position to earn a living in town: as marketeers, as illegal sellers of beer and prepared food, as prostitutes, or in the formal sector as domestic servants, shop assistants, secretaries, etc. Nkoya women who manage to stay in town for any period exceeding a few months are in general those who can depend upon the monetary income derived from men with whom they reside and to whom they are tied through marriage, concubinage or close kinship. Fellow-tribesmen (both men and senior women) exert considerable pressure upon Nkoya women in town towards such dependence upon men. Not only because of standards of propriety: female dependence means that the woman's urban kinsmen can benefit from her domestic labour or (in the case of marriage or concubinage) from profitable relationships with her male partner, involving cash transactions for bride wealth or in lieu thereof.

Independent women from other ethnic groups are fairly conspicuous on the Lusaka scene.[16] Therefore it is unlikely that the social pressures making for dependence among Nkoya women in town would be so successful, if these women were not already debarred from independent urban participation anyway, because of a whole range of factors. Their education is defective: few of them even completed primary school. They are unfamiliar with town life: practically all of them were born and raised in a distant village. Their command of Nyanja and English is very limited. They lack the starting capital necessary for setting up in business. And they lack urban patrons and associates that might introduce them to the formal or informal sectors of the urban economy. In Lusaka access to both sectors is more or less controlled by people from Eastern

Province, from whom the Nkoya are separated by language, culture and regional origin, and who are even too remote to be approached as joking partners.

Male Nkoya's chances or urban monetary income are affected by the same factors, but less severely so. Their education, urban experience and command of essential languages tend to be considerably higher than those of their tribeswomen. The formal sector has few convinced equal-opportunity employers, so many jobs which might be done by women are in fact reserved for men. Often men have had chances of acquiring patrons which, however unpredictably, sometimes do give access to jobs in the formal sector. And once a man is more or less established there (but many Nkoya never reach beyond the stage of low-paid, uncertain and temporary urban employment), he might after a number of years even amass some small capital with which to enter the informal sector (fish-trade, tailoring, etc.). The majority of adult Nkoya men in town have a very low monetary income from uncertain employment in the formal sector (including domestic service). The others are recent arrivals looking for work; not-so-recent arrivals who have lost their jobs or failed to find any, and who prepare for return to the village; a few elderly men who have retired in the households of younger urban wage-earners; and the happy few who have joined the middle and upper classes.

So the men are often in a position to finance the cult sessions for Nkoya women in town, even though sponsorship invariably means a very substantial drain on the household budget. Potential sponsors do not accept ungrudgingly the financial burdens, and the other female claims, associated with Bituma. Some men do not take the cult seriously at all, and mock at it, saying that Bituma is just a silly invention of women who want to assert themselves *vis-à-vis* men, and who want to eat luxury food. This echoes earlier male reactions against this type of cult in the central parts of Western Province where shortly after the Second World War Gluckman[17] found men complaining about these 'abominable cults which make women behave like fools and expose their thighs when in trance'. Yet, among contemporary Nkoya men in town, most comply with the financial claims imposed by Bituma. Some however flatly refuse to pay up, and get away with it:[18]

Jenita, a Nkoya woman in her early twenties, born and raised in the village, was living in a Lusaka compound with her husband Zacharia and their baby daughter Lusha. Zacharia had a job as assistant in a butcher's shop. However, he spent his income on girl-friends, and neglected his family. Jenita and Lusha fell ill and applied to the cult leader Kashikashika, who included them as patients in a Bituma session. Jenita's brothers in town covered the initial expenses. When Jenita's and Lusha's condition subsequently improved, Zacharia refused to pay Kashikashika's main fee. The brothers, claiming that they had already done more than was proper, refused to pay, too. They called their mother from the home village to discuss the future of Jenita's marriage. At the informal family moot held in Lusaka, Zacharia showed repentance; and, largely because of the very close ties between his and Jenita's home villages, the marriage was not dissolved. Meanwhile Kashikashika, still waiting for her fee to be paid, threatened to restore Jenita's and Lusha's affliction. However, since Jenita's mother was also a prominent Bituma healer, she herself, while in Lusaka, staged another Bituma session for these patients. This not only saved them the expense of the leader's fee, but also meant that Jenita left Kashikashika's faction of adepts, and joined that of her mother.

Although this case is exceptional in its outcome (after all, very few Bituma patients have senior healers for mothers), the theme of a woman in town seeking redress for a breach in conjugal relationships via the Bituma cult is a recurrent one (cf. Mary's case, above). It applies to many, although not to all, urban Bituma cases. It must be remembered that the plight of the average Nkoya woman in town is particularly severe. She has to face the many structural disadvantages I discussed above. She is largely dependent on male income for her day-to-day survival, and thus often has to accept treatment at variance with the ideal of respectful male-female relationships, in which she has been brought up in the village. By contrast most women in the village can rely on the support from their male consanguineal relatives in times of crises; moreover, they can by and large feed themselves and their children from their own crops and from gathering – male income is required for larger expenditure, e.g., clothing. Finally, the Nkoya woman in town is deprived of most of the daily economic activities (gathering, cultivation, food processing) for which she was trained in the village and which made her life there both practically and symbolically meaningful.

A minority of male Nkoya wage-earners in town are single; most are married. The urban Nkoya are lapsing behind the general trend in Central African towns after independence[19] in that quite a few of the Nkoya men work in town while their wives and children are staying in the village. It largely depends on a man's employment career whether the family will come to live in town, or whether he will return to the village. With the uncertainty characteristic of the low-grade urban jobs that Nkoya urban migrants tend to have, with the recent tightening of the urban labour market in general, and with the slow rise of economic opportunities in the rural district, the latter outcome is fairly frequent. However, there is a core of one or perhaps two hundred Nkoya men who have managed to remain in town for years at a stretch, success-fully bridging periods of unemployment either by seeking assistance from urban kin or by temporary withdrawal to the village. These men have built up nuclear families in town. Nearly all of them, too, are maintaining close ties with their relatives at home. They attend the funerals of rural kin, keep in touch through letters and oral messages, infrequently forward money, and occasionally visit the village, leaving there part of their town-earned money and possessions (blankets, clothes, an occasional wireless set or bicycle). They very frequently entertain visitors from home (especially male job-seekers). Although many of them have passing affairs with non-Nkoya women, especially in the first years of their stay in town, almost all of them end up with a Nkoya wife, from home.

With the exception of those very few who have joined the middle or upper classes, nearly all of them maintain very intensive contacts with fellow-Nkoya in Lusaka: both through dyadic network relations (along the lines of kinship, joking relationships, friendship and pat-ronage) and at frequent collective rituals and ceremonies held in town. Bituma sessions as described here are only one of these occasions; the others are girls' puberty ceremonies (which may bring together virtually the whole adult working-class Nkoya population of Lusaka), funerary wakes, and informal family moots. For most urban Nkoya, contacts with fellow-Nkoya in town are the main source of assistance in cases of crisis: illness, death, unemployment, marital or family disputes, or conflicts with the authorities.

But of course, they never draw exclusively on intra-ethnic assis-tance. My argument, and indeed the set-up of my research among the Nkoya, would tend to stress intra-ethnic relations. But this hand-ful of Nkoya tribesmen are dispersed over a vast city, where much of the social life in the residential areas is multi-ethnic, and dominated by formal organizations like the party (UNIP) and churches. For their livelihood the Nkoya in town are dependent on wage-labour in bureau-cratic organizations created by industry and the state; and they utilize similar organizations for medical assistance, education, shopping, transport, formal litigation, burial, etc. Their urban life is not exclusively, perhaps not even primarily, organized around ethnic concerns; yet these loom large in their own perception of the urban situation. And although the space is lacking here for a more satisfactory treatment on this point,[20] there is considerable evidence that among working-class Nkoya in Lusaka intra-ethnic cohesion (as reflected in marital choice, network relations, co-residence) is somewhat higher than among the average Lusaka townsmen of the same socio-economic position. Nkoya participation in Zambia's one party (UNIP), their involvement in urban churches (both mission churches and independent ones), and their utilization of outlets of western medicine[21] and of formal Urban Courts of Law, is rather below average. In line with their insecure footing in the urban economy, also on the social and the political level they can be said to be 'in the city, but not of the city'.

Having thus presented descriptive data of the Nkoya urban cult practice against the background of Nkoya urban life in general, I shall now proceed to interpret these data. A review of major current non-Marxist approaches will throw into relief the potential of the approach stressing modes of production and their articulation.

Interpretation: (a) Current non-Marxist approaches

To what extent can current non-Marxist approaches to Central African society, urban-rural relations and ritual yield a satisfactory interpretation of the descriptive material on Bituma as presented in the previous section? In order to answer this question, I shall discuss, in the present section, two inter-related major approaches: the Manchester School, and the more recently emerged regional-cults theory.[22]

The Manchester School

The cult studied here derived from a remote rural area but is practised in the compounds of a modern city. This creates considerable problems of interpretation. A dichotomy between town and countryside has pervaded Central African social research since its beginning – at least in formerly British Central Africa, where research was highly dominated by Gluckman's Manchester School. Early anthropological research in Central Africa took place in a context where, much in the way of present-day Apartheid, urban African migrants were denied the status of urbanites, and were relegated to a position of visiting bachelor peasants. Therefore, the opposite viewpoint taken by Gluckman and his colleagues was, however theoretically one-sided, politically both timely and courageous. 'The African townsman is a townsman', Gluckman proclaimed.[23] While Mitchell[24] and Epstein[25] made an effort to explain urban phenomena like the Kalela dance, ethnicity and tribal elders by almost exclusive reference to the structure and dynamics of what was then still called the 'industrial-colonial complex' of Central African towns, Victor Turner was studying rural ritual with the patience and rapture of the stalker of rare game. As he wrote in his first publication on the subject:[26]

> In many parts of Northern Rhodesia the ancient religious ideas and practices of the Africans are dying out, through contact with the white man and his ways. . . . But in the far north-west of the Territory, this process of religious disintegration is less rapid and complete: if one is patient, sympathetic and lucky one may still observe there the dances and rituals of an older day. . .

Also Elizabeth Colson would study Tonga religion as primarily a rural affair.[27] In the dominant tradition of Zambian social research, non-Christian ritual was something for the rural areas, something dying out anyway, and even (with the exception of Turner and Colson) something rather peripheral to the mainstream of current description and theory. It was probably largely as a result of this research tradition that even Christian religion in Zambia did not receive substantial sociological treatment until after independence.[28] At any rate, rigid distinction was made between urban and rural structures. No detailed and incisive analysis was made of the economic, social and religious *interactions* between village and town. It was not denied that the new urban life emerging in Central Africa (where towns were a colonial creation) owed much to rural inputs, particularly in the more intimate domains (domestic life, kinship and marriage, notions concerning sorcery, witchcraft and healing, judicial notions); yet no systematic attempt was ever made to study the conditions under which these inputs were capable of penetrating the allegedly solid boundaries separating urban and rural structures.

Admittedly, Geoffrey Wilson's pioneer study[29] of the town of Kabwe (Broken Hill) paid some attention to the rural circulation of town-earned money and commodities, the emergence of urban marital patterns differing from rural ones, etc. But his functionalist approach to changing Central African society[30] was not conducive to a viable theory of urban-rural relations. And apart from stressing its considerable prevalence in town, he had very little to say about non-Christian religion:[31]

> Only ten per cent of the Africans in Broken Hill are members of any Christian sect; the remainder are still held more or less loosely by the decaying tribal religions, compounded of the cult of ancestral and other spirits, of fears of witchcraft and sorcery, and of the belief in magic; and Native 'doctors', both resident and visiting, do a considerable trade.

Later Gluckman, summarizing the work of his associates, stressed urban migrants' continued contacts with the rural areas as a means of maintaining rights in rural land.[32] Van Velsen[33] wrote in a similar vein when he claimed that rural, 'traditional' societies were surviving in Central Africa because migrants, urban employers and administrators all shared an interest in such survival. His picture of urban migrants keen to retain a stake in the village, and discussing village politics, keeping in touch through visits, letters, remittances, etc. seems quite compatible with a pursuit of home rituals in town – but the issue did not crop up in his writings.

On the rural side, after specific studies of how one particular institution of rural society, notably marriage, had been affected by 'modern conditions',[34] Watson's *Tribal Cohesion in a Money Economy*[35] was a major effort to show how, given a rural social structure such as prevailed among the Mambwe, 'participation in industry has not led to a breakdown in tribal life'.[36] Over half a century after the imposition of colonial rule, Watson had no difficulty with this conclusion, for[37]

> A society will always tend to adjust to new conditions through its existing social institutions. These institutions will survive, but with new values, in a changed social system.

Watson's essentially functionalist outlook which gave priority to institutions and values over relations of production (i.e., patterns of expropriation and control), made this conclusion fairly inevitable. And presumably, if rural institutions (including ritual) allegedly survived automatically, there would be no *a priori* reason why migrants would not introduce them into town. However, in the paradigm of the articulation of modes of production (cf. below) Watson's conclusion would appear to be much less self-evident. We would rather look at these surviving institutions as devices which an encroaching capitalism (of which Watson's book provides numerous examples) allowed to survive, and actually furthered, for its own benefit: because these institutions maintain a setting for the reproduction of cheap labour, and for the accommodation of discarded labourers, in pre-capitalist, neo-traditional pockets of the world system. Is it possible to find a similar explanation for village-derived urban *ritual*?

Again, a decade later (when the overt effects of change had become even more conspicuous than in Watson's time, and social change had become a major focus of social research), Long's treatment[38] of the transformation of another Zambian rural community (among the Lala) would prove to be rather less blind to the profound infrastructural changes produced by capitalism and the modern state. His discussion[39] of the effect of urban experience upon the villagers' religious responses (conversion to the Watchtower faith) formed a first attempt to pose the question of urban-rural relations in a religious context, at least in Central Africa. But in line with the Manchester tradition of studying either the urban or the rural side of urban-rural relations, his analysis is curtailed by lack of corresponding urban data.[40] It is only in Harries-Jones's study of the town of Luanshya (based on field-work in 1963–5) that we find the first analysis of one urban ritual, the funeral, with a (very brief) discussion of its rural counterpart and of its urban transformation in the hands of the UNIP funeral committee.[41]

Obviously, it is impossible to do justice here to the tremendous achievements of the Manchester studies of Zambian society. Yet even a full treatment would probably lead to the conclusion that the problems posed by our topic in this chapter cannot be solved within that tradition. This is due not only to a fixation on the rural-urban dichotomy and the relative lack of interest in religion and ritual, but also to a failure to develop an integrated theory with which the total modern transformation of Central African society can be grasped in both its rural and its urban aspects. The main attraction of the Marxist articulation approach seems to lie in the hope that it does begin to provide the first outlines of such a theory, whereas rival approaches (e.g., structural-functionalism, neo-classical economics, or methodological individualism[42]) have so far failed to convince. To what extent could migrancy, urban-rural relations between migrants and their home villages, and ritual continuity between town and countryside, all be viewed as aspects of this overall transformation process, in the course of which the capitalist mode of production has linked itself to pre-existing modes?

However, before we consider the extent to which the paradigm of the articulation of cults of affliction does solve the interpretational problems of a cult like Bituma, let us consider a major development in

251

the anthropology of religion -- a development whose stated claims would suggest that it is in fact providing such a solution along non-Marxist lines.

The theory of regional cults

When anthropology was still concentrating on single cultures and societies, development of a theory of cults was hampered by the fact that only some types of cults (e.g., ancestral and royal cults) could be meaningfully dealt with within a framework of bounded and disparate social, cultural and political units. In the tradition of Robertson Smith and Durkheim, which for a long time had been dominating the anthropology of religion, such cults have been analysed with a version of the correspondence theory, which looks for formal and structural analogies and isomorphism between religious and non-religious aspects of the same social group.[43] Secular authority relations were claimed to correspond with particular conceptions concerning the supernatural world;[44] religion was said to be a model both *of*, and *for*, social action;[45] and even Karl Marx claimed the secret of the Holy Family to lie in the earthly family.[46] It is clear that the correspondence theory is inadequate for our topic in this chapter. It would be pointless to try and identify, in a synchronic analysis, the corresponding non-religious referents of a cult which, while of rural origin, is practised simultaneously (and without marked formal differences), in two environments structurally as different from each other as a remote rural community and a modern national capital city.[47] The rural community is still partly based on subsistence farming, with kinship dominating social life to a considerable extent, and fairly homogeneous in its ethnic composition; the town is almost exclusively based on participation in the capitalist sector, with social life largely dominated by formal bureaucratic organizations associated with industry and the post-colonial state, and extremely heterogeneous in ethnic composition.

Within the Central African context, Victor Turner's work, ever since his first major book,[48] has been a forcible attempt to break through the limitations of the correspondence theory, by pointing out the essentially dialectical relations between ritual and non-religious structures,[49] which is altogether more subtle than correspondence theory would suggest:[50]

> Ritual among Ndembu does not express the kinship and political structure as in a firmly organized society; rather it compensates for their deficiencies in a labile society.

The incredible riches of Turner's Ndembu material, as well as its being confined to just one rural group conceived as a viable unit of analysis, prompted him to develop his approach to cults in depth, to ever greater insight in Ndembu society and in human symbolic action in general.[51] However, since for Turner the relation between ritual and society is somewhat more subtle than one-to-one correspondence, he could become a major influence on the development of a theory that would be capable of dealing with that large class of cults (which Werbner[52] was to call 'regional cults') that not only do *not* display a clear one-to-one relation with the non-religious features of any single social group in which they are found, but that in fact extend beyond the political, cultural, economic and linguistic boundaries of any one group. When in later years Turner turned his attention to religious phenomena (particularly pilgrimage) in large-scale societies, he once again gave a powerful stimulus to the development of a theory which, in principle at least, is capable of handling regional cults.[53]

Crucial in this new approach is that, once certain requirements such as internal organization and the development of a distinct cult idiom have been met, cults are claimed to transform the geographical, cultural or social space in which their specific activities take place into a cultic region, normally focusing on a ritual central place, and bound together by the cultic interactions between cult members. These interactions generate flows of goods and services, movements of people, economic and political power, and ideological commitments. All these cut across rather than reflect or reinforce such economic, social, political or moral relations and boundaries as exist locally on the basis of principles other than the cult. Hence Werbner's recent characterization of the regional cult as[54]

> a locally uneven resolution of opposite tendencies, towards exclusiveness on the one hand, and inclusiveness on the other. Together the tendencies make for a mixture, often highly unstable, of the specific, highly parochial along with the transcultural and more universal . . . . In one cult's regions, there may be a great ethnic heterogeneity, in another the greatest cultural differences may be between some people in towns and others in the countryside, but no regional cult is simply homogeneous.

So here is a framework which is at least in theory capable of encompassing both the rural and the urban manifestations of healing cults. In fact, I did analyse my material within this framework.[55] However, in that analysis (see chapter 5), emphasis was on rural cult forms. When I discussed two cults in western Zambia, the large and bureaucratically organized Nzila cult[56] and the Bituma cult which soon fragmented into disconnected small factions, I tried to explain their differences in organization and success by reference to what now appears just another variant of correspondence theory. Nzila, I claimed, acquired such organizational features as both derive from, and are appropriate in, the urban and peri-urban areas which form the centres of gravity of Nzila's cultic region; whereas Bituma fell apart, in line with the fragmented political and economic structure of the rural area where its members are predominantly located. While theoretically hybrid, this interpretation now also seems incomplete in the light of the fact[57] that Bituma's region, too, encompasses urban areas.

Does the theory of regional cults, in Werbner's successive versions, provide the means to overcome these imperfections? Not, I think, in a sense that it would throw light on the inter-relations between religious and non-religious phenomena. As Werbner writes in relation to the Mwali cult,[58]

> The cult's regions are not a replica of the social divisions which exist apart from ritual relations. On the contrary, the cult's regions, like all its ritual relations, have an autonomy of their own. Their transformation must be studied in its own right, therefore, and not as some dependent variable of other phenomena.

It is here that considerable further thinking has to be done, and that we can benefit from a materialist approach like that of the articulation of modes of production. Before regional cults can be taken as relatively autonomous *vis-à-vis* extra-religious structures, and *vis-à-vis* the fundamental contradictions dominating those structures, we have to assess the extent to which these regional cults are actually structures of *material production*, as distinct from circulation. The studies collected in Werbner's *Regional Cults* book[59] do in fact discuss flows of resources and people as contained within the cults. But underlying all these cults is a dependence upon a material production base outside these cults. And the same can be said for the recent Central African studies collected in Schoffeleers's *Guardians of the Land*.[60] In this book, Schoffeleers's introduction as well as my own contribution[61] stress the ecological dimension of these regional cults concerned with the land. The cults are shown to impose extensive constraints on the actual practice of agriculture, hunting, fishing and collecting (a major example being the management of forest fires in Malawi as a fertilizing technique). Yet it is very obvious that the cults never positively stipulate material production as part of their own cultic structures. The relations of production on which the material survival of the Central African societies described in *Guardians of the Land* and *Regional Cults* depends are not cultic relations, nor are the people involved in these relations of production primarily cultic personnel. In so far as these cults are imposing constraints on actual material production, their role is somewhat similar to that of the state under industrial capitalism: they set and maintain some of the judicial and ideological conditions under which relations of production (which in fact exist on a different plane from the cult, i.e. the state) can continue to exist.[62] In other parts of the world a very different situation may obtain. The maraboutic complexes in North and West Africa as described by Gellner or Cruise O'Brien, stressing slavery and agricultural production,[63] suggest that in some cases regional cults *can* in themselves organize production. But in Central and Southern Africa such non-religious contradictions between elders and youth, men and women, masters and slaves, rulers and subjects, and capitalist and workers, around which production revolves in the various specific modes, cannot fail to provide a context within which the distributive aspects of regional cults have to be analysed. If we are to understand such cults, we must primarily understand this extra-religious context, and the approach in terms of the articulation of modes of production attempts to do precisely this.

Meanwhile, we should point out one other development in Central African studies which, without being phrased in specifically Marxist idiom in itself, has paved the way for Marxist interpretation. Much more than the Manchester School and regional cults theory, Marxism amounts to a *historical* approach to social phenomena. In the 1950s and early 1960s, the heyday of the Manchester School, very little research had been done on the history of Central Africa, or on the comparative and historical study of its religious systems. Since these days, enormous progress has been made. For many parts of the area we now have first-class studies of colonial and pre-colonial history, and there are several useful syntheses of this material.[64] Despite the great methodological and theoretical difficulties in this field, religious studies are keeping pace with these developments. We are moving towards a preliminary model of religious forms and changes in Central Africa over the past few centuries.[65] As a result it now becomes possible to fill in, albeit extremely tentatively, the kind of historical data that a treatment of aspects of Central African religion in the context of an articulation approach would require. It is only very recently that professional historians have started to work within this approach, and then only for the analysis of economic and political data which lend themselves much more readily to such application than religion does.[66] What light does this approach throw on religion?

Interpretation: (b) Marxist approaches

The paradigm of the articulation of modes of production as developed by Meillassoux and Rey, and to a lesser extent by Terray, Amin and others over the past fifteen years or so was hardly meant to tackle problems of religious analysis.[67] The primary focus of the authors has been the economic organization of local African communities, trying to identify the material aspects of production, reproduction, and control, as regulated by kinship, marriage, exchange, tribute, etc. Thus they hoped also to arrive at a better understanding of the processes by which these communities were penetrated by world capitalism. The mainstream of Marxist religious studies[68] seems to derive more directly from Marx's theory of ideology, rather than taking the detour of the recent articulation approach. So far, Marxist studies of religion have concentrated upon the ideological elements within any *one* mode of production, instead of a set of articulated modes. Houtart and Lemercinier's stimulating attempt to outline a theory of religion in the tributary mode of production[69] appears to be one of the first along this line; but, unfortunately for the Africanist, the case studies they present to develop this theory[70] all deal with South Asia.[71] Yet, if the articulation approach can safely be said to illuminate crucial aspects of recent economic and social change in Africa, as I have elsewhere claimed it does,[72] it is likely that the student of religion also will find some inspiration here.

A theoretical outline

For our purpose here, it is unnecessary to go into all the theoretical refinements of the articulation of the modes-of-production paradigm, and the fundamental debates its various protagonists have been carrying on since the 1960s. A few working definitions will suffice. A mode of production is a model that stipulates a specific arrangement according to which the productive forces (means of production, resources, labour and knowledge) existing at a particular time and place are subject to specific relations of production such as define forms of expropriation and control between the various classes of people involved in the production process. Each mode of production is characterized by one fundamental contradiction: between elders and youth in the domestic mode of production based on agriculture; between rulers (or the state) and local communities in the tributary mode; and between capitalists and workers in the capitalist mode of production.

A mode of production is in principle capable of reproducing itself: both on the demographic level (by devising ways of coping with the life-cycle of the people involved in it, and by recruiting human personnel from other modes of production through raiding, labour migration, formal education, etc.); and on the political and ideological level, where it creates and maintains the kinship, authority, legal and religious structures which shape, support, express or conceal the central contradiction on which that mode of production revolves. Capitalism, as a mode of production based on the absolute separation between workers and their means of production, reduces all aspects of economic and social life to commodities, to such an extent that the economy becomes not only determinant (setting the confines for the mode's survival and reproduction), but also absolutely dominant, making all kinship, political, legal and religious aspects or levels of the mode of production subservient to the economy. In other modes of production, any of these levels may be dominant. As an abstract model, no mode of production is ever fully realized within a given historic society. All societies consist of a combination of several modes of production in varying degrees of actual realization; such a combination is called a social formation.

Articulation between co-existing modes of production provides the internal structure within a social formation: surpluses generated in one mode are extracted so as to reproduce another dominant mode. Thus long-distance trade in pre-colonial Africa can be seen as a device to link ('articulate') a tributary mode of production to the mercantile capitalist mode as existing in distant metropoles. Labour migration in colonial and post-colonial Africa is a similar device, linking domestic communities to industrial capitalism as existing in the African submetropoles (e.g., mines, towns and commercial farms of South Africa, and the Zambian line of rail). In general, the articulation of pre-capitalist modes of production to capitalism is considered the major historical process having taken place in Africa over the last few centuries, and the necessary background for case studies of social, political or religious change.

257

In two crucial ways this approach helps us to understand the Bituma cult. First, it sheds light on the cult's history: the emergence of non-prophetic cults of affliction; the subsequent transformation of this non-prophetic substratum into such prophetic cults as Nzila, Bituma and Moya; and perhaps even the final decline of Bituma when it reverted to the form of the non-prophetic cults. Second, this approach enables us to understand somewhat better the practice of Bituma among contemporary urban Nkoya, as an aspect of urban-rural relations springing from the articulation between the capitalist and the domestic mode of production.

Cult history and articulation

In the nineteenth century dramatic changes took place in the social formation of Kaoma district. By the end of the eighteenth century, the social formation was already a highly complex one, in which, as a result of the emergence and articulation of various modes of production in previous centuries, various mutually dependent branches or forms of production[73] co-existed: highly developed hunting and gathering; rather crude fishing and farming; a limited form of domestic slavery;[74] and petty commodity production (particularly ironware) for local trade circuits. Clan chieftainship was largely concerned with ritual functions concerning the land, and with exclusive claims to certain proceeds from hunting, which were locally consumed or hoarded but were not yet circulated in long-distance trade and tribute.

Oral tradition, and written documents relating to the late nineteenth and early twentieth centuries,[75] as well as the converging evidence from scholarly studies of neighbouring areas,[76] suggest the following trends for the period starting *c*. 1800. Small militant groups coming in from the north brought a new, more exalted style of chieftainship, as well as some of the economic prerequisites (better crops, cattle, and cattle-raiding) with which to generate a surplus on which such chieftainship could thrive. Domestic slavery was greatly increased, and lost the earlier kinship connotations of pawnship. Between local communities and the emerging chiefly courts, and between courts of different importance, tributary networks were developed, along which travelled not only the products of local branches of production, but also slaves in increasing numbers. This process was further intensified by the advent, around 1850, of long-distance trade in the hands of Mambari and Swahili caravan traders, and the marked ascendance, some 200 kilometres to the west of the Luyana/Kololo state. In the last quarter of the nineteenth century the economy of that state became largely dependent upon slave labour; hence large raiding expeditions for slaves and cattle were organized, and they extended well to the east of the Nkoya lands. Whereas in the social formation before 1800 a domestic mode of production could be said to be dominant, the later period saw the gradual subordination of this mode to tributary and, via long-distance trade, mercantile-capitalist modes of production.

The boundaries of the local community, which until then had contained most of the production process and its ritual counterparts (ancestral cult, hunters' cults and land cults), ceased to be relevant. There was place for new cultic forms, which could incorporate increased stranger contacts and extension of economic and political scale, and which provided a new explanation of illness and misfortune where those ideologically referring to the domestic community were no longer convincing.[77] Cults of affliction formed an ideal solution, with their connotations of impersonality and alienness, and their explanations in terms of whimsical a-moral possession agents rather than in moral terms of breach of kin relations, or sorcery, within the domestic community. If the negation of the subjects' autonomous community by the state (in this case emergent chiefly states) is the basic contradiction underlying the tributary mode of production,[78] this negation is also reflected in the nature of the new cults, which ignore or transcend the ideological components of the domestic community.[79] Ancestors, evil fellow-men, and spirits of the wilds become supplanted by impersonal alien spirits as causes of misfortune. The commodity transactions of the caravan trade, clad as they were in an idiom in which the traders continued to observe elements peculiar to the older modes of production,[80] are reflected in the healer/patient relationship within the cults. For this relationship is ideally between strangers. Patterns of recruitment in the cult cut across existing social contacts. The cults involve entrepreneurial attitudes and cash transactions.

If the negation of the slave's link with his original community is at the root of the type of slavery widespread in late pre-colonial Central Africa, then the same negation can be seen in the impersonal, free-floating, alien agents venerated in the cults. The new modes of production emerging in the nineteenth century were closely linked to each other. Most if not all slaves were controlled by chiefs and their office-bearers; this gave these nobles unique opportunities to have a local surplus generated, available for long-distance trade. It appears that domestic slavery rapidly declined to a trade in humans from which even close kinsmen (notably sister's sons) were not excluded.

The precise inter-relations between the tributary and the mercantile-capitalist mode of production await further research. Both were still groping to establish themselves, and both never attained the full realization of their respective models. But what is important here, and fairly well documented, is the subordination of the domestic mode of production to other modes. The cults of affliction coming up in this period are the ideological counterparts of this *articulation process* – rather than any of the distinct modes of production involved in the process. But they are not just a secondary expression of non-religious structural change; they themselves helped to undermine the domestic mode by providing alternatives to its ideological aspects, by introducing new forms of circulation and interaction of people and goods beyond the group boundaries set by the domestic mode, and by adding to the extraction by chiefs and traders that by healers.

As the penetration of the capitalist mode of production in the social formation of Kaoma district proceeded (and as this social formation itself became integrated in a much wider formation: Northern Rhodesia, the capitalist world), the tributary and mercantile-capitalist modes of production (having gained dominance in the nineteenth century) were encapsulated and largely destroyed. That colonial rule was committed to the spread of capitalist relations of production no longer requires a lengthy discussion. Very soon after its imposition (1900) the flow of commodities into the area would be channelled through the rather ill-equipped rural trading stores, but particularly through the purchases by labour migrants at their distant places of work. Long-distance trade was forced to an end. The tributary mode of production was destroyed by colonial legislation abolishing slavery and tributary labour. Government subsidies allowed some of the chiefs and aristocrats to keep up the remnants of a political and ideological pre-capitalist structure, after the relations of production underlying that structure had been radically altered.[81] These subsidies were paid out of the revenues from hut tax, a direct form of surplus extraction imposed by the colonial administration, and one that soon forced people to sell their labour for money, after the rapid breakdown of local participation in the agricultural market.[82] Now that the circulation of traders, commodities and slaves (the local manifestations of extraction by an as yet invisible mercantile capitalism) had given way to the circulation of money and of labour migrants, and many people had become directly (though seldom permanently) involved in capitalist relations of production, the new cults of affliction, although they kept spreading, were no longer truly in line with the dominant social and economic contradictions in the social formation. The articulation processes they had been part of had become obsolete.

Mission Christianity, preached in Kaoma district since the 1910s, in many ways provided an ideological response appropriate to capitalist relations of production.[83] In addition to Christianity there remained room for new religious responses which, working on the locally available cultic material, offered new solutions that were somewhat less divorced from the local religious tradition, while adopting those aspects of Christianity (individual-centredness, universality) which fitted in with capitalist relations of production. Thus after 1930 a few local prophets, all of them amply exposed to Christian teaching and to labour migration, came up with radically redefined prophetic cults of affliction, that no longer conveyed just another form of anonymity and alienness along with the many outside influences people had become acquainted with in the nineteenth century. These prophets' main innovation (which made their prophetic cults the ideological counterpart of the process of direct industrial-capitalist articulation that was going on) was to claim an all-encompassing affliction agent: the High God or notions associated with him (Angel, Holy Spirit). While the non-prophetic cults were copied in their denial of the local domestic community and their entrepreneurial relations between healer and patient, a unique and exalted principle of legitimation and identification was proclaimed. This was in line with the universality and abstraction typical of the commodity-centred capitalist relations of production. In the light of the progressive encroachment of these relations of production, such forms of ethnic distance and alienness as associated with the non-prophetic cults were becoming irrelevant, as people were increasingly peasants, migrants and proletarians rather than tribesmen.

Bituma in town as articulation

These new, exalted affliction agents offered the possibility of monopolizing charisma as the basis for an inter-local cult organization.[84] All three cults referred to here initially developed such an organization, but whereas Nzila retained and greatly expanded its organization, Moya remained fairly small, and Bituma lapsed back virtually to a non-prophetic form. Above[85] I indicated weaknesses in my earlier analysis[86] of this differential development. I would now submit that it is not the urban environment of the cult members as such, but the extent of their actual commitment to capitalist relations of production, which is the crucial factor.

From my description of urban Bituma earlier in this chapter it is clear that Bituma forms one major way in whch male participants in the capitalist sector, and the monetary income generated there, are linked to people who are not themselves involved in such participation: female urban migrants, rural-based healers, and by extension the wider rural kin-group over which the revenues of the healers are distributed. Bituma is both an aspect of the articulation of the domestic and the capitalist mode of production, and a telling indication that even the male urban migrants are not so effectively steeped in the capitalist mode of production that they can afford to reject the claims which, via Bituma, the domestic mode of production is making upon their limited resources and their commitment. The fact that most male Nkoya migrants in town end up with Nkoya wives from the village (rights over whom are secured through marital payments about four times an urban healer's fee) points to the considerable parallels between the Bituma cult and marriage. Both constitute articulation. Both provide means through which the domestic mode of production, made dependent upon the capitalist mode, can yet reproduce itself – after producing the male labour force for the capitalist sector.

In the Nzila case, by contrast, one would expect not so much a large urban membership (which certainly exists), but particularly a membership which is deeply involved in capitalist relations of production, and which no longer has to rely largely on the maintenance of ties with the domestic, rural sector. What little information we have on the economic background of the Nzila members[87] seems to confirm this hypothesis. For example, Muntemba refers to the fact that in the town of Livingstone church elders in the main established Protestant church (the United Church of Zambia) also participate in Nzila; these elders are likely to be urban notables of some kind, integrated in urban capitalist and bureaucratic structures. But the data are altogether too scanty for definitive conclusions. In any case, the Nzila members do not need to reside in town for my hypothesis to be confirmed. As has been repeatedly argued,[88] the urban-rural distinction is only a secondary derivation from the more fundamental distinction between capitalist and non-capitalist modes of production. Due to the rise of cash cropping, agricultural wage labour, and civil service jobs (agricultural extension workers, game guards, etc.) in the rural areas in recent years, a growing number of rural dwellers of western Zambia have become involved in capitalist relations of production as well. In the areas where Nzila and Bituma exist side by side,[89] it is the people involved in capitalist relations of production whom one would expect to be adepts of Nzila (or of Christian churches), rather than of Bituma in its latterday, post-prophetic form.

The contemporary Nkoya situation provides a good illustration of the articulation of a domestic mode of production, stripped, to a considerable extent, of the remains of the tributary mode, and articulated to the dominant industrial capitalist mode. The old branches of production organized by kinship are more or less surviving, although they have been encroached upon by state control (alienation of land for game reserves and (para-)statal agricultural enterprise; and prohibitions on hunting). Likewise they have been eroded by the exodus of male labour; [90] the penetration of capitalist consumer markets (all clothing, most implements, and some food, are now bought from outside); and the introduction, at a limited scale, of cash cropping and agricultural wage labour.

Adult males participate as migrants in the urban capitalist economy, and a minority of them manage to set up and maintain urban nuclear families which, if continuously successful in town, are going to contribute directly to the reproduction of the capitalist sector. However, the footing of these urban migrants is particularly insecure; and many of the members of their households may ultimately end up in the rural sector. While remaining in town, these migrants can find greater security in the domestic domain by participation in dyadic networks as well as collective ceremonies and rituals, which encompass both urban wage-earners, recent arrivals, urban drop-outs about to return home and people without any participation in the urban relations of production: women and villagers. The domestic sector extends well into the urban areas, and into the households of the urban wage-earners. Bituma provides a setting for this interpenetration, as well as a means to re-circulate money earned in the urban capitalist sector to those debarred from it. It is an instrument of articulation, and notably one which syphons resources back into the domestic sector, contributing to the latter's reproduction rather than to its exploitation.

Conclusion

This perspective upon a Central African cult of affliction in its historical development and its urban manifestations may suggest the potential of the articulation approach for religious analysis. However, we should not overlook the many great problems which remain.

One would like to be able to make more precise pronouncements as to the symbolic and structural transformations which lead to a specific form of religious innovation, given a specific articulation of modes of reproduction. Why does the articulation of domestic mode of production with a tributary or mercantile-capitalist mode produce non-prophetic cults of affliction of precisely the type generated in Central Africa since about 1850? Only a much more specific spelling-out of the transformations, forward and backward, between relations of production and specific ideas concerning supernatural entities, mechanisms of causation, etc. can help us here. And in addition to this theoretical exercise, much wider comparison is needed. The apparent spate of cults of affliction in many parts of Africa in a context of articulation between the domestic mode and other modes apart from industrial capitalism,[91] suggests that over a considerable part of the continent similar mechanisms have been at work. But as it is, such historical explanations as I can tentatively offer here are not only curtailed by the obvious limitations of a mere chapter, but also seem to have a certain *ad hoc* element about them.

If one were to move deeper into the conceptual framework and the symbolism of these new cults arising out, and partly constituting, the coupling of modes of production, one would no doubt be drawn in the direction of analyses in the manner of Victor Turner or Richard Werbner. How could both approaches be brought to cross-fertilization, rendering those authors' analyses more sensitive to relations of production, and an analysis like the present one more sensitive to 'inclusiveness/exclusiveness', 'focusing', and 'processual symbolic analysis' (the catchwords of Werbner's and Turner's recent work)?

In a broader context than religious studies, one might well wonder whether the articulation approach to urban-rural relations does do full justice to the cultural and psychological dimensions of urban ethnicity. Is not an element involved of identity, subconscious orientation as instilled through experiences early in life? And if so, does that identity directly spring from the articulation process, or does it constitute an independent factor to be reckoned with? The case of A. L. Epstein gives us something to think about. Twenty years after *Politics in an Urban African Community*,[92] he reassessed his Zambian ethnicity data, and, after all the manipulation and networks that was Manchester, came up with an analysis stressing[93]

methods and approaches more fine-grained than those adopted hitherto which take full account of the interplay of the external and the internal, the objective and the subjective, and the sociological and psychological elements which are always present in the formation of ethnic identity.

I am not for a moment meaning to come back on my steps and to claim that, when all is said and done, Bituma in town is simply an 'expression of ethnic identity', the penetration, in town, of, e.g., 'rural forms so deeply anchored in the Nkoya collective subconscious that these tribesmen cannot do without'.[94] I am convinced that the notion of the articulation of modes of production gives us a genuine insight in crucial aspects both of this cult and of the situation of the people engaged in it. But I am also convinced that this is not the last word. As we continue to collect data, and to refine what is still a very unsatisfactory theory, a more mature approach will emerge in which all these perspectives which as yet I have been unable to integrate into my argument will converge.

Chapter 8

Religious innovation and political conflict in Zambia: the Lumpa rising[1]

The Lumpa problem

When in January 1976, in response to a complex national and international crisis, President Kaunda of Zambia announced a state of public emergency, he in fact merely re-activated the dormant state of emergency that had been declared in July 1964 by the then Governor of Northern Rhodesia, in connexion with the rising of Alice Lenshina's separatist church, commonly called 'Lumpa'. In the rural areas of north-eastern Zambia the fighting between state troops and the church's members had ceased in October 1964, leaving an estimated death toll of about 1,500.[2] But the state of emergency (implying increased powers for the government executive) was allowed to continue. It was renewed every six months and lived through both the attainment of territorial independence (October 1964) and the creation (December 1972) of the Second Republic under the exclusive leadership of Kaunda's United National Independence Party (UNIP). The Lumpa aftermath, including the continued presence of thousands of Lumpa refugees in Zaïre just across the Zambian border, was repeatedly cited as a reason for this continuation.[3]

It is not only in this respect that the Lumpa rising at the verge of independence appears as a key episode for an understanding of post-colonial Zambia. The event lives on as an important reference point in the idiom of the Zambian elite. Sometimes reference is made to it to express governmental and party assertiveness, as in Kaunda's remark at a mass rally in January 1965:[4]

> We have no intention whatsoever . . . of legislating against the
> formation of any other party, so long as their behaviour inside

Parliament and outside is responsible. If they misbehave, in accordance with the law of the country we shall ban them. If they misbehave, I repeat misbehave, we shall ban them as we banned the Lumpa Church.

More often, the Lumpa example is used to point out the dangers of religious sectarianism for national unity and stable government. This is most clear in the case of African Watchtower, one of Zambia's largest religious groupings, with a long history of clashes with the colonial government. Shortly after independence, Watchtower adherents incurred the wrath of government and the party for their refusal to register as voters, buy party cards or honour the Zambian flag and national anthem. In that context, comparisons with the Lumpa Church were frequently made, partly in justification of the tough measures taken against Watchtower.[5] The use of Lumpa as a reference point, and the comparison between Lumpa and Watchtower, have become so commonplace that the Zambian historian Meebelo,[6] himself a government official, somewhat anachronistically reaches for the Lumpa example (1963–4) in order to stress features of early Watchtower in 1918.[7] Likewise, reference to the Lumpa events played an important role in the discussion, within the Zambian government, that led to the final banning of the Zambian wing of the Zaïre-founded 'Church of Christ on Earth through Simon Kimbangu'.

But the most typical attitude towards the Lumpa episode among the Zambian elite has been one of embarrassment and silence. One gets the impression of a home truth that one is not at all keen to share with outsiders. The rising was not only a national crisis but also a crisis in the home ties and kin relations of UNIP's top leadership. Chinsali district, where the conflict concentrated, was the home both of the nationalist leaders Kaunda and Kapwepwe, and the Lumpa foundress, Lenshina. Kaunda and Lenshina had been at the same school. Robert Kaunda, the President's elder brother, was a top-ranking Lumpa leader, whilst their mother, the late Mrs Helen Kaunda, was reported as having been 'close to the movement'.[8] But it was not just childhood reminiscences and family ties that made Kaunda's decision, three months before independence, 'to use force against the Lumpas . . ., as he told me at the time, the hardest decision he had ever taken in his life'.[9]

The long and hard struggle for independence had seemed over with the January 1964 election, which gave the then Northern Rhodesia its first African party government under UNIP.[10] The world's eyes were on what was soon to be Zambia. After campaigning for black government for years, UNIP, Kaunda and his cabinet, however 'well-balanced and extremely capable',[11] now had to prove themselves. The country was ready to reap all the economic, social and moral benefits that self-government was expected to entail.

At this extremely inconvenient moment the Lumpa rising had to occur. It demanded a death toll far exceeding that of the general clashes (commonly called 'Chachacha') between the colonial government and the nationalists in 1961.[12] The rising manifested the existence of massive and intransigent opposition to UNIP and to an African government, in the part of Zambia that had been UNIP's main rural stronghold. For years the UNIP leadership, and foremost Kaunda, had through tremendous efforts rather successfully attempted to keep the rank and file of their party membership from violent anti-white agitation; but now the Lumpa rising forced an African government to direct a predominantly African military force against fellow-Africans. Kaunda was compelled to suspend his Gandhist principles of non-violence, which until then had been such an integral aspect of his identity as a nationalist leader, and of his splendid international image. Also, the rising could not fail to focus attention on such acts of violence by local UNIP members as were, from the beginning, recognized to constitute part of its causes.[13] An extensive process of attempted reconciliation, undertaken by Kaunda and other senior UNIP leaders in the months preceding the final conflict, had failed. Instead of the nationalists' promise of a new, proud African order there was chaos and fratricide. White racialists, and critics of nationalism, could sit back and rejoice. The blow to nationalist self-confidence was almost fatal.

While the insurrection was effectively quashed, angry declarations of the obvious juridical justifications of this state action, as issued by Kaunda and his cabinet, could barely hide the distress and embarrassment of the nationalist leaders. In the terrible dilemma, it was soon realized that reconciliation not retaliation was the only way out. Whilst Lumpa's alleged fanaticism, criminality and heresies were vehemently condemned, measures were taken to limit the number of casualties to an absolute minimum. Local people who were loyal to the state and the party were urged to refrain from all retaliation. Rehabilitation camps were erected and resettling campaigns were vigorously undertaken. When captured, the Lumpa Church's senior leadership, including Lenshina, were treated respectfully. An amnesty for the Lumpa rank and file was declared in 1968. However, the ban on the Lumpa Church imposed in August 1964 was not lifted, and Lenshina remained in custody.

After the rising the Lumpa adherents found themselves dispersed all over north-eastern Zambia. Because of difficulties in resettling in their home areas, among people with whom they had fought, a gradual exodus took place to Zaïre. In the years 1965–8 the number of Lumpa refugees in that country increased to about 19,000, and only about 3,000 returned to Zambia after concentrated governmental effort in 1968.[14] The Lumpas in exile have continued to form a reminder of what by now has taken the proportion of a major trauma of the Zambian nationalist dream. The main other reminder consists of the occasional trials of individuals who within Zambia were caught in the act of reviving the Lumpa Church's organization and ritual (revolving particularly around Lenshina's talented hymns). Such trials, in which again a reconciliatory attitude prevails, occurred in small numbers throughout the 1960s and early 1970s.[15] The final gesture of reconciliation was Lenshina's release in December 1975.[16]

The extent to which the Lumpa rising and its aftermath does constitute a collective trauma for the Zambian elite can also be gauged from the silence surrounding it. The occasional vindications by the UNIP leadership at the time of the rising, justifying state action, and Meebelo's cursory reference as cited above are virtually the only published statements on the subject by members of the Zambian elite. The 1965 official _Report of the Commission of Enquiry into the Former Lumpa Church_[17] is not easily available within Zambia. Expatriate writers who covered the details of the creation of independent Zambia, and who therefore for their data collection and publication were highly dependent on official introductions and clearances, are remarkably reticent on the subject.[18] They have certainly not attempted any interpretation of the significance of the Lumpa rising. The final conflict, and the preceding rise and development of the Lumpa Church, are still considered topics too sensitive for research within Zambia.

Thus in this time of rapidly expanding insights into African religious innovation, our knowledge of and insight into the Lumpa episode remains rather stagnant. At present, the literature on the subject mainly consists of the following categories of publications:[19]

1 Exploratory scholarly studies of the Lumpa Church as an independent church in colonial Northern Rhodesia, written before the final conflict broke out.[20]
2 A host of journalistic pieces covering the events of the 1964 rising.
3 Scholarly articles and notes in which soon after the rising a considerable number of specialists on African religious innovation and Central African society interpreted the conflict, thus providing often

hurried attempts to add a scientific background to the journalistic accounts. Publications in this category mainly refer to the pre-conflict studies under 1.[21]

4   A few scholarly publications in which the available material, including some unpublished data, is synthesized, and attempts are made at more comprehensive interpretation.[22]

The empirical basis is still rather scanty, and so far there is no accomplished full-size study[23] interpreting the Lumpa episode within a widely acceptable theoretical framework. Yet the literature is sufficiently voluminous for the Lumpa Church to become a standard reference in Africanist writing over the past two decades. Here, to give a few instances, Lumpa is cited as an institutionalized witchcraft-eradication movement;[24] as a case in point for the claim that independent churches re-enact traditional opportunities for female leadership;[25] as an example of the religious expression of nationalism;[26] as a 'stark corrective [of the view that] all anti-administration movements were forerunners of mass nationalism';[27] and, finally, as an example of the post-colonial rivalry between state and church.[28]

As this selection of contradictory references makes clear, the relations between the Lumpa Church and the power structure of Zambian society, both before and after Independence, constitute a major interpretational difficulty. It is in this respect that Lumpa forms a key to the understanding of contemporary Zambia.

My claim of Lumpa's significance is somewhat at variance with the attention given to the rising in the two main recent studies of Zambian politics.[29] Both studies summarize the basic facts concerning the rising and its aftermath. However, in their interpretation they are rather reserved.

Pettman writes:[30]

Subnational threats to Zambia's unity and security are not only seen in tribalism, regionalism, and other sectional interests, but also in group loyalties like those of the Lumpas and the Watchtower Sect. These religious groups are held to differ from others in that their behaviour and beliefs are 'political', a perceived challenge to the existing or desired authority of the party and government.

Correct as this assessment may be, as an analysis of a major episode in modern Zambian politics it remains on the surface. In what respect are such primarily religious phenomena as Lumpa and Watchtower, *political*? Why do they represent a threat to the political establishment, and why is the latter's perception of this threat sufficient reason for suppression and violence? These are some of the questions Pettman ignores, and to which the present chapter attempts to give an answer.

In Tordoff's book, *Politics in Zambia,* Molteno's brief discussion of Lumpa and Watchtower[31] revolves around the question: what cleavages exist in modern Zambian society that could be a mobilization basis for political conflict *within* the existing, formal party organization and the representative institutions of the Zambian political system? For Molteno, religious affiliation 'could form the social basis for political conflict, but . . . has not done so'.[32] Within the context of his argument, Molteno's narrow conception of political conflict is justified; and it conveniently excludes Lumpa and Watchtower troubles from a discussion of political conflict. Yet conflict it remains, and with far-reaching implications for the distribution of power – the subject matter of politics. Therefore, Molteno's explanation of why the unmistakable religious cleavage has failed to precipitate political conflict in the narrower sense of the word, does not convince:[33]

> The reasons are that Watch Tower and Lumpa together form less than 5% of the population, and both movements in any case reject political participation.

Is Molteno suggesting that if there had been more Lumpa adherents, they would have challenged UNIP in the arena of Zambia's formal political institutions, instead of engaging in battle against government troops, brandishing their battle axes and spears and firing an occasional muzzle-loader?

What makes Molteno's approach unhelpful for an understanding of Lumpa, is that it takes the existing, formal political system, such as defined by the political elite themselves, as its exclusive frame of reference. This would deny us the possibility of exploring the limits of that system, and of identifying such social groups and institutions as, peripheral to or outside the formal political system, may legitimate it, challenge it, or opt out of it. If it is true that any political system can only be understood in its wider social context, this is particularly so in the case of a post-colonial state that still has to consolidate itself through processes of incorporation and legitimation. The significance of Lumpa (and of Watchtower) is that it demonstrates the limits of these processes. Beyond these limits a considerable number of Zambians refuse to be drawn into the post-colonial state, and reject its claims to legitimate power. Studying the Zambian political system from this

271

angle helps to reveal its dynamic, even precarious nature – instead of taking this system for granted as an established and self-contained fact.

The Zambian political system is of recent date. It is not yet so deeply rooted in every part of the Zambian soil and population that it can afford to ignore challenges from outside this political system, challenges that undermine its legitimation and threaten its most fundamental assumptions. It is along such lines that I will attempt, in this chapter, to interpret Lumpa's relations with nationalism and the state against the background of the process of class formation. Such an approach is only meaningful if the following related problems are discussed at the same time. Because of what structural conditions should the post-colonial state experience difficulties of incorporation and legitimation, particularly with regard to peasants in remote rural areas? For the rural adherents of Lumpa form only a small part of the large class of Zambian peasants; and difficulties similar to Lumpa exist elsewhere in rural Zambia, although without the specific Lumpa features of a large, rural-based independent church and armed mass resistance.[34] Moreover, we shall have to identify Lumpa's specific dimensions of power, particularly in terms of class and class struggle. Thus we may begin to understand Lumpa's relations with nationalism and the state, including the final conflict. Finally, as a religious movement, Lumpa is only one in a long series of religious innovations that have occurred in Central Africa during the last centuries. The latest decade has seen considerable growth of our insight into these religious innovations, their inter-connectedness, and their causes. What new light does this emerging, comprehensive analysis of Central African religious innovation throw upon the Lumpa movement?

As my argument develops, it will become clear that these several problems are intimately related, mainly through the themes of urban-rural relations, incorporation processes, and class formation – which are in fact three different terms for the same phenomenon. Meanwhile, the relations between religion, politics and the economic order, as exemplified by the Lumpa problem, constitute a core problem of society and history. The present argument, however ambitious, does not pretend to solve the problem. But perhaps it rearranges the pieces in a way that may be helpful towards a future solution.

Reserving the order in which the specific problems raised by Lumpa were mentioned above, I shall now first discuss the background of religious innovation in Central Africa; then place Lumpa in this context; finally, after a discussion of its confrontation with nationalism, I shall deal with the problems of incorporation and legitimation of the Zambian state from a more general point of view.

The background of religious innovation in Zambia

Superstructural reconstruction

In every society the members have explicit and mutually shared ideas concerning the universe, society, and themselves. These ideas are supported by implicit, often unconscious cognitive structures such as are studied by structural and cognitive anthropology. The total arrangement of these elements can be called the symbolic order, or the super-structure. The superstructure defines a society's central concerns, major institutions, and basic norms and values. Against these, actual behaviour can be evaluated in terms of good and evil, status and success. The superstructure is the central repository of meaning for the members of society. It offers them an explanatory framework. While thus satisfying the participants' intellectual needs, the superstructure also, on the level of action, patterns behaviour in recognized, predictable units (roles), which the participants learn in the course of their socialization. Thus the superstructure provides the participants with a sense of meaningfulness and competence in their dealings with each other and with the non-human world. Ritual and ceremonies, as well as internalization in the personality structure of individual members of society, reinforce the superstructure and let it persist over time.

On the other hand, every society has what we can call an infrastructure: the organization of the production upon which the participants' lives depend, and particularly such differential distribution of power and resources as dominate the relations of production.

There is no simple solution for the long-standing problem of the relation between superstructure and infrastructure. The problem is particularly manifest in the study of religious innovation, political ideology and mass mobilization. When studied in some concrete setting, it is often possible to determine the infrastructural conditions accompanying these phenomena; yet superstructural elements – the participants' explicit or implicit ideas – often appear as direct and major factors in these contexts. The problem becomes acute in situations of rapid change. For in a relatively stable situation infrastructure and superstructure are likely to be attuned to each other. The superstructure conveys meaning and competence, which are ultimately derived from the way in which the superstructure expresses, reinforces and legitimates the infrastructure.

But in situations of rapid change the relative autonomy of infrastructure and superstructure becomes more pronounced. As the infrastructure undergoes profound changes, the superstructure has no longer a grip on, is no longer fundamentally relevant to, the practical experience of participants in economic life. The superstructure therefore ceases to convey meaning and competence. This creates in the participants existential problems: the subjective experience of alienation. For these problems two solutions exist. Upon the debris of an obsolete superstructure, the participants may try to construct a new superstructure that is more in line with the altered relations of production; I shall call this *superstructural reconstruction*. Alternatively, participants may attack the alienation problem on the infrastructural level: reversing or redefining, once more, the altered distribution of power and resources and the production process as a whole, so as to bring it in line again with their superstructure that has remained virtually unaltered.

A dialectical relation exists between such infrastructural reconstruction and the superstructural solution. For infrastructural reconstruction requires the co-ordinated action of a large number of individuals; to enable this, new superstructural elements (ideology, new roles within new groups) have to be created. On the other hand, participants take to superstructural reconstruction in response, in the first instance, to their individual existential problems, and not on the basis of a detached scientific analysis of their society's changed infrastructure; in other words, the new ideas the participants produce derive at first from the symbolic order and do not necessarily correspond closely with the altered infrastructure. Therefore, their experiments with new ideas, even if ultimately called forth by infrastructural change, may often miss the mark and, failing to restore the correspondence between superstructure and infrastructure, may instead lead on to a new symbolic order that is just as remote as their old superstructure from current infrastructural conditions.

The emergence of a new superstructure is a highly creative process. It requires the efforts of visionary individuals who experiment with both old and new symbols (the latter invented, or introduced from elsewhere). The innovators generate new combinations and permutations of their symbolic material, and offer their tentative results to the surrounding population. This population shares with the innovators in their midst problems of interpretation and competence, as caused by the divorce between infrastructure and superstructure. Therefore, an innovator's proposal of a new superstructure (as one individual's solution to his own problems) may yet appeal to the population at large as a likely solution of their own, similar problems of alienation. The visionary's proposal is therefore likely to be adopted at first. On the subjective level, it may give psychological relief, as long as the participants are confident that the longed-for solution has been found. But whether the proposed superstructural innovation actually does or does not correspond more closely than the old superstructure with the altered infrastructure will not be immediately clear. The participants will find this out gradually, by on the one hand living through their superstructural innovation, on the other hand continuing to participate in the altered relations of production. In most cases the superstructural reconstruction attempt will turn out to be off the mark. After initial success it will die down, as the people become increasingly aware that the new ideas do not fundamentally relate to the actually prevailing structure of production. Sometimes, however, superstructural innovation may tune in with the altered relations of production, and in this way the subjective experience of alienation may be dissolved. A truly revolutionary situation occurs when superstructural innovation at the same time stipulates such infrastructural changes as curb alienation at the infrastructural level, i.e., in terms of expropriation and control. Then a lasting change of the society becomes possible.

Meanwhile, in order to work at all if only during a short time, attempts at superstructural reconstruction apparently have to do three things. First, they have to propound a new arrangement of symbols. Thus they can restore the sense of meaningfulness, subjectively and temporarily, even if the infrastructure from which such meaningfulness ultimately derives is left unaffected. Such a new arrangement of symbols must then focus on symbols that are eminently effective and unassailable in the eyes of the participants. The new superstructural reconstruction may be predominantly religious (e.g., Lumpa), political (e.g., Zambian nationalism), or presumably take some other course; essential is, in all these cases, that the central symbols appear absolute to the participants.

Second, superstructural reconstruction must restore the sense of competence by stipulating new forms of action. This action may vary from collective ritual to campaigns to check party cards (such as have been conducted by UNIP members in Zambia). It is important that participants are brought to look upon such action as bringing about the new, desired social order where their alienation problems will no longer exist. At the same time these actions translate the movement's central symbols into the context of tangible, lived-through reality, thus reinforcing them.

Finally, attempts at superstructural reconstruction, in order to be at least initially successful, cannot stop at the level of merely individual interpretations and actions, but must create new group structures (e.g., restructured rural communities, churches, political parties) within which the participants can lead their new lives once their alienation problems have been solved subjectively. The agents of superstructural reconstruction will have to present recruitment into these new groups as the solution to the alienation problems of individual people. Expansion of the new group is often considered the main method to create a new society.

Religious innovation in Zambia as superstructural reconstruction

As Vansina pointed out,[35] throughout Central Africa a fairly similar superstructure prevailed before the recent processes of social change made their impact. On the infrastructural level, two major changes occurred since the eighteenth century. The first consisted in the increasing involvement of local farming, fishing and hunting communities (which until then had been largely self-contained) in a new mode of production that was dominated by long-distance trade and by the payment of tribute to the states that emerged in Central Africa, partly as a result of such trade.

The second major infrastructural change was the penetration of capitalism. Directly, capitalism induced the rural population to leave their villages and work as migrant labourers in the mines, farms and towns of Central and Southern Africa; to adapt their rural economy, and increasingly their total life, to the consumption of manufactured commodities; and, in selected areas, to embark on small-scale capitalist agricultural production. Indirectly, the infrastructural accommodation to capitalism was promoted by the colonial state; e.g., by the imposition of hut tax; the destruction of pre-existing networks of trade and tribute; the transformation of indigenous rulers into petty administrators for the colonial state; the regulation of migration between the rural areas and the places of work; the provision of schools to serve the need for skilled workers and clerks; urban housing; medical services; the occasional promotion of African commercial farming, etc. Admittedly, the relations between the colonial state and capitalism are rather more complex than suggested here, and failure to work out these relations (even although such had been impossible within the scope of the present chapter) is one of the shortcomings of my argument.

The emergence of the trade-tribute mode of production and the expansion of capitalism both constituted infrastructural changes of sufficient scope to provide test cases for my provisional theory of superstructural reconstruction. There is no *a priori* reason why disjunction between an altered infrastructure and an old superstructure should lead to predominantly *religious* superstructural reconstruction. Historical evidence on Central Africa is still rather scanty for the precolonial period, but rather abundant for the colonial era. From this evidence one gets the impression that religious innovation has for long constituted the main response to recent infrastructural change. Only after the Second World War mass nationalism appeared as a political form of superstructural reconstruction, in addition to current religious innovation. Probably this preponderance of religious superstructural reconstruction has systematic reasons which a more developed theory may identify in future.

An important *ad hoc* explanation seems to lie in the fact that among twentieth-century Zambians the concepts of politics as a distinct sector of society is a recent innovation. The modern concept of politics, just like that of religion, can only be meaningful among the members of a highly differentiated, complex society, where institutional spheres have acquired considerable autonomy *vis-à-vis* one another. Contemporary Zambia has become such a society. But sections of the rural population continue to reject this differentiated view of politics. Instead they have a rather holistic conception of society, in which religious, political and economic power merge to a considerable extent.[36] In this respect many peasants have retained the basic outlook of the old superstructure, in which religious and non-religious aspects appear to have merged almost entirely.

In the old superstructure, the link with the local dead was the main legitimation for residence, political office, and for such a variety of specialist roles as divining, healing, hunting, ironworking and musical crafts. Through residence, veneration of the local dead, and ritual focusing on land spirits, a special ritual link with the land was established. Without such a link no success could be expected in economically vital undertakings such as agriculture, fishing, hunting and collecting. The participant's view of the society and of an individual's career arranged village life, the economic process, politics and ritual in one comprehensive framework, where each part had meaning by reference to all others. This view was, therefore, religious as much as it was political or economic.

When the trade-tribute mode of production expanded, the emergent major chiefs initially had to legitimize their political and economic power in terms of this same view of society. Chiefly cults came up which enabled the chiefs to claim ritual power over the land's fertility, either through ritual links with deceased predecessors, or through non-royal priests or councillors representing the original 'owners of the land'.[37] Thus, as a result of infrastructural change, symbolic themes already present in the superstructure were redefined; a new power distribution was acknowledged in the superstructure; and a pattern that in the old superstructure referred to merely local conditions was now applied to extensive regional political structures which often comprised more than one ethnic group. However, in this altered superstructure the merging between religious and political aspects was still largely retained.

Along with these chiefly cults, two other types of religious innovation can be traced back to the late precolonial period and to the infrastructural changes then occurring: the appearance of prophets and the emergence of cults of affliction. Cults of affliction concentrate on the individual, whose physical and/or mental suffering they interpret in terms of possession by a specific spirit, whilst treatment mainly consists of initiation as a member of the cult venerating that spirit. Central African prophets and the movements they trigger fall into three sub-types: the ecological prophet whose main concern is with fertility and the land; the eschatological prophet who predicts the imminent end of the world such as it is known to his audience; and the affliction prophet who establishes a new, regionally-organized cult of affliction, which in many respects resembles an independent church. For an initial treatment of these main types, and references, I refer to Carter[38] and my own work[39] as collected in the present volume. Prophetic cults of these sub-types, and cults of affliction, have continued to appear in Central Africa during the colonial period, and still represent major forms of religion among the Central African peasants. But in addition the colonial era saw new types of religious innovation. Preachers and dippers (advocating baptism through immersion) appeared. They were connected, some more closely than others, with the African Watchtower movement, which in itself derived indirectly from the North American Jehovah's Witnesses. There were other independent churches which pursued more or less clearly a Christian idiom. Finally, mission Christianity had in fact penetrated before the imposition of colonial rule (1900), but started to gain momentum much later.

Let us first consider all these cases of religious innovation as superstructural experiments, which propounded a new symbolic order.

278

Despite their differences in idiom, ritual and organizational structure, it is amazing to see how the same few trends in symbolic development dominate them all.[40] All struggle with the conception of time. The cyclical present implicit in the old superstructure (highlighting agriculture, hunting, and gathering on the scale of the small village community) becomes obsolete. In the course of these religious innovations, it gives way to a linear time perspective that emphasizes personal careers and historical development, even to the extent of interpreting history as a process of salvation in the Christian sense.[41] In some of these religious innovations, the linear perspective is again supplanted by the eschatological: the acute sense of time drawing to an end. Moreover, almost all these innovations try to move away from the 'ecological' concern for the land and fertility that dominated the old superstructure. The village dead as major supernatural entities venerated in ritual give way to other, less particularistic entities, especially the High God.

In line with this, all these innovations tend to move away from taking the old village community, in its archetypical form, as the basic concept of society. In the cults of affliction this process manifests itself in their extreme emphasis on the suffering individual, and their underplaying of morality and social obligations. In some of the other religious innovations the same process reaches further: they explicitly strive towards the creation of a new and fundamentally different community, a new society to be brought about by the new religious inspiration and new ritual.

Finally, in so far as in the old superstructure sorcery was considered the main threat to human society, these religious innovations each try to formulate alternatives to sorcery. The cults of affliction and the mission churches attribute misfortune and suffering to causes altogether different from those indicated by sorcery. Most of the other innovations continue to accept the reality of sorcery but try to eradicate it once for all so as to make the new, transformed community possible.

The constant occurrence of these themes throughout recent religious innovation in Central Africa suggests that underneath the several types, each representing scores of individual religious movements, one overall and persistent process of superstructural change took place, in which the same symbolic material was manipulated within rather narrow limits.

When we try to relate these superstructural experiments to infrastructural change, it becomes necessary to distinguish between two main streams of superstructural reconstruction. One stream is of exclusively rural origin; the religious innovators and their followers are peasants. This applies to cults of affliction, and to the cults created by ecological, eschatological and affliction prophets. The other stream springs from what we can provisionally call the 'intensive contact situation'. This comprises the places of work which attracted labour migrants from throughout Central Africa (mines, farms and towns) and the rural extensions of these centres: district administrative centres (*bomas*); rural Christian missions; and military campaigns involving thousands of African carriers, and fewer soldiers, near the Zambian–Tanzanian border in the First World War. Watchtower dippers and preachers, other independent churches, and mission Christianity are the religious innovations belonging to this second stream. The two streams roughly coincide with the division rural-urban. But the following argument will make clear that much more is involved than a purely geographical or demographic criterion. This justifies my classifying of such countryside phenomena as *bomas*, missions, farms and military campaigns in the scond stream.

Typical of the first, truly rural stream is that it comprises people still largely involved in a pre-capitalist mode of production: shifting cultivation, hunting and gathering. State expansion (before and after the imposition of colonial rule) and the impact of capitalism have infringed on their local autonomy, draining their products and labour force (through slave-raiding, tribute, forced labour and urbanization) and encroaching on their rights on local land, hunting and fishing (e.g., by the creation of chiefs' hunting reserves, and later by the founding of commercial farms, town, mines, native reserves and forest reserves). The infrastructure of their local society has been deeply affected by these developments. From free, autonomous farmers whose system of production was effectively contained within their social horizon and subject to their own control, they became a peasant class in a worldwide society.

But while the facts of this process of incorporation and expropriation are unmistakable and have come to affect every aspect of village life, the agents of control in their new situation have largely remained invisible at the village level. The physical outlets of the state and of the capitalist economy were confined to the district centres and the towns along the line of rail, outside the everyday experience of the peasants. Particularly after the creation of indirect rule (around 1930), administrators and peasants alike could foster the illusion of an essentially intact 'traditional' society whose time-honoured social institutions, though heavily assailed (after all, there was the reality of incorporation and alienation), were still functioning. Under these circumstances, the rural population's reaction against being forced into a peasant class position could hardly be expected to confront directly the outside forces responsible for their expropriation. One does not expect strongly anti-colonial responses in this context. A pre-condition for such responses would have been that the peasants had acquired some explicit assessment of the power situation in the wider society in so far as this affected their situation – and were prepared to challenge these structures. But as Gluckman pointed out in one of his most comprehensive analyses of political change in Southern and Central Africa:[42]

> There were plenty of hostilities [between black and white] ; but
> they did not continually affect the daily life of Africans; and the
> picture of Africans in constant and unceasing antagonism to whites
> is false for the rural areas.

Instead, the peasants sought a solution for their predicament of alienation entirely at the local level; and not primarily through the creation of new relations of production, but mainly through the formulation of a new superstructure. The innovators' messages and their ritual, though explicable from the predicament of 'peasantization', in nearly all cases remained without overt references to this predicament. The various rural-based religious innovations were attempts to render, on a local scale, village life once again meaningful by reference to new symbols, restoring the sense of competence by new ritual. Whereas the cults of affliction attempted to do this on the exclusively individual level (and thus dealt with only part of the problem, even at the mere superstructural level), the various prophetic cults went further; they aimed at ushering the local population into a radically new community. Usually this community was conceived entirely in ritual terms. Most prophetic cults did not attempt to work out the infra-structural requirements, in terms of relations of production, by which such a new community might really have formed a lasting answer to the predicament of peasantization. Lumpa was an important exception to this. Divorced from a production base, in other words entirely based on an illusion, most cults of affliction and prophetic cults soon lost their vigour. But their idiom remained attractive: in many regions we see a succession of such cults, at intervals of a few years or decades.

The second stream of superstructural reconstruction sprang from a quite different social situation. In the places of migrant work, the *bomas*, the missions, and while involved in a military campaign, the Africans experienced the distant effects of the expansion of state systems and capitalism. In general, they were born and raised within the peasant context indicated above, retaining more or less close links with their rural kin. Yet they had entered into a different class position, or were on their way to doing so. They lived outside their villages, in a social setting dominated not by the inclusive, reciprocal social relationships typical of the village, but by formal organizations, patterned after those of modern North Atlantic society. Their daily working experience was determined by forms of control characteristic of capitalist relations of production. In this situation, their livelihood was entirely dependent upon their taking part in the production process as wage-labourers. Therefore their class position was largely that of proletarians, even though the majority attempted to keep open the lines back into the village, and still had rights to rural land should they return home.

The forces of the state and capitalism, that in the villages remained distant, anonymous and often below the threshold of explicit awareness, were in this proletarian situation blatantly manifest. These forces pervaded every aspect of the worker's social experience, and found a personified manifestation in concrete people: white employers, foremen, administrative officers and missionaries. Exploitation, economic insecurity, humiliation and racial intimidation were the specific forms in which the causes of the African predicament were visibly driven home in this situation.

Essentially all this applies equally to the rural Christian missions. I am not denying that the flavour of human relations in the missions may have been somewhat more humanitarian than at the migrants' places of work. But infrastructurally the missions represented a social setting very similar to the latter, in such terms as: formal, bureaucratic forms of organization and control; race relations; predominance of capitalism, as manifested in exclusive land rights, wage labour, and distribution of manufactured commodities.[43]

Africans in the intensive contact situation were experiencing problems of alienation rather similar to those of their kinsmen in the village. But their response had to be different. Well advanced in the process of proletarization, they had acquired a working knowledge and understanding of capitalist structures. They could no longer take the strictly local, rural scene as their exclusive frame of reference. Like the peasants, they felt the existential need for reconstruction, but then reconstruction of the wider society and particularly of those manifest (albeit often secondary) aspects of the power distribution therein that had caused their most bitter experiences.

For many thousands of people in colonial Zambia, mission-propagated Christianity seemed to provide the solution they were looking for. This religious innovation promised a new life and a new society. Its organizational structure as well as its moral and ethical codes were, not surprisingly, well attuned to colonial society and capitalism. However, for this very reason conversion did not solve the predicament of alienation; it added but a new dimension to it. A substantial proportion of independent Christian churches in Zambia were founded as a result of African converts realizing that joining a mission church had by no means offered them the solution for the problems engendered by the intensive contact situation.

In this intensive contact situation a general and explicit reaction was generated against white domination in both the political and the religious field. Springing from the same setting, the political and religious responses were rather parallel and initially merged to a considerable degree. African Watchtower and other independent churches (along with the black-controlled African Methodist Episcopal Church, as introduced from North America via South Africa), are the more predominantly religious manifestations of the second, non-rural stream of superstructural reconstruction. The political manifestations led through Welfare Societies and labour agitation at the Copperbelt to the nationalist movement which took a concrete form after the Second World War.

Given the fact of circulatory labour migration, in which a large proportion of the Central African male population was involved, the two streams of superstructural reconstruction could not remain entirely screened off from each other. Significant exchanges took place between the superstructural responses of peasantization and those of proletarization. The introduction of peasant cults of affliction into the intensive contact situation is a common phenomenon in Central Africa.[44] Alternatively, the 'proletarian' superstructural responses were soon propagated in the rural areas as well. As the social settings of proletarization and peasantization were very different, the innovations had to undergo substantial transformations as they crossed from one setting to the other. The case of the Zambia Nzila sect shows how a cult of affliction, when introduced into the setting of proletarization, could take on a formal organizational structure and develop into a fully-fledged and exceptionally successful independent church.

African Watchtower shows the opposite process, by which a religious innovation properly belonging to the proletarian context is greatly transformed so as to fit the context of peasantization.[45] In the late

1920s and the 1930s Watchtower was propagated in the rural areas of Central Africa on a very large scale. The proletarian preachers and dippers expressed anti-colonial attitudes, and attracted state persecution on this basis. However, the massive peasant audiences they inspired and brought to baptism seemed to respond less to their anti-colonialism and their analysis of the wider society. Instead the peasants were looking for reconstruction of just the local, rural society by ritual means, and therefore chose to emphasize selectively the eschatological and witch-cleansing elements in the preachers' messages. And the latter were not hesitant to oblige. A case in point is the rapid transformation of Tomo Nyirenda ('Mwana Lesa') from an orthodox Watchtower adherent in the typical intensive contact situation, to a self-styled rural witch-finder whose lethal efficiency cost scores of lives (and finally his own).[46]

Nyirenda's case appears to have been only an extreme example of what seems to have happened to many Watchtower preachers. Their messages, deriving from a different class situation, were rapidly attuned to the idiom in which the peasants were phrasing their own attempts at superstructural reconstruction. The specific Watchtower message, including its anti-colonial overtones, got lost behind the peasants' perception of the preachers as predominantly engaged in the eradication of sorcery. They were supposed to usher the local society into a radically new state, but on a strictly local scale and ignoring the wider colonial and capitalist conditions which had both intensified the predicament of peasantization, and had originally triggered the proletarian Watchtower response.

By no means all religious innovators who exhorted local rural communities to cleanse themselves from sorcery had Watchtower connotations. Some were channelled into other independent church movements. Others were individual innovators who adopted elements from the current idiom (dipping, hymn-singing, or the use of a Bible and other material paraphernalia for the identification and cleansing of sorcerers) without identifying themselves as belonging to any specific movement. Many claimed, or were regarded, to belong to the *Mchape* movement, which from Malawi spread over Central Africa from the 1920s onwards. Several other such movements have been described for Zambia and the surrounding areas.[47]

Willis[48] has aptly characterized the common purpose of all these rural movements with the phrase 'instant millennium'. Unlike cargo cults and many other millennarian movements, these Central African witch-cleansing cults not only contained the expectation of a radically different new society: they actually claimed to provide the apparatus and ritual that was to bring about this new society. Despite waves of religious innovation that had temporarily superimposed alternative interpretations, sorcery had remained the standard explanation for misfortune. In such a context the claim to remove all sorcery from the community inevitably amounts to nothing less than the creation of a realm of eternal bliss, of a community that belongs to a totally different order of existence. Mary Douglas[49] suggested that recurrent witch-cleansing cults form part and parcel of the 'traditional' set-up of Central African rural society. My interpretation would be rather different.

Admittedly, the well-known debate[50] on the methodological difficulties involved in the hypothesis that modern social change had led to an increase of sorcery and sorcery accusation, discourages any further argument along that line. Instead of a change in the incidence of sorcery or alleged sorcery, I would suggest that the significant element of change lay in the personnel and the idiom of witch-cleansing. This is again not something that is easily assessed for an illiterate past, but at least it is a qualitative instead of an unsolvable quantitative problem. In the old superstructure, sorcery formed the central moral issue. The necessity to control sorcery and to expose and eliminate sorcerers was fully acknowledged. These functions were the prerogatives of those exercising political and religious authority, or were largely controlled by the latter. The battle against sorcery was waged continually, and formed a major test for the amount of protection and well-being those in authority could offer their followers.

The removal overnight of all sorcerers, as in eradication movements, does not by any means fit into this pattern. The cyclical time perception characteristic of the old superstructure is likewise incompatible with the idea of 'instant millennium'. These millennarian expectations, the recruitment of witch-cleansing agents from amongst outsiders divorced from local foci of authority (even if often invited and protected by chiefs), the new symbols (dipping, the High God, hymns and sermons), the massive response which made the populations of entire villages and regions step forward, hand in their sorcery apparatus, and get cleansed – all this suggests not a recurrent 'traditional' phenomenon, but a dramatic attempt at superstructural reconstruction that properly belongs to the chapter of recent religious *innovation* in Central Africa.

Superstructural reconstruction, class struggle and the state
On the descriptive level, I have now prepared the ground for an inter-

pretation of Lumpa against the total background of recent religious and political movements in Central Africa. For a fuller understanding it is necessary to examine this material in the light of two fundamental issues: class struggle and the overall distribution of power. We touch here on basic problems of both modern African society and social theory. Therefore, as I rush in where angels fear to tread, the following ideas are offered as extremely tentative.

I have argued that the various superstructural reconstruction movements were peculiar to the two specific class situations of peasantization and proletarization. However, they were much more than mere sub-cultural traits contributing to the life-style of a social class (such as diet, fashion in clothing, patterns of recreation, etc.). Directly springing from the predicament of alienation, and trying to solve it, these movements should be recognized as manifestations of class struggle.

Here the broad distinction between the peasant stream and the proletarian stream is relevant, again. The various peasant responses reveal the attempt to reconstruct a whole, self-supporting, autonomous rural community. Trapped as they usually were in superstructural illusions, ignoring the infrastructural requirements (in terms of relations of production) for such a reconstruction, most of these attempts were unrealistic and failed entirely. Yet in essence they are extremely radical in that they attempt to reverse the process of peasantization, by denying the rural community's incapsulation in a wider colonial and capitalist system. By contrast, the 'urban' responses were decidedly less radical. For they took for granted the fundamental structure of capitalism, and aimed not at an overthrow of capitalist relations of production, but at material and psychological improvement of the proletarian experience within this overall structure. Thus in Zambia the proletarian class struggle in the trappings of African nationalism was fought within the terms of the very structure that had brought about the process of proletarization; it was reformist, not revolutionary. Thus Zambian nationalism, having emerged as the main response to proletarization,[51] entirely lost its aspect of class struggle. After UNIP brought about territorial independence, this nationalist party and its leaders have instead greatly enhanced state control as a means to consolidate the capitalist structure of Zambian society. The capitalist infrastructure was left intact, and after the replacement of this structure's white executive personnel by Africans, its further expansion was stimulated. The growth of UNIP in the rural areas, where the party increasingly implements and controls state-promoted projects of 'rural development', represents a further phase in the domination of rural communities by the state and capitalism.

Within the proletarian response Watchtower came closest to radical class struggle. It did not analyse and counteract the capitalist relations of production. On the contrary, Watchtower adherents have been described as quite successfully adapted to capitalist production. This was particularly the case when the movement, introduced into the rural areas, could resist the peasants' redefinition of its idiom in terms of witch-cleansing, and enduring Watchtower communities emerged.[52] However, Watchtower radicalism did show in its theocratic rejection of the authority of the state – both colonial and post-colonial. Watchtower has thus opposed a structure of domination that, as I indicated above, was closely linked to capitalist structures.

This rejection of the state also brought Watchtower close to the peasants' reconstruction attempts. For although the latter were not explicitly anti-state or anti-colonial, their insistence on a strictly local rural society left no room whatever for structures of control beyond the local level.

Most Central African peasant reconstruction movements were of limited scope, organizationally weak, and lacked infrastructural initiatives. This caused them, in general, to yield and die down as soon as effectively confronted with the power of the state. Lumpa, however, shows the great potential of these movements, once they comprise a sufficient number of people and explore, in addition to superstructural reconstruction, the possibility of infrastructural reconstruction.

Incorporation of rural communities in a system of state control under capitalist conditions is not only an infrastructural problem. The superstructural innovations discussed here emphasized the importance of people's conceptualization of their society, and of their own place therein. It is impossible to build a state on sheer coercion alone, and anyway the Zambian leaders would seem to abhor the very idea. In addition to actual control through effective structures, the Zambian state seeks legitimacy in the eyes of its subjects. In the present-day context it is therefore of great importance that the state, as the culmination of supra-local control, has remained a distant and alien element in the social perception of many Zambian peasants, also after independence. The colonial state, for various reasons, was contented to have only a distant grip on rural villages, and concentrated its efforts in the *bomas* and in the urban centres. The post-colonial state is now struggling for both effective domination and acceptance right down to the grass-roots level of the remotest villages. Expansion of the party and of other rural foci of state control (schools, clinics, agricultural extensions and courts) in itself cannot take away the fact that the state still has not legitimated itself entirely in the eyes of a considerable portion of the Zambian peasantry. This situation causes strain and insecurity among the Zambian leaders, and they tend to react forcibly against rural (or whatever other) challenges of their power and legitimacy. Of this Lumpa, again, offers an example.

Lumpa and its development in rural north-east Zambia

We have now reached a stage where we can assess the position of the Lumpa Church as a case of religious innovation, against the general background of superstructural reconstruction in Central Africa, and where we can begin to analyse the conflicts this church gave rise to.

The story of Lenshina's first appearance as a prophet and of the founding years of her church has been told often enough.[53] We can confine ourselves here to a broad outline. Lenshina was born around 1920, as the daughter of a Bemba villager who had fought against the Germans near the Tanzanian border, and who had later been a *boma* messenger. Though growing up near Lubwa mission, Lenshina was not a baptized Christian when she received her first visions in 1953. Her husband had been a carpenter at Lubwa mission but by that time was no longer employed there. Lenshina referred to the mission with an account of her spiritual experiences. The white missionary-in-charge took her seriously, saw her through Bible lessons and baptism (when she received the name of Alice), and encouraged her to give testimony of her experiences at church gatherings. When this missionary went on leave abroad, and Alice began to develop ritual initiatives on her own, even receiving money for them, the African minister-in-charge felt that she could no longer be contained within the mission church.

From 1955 onwards Lenshina propagated her message on her own behalf, thus founding an independent church. She collected a phenomenal following around her, which by 1958 was estimated at about 65,000.[54] Many of these were former converts of Lubwa mission and of the neighbouring Roman Catholic missions. In Chinsali district and adjacent areas the great majority of the population turned to Lenshina's church, which was soon known as Lumpa ('excelling all others'). An organizational framework was set up in which Lenshina's husband Petros Chitankwa and other male senior deacons held the topmost positions. Thousands of pilgrims flocked to Lenshina's village, Kasomo, which was renamed Sioni (Zion); many settled there permanently. In 1958 the Lumpa cathedral was completed to be one of the largest church buildings of Central Africa. Scores of Lumpa branches were created throughout Zambia's Northern Province. In addition, some appeared along the line of rail, and even in Zimbabwe. The rural membership of the Church began to drop in the late 1950s from about 70 per cent to about 10 per cent of the local population.[55] After various clashes with the chiefs, local missions, the colonial state and the anti-colonial nationalist movement armed resistance against the state precipitated the 1964 final conflict which meant the end of the overt existence of Lumpa in Zambia.

Against the background of previous religious innovations in Central Africa, Lumpa offered a not very original combination of recurrent symbolic themes. Lumpa laid strong emphasis on the eradication of sorcery, mainly through baptism and the surrender of sorcery apparatus. It displayed the linear time perspective implicit in the notion of salvation, while eschatological overtones became very dominant only in the few months preceding the final conflict. Lenshina assumed ritual ecological functions such as distributing blessed seeds and calling rain, but on the other hand imposed taboos on common foods such as beer. The Church's idiom highlighted God and Jesus, while denouncing ancestors, deceased chiefs and affliction-causing spirits as objects of veneration. The Church aimed also at the creation of a new, predominantly rural society – but this time not only by the ritual means of witch-cleansing but also by experiments with new patterns of social relations and even with new relations of production and control which at least went some way towards infrastructural change. In this last aspect lies the uniqueness of Lumpa – as well as its undoing.

But before we discuss this aspect, let us try to identify the position of Lumpa within either the 'urban' on the 'rural' stream of superstructural reconstruction. The class position of the Lumpa foundress and of the great majority of Lenshina's adherents was that of the peasantry. Yet Lenshina's background (particularly the labour history of her father and of her husband), and Lumpa's period of 'incubation' at Lubwa mission (1953–4), suggest the importance of elements deriving from the intensive contact situation. Negative views concerning the missionaries, the whites and colonialism were initially quite strong in Lumpa. Lenshina's first visions occurred around the time that the Central African Federation was created, a controversial step that had greatly enhanced the political awareness of the African population, representing the first major defeat of Zambian nationalism. There is, moreover, specific evidence of the nationalist element in Lumpa in the early years (mid-1950s). Many of the early senior leaders of Lumpa were nationalists who for that reason had left the Lubwa mission establishment. Lumpa gatherings were used for nationalist propaganda. In 1954 even the then leader of Zambian nationalism, Harry Nkumbula, had a meeting with Alice to enlist her support for the nationalist cause.[56] Lumpa seemed to develop into a textbook demonstration of Balandier's well-known view that independent churches are 'at the origin of nationalisms which are still unsophisticated but unequivocal in their expression'.[57]

Lumpa's closeness to the nationalist movement was emphasized by the authors of the most authoritative early studies of Lumpa.[58] On the basis of their field-work, which took place in the late 1950s, these researchers were entirely unable to predict Lumpa's clash with UNIP in the early 1960s.

From the very beginning, however, the symbolic idiom in which Lenshina expressed her message belonged not to the stream of proletarization, but to that of peasantization. This is clear from Lenshina's emphasis on ecological ritual (which in the 1950s must be considered almost an anachronism within the development of Central African religious innovation), sorcery-eradication, and the construction of a new, exclusively local, rural society. As the movement spread over northeastern Zambia, these peasant elements became more and more dominant. Lumpa became primarily a means to overcome the predicament of peasantization. In its emphasis on the creation of a new, local society, Lumpa was not interested in modifying and improving the incorporation of that society in the wider structures of capitalism and the colonial state (the frame of reference of the proletarization response, including nationalism); instead, the entire reality of this incorporation came to be *denied* within Lumpa. Whereas it could be maintained that Lumpa initially straddled both the urban and the rural streams of superstructural reconstruction, it gradually went through a process of accommodation to the peasant outlook. This was rather analogous to the rural transformation of Watchtower a quarter of a century earlier. The constitution of the Lumpa Church, drawn up in 1957, fore-shadows the outcome of this process: the Church is there presented as nonracial, not a political party and not opposed to the laws of the country, thus opting out of the nationalist position.[59]

By becoming more and more specifically a peasant movement, Lumpa could no longer accommodate those of its members whose experiences at rural missions, *bomas*, and in town were more deeply rooted in the proletarization process. This partly explains the decline of Lumpa in north-eastern Zambia since the late 1950s. By that time many of the Lumpa adherents had returned to their mission churches. Others heeded the call of the rapidly expanding rural branches of UNIP. Entrenched in its exclusively rural and local outlook, Lumpa was working out a form of peasant class struggle quite incompatible with the nationalist emphasis on wider incorporation and on the state. By the same token, the urban branches of Lumpa became increasingly divorced from the developments in the Church in Chinsali district. While their relation to nationalism remains a subject for further study, it is clear that the urban branches did dissociate themselves from rural Lumpa in the latter's final conflict with the state.[60]

If Lumpa gradually defined itself as a peasant movement aiming at a radical reversion of the process of peasantization, let us now consider the non-ritual ways in which Lumpa attempted to achieve this.

On the level of sorcery relations, the belief in the eradication of sorcery created a new social climate where the very strict moral rulings of the Lumpa Church were observed to an amazing extent. This was, for instance, noticeable in the field of sexual and marital relations.[61] In many respects, moreover, Lumpa tried to revive the old super-structure, in which concern for the land and fertility, protection against sorcery, general morality, and political and economic power had all combined so as to form one holistic conception of the rural society. However, the new society was to be a theocratic one, in which all authority had to derive from God and his prophetess, Lenshina. The *boma*, chiefs and Local Courts, as they had no access to this authority, were denounced and ignored. In the judicial sphere, cases would be taken to Lenshina and her senior church leaders, who tried them to the satisfaction of the Lumpa adherents involved. For some years Chinsali district was in fact predominantly Lumpa. Very frequent communication was maintained between the various branches and headquarters, e.g., by means of pilgrimage and the continuous circulation of church choirs around the countryside. Under these conditions the creation of an alternative, church-administered authority structure was no illusion, but a workable reality. Two comprehensive studies of Lumpa[62] emphasize this aspect of the effective reconstruction of the rural society.

These indications are already highly significant, as they demonstrate Lumpa's temporary success in functioning as a focus of control independent from the state. The nationalist leaders were not so far off the mark when they denounced Lumpa for attempting to form 'a state within the state'. For while Lumpa implicitly denied the legitimacy of the colonial state and its post-colonial successor, it attempted to create a structure of control comparable to the state, if at a much smaller scale geographically.

The superstructural achievements would have been meaningless, even impossible, without some infrastructural basis. Did Lumpa actually experiment with new relations of production which counteracted incorporation of the local community into capitalism and the state? As no primary data on Lumpa have been collected with this specific question in mind, the evidence is scanty, but does contain some interesting points. The very substantial donations from Lumpa church branches, individual members, and pilgrims, accumulated at Sioni. They were used not only for Lenshina's household and retinue, but also towards the creation of a chain of rural stores. Trucks were purchased both to stock the stores and to transport church choirs between the branches and headquarters. Without further information it is difficult to say whether this represents merely the attempt of Lumpa leaders to launch themselves as entrepreneurs, or rather a move to create a self-sufficient distribution system as independent as possible from outside control.

Further examples bear out Lumpa's experiments with economic relations that were widely at variance with capitalism and that remind much more of the economic ideals of the old village society. The huge Lumpa cathedral was built in 1956-8 by the various church branches in a form of tribute labour, with no outside assistance. The continuous circulation of pilgrims and choir-members through the countryside of north-eastern Zambia represented another interesting economic feature. These Lumpa adherents had to be fed *gratis* by the local villagers, to whom they were often strangers. They were not always welcome and were likened to locusts. Yet this institution suggests the potential of the economic network created by Lumpa.

The most significant move towards a new infrastructure revolved on land and land rights, as befits a peasant movement. In this context it is important to note that for the population of north-eastern Zambia the process of peasantization started not with the imposition of colonial rule, but with the formation of the Bemba state, in the eighteenth century.[63] Chiefs occupying various positions in the Bemba chiefly hierarchy had assumed rights over the allocation of land. The colonial state had largely reinforced these rights, while claiming for itself the power to acknowledge or demote the chiefs. Lumpa's attempt to create a new rural society and (to some extent) new relations of production, inevitably called for a territorial basis on which a contiguous, exclusively Lumpa population could pursue their new social, economic and religious life. Lumpa adherents began to resettle, primarily around Sioni, where apparently hundreds of them concentrated. Accepting only theocratic authority, they did not ask permission from the chiefs. In this way they challenged the fundamental property rights on which their rural production system had been based for two centuries or more.

That the issue was indeed vital not only in terms of my theory but also for the Lumpa adherents, the chiefs and the colonial state, is clear from the fact that this conflict of 'unauthorized' settlement led to the first violent clashes between Lumpa and the police in 1959.[64] In the years that followed, land as a key issue in rural relations of production continued to play the role one would expect it to play in a peasant movement struggling to create a new infrastructure. Soon, Lenshina tried to purchase land, which was greatly opposed and resented by the chiefs and by the increasingly non-Lumpa population. As UNIP/Lumpa tensions mounted (see below), Lumpa adherents withdrew into a number of exlcusively Lumpa villages, which were again 'unauthorized' from the point of view of the chiefs and the state. In July 1964 Kaunda's ultimatum to abandon these villages expired. Police officers on patrol visited one such village; the inhabitants allegedly understood that they came to demolish the village, and killed them. This started the final conflict, whose outcome was, *inter alia*, the demolition of all Lumpa villages and of the Lumpa cathedral.

The conflict with the chiefs over land shows how Lumpa, in its creation of a new rural society, clashed with individuals and groups who opted out of the Lumpa order and who, at the same time, were in a position to mobilize the forces of the colonial state against Lumpa. Mere ordinary villagers who were opposed to Lumpa were not in such a position. If they did not want to join Lumpa, strong social pressure was brought to bear on them: foremost the allegation that they were sorcerers and for that reason shunned a church concentrating on sorcery eradication; also, occasionally, they were exposed to downright violence from the Lumpa side.[65] Among many joiners, the obligations (in terms of time, money and commitment) imposed by the Church were increasingly felt as a burden; but while Lumpa was still strong these dissenters risked serious conflicts and ostracism if they defected to the mission churches or the nationalist party.

A group which, besides the chiefs, successfully mobilized the colonial state against Lumpa was the Roman Catholic Church. This Church had been the first to establish missions in the area, and was by far the greatest Christian denomination in north-eastern Zambia on the eve of Lenshina's appearance as a prophet. Lenshina initially operated in a Protestant environment, whose strong anti-Catholic feelings had not yet given way to the ecumenism of later decades. Moreover, Lumpa was opposed to sorcery and to all ritual objects that could be considered sorcery apparatus; therefore it found much more fault with the very elaborate Roman Catholic devotional paraphernalia than with the austere, mainly verbal Protestant worship.[66] These two factors made Lumpa particularly inimical to local Catholic missions and their senior personnel. The rapid spread of Lumpa virtually exterminated a major Catholic stronghold in Central Africa, and so caused bitter animosity among the Catholic leaders. Catholic mission-workers on tour were increasingly harassed. In 1956 an African Catholic priest, when visiting a village, was called a sorcerer. He set in motion the judicial machinery (accusation of sorcery is a criminal offence under the Witchcraft Ordinance). The offending party was detained at the district head-quarters. A crowd of Lumpa adherents headed by Lenshina's husband protested against this, and a confrontation with the administration ensued which eventually led to Petros Chitankwa, Lenshina's husband, being sentenced to two years with hard labour.[67]

The last and most important conflict between Lumpa and a local group was with UNIP. After Lenshina had been away for over a year, visiting the urban Lumpa Churches, she returned to find her Church declining and UNIP increasingly controlling the countryside. She reacted very strongly to this state of affairs. In 1962 she forbade Lumpa adherents to join UNIP, publicly burned party cards, and instead issued Lumpa membership tickets which may well have been regarded as the counterpart of party cards. She was even reported to say that the nationalist activists killed during 'Chachacha' would not go to heaven. From the time of preparation for the 1962 general election, bitter feuding between UNIP and Lumpa took place, resulting in the sad official statistics contained in Table 8.1.[68]

The resettling in exclusively Lumpa villages was no longer, positively, the creation of a viable territorial basis for the new society. Instead, it had become a retreat from an increasingly hostile environment. There are indications that in the year preceding the final conflict eschatologi-cal expectations gained momentum among the Lumpa adherents. They prepared to defend whatever was left to their short-lived new world. They surrounded their villages by stockades, manufactured simple weapons, and prepared magical substances intended to make them-selves invulnerable. There were repeated attempts by the UNIP top

Table 8.1 *Official figures concerning UNIP/Lumpa feuding in north-eastern Zambia prior to the final conflict*

	UNIP attacks on Lumpa adherents	Lumpa attacks on UNIP members
Murders	14	7
Houses destroyed by arson	121	2
Churches destroyed by arson	28	no information
Grain bins destroyed by arson	28	2
Assaults	66	10
of which serious	22	no information
Intimidation cases	22	no information
Cattle kraals destroyed by arson	1	no information
Goats burned	18	no information

leadership to bring about a reconciliation between their local rank and file, and Lumpa. These attempts proved unsuccessful. When fighting between UNIP and a Lumpa village broke out, as a result of a quarrel over school attendance (in 1964 Lenshina had forbidden her followers to send their children to school), government decided that Lumpa villages could no longer be tolerated, and issued the ultimatum leading to the final conflict.

Why did Lumpa at first accommodate nationalism, to reject it later on, engaging in bitter feuding with local nationalists, which eventually lead to Lumpa's virtual extermination? The answer Roberts gives,[69] and which Ranger cites approvingly,[70] is that

Both Church and Party were competing for total allegiance. As I have argued, it was their similarities as much as their differences which brought them into conflict.

In the light of the tentative theoretical position I have developed here, a detailed assessment of the validity of this answer has become possible.

In defining itself more and more as an exclusive peasant movement, Lumpa had gradually to shed such traits as it had initially shared with the nationalist movement and with the proletarian response in general. These traits were without solid roots in the peasant experience. Lumpa had subsequently struggled to regain local, rural control and to create new relations of production not dominated by the rural community's wider incorporation in capitalism and the state. Once Lumpa had taken this road, the (secular) state, and nationalism (as a set of political ideas on the nature and the personnel of the state), could no longer find a place in the Lumpa world view. Alternatively, nationalism, as a response to the proletarian situation, had found a final outcome in UNIP in 1959. UNIP accepted the basic infrastructural conditions of modern Central African society, including the incorporation of rural areas by the state and by capitalism. Less radical than Lumpa, therefore, UNIP's blueprint of the future society was almost diametrically opposed to Lumpa's. But if the incompatibility between UNIP and Lumpa derived from a difference in class situation and from a difference in degree of radicalism in the context of class struggle, we still have to explain why these two different movements confronted each other with deadly hostility among the *same* rural population of north-eastern Zambia.

I have argued that the proletarian response is not confined to places of migrant work, but may also be found in specific rural settings: missions, *bomas* or military campaigns. Could the UNIP/Lumpa opposition reflect a class difference within the rural population of Chinsali district, in such a way that the persistent Lumpa adherents were more truly peasants, whereas those who filled the ranks of the rural UNIP branches were more involved in the process of proletarization? Again, the evidence is scanty, but this time it seems not to support the hypothesis. Lumpa and UNIP villages were often adjacent. The UNIP/Lumpa division often ran across close kinship ties, as in the school conflict referred to above.[71] We must conclude that in the early 1960s Lumpa and UNIP represented rival options for social reconstruction amongst members of the same peasant class in Chinsali district.

Perhaps we come closer to an answer when we try to understand the position of UNIP as a proletarian response among a peasant population. Let us recall the process of accommodation to the peasant class situation, such as happened with Watchtower and, to a lesser extent, with Lumpa itself. Did not UNIP, too, undergo a transformation before it could make an impact among the peasants? Superficially, there are indications in that direction. At the village level UNIP was much more than a strictly political movement aiming at territorial independence. It became a way of life. It created, apparently, a state of millennarian effervescence similar to that of more specifically peasant responses such as sorcery-eradication and Lumpa. Already years before the new nationalist order was realized at a national scale (with the attainment of territorial independence), UNIP produced what Roberts called a 'cultural revival' in the villages.[72] Thus, like Watchtower and Lumpa, UNIP seems to have yielded to the model, so persistent among Central African peasants, of superstructural reconstruction at the local scale of the rural community. If this were a correct assessment, the peasants siding with Lumpa would have had very much in common with those siding with UNIP; they would have acted on the basis of the same inspiration of rural reconstruction, and Roberts's explanation would be basically correct. In this line of argument, the explanation of UNIP/Lumpa feuding would lie in the alleged fact that both were rival attempts at rural superstructural reconstruction. The ultimate drive behind both movements, at the village level, would then have been against peasant alienation and towards the primarily local restoration of meaning and competence. The solution that each of the feuding groups was propounding would only have the power to convince its adherents as long as it remained, in the latters' eyes, absolute and without alternatives. People on neither side could afford to yield – as they would be asserting, and defending, the very meaning they were giving to their lives.[73]

This approach to UNIP-Lumpa feuding has three implications which make us seriously doubt its validity. First, the different class references of Lumpa and of UNIP, as peasant or proletarian responses, would have to be immaterial: both would have to be transformed to serve a strictly local peasant response. Second, UNIP in Chinsali district in the early 1960s would not have functioned primarily as a nationalist movement aiming at territorial independence; rather, it would have adopted the nationalist symbolism and idiom merely to serve some peasant movement of local scope. Third, equally immaterial would have to be the fact that UNIP's solution to the peasants' predicament was no solution at all, as its insistence on the state and its acceptance of capitalism could only lead to a further incorporation and dependence of the rural community.

Although class formation in modern Africa follows notoriously devious dialectics, these implications do appear too preposterous for us to maintain Roberts's explanation wholesale. The crucial issue is the mobilization process by which UNIP established itself among the peasant of Chinsali district. But as long as no new, detailed material is available on this point, let us try to modify Roberts's analysis in a way that takes the above implications into account.

Let us grant that UNIP in Chinsali district initially contained an element of superstructural reconstruction at the purely local level – thus somewhat accommodating to the typical peasant response. However, this element may soon have worn out, as it became clear that UNIP aimed at intensifying, rather than counteracting, wider incorporation, and that therefore UNIP was a powerful mechanism in the very process of peasantization which the peasants were anxious to reverse. Is it then not more realistic to explain UNIP/Lumpa feuding from the fact that Lumpa, as rather successfully realizing a local, rural reconstruction of both superstructure and infrastructure, represented in north-eastern Zambia the main obstacle to UNIP's striving towards wider incorporation? Those peasants siding with UNIP would then be the instruments to curb the class struggle of the Lumpa peasants. In that case not only the final Lumpa/state conflict, but also the preceding Lumpa/UNIP feuding at the local level, would revolve around wider incorporation, much more than around 'total commitment' (Roberts) at the village level.

There are indications that the local feuding, and the final clash between Lumpa and the state, were two stages of the same overall conflict. Not only was Lumpa in both cases confronted with UNIP, first in the form of rural branches, finally in the form of a UNIP-dominated transition government. There is also the suggestion that the rural feuding was accepted by the UNIP top leadership as rather compatible with UNIP's basic orientation. With UNIP rural aggression heavily outweighing Lumpa's (Table 8.1, based on a state-commissioned enquiry), is it not significant that no extensive records seem to exist of UNIP members in Chinsali district having been tried, after independence, for offences just as criminal as those so loudly decried when committed by Lumpa? Let me emphasize that there is not the slightest indication whatsoever that rural UNIP aggression was *instigated* by the national UNIP leaders; in fact, the latter tried repeatedly to stop the feuding – if only Lumpa were prepared to accept UNIP control. However, the necessity to exterminate Lumpa, and movements like it, is at the root of UNIP and similar reformist nationalist movements, irrespective of personal standards of integrity and non-violence of the leaders involved. Far from transforming UNIP into a peasant movement of purely local scope, UNIP adherents in Chinsali district attacked Lumpa on the basis of a consistent application of the logic of UNIP nationalism. However regrettable, and however deeply regretted by Kaunda and his colleagues, the feuding as well as the final conflict were fairly inevitable.

Religion and the state in modern Zambia: the problem of legitimation

Having attempted to explain the reasons of the conflict between Lumpa and various other groups in rural north-eastern Zambia, my argument already contains the elements on the basis of which the final conflict between Lumpa and the state can be understood. It is useful to discuss this issue *in extenso,* as such a discussion may also throw light upon the relations between the Zambian state and contemporary churches in general.

In my introduction to this chapter I pointed out that the Lumpa rising was a bitter disappointment for the Zambian nationalists, and a threat to their international public image. Meanwhile we have identified more profound reasons for the state's stern reaction to Lumpa.

The primary reason was, of course, that Lumpa did represent a very real threat to the state itself. Although declining and greatly harassed by conflicts with other groups in north-eastern Zambia, Lumpa represented to the end a successful peasant movement, comprising many thousands of people and binding these people in an effective organization that radically rejected state control and that was beginning to define its own infrastructure. With the years rural Lumpa did not settle down as a tolerant denomination attuned to the institutions of the wider society. Here Lumpa differs from most rural Watchtower communities founded before the Second World War. Under the mounting attacks by rural UNIP, Lumpa became increasingly intransigent *vis-à-vis* the outside world. Short of giving up the modern conception of the national state, or at least embarking upon a fundamental discussion of this conception, the logic of the state left no option but breaking the power of Lumpa once for all. And this is what happened.

Additional reasons helped to shape the course of events. Taking the fundamental assumptions of the modern state for granted, the nationalists, once in power, proved as staunch supporters of state-enforced law and order as their colonial predecessors had ever been. A major justification for the sending of government troops was that the Lumpa adherents, in trying to create 'a state within the state', had become criminals.[74] Moreover, there were tenacious rumours as to Lumpa's links with Welensky's United Federal Party (the nationalists' main opponent), and with Tshombe's secessionist movement in Zaïre. So far the evidence for this allegation has been slight.[75] It seems difficult to bring in line such political manoeuvring with the situation of the Lumpa church, which in 1963–4 increasingly entrenched itself in a retreatist and eschatological attitude. But whatever the facts, belief in these links with UNIP's enemies appears to have influenced the UNIP-dominated government on the eve of independence.

A third complex of reasons revolves around the problem of legitimation of the modern state. The following extracts from a speech of Kaunda show that the UNIP government was not merely trying to enforce its monopoly of power, but also tried to underpin its own legitimacy in the eyes of the Zambian population by presenting itself as the supreme guardian of religion and morality. Speaking about Lumpa, Kaunda says:[76]

> They have become anti-society. They have been known, husband and wife, to plan to kill their own parents because they were non-Lumpa Church members and this they have done. . . .
>
> Innocent villagers and children trying to escape from their burning homes have been captured by the followers of Lenshina and thrown back alive into the flames. Senior men in the country's security services have reported that the Lumpa followers have no human feelings and their ferocious attacks on security forces bear out the fanatical nature of what I can only describe again as lunatics. . . .
>
> I have no intention whatsoever of again unleashing such evil forces. Let me end by reiterating that my Government has no desire whatsoever to interfere with any individual's religious beliefs but . . . such a noble principle can only be respected where those charged with the spiritual, and I believe moral side of life, are sufficiently responsible to realize that freedom of worship becomes a menace and not a value when their sect commits murder and arson in the name of religion.
>
> No clean-living and thinking man can accept the Lenshina 'Passports to Heaven' as anything more than worthless pieces of paper – a usurping by an imposter of the majesty of God Almighty. Such teaching cannot be allowed to continue to corrupt our people and cannot and would not be tolerated by any responsible government.

In the context of modern Zambian society there can be little misunderstanding that here Kaunda is describing the Lumpa adherents as sorcerers, and tries to mobilize all the abhorrence that the general population feels with regard to sorcerers. Kaunda even points out, in the same passage, the need for the Lumpa members to be cleansed (as in witch-cleansing movements so popular in twentieth century Central Africa) before they can return to human society:[77]

> When they have surrendered and look back at their actions, some of these people realize the horror, damage and sadness they have brought to this young nation and say plainly that they require

some treatment to bring them back to sanity. They just cannot understand why they acted as they did.

Kaunda presents and justifies state action in terms of religious and moral beliefs: the anti-social nature of sorcerers, and the 'majesty of God Almighty'. These beliefs have a very strong appeal among the great majority of the modern Zambian population. By invoking them, Kaunda is in fact claiming implicitly a supreme moral and religious legitimation for his government. Yet his government has already, secularly, the fullest possible legitimacy in terms of the constitutional and democratic procedures from which its mandate derived. Why, then, this need to appeal to a religious basis for the legitimation of the Zambian state?

Here we have reached the point where Lumpa illustrates the precarious situation of the modern, post-colonial state in Zambia, due to the latter's incomplete legitimation in the eyes of a significant portion of the Zambian population.

Whatever its access to means of physical coercion, the ultimate legitimation of a bureaucratic system like the state lies, in Weber's terms, in[78]

a belief in the 'legality' of patterns of normative rules and the right of those elevated to authority under such rules to issue commands (legal authority).

Now how does one establish and maintain such a legitimation if part of the state's subjects are peasants for whom such an abstract, universalist 'legal authority', and the formal bureaucratic organizations based upon it, virtually have no meaning, in whose social experience at any rate they play no dominant part?

In Zambia this problem has been duly acknowledged, if in different terms. Under the heading of 'nation-building', a tremendous effort has been launched along such lines as political mobilization; youth movement; women's movement; specific school curricula incorporating training for citizenship; rural development, etc. Populism, here in the form of the ideology of Zambian humanism, emerged as an attempt to overcome, if not to ignore, the fundamental contradictions inherent in the situation. The careful management of relations with the chiefs is part of the same effort. At the district level chiefs have retained considerable authority and state stipends, and nationally they are represented in the House of Chiefs. These arrangements (which, incidentally, strikingly contrast with the position assigned to chiefs in the

Lumpa blueprint of society) constitute an attempt to incorporate rural, local foci of authority into the central government structure, so as to let the government benefit from the additional legitimation which this link with traditional authority may offer. Where this attempt fails, the state curtails the chiefs' privileges,[79] but such moves do not necessarily reduce the chiefs' actual authority among the rural population. Ethnic and regional allegiances, as threats to 'nation-building' and as challenges, either implicit or explicit, to the supremacy of the state, are likewise denounced by the ruling elite.

Lumpa, as the largest and most powerful peasant movement Zambia has yet seen, drove home the fact that large sections of the Zambian peasantry still opt out of the post-colonial national state. Lumpa antagonized precisely the grass-roots processes by which the post-colonial state expects to solve its problem of incomplete legitimation. For a national elite who find, to a great extent, in the state not only their livelihood but also the anchorage of their identity, this is a disconcerting fact, which hushing-up and ostentatious reconciliation may help to repress from consciousness. For the elite the situation is uncomfortable indeed, for the extermination of Lumpa has by no means solved the much wider problem of the incorporation of peasants into the Zambian state. New peasant movements are likely to emerge which, like Lumpa, may employ a religious idiom in an attempt to regain local control and to challenge wider incorporation.[80]

Meanwhile, given the general problem of legitimation, it is obvious that religion has a very significant role to play in Zambia and other Central African states. On the basis of a rather widespread and homogeneous cultural substratum, similar religious innovations (of the kinds I have discussed above) occurred throughout Central Africa. Sorcery beliefs and the prominence of the High God form the two main constants in the emerging supra-ethnic religious systems of modern Zambia. These two religious elements are subscribed to by virtually the entire African population of the country, no matter what various specific ritual forms and organizations the people adhere to. The process of secularization, so marked in North Atlantic society, has not replicated itself in Central Africa – yet. Therefore, some form of appeal to this shared religious framework could provide extensive legitimation for contemporary authority structures,[81] albeit along lines rather different from those stipulated by Weber under the heading of legal authority. For the result would be neither legal nor traditional authority, but charismatic authority.

In the speech cited above, and in numerous other instances, Kaunda and other Zambian political leaders have employed a religious idiom to underpin the authority of themselves and of the state bureaucracy they represent. The situation is complicated by the existence, besides the party and the state, of specifically religious organizations, mainly in the form of Christian churches. These churches, having reached various stages in the process of the routinization of charisma,[82] have a rather direct access to religious legitimation. They generate a considerable social power, through their large number of adherents, the latters' effective organization, loyalty, and above-average standards of education and income. Of course, the churches use their legitimating potential in the first instance for their own benefit. Therefore their social power is, at least latently, rival to that of the state and the party.

Between the established Christian churches (Roman Catholic Church, United Church of Zambia, Reformed Church in Zambia, Anglican Church, etc.) and the Zambian state a not always easy, but on the whole productive, symbiosis has developed.[83] The churches lend both their expertise and their legitimating potential to the government, in exchange for very considerable autonomy in the religious field. The settings in which this interaction takes shape include: public ceremonies in which political and religious leaders partake side by side; the implementation of 'development'; the participation of religious leaders in governmental and party committees; and informal consultations between top-ranking political and religious leaders. An important factor in this pattern seems to be the fact that the established Zambian churches derive from North Atlantic ones which, in their countries of origin, had already solved the problem of the relation between church and state prior to missionary expansion in Africa. Even so, there have been minor clashes, and more serious ones may follow in the future. For state-church symbiosis cannot really solve the problem of the state's incomplete legitimation in terms of legal authority. A religious underpinning of the state's authority automatically implies enhancing the authority of the religious organizations, which may thus come to represent, through a feed-back, an even greater challenge to the state's authority. Ultimately, a shift towards purely legal authority for the state may require a process of 'disenchantment' (already noticeable among the Zambian intellectuals). Such a process would undermine the churches' authority and would be likely to bring the latter to concerted remonstrance in one form or another.

For the independent churches the situation tends to be more acutely difficult. Although it is still far too early to generalize, these independent churches seem to cater typically for Zambians in the early stages of proletarization. The independent churches are most in evidence at the local level: the *bomas* and the urban compounds. The superstructural reconstruction they offer their adherents, and the extensive extra-religious impact they make on the latters' lives (e.g., in the spheres of recreation, marriage, domestic conflict, illness, death and burial) not infrequently clash with the local party organization which often works along similar lines. Despite instances of felicitous co-operation between independent church and party at the local level,[84] conflict remotely reminiscent of the UNIP/Lumpa feuding seems more frequent.

Among the Zambian elite there is little knowledge of and less sympathy for the independent churches. Not only the party, but also the established churches tend to see them as a threat. It is therefore unlikely that the independent churches will ever be called upon, to any significant extent, to play the religiously-legitimating role which the established churches now regularly perform for the state. The Lumpa rising provides an extreme example of what form church/state interaction can take in the context of independent churches. On the other hand, the organizational and interpretative experiments still going on in the Zambian independent churches may represent a major form of superstructural reconstruction in the decades to come – with presumably profound repercussions for the state and the nationalist movement.

Conclusion

This chapter represents an attempt to explore the deeper structural implications of the Lumpa rising in the context of religious innovation, class formation and the state in Zambia. In presenting a tentative interpretation, my main ambition has been to highlight a number of problems, and to indicate a direction in which some answers may be found in the future.

Meanwhile, many important problems have not even been mentioned in the present argument. If Lumpa was essentially a peasant movement, pursuing an idiom of religious innovation that was far from unique in the Central African context, why was it unique in its scope and historical development, and why did it occur precisely among the Bemba of north-eastern Zambia? Another important problem, that can throw light both on Lumpa and on the relations between the state and the established churches, is the development of relations between the established churches and Lumpa during and after the rising. The churches organized a rehabilitation mission right into the areas of combat, and afterwards the United Church of Zambia (into which Lubwa's Church of Scotland had merged) even tried to win Lenshina back into its fold. As more data become available, these issues may be tackled successfully.

At the moment, many essential data on the Lumpa episode are still lacking. The sociology of contemporary Zambian religion still largely remains to be written. And the whole Lumpa tragedy and its aftermath is still a cause of grief for thousands of Zambians from all walks of life. Under these circumstances, nothing but the most preliminary analysis is possible; but even such an analysis may be helpful in defining tasks, and not just academic ones, for the future.

Postscript

J.-L. Calmettes's recent contribution to Lumpa studies

The interpretation of the Lumpa rising as advanced in this chapter has been subject to a careful re-analysis by Jean-Loup Calmettes, in his recent MSc Econ thesis submitted to the University College of Wales.[85] As a Roman Catholic missionary working in north-eastern Zambia in the late 1960s and early 1970s, Calmettes was fortunate to have virtually unlimited access to three sources of data which hitherto have been lacking in the study of the Lumpa Church: extensive oral-historical evidence; missionary documents and missionary publications of limited circulation; and an almost complete set of Lumpa hymns. Calmettes must be congratulated on the competent way in which he has used and presented these new materials.[86] Particularly on the descriptive side his work goes a long way towards resolving some of the major puzzles of the Lumpa Church. However, I must resist the temptation to quote extensively from his text. I understand publication is currently being prepared. Moreover, in the field of Central African religious studies, extensive quotation from unpublished scholarly work has since long been the established privilege of Terence Ranger. Let me therefore limit myself here to those passages in Calmettes's thesis which explicitly criticize my own Lumpa analysis. This critique is contained in the ten concluding pages of his work.

While Calmettes does agree with the main thrust in my argument, his specific emphasis is substantially different. In the light of his analysis I can now see that my argument tried to explain the Lumpa crisis largely as the confrontation between two monolithic protagonists: on the one hand the state (in the liminal stage between the colonial and the post-colonial phase) and the United National Independence Party, which at the time of the rising was holding a majority in the Zambian transition government; and on the other hand the Lumpa Church, which in the years 1963–4 consisted of Lenshina, the senior Church leaders including her husband, and about 20,000 faithful followers – all that had remained after about four-fifths of the membership of the late 1950s had defected. According to my analysis, Lumpa had increasingly defined itself as a peasant movement defying peasantization, i.e., incorporation (both economically through capitalist relations of production, and politically through UNIP) in the wider capitalist order and the nationalist state. The basic force behind the Lumpa uprising, I claimed, was the peasants' class struggle. The logic of capitalism, as mediated through the state, left no option but to confront this struggle violently with military means. Put thus crudely, it is certainly somewhat too simplistic, and I am grateful to Calmettes for providing the elements with which we may yet arrive at a somewhat more penetrating analysis.

Towards new relations of production

In my analysis I stressed how Lumpa was an exception among Central African forms of religious innovation, but not because of its size, ritual or beliefs. As a form of 'superstructural reconstruction', Lumpa showed a combination of themes of religious innovation which to the student of Central African religious change are familiar: witchcraft eradication, millennarian fervour, a certain concern for ecological ritual, etc. What was exceptional in Lumpa, I claimed, was its ability to move towards the creation of alternative relations of production which could serve as a negation of the capitalist relations into which the population of north-eastern Zambia had increasingly been drawn. In other words, for the alienation produced by incorporation, Lumpa tried to provide not only ideological and ritual, but also infrastructural remedies – a state of affairs which I called revolutionary.[87]

Calmettes writes: 'I agree with Van Binsbergen's insistence on the significance of the creation of new relations of production.'[88] But he is critical of the way in which I worked this out in detail. He claims that I give a partly false picture of Lumpa attempts at redefinition of relations of production prevailing in the countryside of north-eastern

Zambia around 1960; moreover, he feels that I exaggerate the significance of these attempts.

Thus he denies that the resettlement of a considerable Lumpa
membership around Sioni, without formal permission from the chiefs,
constituted the challenge to the rural production system I claimed it
to be. For tribute labour to chiefs, Calmettes tells us, had gone into
disuse several decades before the Lumpa church was established. I
must reject Calmettes's point here. I did not say that unauthorized
resettlement of peasants upset a tribute-labour system which clearly
no longer existed. I said it challenged fundamental property rights in
land, which ever since the rise of the Bemba chiefly dynasties had been
vested in the chiefs. Colonial administration would of course infringe
on these rights in the interests of itself and allied outsiders (claiming
sites for administrative premises, missions or the odd European settler);
but *vis-à-vis* local peasants the colonial state would uphold the chiefs'
control over land.

Creation of new villages, or individual changes of residence from one
chief's area to another, was subject to the formal approval of the
chiefs involved. Clearly this constitutes a major aspect of the articulation between the domestic community in north-eastern Zambia and the
capitalist mode of production as mediated through the colonial state.
By underpinning chieftainship (which could be termed an incapsulated,
neo-traditional tributary mode of production), the colonial state
backed a system of chiefly power and prerogatives which to a considerable extent denied the peasants control over their main means of
production, land. It remains to be analysed how precisely this system
of rural control was instrumental in forcing a considerable portion of
the labour force in the domestic communities of north-eastern Zambia
to be involved in labour migration. But in the light of Rey's analysis
of similar processes elsewhere in Africa,[89] it seems very likely that the
class alliance between those European classes controlling the colonial
state (white settlers, metropolitan capitalists, etc.) and local chiefs
enabled the system of circulatory migration to impose itself on the
countryside of north-eastern Zambia. Although I admit that I should
have spelled this out in my main arguments, this is what I meant by
the phrase 'rural production system'. In this rural context, much as
in the numerous squatments around the Zambian line of rail, *unauthorized* settlement means, essentially, a form of active class struggle.

Calmettes goes on to point out that Lenshina never attempted to
purchase land, as I wrote, but that she merely applied for a *lease* on
a piece of land. Calmettes adds[90] that he does 'not think that she wanted

to buy a huge estate on which she would have regrouped her thousands of shifting cultivators'. I am grateful to Calmettes for pointing out this monstrous slip of the pen. The main source on this point[91] mentions 'lease', not 'purchase'. And anyway, given the legal structure of land tenure in north-eastern Zambia around 1960, it would have been almost inconceivable that Lenshina could have bought land. Yet I would maintain that from the point of view of Lumpa's attempt at redefining existing relations of production, the difference between purchase and lease may not be all that important. What is essential is that the Lumpa Church attempted to gain autonomous control over land, and this, as Roberts writes,[92]

> was taken as proof that she wished to set up a kingdom of her own. Whatever the political implications of her request [for land – WvB], there can be little doubt that its rejection had important economic implications: her followers now felt that their livelihood as well as their religious and political autonomy was threatened.

Calmettes is likewise critical of my claim that the final conflict developed out of another aspect of the land theme in the Lumpa drama: the refusal to demolish the stockaded villages into which the Lumpa membership had retreated in 1963. Here again I think there is no need to give in too readily to Calmettes's criticism. The demand to abandon these 'illegal settlements' was a central issue in all negotiations between the Lumpa Church, the UNIP leadership and the state, in the months preceding the final conflict. And an eye-witness of the Lumpa final conflict in Lundazi even started his account of the Lumpa episode thus:[93]

> It was ironic that the 'Independence' Constitution should grant the right of every lawful inhabitant of Northern Rhodesia to reside where he wished. The members of the 'Lumpa' Sect, followers of Alice Lenshina, exercised this right with results to themselves that will be described.

In the light of all this I would still maintain that, particularly in the context of land and relations of production focusing on land, my analysis essentially (although not in all details) holds out against Calmettes's criticism.

Let us now turn to those other indications of what I claimed to be Lumpa's experimenting with new relations of production alternative to the form of capitalist relations of production to which the local peasants were then subjected. Rightly, Calmettes points out that in the Lumpa Church, tribute labour was not *only* revived for the building of the Lumpa cathedral (as mentioned in my article), but also for agricultural work in Lenshina's gardens; the produce she sold. She also received tribute in kind.[94] Calmettes agrees that this is a form of production which opts out of the relations of production as defined by the chiefs, modern industry, or the state. While a Marxist analysis would tend to stress production over circulation and distribution, we should also look at the latter aspect. Here Calmettes helps us to detect a fundamental contradiction within the Lumpa Church, although in his own re-analysis this remains only implicit. Whereas the Lumpa adherents as direct producers were joining in new, alternative relations of production as defined by the Lumpa Church, in the sphere of distribution the contradiction between them and the Lumpa leadership became very marked and took on class-like elements.

In my earlier analysis I stressed how the continuous circulation of multitudes of choir members and pilgrims over the Lumpa countryside imposed upon local villagers the obligation to feed and accommodate these outsiders. The Lumpa Church, as an organization, thus created a structure through which a local surplus was extracted and was made to benefit Lumpa members from elsewhere. If all Lumpa members had had a chance of touring the countryside in this way, the inequalities thus created might have levelled out. In practice, it seems that some groups (those living around Sioni, the Church's headquarters; those in younger age cohorts) were more likely to be on the receiving side of this regional distribution system. And their continuous parasitism did create resentment. However, most surplus extraction by the Lumpa organization benefited not the rank and file of the Church, but its leadership.

In addition, of course, much was invested in prestigious and ritual objects, like the Lumpa cathedral. The purchase of two lorries, bought from similar sources, is very interesting since on the one hand they served the circulation of choirs and thus the regional extraction process in the interest of the rank and file (in addition to the strengthening of ritual ties throughout the region); on the other hand they served the entrepreneurial interests of the Church leadership, through trips to the Copperbelt where produce would be sold.[95] Calmettes provides the answer to my earlier queries concerning the economic network the Lumpa Church could maintain with the aid of these trucks. Rather than creating 'a chain of rural stores', as 'a move to create a self-sufficient distribution system as independent as possible from outside control', the trucks turned out to represent what I suggested as the alternative possibility: 'merely the attempt of Lumpa leaders to launch themselves as entrepreneurs'.[96]

Before Calmettes's thesis, we had to accept as authoritative Roberts's resigned statement:[97]

> There is very little information of any kind on the internal organization of the Lumpa church – a most important subject which perhaps will never properly be elucidated.

Against this background I was tempted, perhaps justifiably, to treat Lumpa as a monolithic whole. But it is here that the strength of Calmettes's work lies. The evolving relations between leaders and followers within the Lumpa Church, and between the leaders themselves, are now for the first time discussed in terms that are no longer hazy and conjectural.

Already on theoretical grounds the deficiencies in my earlier interpretation could have been detected. If we accept that the impetus behind Lumpa, up to and including the final conflict, was a peasants' class struggle against incorporation, then it should have been clear that these peasant's experimenting with new, alternative relations of production did not amount to a dissolution of all class-like relations. Only then could Lumpa have been treated as a monolith. But what we should have expected, instead, was the creation of a new type of class-like relations: contradictions and patterns of expropriation and control which, at least initially and at least for the Lumpa followers themselves, would be hidden from the eye by the theocratic assumptions of the Lumpa organization and beliefs. This is precisely what happened. Lumpa channelled peasants' rejection of current relations of production, offering them a form of superstructural reconstruction by which to battle against the alienation springing from current conditions. But meanwhile, by involving these peasants in new Lumpa-defined relations of production (such as tribute in labour and kind, resettlement in Lumpa-controlled settlements, and circulation of pilgrims and choirs), the Lumpa leadership began to act as an exploiting class themselves.

In this light many aspects which my earlier analysis could not accommodate fall into their proper place. Lumpa imposed what could be termed a *theocratic* mode of production; or perhaps, in line with a recent theoretical development hallmarked by the publication of the ASA volume on *Regional Cults*,[98] a *regional-cultic* mode of production. The internal structure of expropriation and control hinged on the contradiction between sect leaders and followers. This emergent, cultic mode of production, whose outlines are now becoming much clearer thanks to the work of Calmettes, defined itself *vis-à-vis* the other modes of production represented in the area. Unauthorized settlement, claims to judicial powers and to tribute challenged the tributary mode; through unauthorized settlement again, opposition against polygamy, the mobilization of labour for tribute work and ritual activities, and financial contributions, the Lumpa organization made significant inroads into what by the 1950s was left of the domestic mode of production.

While the desire for superstructural reconstruction as felt among the peasants may ultimately have been the main inspiration of the Lumpa beliefs, I must agree with the suggestion contained in Calmettes's work that the Lumpa *leadership* was *not* fundamentally opposed to the capitalist mode of production, as long as it fell into line with their own perceived material interests. Lumpa did not issue pronouncements against wage labour or migrancy. On the contrary, it set up Lumpa branches in the industrial areas along the distant line of rail, persuaded migrants to make the pilgrimage to Sione, and maintained profitable relations with the thoroughly capitalist Copperbelt commodity markets. While I would still maintain that the original inspiration of Lumpa, and the continuing orientation of its rank and file, was against incorporation into capitalist relations of production, the conclusion is now forced upon us that the Lumpa leadership struck a class alliance with the forces of capitalism as dominant along the line of rail. Lumpa became a structure of rural extraction, and the Lumpa leadership acquired material privileges worth defending.

There is much to be said for Calmettes's view that the leaders' struggle to defend privileges as derived from the internal set-up of the Lumpa Church was an important factor in the feuding which arose in north-eastern Zambia between Lumpa and the United National Independence Party. Much as the increasingly oppressive nature of the Lumpa organization brought up to 80 per cent of the original membership to defect in the early 1960s (so that these peasants had little reason left to resist the UNIP pressure to join the party), the fear, among the Lumpa leadership, of a further eroding of their privileges seems to have suggested the strong anti-UNIP pronouncements made by this leadership as from 1962. In fact, the Lumpa leaders had changed their attitude *vis-à-vis* nationalism and the colonial state much earlier than this: after having served as a nationalist platform for some years, already the 1957 Lumpa constitution virtually pledged allegiance to the colonial state.[99] I would suggest that already by that time the Lumpa

311

leadership had come to understand that, in upholding the *status quo*, the colonial state (as the expression, and protection, of the totality of class contradictions existing within its territory[100]) would be an essential factor in the continuation of the very privileges the sect leaders were building up by means of the Lumpa organization.

Thus it could be claimed that in the final conflict leaders and followers were fighting the same enemy but for very different reasons. The peasant rank and file were still, with remarkable courage as well as occasional atrocity, fighting the destruction of their reconstructed new society; the Lumpa leadership, which *de facto* had acquired the status of a local religious bourgeoisie, was fighting against the annihilation of their privileges. The complexities of this situation are perhaps reflected in the fact that Lenshina and her top leadership took little or no part in the actual battles, and were in a remarkably confused state when finally apprehended.

In the light of this reinterpretation, it does not seem as if I exaggerated the significance of Lumpa's striving towards new relations of production. Of course, even these new relations of production never reached maturity; I never claimed they did, and in a context of international dependency it is extremely unlikely that a relatively small peasant movement could ever succeed in escaping a structure of peripheral capitalism controlled from powerful metropoles. But notwithstanding all this, Lumpa's attempts at new relations of production were both even more complex and more fundamental to Lumpa's development than I claimed in my original argument.

Having criticized my analysis of Lumpa attempts at creating new relations of production, and having pointed out (correctly) that my analysis is only partial, Calmettes goes on to overstress the significance of the internal cleavage within Lumpa. He plays down entirely the struggle for both superstructural and infrastructural reconstruction, which I continue to see as the main inspiration of the Lumpa rank and file, up to and throughout the final conflict. For him, 'The conflict resembles more the wars which took place when the Bemba chiefs defended their privileges.'[101]

Following the line of Lehmann's early analysis,[102] Calmettes considers Lenshina to be a self-styled female Bemba chief. The fact that she surrounded herslef with tribute labour and claimed judical powers, Calmettes does not see as the selective borrowing of redefined historical institutions into a totally new set of relations of production, social relations and ritual relations: instead, he considers it a 'return towards the past',[103] in other words as an attempt to revive the tributary mode

of production – an attempt which, without much conceptual discussion, he calls, 'messianic sect'. Thus he becomes the victim of his
own, in itself illuminating, emphasis on the internal dynamics of the
Lumpa Church.[104]

> I would rather insist on the implications of the type of relations of
> production which had been evolved within the sect itself. I think
> that they explain the ideology of the leadership of the sect and the
> final conflict.

After what I have said above I do not think we need a detailed spell-
ing out of the tributary mode of production in Bembaland in the two
or three centuries of its pre-colonial existence[105] or in its incapsulated
neo-traditional colonial form[106] to make the point convincingly that the
essence of the Lumpa Church was *not* a revival of the tributary mode of
production. Moreover, the final conflict was between the Lumpa
Church (with all its internal contradictions) and an outside enemy, and
cannot be adequately explained by reference to the Lumpa internal
structure alone.

UNIP and the state

Calmettes's criticism has thus helped us to deepen our understanding
of Lumpa in terms of relations of production, even though we cannot
accept his own alternative analysis. Let us now proceed to re-examine
the other quasi-monolithic block in my original argument: that of
UNIP and the state, in an attempt to re-interpret both the nature and
the timing of the final conflict that led to Lumpa's annihilation.

We would do well to heed Cross's warning in the context of the
clashes between the Jehovah's Witnesses and the state in Zambia and
other African countries. In his view,[107]

> The course of events would appear to be determined more
> by the kings of the State than by the state of the Kingdom . . . .
> The clashes and restrictions may be more accurately explained
> by an examination of the particular demands of politicians.

Towards an understanding of the party side in the conflict Calmettes
has very little to contribute. He promises[108] to provide an analysis
of the class base of UNIP in north-eastern Zambia in what could have
been an answer to an urgent question I had raised:[109]

> The crucial issue is the mobilization process by which UNIP esta-

313

blished itself among the peasants of Chinsali district. But . . . no
new, detailed material is available on this point.

Calmettes reflects[110] on a handful of educated and politically-minded
activists who passed through Lumpa (in its pro-nationalist phase),
only to opt out of that organization when it could no longer identify
with the nationalist cause and/or serve their personal interests. But he
has hardly anything to say concerning the thousands of uneducated
peasants whose allegiance shifted from Lumpa to UNIP without,
apparently, any significant class differences between them and faithful
Lumpa adherents being involved.

Studies of class formation in Africa,[111] against the background of
a renewed interest in the theory of the state among Marxist general
theorists,[112] have stressed how in modern Africa the struggle between
classes over the control of the post-colonial state has become the
major form of class conflict. This state of affairs is attributed to such
factors as: the expansion of state control in all sectors of economic and
social life; the decline or removal, after independence, of those classes
which had firmly controlled the colonial state; and the fact that after
independence the state has become political, i.e. susceptible to processes of mass mobilization, factional strife and representational government. This insight may prove helpful to understand the timing and the
impetus of the final Lumpa conflict. Thus we might be able to proceed beyond the idealist, Weberian approach as pursued in my original
Lumpa study, which appears to attribute too much weight to the
problem of the legitimation of the post-colonial state as if this were
an independent input in the development of political processes in the
Third World (or anywhere else).

From the point of view of Lumpa members experiencing violent
persecution in rural north-eastern Zambia, the feuding as waged by
local branches of UNIP, and the final battles with state troops armed
with automatic weapons, all may have been part of the same process
of escalating violence. UNIP's president Dr Kaunda was leading the
UNIP transition government when negotiations to give up the fortified
villages broke off, and the order for military action was given. But in
fact the state and UNIP had only very recently merged into *one* force
confronting Lumpa. Nor did formal authority over the government
executive and the armed forces mean that UNIP had yet gained *de
facto* control over the entire state. The civil service was still largely
staffed with people who, until very recently, had opposed the nationalist movement and had assisted in its repression. Among them, anti-

Lumpa feelings may not have been so very strong. Thus, police officers in Lundazi (as a Lumpa area surpassed only by Chinsali district) ate their 1963 Christmas dinner inside a Lumpa stockaded village, where they were stationed in order to protect it against violent attacks from the local UNIP branch.[113] Short's claim[114] that Lumpa 'relations with the Police were good, as they spent much time protecting them from attack', may only apply to Lundazi.

In any case, UNIP's attainment of political supremacy with the creation of the transition government must have tipped the balance of UNIP/Lumpa feuding in a decisive way. Lumpa could no longer look to the state for protection against UNIP. State officers now had to obey orders given by leading UNIP politicians who, while not themselves involved in the UNIP/Lumpa feuding, yet had an emotional stake in the matter in so far as they hailed from Chinsali district (Kaunda, Kapwepwe) and politically could not afford to disavow the violence of their Chinsali UNIP branches. On the other hand, UNIP now had access to mobilization methods (state troops and their automatic weapons) which before they could not have brought to bear on Lumpa. And while these methods did not prove to be persuasive (1,500 killed and 20,000 emigrated bear witness to this) they were effective none the less.

Clearly, Lumpa leaders were not competing with the nationalist petty bourgeoisie that constituted UNIP's leadership, over the control of the entire Northern Rhodesian or Zambian state. However, on a more limited geographical scale, Lumpa's rejection of UNIP in north-eastern Zambia certainly amounted to a serious challenge of that bourgeoisie's position. My re-analysis in the light of Calmettes's criticism has shown how overall rejection of peasant incorporation, stressed as a sole factor in my earlier analysis, may have been only one side of Lumpa. The struggle of the Lumpa leadership to safeguard its own privileged position (which depended on the continued functioning of the structure of domination that Lumpa, as a regional-cultic mode of production, had imposed upon the countryside) may be another side. If so, another dimension of class conflict in Lumpa is revealed which so far has found little mention in the literature on class formation in modern Africa: the struggle between a secular bourgeoisie and a religious bourgeoisie. The issue at stake was not directly control of the state, but on the one hand a network of economic, political and social relations as existing in a significant part of the state's territory; on the other, the self-esteem and credibility of a political petty bourgeoisie uncertain of its recent hold on the state. Lumpa represented a threat to processes of mass mobilization at the grass-roots level, so crucial for a bourgeoisie aspiring to control the post-colonial state; at the same time, the state contained the military means to exterminate such threats. Therefore, once having secured a considerable degree of control over the state, the secular protagonist in this conflict could effectively crush its religious adversary.

Notes

Chapter 1 Introduction

1. For comments on earlier drafts of this chapter I am indebted to J.M. Schoffeleers, H.U.E. Thoden van Velzen, T.O. Ranger, A. Kuper, R.J. Papstein, J. Tennekes, R.P. Werbner, R. Buijten-huijs, H.L. van der Laan, R. Devisch, A. Droogers and J. de Wolf.
2. Murdock (1949); Köbben (1961, 1970); for a pioneer application of this approach to religion, see Swanson (1964).
3. Schapera (1956); Douglas (1964a); Kuper (1970); Richards (1950).
4. Taylor and Lehmann (1961); Fabian (1971); or the essentially sociological study by Wylie (1969).
5. Cf. Kuper (1973); Van Teeffelen (1978); Magubane (1971); *African Social Research*, no. 24 (December 1977) was entirely devoted to the history of the Rhodes–Livingstone Institute and contains much valuable material towards the understanding of the Manchester School in the Zambian context.
6. Marwick (1965a); Colson (1962, 1969); Turner (1957 and especially 1962, 1967, 1968, 1969).
7. Colson (1969), Long (1968) and White (1949a) are notable exceptions; as is, from the urban areas of Zimbabwe, Mitchell (1965).
8. Rotberg (1961, 1965, 1967); Ranger (1967); Bolink (1967).
9. Shepperson and Price (1958); Murphree (1969); Daneel (1971). Part II of Daneel's study was to appear in 1974; cf. Daneel's earlier, shorter studies of aspects of Zimbabwean religion (1970a, 1970b).
10. Werner (1971).
11. Langworthy (1969); Roberts (1973, based on his PhD thesis, Wisconsin, 1966); Mainga (1973, based on her PhD thesis,

London, 1969). At this stage in my argument, there is no point
in discussing the relative merits of these works, which of course
are hardly comparable.

12. Mainga (1972); Langworthy (1971).
13. Roberts (1970b, 1972; in this book the 1972 edition has been
used).
14. Werbner (1979). Robert J. Papstein's research in north-western
Zambia concentrated on religious historiography of the period
AD 1000–1900, but so far only his social and economic data
have been written up (Papstein, 1978).
15. Ranger (1967, cf. 1966).
16. Ranger (1979a) and references cited there.
17. Ranger and Kimambo (1972a).
18. Turner (1967, 1969); Shorter (1972); Alpers (1972): 179f;
Posnansky (1972): 51, 59; Ranger and Kimambo (1972b): 11.
19. Lewis (1966, 1971); Beattie & Middleton (1969b).
20. Ranger and Kimambo (1972b): 11.
21. Horton (1971, 1975); Ranger and Kimambo (1972b): 15f.
22. Gilsenan (1972): 64f; De Heusch (1964, 1966); the latter's
Le Roi ivre ou l'origine de l'état (1972) appeared too late to
have an impact on the Ranger and Kimambo volume.
23. Wright (1972): 156f; G. Wilson (1936, 1939); M. Wilson (1959).
24. E.g., Horton's theory (1971, 1975), or Schoffeleers's reconstruction of the history of the M'bona cult (1972a, 1972c).
Ranger's publications in this connexion include Ranger 1972a,
1972b, 1973b, 1974, 1978a, 1978b, 1979b.
25. The best recent overview of the field is Fernandez (1978a).
What falls specifically outside the scope of this volume are
recent studies of Central African churches and religious movements which stress symbolic and/or organizational patterns over
historical aspects and social change: Fabian (1971), Jules-Rosette
(1975), Johnson (1977).
26. Cf. p. 89: 'The participants of a given society have their systems
of explicit categories and definitions with which they attribute
meaning to their environment and their actions, and it is a major
task of social-scientific (and historical) research to identify these
systems and describe them in their internal coherence.' This is,
however, not what I have done in this book. I suppose I have concentrated on other 'major tasks', considering those more urgent,
or more neglected by others.
27. Turner (1969): 9.
28. M. Wilson (1957): 6.
29. Cf. Vansina (1968).
30. Prins (1978b): 312; my italics.
31. I have not yet published a full account of the Nkoya complex

of ancestor worship (cf. Van Binsbergen, forthcoming (a)),
but preliminary descriptions are available in Van Binsbergen
(1977c) and (1979c).

32. The Chewa case may illustrate this point. Around 1830, when
Gamitto (1960) passed through the Chewa lands in what is now
eastern Zambia, he encountered a form of ancestor veneration
in which baskets containing sacred snakes played a major part.
Nothing remained of this when, little more than a century later,
Bruwer and Marwick made anthropological studies of the Chewa.
For the Nkoya, such nineteenth-century sources are lacking,
but had they existed, what would they have left of our recon-
structions?

33. Cf. Shimunika, forthcoming; Van Binsbergen, forthcoming (a).

34. Cf. chapter 4, especially note 97.

35. Cf. section on 'The potential of the emerging theory', pp. 61 ff.

36. Cf. De Leeuwe (1973).

37. See pp. 116–32.

38. See pp. 61, 221–4, 327 n.7.

39. One area, however, where this book should have offered more
theoretical and conceptual reflexion, is that of witchcraft and
sorcery (cf. chapter 4). For a discussion of core problems in this
field, see Van Wetering (1973).

40. Prins (1978b): 311.

41. Lewis (1966, 1971); Wilson, P. (1967); Aberle (1970). For a
general theoretical discussion of the concept of relative deprivation, cf. Runciman (1972); echoes of these views in the context of Central African religious change are cited in chapter 2.

42. However, cf. note 26.

43. McKillop Wells (1978): 12.

44. Bourguignon (1973, 1976).

45. Greenbaum (1973).

46. Douglas (1970b): 116f.

47. Van Binsbergen 1971a, 1971b, 1976d, 1980, and forthcoming (b).

48. Werbner (1977a).

49. Cf. Ranger (1973b); Schoffeleers (1979b). The latter book is
mainly a collection of papers on shrine cults, presented at the
1972 Lusaka Conference on the History of Central African
Religious Systems.

50. Colson (1960, 1962).

51. Smith and Dale (1920); Jaspan (1953).

52. Gellner (1969).

53. At the time (1972–3), there was some confusion among historians as to the identification of the ethnic background of
aspirant rulers migrating into Zambia: were they Luba, Lunda,
or Luba-Lunda? Lacking the historical background to sort this

matter out, I followed Marcia Wright's advice and called them all Luba. I am not sure if this is still a tenable solution. For a recent study of Luba/Lunda intricacies, see Reefe (1977).

54. Vansina (1966).
55. De Heusch (1972).
56. Miller (1972, 1976).
    Van Binsbergen, forthcoming (a); Shimunika (forthcoming); Papstein (1978); Sangambo (1979).
58. See p. 334 nn. 47, 48, and Schoffeleers (1979b).
59. The outlines of the recent history of western Zambia from the perspective of the articulation of modes of production, which I present in this chapter as well as in chapter 7, are empirically based to a larger extent than the pious application of neo-Marxist catchwords might suggest. Admittedly, my main field-work among the Nkoya (1972–4) was not yet organized along the lines of this approach. But even so it did yield oral-historical data which, on second analysis, corroborate the views presented here. During shorter field-work trips in 1977 and 1978 my data-collection was specifically oriented towards the articulation approach. For a very preliminary analysis, see Van Binsbergen (1978). A wealth of relevant detail is moreover available in four collections of oral-historical data on Kaoma district: Clay (1946); Ikacana (1971); Shimunika (n.d.); and particularly in *Likota lya Bankoya*, an extensive collation of oral traditions by the Rev. J.M. Shimunika, which M. Malapa and I translated into English and which I am currently preparing for publication in both Shinkoya and English.
60. Horton (1971, 1975). The initial capitals of 'Intellectualist Theory' are Horton's. While his specific argument in these articles is in line with a host of related publications from his hand, on West African religion, philosophy, science, etc., his theory was particularly prompted by the publication of Peel (1968).
61. See Ranger and Kimambo (1972b): 15f; Ranger (1978a): 491f; Fisher (1973); Groff (1978); Fernandez (1978a) and references cited there.
62. Horton (1971): 101.
63. Horton (1975): 394f.
64. M. Wilson (1971).
65. E.g., the list of contributors of the most recent standard work on *Christianity in Independent Africa* (Fasholé-Luke *et al.*, 1978) contains forty-six people, of whom twenty-three hold titles of Christian religious office (Reverend, Pastor or Sister), while of the remaining scholars at least half are generally known to be practising Christians or Muslims.

66. Ranger (1978a): 495f.
67. Cf. note 35.
68. De Craemer *et al.* (1976).
69. De Craemer, *et al.* (1976): 465, as quoted in Ranger (1979b): 3.
70. Fernandez (1978a): 226.
71. Van Binsbergen (1976c): 111; see also p. 279 below.
72. Mary Douglas's cyclical view of witchcraft eradication (1963) comes close to the position of De Craemer *et al.*; see also p. 285 below.
73. Ranger (1978a): 497.
74. Ranger and Kimambo (1972b): 11f; Carter (1972), quoted approvingly in Papstein (1978): 218.
75. See pp. 95, 151–2, 181–93 and nn.
76. Cf. Ikacana (1971).
77. E.g., by Matthew Schoffeleers, when I presented a condensed version of chapter 4 at the Leiden Africa Seminar, spring 1976.
78. Ranger (1979b).
79. Ranger (1979b):20.
80. Vansina (1973, 1978).
81. Miller (1976).
82. A. Wilson (1978).
83. Janzen (1978).
84. Ranger (1979b):1f.
85. Ranger (1979b):20.
86. Skorupski (1975).
87. Skorupski (1975):207.
88. Horton (1971, 1975).
89. Fernandez (1978a):220f.
90. Fernandez (1978a):212f., 220; (1978b):4f; his main reference in this connexion is to my analysis of the Lumpa rising in terms of class conflict: see below, chapter 8.
91. Fernandez (1978a):222.
92. Turner (1968, 1969); Jules-Rosette (1975).
93. Fernandez (1978a):222.
94. Horton (1967).
95. Cf. Horton (1975):220, note 3; 224, note 12; section on 'Sharpening our tools' in the present Introduction, as well as my preface; and Van Binsbergen (1979a).
96. Fernandez (1978a):214.
97. See p. 84.
98. Turner (1968).
99. Ifeka-Moller (1974).
100. Horton and Peel (1976).
101. Werbner (1977a).

102. One aspect of the structure of the regions of Nzila and Bituma could have been stressed more than in the original article. Nzila's regions appeared to be far richer than Bituma's, and the fees circulating within the Nzila cult far higher than those in Bituma in the early decades of the latter cult. Nzila adepts are reported to pay in livestock (Reynolds, 1963:137), whereas Simbinga initially declined fees, and later tried to keep down the fees demanded by his senior officials. It is likely that this difference in wealth partly explains the greater success of the Nzila cult in building up and retaining an inter-local cult organization.

103. Prins (1978b):508.

104. Fisher (1973).

105. Horton (1975):375f.

106. Werbner (1977c):xviiif.

107. Matthew Schoffeleers (1972b; 1979c; cf. Ranger, 1973b: 590f.) draws my attention to what might be an example of such dialectics in the Central African context. As in various parts in Africa (cf. this book, chapters 4, 5, 7 for central western Zambia; Fisher, 1973:32 for West Africa), penetration of the macrocosm in the form of expansion of trade does not seem to lead at first to greater prominence of the High God, but to veneration of rather particularistic traders' spirits, with connotations of luck, misfortune, and (in the eyes of non-traders) alienness. While in the central Zambezi valley, a major trading area for many centuries, such traders' cults have flourished, the main centres of the High God cult are projected, in mirror-fashion, on the remote highlands to the north-east (Kapirinthiwa) and south-west (Mwali): i.e., where the macrocosmic penetration through trade was much less advanced.

108. Fisher (1973):39.

109. Horton (1975):381.

110. This reflects a phase in the growth of insight into the nature of ethnicity, both in my own work (Van Binsbergen, 1975a and forthcoming (a)), and generally. In the earlier chapters of this volume (2, 3), 'tribes' or 'ethnic groups' are still taken as viable, self-contained units of social analysis. In chapter 6, ethnicity is largely seen as part of a transactional structure hinging on individual self-interest. In my forthcoming analysis of the Nkoya social experience, I try to go beyond these points of view, presenting ethnicity both as a manipulable product of incorporation, and as an aspect of historical self-awareness, or identity.

111. Cf. Neckebrouck (1978:453), who cites my argument in a discussion of the same theoretical problems, such as they are

posed by his case study of a Kenyan independent church.

112. Interestingly, when Ranger (1979b) attempts to proceed beyond the limitations of the Hortonian model, he finds himself also struggling to apply a concept of relations of production, as derived from Godelier. Regrettably, Ranger's picture of my work (1979b:20) takes too little into account such progress in the same direction as I have made since chapter 4 was written. Of this progress, chapter 8 (which was published in 1977, and which Ranger cites) contains already sufficient indication that 'the transition from closed societies to open ones' is no longer an adequate summary of my evolving views.

113. See pp. 256-7.

114. Cf. note 59.

115. Meillassoux (1975); cf. Gerold-Scheepers and Van Binsbergen (1978):25f.

116. See pp. 226-8.

117. See p. 223.

118. See p. 277.

119. Also see pp. 261-3, 228-34.

120. Shifts of this nature are recorded in my field-notes. Cf. Van Binsbergen (1975a).

121. See Table 4.1.

122. See p. 273.

123. One could criticize the use of the concept of alienation in this connexion on two counts. First, it has a psychologistic ring which suggests that the essential enactment, and solution, of class struggle is at the level of the individual consciousness. And second, one might wonder whether the specific suffering created under specific relations of production is not exaggerated here as the main or perhaps even unique basis of religious innovation. Would not the more universal human experience of socialization, the taming of the human individual to become an adjusted and (inevitably) exploitable member of society, be a source of suffering of sufficient depth and scope to rival alienation as the root cause of religious innovation? The debate between Marx and Freud, as staged by their numerous pious or rebellious partisans, is however too central to the social sciences, and to the North Atlantic cultural tradition as a whole, to be dealt with in a note.

124. I am aware of recent writings which advocate a more diversified and complex view of African peasantries, claiming that current usage (see Saul and Woods, 1973; Palmer and Parsons, 1977) is too blunt and programmatic to serve the purposes of historical analysis (Ranger, 1977; 1978c:101f; McCracken, 1978). However, I would suggest that the modes-of-production

approach, which none of the authors mentioned here pursues, allows us that precision of definition, and that degree of shading of various class positions within the peasantry (in terms of their involvement in capitalist relations of production, and alternative modes) necessary to overcome Ranger's and McCracken's well-taken criticism; in fact, Ranger himself seems to be moving in this direction (1978c; 123f.).

125. My analysis of Lumpa shows the potential of a contextualized, materialist rather than idealist/symbolic, religious analysis. There are precious few sources on what Lumpa members actually felt and thought, what their specific religious beliefs were and what their motivations were when engaging in armed combat. Even Alice Lenshina's own religious notions are inadequately documented so far. Collections of the hymns she composed are hard to come by. Thus considered, my analysis in terms of class struggle against the process of peasantization or incorporation may appear to amount to an unwarranted imputation of radical ideas and intentions into the minds of Zambian peasants whose conscious views of their own situation may have been primarily religious rather than political. These peasants are unlikely to have had a thorough understanding of their own situation anyway. (Would they otherwise have pursued a predominantly religious idiom?) So whatever they might have told us about their own motives would always have to be augmented by a more structural analysis. Moreover, while we do not know what they felt and believed, we do know in considerable detail what their adherence to the Lumpa Church led them to do, in the way of political and military action. In addition, the material is there that enables us to sketch the outlines of their social, political and economic situation. Against that background, I believe one is justified in attempting to explain the Lumpa episode in terms of class struggle. But of course my tentative analysis has to be further developed in the light of at least the following two questions: why should this class struggle take a religious form; and suppose we manage to obtain better documentation on the subjective orientation of Lumpa adherents (cf. Calmettes, 1978; and pp. 305–16 below), how is the class struggle element reflected in the individual, subjective consciousness of the believers?

126. Calmettes (1978).
127. Godelier (1975a, 1977).
128. Van Binsbergen (1977b); cf. Bates (1976).
129. Werbner (1979b).
130. Fernandez (1978a; 1978b; 1978c).

131. Fernandez (1978a):213.
132. Ogburn and Nimkoff (1947).
133. In 1976, when chapter 8 was written, this way of looking at religious innovation in Africa seemed to be very much in the air. In our introduction to a collection of studies mainly of the political dimension in religious movements, Robert Buijtenhuijs and I perceived a 'shared trend towards the interpretation of modern religious innovation as local attempts to reconstruct a disrupted social order' (Van Binsbergen and Buijtenhuijs, 1976b: 10). It now looks as if this was rather a passing phase on the one hand towards more exclusively cultural and symbolic approaches (cf. Fernandez, 1978a:208f, 215f, 225f; Fabian, 1978; and references there), on the other hand towards more strongly Marxist analyses, as in my own recent work.
134. Schoffeleers (1979a).
135. Schoffeleers (1978); cf. Schoffeleers (1972a, 1972c).
136. Cf. Godelier (1973, 1975b); Houtard (1977); Houtard and Lemercinier (1977a); Schoffeleers (1978). Attempts to formulate the sort of symbolic theory which such a Marxist approach would need in order to reach maturity, include Augé (1975), Baré (1977), Sahlins (1976), Bloch (1977) and the exciting, rather underestimated book by Burridge (1971).
137. Cf. Wertheim (1964).
138. There is an underlying conceptual problem here. Modes of production are models or ideal-types, and as such defined to be distinct and irreducible. However, within concrete social formations various sub-systems, organized around specific relations of production, and tending towards one mode of production rather than the other, go through a process of development where the theoretical outlines of the mode of production, and its potential to organize social life, are only fully realized towards the end.
139. In my emergent theory of religious change along the lines of the modes-of-production approach, perhaps too little attention is paid to the effects of changes, not in the *relations of production* in which people are involved, but in the *productive forces,* which form a necessary condition for these relations. As a result, my treatment of the ecological factor throughout this book may have been more static and self-explanatory than would be justified by the actual historical processes productive forces have undergone in Africa during recent centuries. Thus in a recent study Kjekshus (1977) has stated the case for the possible disruption of East African ecologies at the level of one of the productive forces

(natural resources), in the late nineteenth century, when mainstream Marxist studies of the penetration of capitalism in
Africa would stress changes in the relations of production. In
the field of religious studies, this ties in with the debate about
the 'crisis explanation' of religious innovation (Ranger, 1979a).
In the present book I have virtually ignored this point of view.
Yet a rethinking (cf. chapter 4) of prophetism in western
Zambia in the 1910s (Ila prophets, Mupumani) and the 1930s
(eschatological and affliction prophets, including Simbinga),
against a background of evidence on droughts, locust plagues,
etc., would open up a whole new range of questions – and
perhaps answers.

140. In this respect the emerging, stratified model of contemporary
Central African religion may explain not only the retention
of historical religious forms, but also their resilience. As
declining urban conditions force people away from the towns
and back into the rural areas, they will engage, rather more
extensively than while still in town, in non-capitalist relations
of production. Under these circumstances it is likely that they
will opt out of more 'modern', articulation–centred religious
forms, and be drawn towards ancestral and chiefly cults.
For a quantitative analysis of this hypothesis, cf. Van
Binsbergen, forthcoming (a). For an argument in which the
continued participation in the domestic mode of production
is linked to the continued adherence to local medical systems
(including ancestor worship and cults of affliction) as rivals
of cosmopolitan, scientific health care, cf. Van Binsbergen
(1979c).

141. These processes will be discussed in detail in Van Binsbergen,
forthcoming (a).

142. Cf. Meillassoux (1964); Terray (1969); for a discussion of
this debate and its implications, cf. Pouillon (1976).

143. This is suggested not only by Meillassoux (1964, as compared
with 1975), but also, e.g., by the limited theoretical sophistication of the empirical contributions in two collections
edited by leading French Marxist anthropologists (Rey, 1976;
Amselle, 1976b); cf. Gerold-Scheepers and Van Binsbergen
(1978):29f.

144. Cf. Richards (1950).

145. See pp. 116–32.

146. Cf. Colson (1968); Lancaster (1974); Van Binsbergen (1975a).

147. See especially Godelier (1973).

148. See pp. 96, 172–3, 191–4, 201–3, 207, 226, 230, 274,
289–90.

149. See p. 171.

150. Ranger (1979b):20.
151. Schoffeleers (1979b).
152. Their partial nature is especially clear in the treatment of historical and independent Christian churches. While the available literature on religious change in Zambia would suggest that these churches constitute the main form that religious innovation has taken in this part of the world, yet in the present book they are never treated extensively and separately; and other forms of religious innovation, notably the chiefly cults, cults of affliction and witchcraft eradication movements, receive more systematic attention here than Christian churches.
153. See p. 220.

Chapter 2 Possession and mediumship in Zambia

1. I am indebted to Q. Neil Parsons, H.E. van Rijn and A. Turner for their stimulating criticism of this paper at various stages of its completion.
2. Murdock (1949); Lévi-Strauss (1949); Whiting and Child (1953).
3. Cf. Köbben (1970).
4. Department of Anthropology, University of Amsterdam.
5. Swanson (1964).
6. Cf. Köbben (1960); Fernandez (1964a); Beattie and Middleton (1969); Lewis (1971).
7. In order to avoid frequent repetition of a rather awkward formula, throughout this chapter the phrase 'religion and society' will stand for 'religion and the non-religious aspects of the society in which this religion occurs'; the abbreviated phrase by no means implies that religion is not an integral part of society. Meanwhile, if we want to study possession and mediumship as particular forms of *religion,* we should of course first devise a clear and widely acceptable definition of religion and its various aspects (ritual, cult, belief, movement, system, etc.). This however falls outside the scope of the present chapter (See pp. 23, 61).
8. Fromm (1952) develops an analogous argument with regard to the world of dreaming.
9. Firth (1959); Beattie and Middleton (1969b):xxvii; Fortes (1965); for Zambia: White (1949b, 1961).
10. For a fascinating discussion of the problem, with special reference to possession and mediumship, see Firth (1959): 141f.
11. Geertz (1966):34, 40.

12. Turner (1953, 1957, 1962, 1964, 1966, 1967, 1968, 1969).
13. Apart from his interesting, but difficult to evaluate, excursions in the field of comparative colour symbolism: Turner (1962, 1966). In his later works (1969, 1974a) Turner draws freely from comparative material from all over the world; but I believe it is fair to say that there his method is more that of a historian of religion (in the line of Eliade, Van der Leeuw, etc.) than of systematic, comparativist anthropology – and hence adds little directly to our comparative understanding of the Central African region.
14. Colson (1962):84f.
15. Spring Hansen (1972):27f; Turner (1968); Frankenberg (1969): 582f; Colson (1969):89f.
16. Turner (1957): 295.
17. Turner (1957):297.
18. Colson (1962):87; Turner (1957): chapter 10.
19. Turner (1957): chapter 10.
20. Langworthy (1971).
21. Turner (1957):291.
22. Turner (1968).
23. Durkheim (1912).
24. Cf. Goody (1961); Evans-Pritchard (1965); Van Binsbergen (1968).
25. Cf. note 12, and Colson (1962, 1969).
26. Geertz (1966):36.
27. Swanson (1964):62f.
28. Sundkler (1948).
29. Gluckman (1935, 1942); cf. (1958):69.
30. Cf. Sundkler (1961):22, 140.
31. Long (1968):229 and *passim*; Watson (1959):214; Rotberg (1967): chapter 6.
32. Cf. Beattie and Middleton (1969b):xxvf; Lewis (1971).
33. Frankenberg (1969).
34. Cf. Colson (1969):97f.
35. Langworthy (1971); Alexander and Rau apply the same reasoning to the offspring of Ngoni warriors (1972:1), but do not give references.
36. Colson (1958):140; Smith and Dale (1920):II, 74; Turner (1968): 149, 192.
37. Turner (1957, 1968); White (1949b, 1961); Spring Hansen (1972).
38. White (1961:48) advances, for the Luvale, the hypothesis that the significant factor underlying the preponderance of women in ancestral possession is the fact that women, due to virilocal marriage, tend to be more remote from their ancestors (ancestral

shrines). This hypothesis has the advantage that it can easily be tested with quantitative material. Though extremely limited in its reliance on one structural aspect of society, White's hypothesis even seems applicable to peoples like the Tonga, amongst whom post-marital residence (at least according to Colson) is not subjected to formal norms, but where statistical tendencies towards virilocality do exist (cf. Colson, 1958:23f; 1960:97).

39. Langworthy (1971).
40. In line with general usage: Firth (1969); Beattie and Middleton (1969b).
41. Richards (1969):48; McCulloch (1951); White (1949b, 1961); Colson (1962):4; Whiteley (1950).
42. Doke (1931):244f; White (1949b, 1961); Smith and Dale (1920): II, 137f; McCulloch (1951).
43. Langworthy (1971).
44. Colson (1962):lf., 84f; Jaspan (1953):60f.
45. Cunnison (1959); Richards (1939):48, 241; Doke (1931):243f; Stefaniszyn (1964):156f; Werner (1971); Slaski (1951).
46. Colson (1958, 1960, 1962, 1969); Scudder (1962):111f; Doke (1931); Reynolds (1963): chapter 5; Jaspan (1953):41f; Langworthy (1971); Watson (1959):162f; on the absence of the rain cult among the Bemba: Richards (1939):380.
47. Doke (1931):203f; Kuntz (1932); Turner (1968); Brelsford (1950); White (1949b, 1961); McCulloch (1951).
48. Richards (1939); Cunnison (1959).
49. Malinowski (1954):44f.
50. Kuntz (1932); Turner (1952); McCulloch (1951).
51. Rotberg (1967):137f; Taylor and Lehmann (1961); Colson (1969):101f; my urban field-notes.
52. Gluckman (1951); White (1949b, 1961); Colson (1969); Turner (1952, 1957, 1968); McCulloch (1951); Stefaniszyn (1964); Reynolds (1963); Kuntz (1932); Spring Hansen (1972); Doke (1931):254f.
53. E.g., between Upper and Middle River Gwembe Tonga: Colson (1960):24.
54. Colson (1969):94f; (1964):4; Hugo (1935); White (1949b); (1961):49f; Kuper (1955); Tracey (1934); Stefaniszyn (1964): 156f.
55. Such an analysis is offered by Colson (1969):96f.
56. White (1949b); (1961):46f.
57. McCulloch (1951); Colson (1969); see also chapters 4, 5 and 7.
58. White (1949b, 1961).
59. Colson (1964, 1971).
60. Werner (1971).
61. Daneel (1970a, 1970b, 1971, 1974); Murphree (1969).

62. Ranger (1966, 1967, 1970); Garbett (1966).
63. Though there is already some literature on the colonial political role of Tonga and Ila mediums: Rotberg (1967):75; Smith and Dale (1920):II; Schlosser (1949):44f; Colson (1962):223f.
64. In addition to the attention they already received from the medical side: Leeson (1969); Savage King, personal communication.
65. Colson (1969):85.
66. Cf. Beattie and Middleton (1969b):xxviiif.
67. Sundkler (1961):302.

Chapter 3 The history and sociology of territorial cults in Zambia

1. The material for this chapter derives from the following sources: (a) most available written material relevant to territorial cults in Zambia, with special emphasis on academic publications and with virtual neglect of two important categories of data: archival sources and early accounts by European travellers and missionaries; (b) my own research on various forms of religion in contemporary Zambia, and on urban-rural relationships among the Nkoya. I am indebted to T.O. Ranger, J.K. Rennie, J.M. Schoffeleers, J. van Velsen, R.P. Werbner and M. Wright for criticism of earlier drafts; and to R.S. Roberts for final editorial efforts.
2. Schoffeleers (1972b).
3. Smith and Dale (1920):II, 140f; Schlosser (1949):29f., 44f; Colson (1960):165; (1962):84-5; (1969):69-103, especially 77; (1971):226-7; Cunnison (1950):31; Torrend (1906-9): 548-9; Doke (1931):230-1. For a Malawian parallel of the prophetic alternative to shrine cults, see Schoffeleers (1972c).
4. For a summary of the relevant literature on Zambian non-communal rain-calling specialists, see Reynolds (1963):128-9.
5. White (1960):46; Turner (1957):319-20.
6. Schoffeleers (1979b).
7. Typical examples are found in Stefaniszyn (1964):155-6; Brelsford (1946):135; Doke (1931):239-40.
8. Vansina (1966):19.
9. Vansina (1966):30-1.
10. Richards (1939):356-7.
11. Richards's identification of the normal dwelling hut as just another type of shrine is quite justified and equally applies to Zambian peoples other than the Bemba (see Colson, 1960:53). For the purpose of analysis in this chapter, however, I shall

concentrate on those shrines that do not primarily serve such a
clearly utilitarian purpose as a house does.

12. An account of the periodical erection of temporary 'shade
huts' at permanent sacred spots is given by Stefaniszyn (1964):
155–6.

13. Turner (1957):119, 126ff; McCulloch (1951):72–3; White
(1960):12. On the Luchazi, see note 87 below.

14. See Declé (1898):239 for a Mambwe example.

15. See Melland (1923):138 for a Kaonde example.

16. See Melland (1923):133, for a Kaonde example; Smith and
Dale (1920):I, 162 for an Ila example; my field-notes contain
Nkoya examples.

17. I shall not dwell here upon the subject of spirit provinces: the
division of the landscape into areas where each area is supposed
to be associated with a particular spirit, the spirits being arranged
in some hierarchical relationship with one another. For Zambia,
the subject is properly documented only for the Mambwe; see
Werner (1979). There are some indications of similar notions
in the accounts of the Tonga shrine cults (see Colson, 1960:
187–8; *passim*; and Scudder, 1962:111–2). On the other hand
we can assume that Garbett's description of spirit provinces
among the Korekore south of the Zambezi also applies to the
Zambian Korekore (Goba), about whose religion very little is
known; see Garbett (1966, 1969) and Mvula (1973). In view of
my discussion of shrines, ecology and the landscape, more
information on a spiritual partition of the landscape would be
extremely valuable.

18. They are reported to be absent among the Ila (see Smith and
Dale, 1920:I, 139).

19. Or, under modern conditions, where he identifies himself as a
member of the village when, born in town, he visits his village
home for the first time.

20. Turner (1957):292–3; (1968):52ff; White (1949b); (1961):46–7;
my field-notes contain Nkoya examples.

21. See Brelsford (1949) for Chisinga ironworkers; White (1956b)
for Luvale fishing and hunting and (1959):14 for Luvale honey-
collectors; Doke (1931):242–3 for Lamba hunters and
dancers; my field-notes contain Nkoya hunter examples.

22. Cunnison (1959):220–1; Slaski (1951):93; Werner (1971):1–2;
(1979); Richards (1939): 358; Oger (1972a).

23. Stefaniszyn (1964):156–7; Doke (1931):242–3.

24. The term 'culture hero' could be used for named, anthropomorphic a-historical beings who are considered to have introduced the local culture or an important element of it; e.g.,
Mulenga, who first domesticated animals, and Kapinda, the

first hunter, among the Bemba (see Oger, 1972a), and Kanyanyu Mangaba among the Tumbuka (see Banda, n.d.).

25. The High God can be defined as an invisible entity, postulated by the members of a society, and to whom they attribute the following characteristics: he is thought of as a person; he is the only member of a unique class of invisible entities; he may be considered the ultimate creator; he tends to be associated with the sky and with meteorological phenomena.

26. See Van Binsbergen (1972b, chapter 2 of this volume), (1976a, cf. chapter 4); and references cited there.

27. Melland (1923):155–6. Melland emphasized that the rain ritual is the only occasion in Kaonde religion known to him where ritual is directed to the High God. It is possible that what he takes to be 'traditional' is in fact a recent innovation, particularly an aspect of the prophetic movement of Mupumani which reached the Kaonde at about the same time that Melland became their administrator; cf. below.

28. Mainga (1972):96.

29. See Langworthy (1971); (1972):30, 34, 55; Schoffeleers (1972c).

30. However, among the Luvale the 'clan formula' used in the village shrine ritual reinforces identification (though not effective interaction) with widely dispersed clan members, on the inter-local level; see White (1960):12.

31. See Werner (1979) for Kapembwa; Brelsford (1946): 136–7, for the Ikoma pool; Colson (1960):166, 187 for examples from southern Zambia.

32. Colson (1960):61–2, 163–4, 20f; Scudder (1962):112–3 and *passim*.

33. Cf. Carter (1972); and chapter 2 of this volume.

34. See Bruwer (1952) for the *Chauta* institution among the Chewa; Werner (1979) and Declé (1898):293–4 on the Mambwe; Richards (1951):185; (1939):385f and Brelsford (1944):28–9 on female custodians of the Bemba royal relic shrines; and Oger (1972a) on *ngulu* wives.

35. The religion of north-western Zambia is exceptionally thoroughly researched (see, for example, Turner, 1953, 1957, 1962, 1967, 1968, 1969; White 1949b, 1961; McCulloch (1951): 72–83 and references cited there; Melland (1923): 127–236), but no evidence of a priestly inter-local shrine cult has been reported.

36. See Turner (1957):25f, and (1967):280–98 for the Southern Lunda; Melland (1923): 91, 96, 229, 243, 256f. for the Kaonde; Richards (1939):344–5 for the Bemba; my field-notes contain Nkoya examples.

37. It could be suggested that my tentative interpretation here is just a lapse back into the old 'explanations' of magic and religion

such as offered by Frazer, Lang and Freud. I doubt whether this
is the case. The interpretation of religion faces at least two
major problems: first, the recognition of some correspondence
between certain religious and non-religious phenomena; and
second (once the general idea of such correspondence is agreed
upon), the detailed explanation of this correspondence which,
among other aspects, involves the attempt to account for the
selection, in a given society, of particular religious forms which
have a specific, systematic relationship with particular non-
religious aspects. The recognition of *some* correspondence
between religious and non-religious aspects has been one of the
main achievements of the nineteenth-century studies of such
authors as Feuerbach, Marx, Fustel de Coulanges and Durkheim.
It is the second problem that dominates many modern religious
studies. Here it becomes necessary to examine and contrast the
formal structures of corresponding religious and non-religious
forms in an attempt to develop a systematic and generalizable
approach which will take us beyond the psychologism and
ad hoc interpretation based on one society only – fallacies to
which so many pioneers in this field have fallen victim. My
attempt is along these lines. It does not stop at the trivial claim
of some correspondence between everyday 'ecological' activities
and 'ecological' shrine ritual, but tries to point out the underlying *specific* correspondence between the constituent formal
properties of these two socio-cultural systems.

38. See Kay (1967):21-2.
39. As denounced by such early sociologists as Durkheim (1897)
     and Sorokin (1928).
40. See Colson (1962):92-3, 217 for a discussion of the Tonga
     village founder raised to the status of land spirit.
41. In other words, she fails to give attention to the second inter-
     pretational problems as outlined above, note 37.
42. For a study of the communal functions of the shelter, particularly
     in defining the village as an effective though rapidly changing
     group, see Watson (1954), based on research by Watson and
     Van Velsen among the Kaonde.
43. This is the general situation in north-western Zambia. See
     Turner (1957), especially Map 4, for the Lunda; Mwondela
     (1972):34-5 for the Luvale; my field-notes contain Nkoya
     examples.
44. Among the Nkoya the erection of a new village shrine is the
     first task when making a new village.
45. See Colson (1960):98.
46. For example, the ruling Kazembe in 1914 removed the royal
     cult from Lunde, where the first Kazembe was buried, to this

capital, by making replicas of the old graves (even of those of the Mwaat Yaavs) and planting new trees on them (Cunnison, 1961:112).

47. See, for example, the eastern Lunda's destruction of the Aushi national shrine Makumba, below, note 94; the Ngoni's destruction of rain shrines (McCracken, 1968a:103, 121; 1968b:196).

48. Schoffeleers (1972a):73–94; (1972c); Ranger and Kimambo (1972b):6–7.

49. Cunnison (1951):24 relates the following Luapula tradition on the pygmies preceding the Bantu population around Lake Mweru: 'They are believed to have been of the same clan as Kaponto, the man who invaded the island Kilwa. There are believed to have been two survivors . . . who made Kaponto promise to keep up the modes of *prayer to ancestors, of rain ritual,* and of the Butwa society which was peculiar to the pygmies' (my italics). For hypotheses concerning the role of Batwa shrine cults, see Linden (1979).

50. Clarke (1950); Fagan and Philipson (1965).

51. White (1962); (1960):46; Vansina (1966); Watson (1959):12–13; Cunnison (1950):7–8, 12; (1951):23–4.

52. See, for example, Evans-Pritchard (1940); Fortes (1945, 1953); Southall (1956); Middleton and Tait (1958).

53. Peters (1967).

54. Barnes (1962).

55. Gluckman (1950).

56. Colson (1962):102–3; Turner (1957); Van Velsen (1964).

57. Gellner (1963, 1969); Van Binsbergen (1971a); (1980); see also my critique of Gellner (1969): Van Binsbergen (1971b).

58. Smith and Dale (1920): II, 186–7.

59. Ibid.

60. Colson (1960):164, 166. On a more limited scale the institution has continued to exist: the payment of a chicken or goat by the person divined as having caused the wrath of the spirit of the shrine.

61. Colson (1962):113, where it is mentioned as one of several factors giving high status to a local leader.

62. Colson (1962):100.

63. Colson (1962):218.

64. Garbett (1966, 1969).

65. Durkheim (1912):*passim.*

66. Cf. chapter 2.

67. Vansina (1966):82–3.

68. See White (1949a), Vansina (1966):85–6, especially in relation to north-western Zambia and adjacent areas.

69. Roberts (1973):38–93; Cunnison (1950):11–12; (1959):30f., 147f; these refer to north-eastern Zambia, where the growth of Luba and Lunda kingship in the eighteenth century formed the culmination of a process of gradual immigration and political development that had been going on for several centuries.
70. Tweedie (1966):204 (my italics). The passage on cleaning the shrines is not included in Roberts's synthetic account (1973:40) of Bemba myths of origin.
71. Probably the construction of the high tower, as recorded in many other myths from the Bemba and neighbouring peoples in Central Africa; see Roberts (1973):30f., 147f.
72. For references on Luchele, see, e.g., Hall (1968): 11f., and Roberts (1973):346f. *Nganga* means doctor.
73. Brelsford (1946):130–1; Werner (1979); Cunnison (1959):218ff.
74. For Luchele see note 72; for the theme of hitting the tree, see Chimba (n.d.); Chiwale (1962):50. Even what is claimed to be the most important (tree) shrine of the Ila has a spearhead embedded in its bark: Anonymous (1973); although, as we shall see in a later section, Luba-ization of the Ila has not been successful.
75. Werner (1971).
76. See Richards (1939):359–60.
77. Roberts (1973):69–71.
78. Werner (1971):14–15; see Oger (1972a) for a similar view.
79. Oger (1972a); Werner (1971); Slaski (1951):93; Richards (1939): 358; (1951); Whiteley (1950):30.
80. Apthorpe 1960.
81. Apthorpe 1960:20; Northern Rhodesia was the colonial name for Zambia.
82. Apthorpe (1959b).
83. Richards (1939):358; and especially Oger (1972b). Oger has written a paper in Bemba on this and related subjects which unfortunately was not available for the present study.
84. Brelsford (1942):1f., 15, 21; (1944); Oger (1972b).
85. Mainga (1972): 96–7; Clay (1946):3; my field-notes on Luchazi history; on the Luchazi, see also note 87.
86. See the prominence of the royal bracelet in early Lunda traditions, in Cunnison (1961):2, 6–7.
87. It is attractive to view *Mukanda* (boys' puberty ritual), a central religious institution among Luvale, Luchazi, Chokwe, Mbunda and Southern Lunda, as an alternative to the priestly inter-local shrine cult: see White (1961):1–27; McCulloch (1951):85f; Mwondela (1972):*passim*; Gluckman (1949); Turner (1967):151–279. *Mukanda* certainly provides inter-local communications, sometimes over hundreds of kilometres, and

ceremonial specialization which might take on political functions
comparable to those of the inter-local priestly shrine cults (see
White, 1956a; 1961:1-2). The idea of *Mukanda* forming an
alternative to the territorial cult is further corroborated by
Colson's data on Tonga immigrants: while in the past immigrants
to Tongaland had always organically been assimilated into
Tonga society – including adoption of Tonga ritual – Luvale
immigrants who have penetrated the area since the early decades
of this century remained in separate villages and, far from
adopting Tonga inter-local territorial cults, continued to send
their boys to *Mukanda* initiation camps in the west (Colson,
1970:35–54, especially 38). *Mukanda*, not unlike *Nyau* in
eastern Central Africa, seems to represent an even older stage
than the priestly territorial cult, and to be associated with a
hunting and gathering economy rather than with more developed
agriculture or husbandry (see White, 1949a:30). Much more
research is needed before the place of the *Mukanda* complex
in Central African religious history can be determined. Meanwhile, it should be noted that the Chokwe and Luchazi, while
belonging to the ethnic cluster practising *Mukanda,* have
their homelands not in Zambia but in south-western Zaïre and
north-eastern Angola. The Chokwe and Luchazi (as shown in
Maps 1 and 2) on the Zambian/Angolan border between
Zambezi and Mwinilunga, are isolated groups of recent
immigrants. From the late 1910s, hundred of thousands of
Angolans (mainly belonging to the ethnic groups of Luvale,
Chokwe, Mbunda, Luchazi, Ovimbundu) have migrated into
Zambia.

88. White (1949a):30, 33–4; (1960):46, approvingly summarized
in Vansina (1966):85–6.
89. Richards (1969):23–5; (1939):359–60; (1951); Brelsford
(1944): especially 37–8.
90. Brelsford (1942); (1944):2–3.
91. Werner (1971); Oger (1972a).
92. Gluckman (1951):1–93, especially 85; Mainga (1972):102f;
Turner (1952):50; Langworthy (1971):1–23 especially 9;
(1972):28–9, 55–6, for the Undi Kingdom; Linden (1979).
93. Cunnison (1959):217–18.
94. Cunnison (1959):219–20; Chimba (n.d.):6–7; Kay (1964):16;
Philpott (1936).
95. Werner (1979).
96. Brelsford (1946):136–7.
97. Vansina (1966):245–6.
98. Vansina (1966):245–6.
99. Brelsford (1944):3.

100. See Colson (1962):207, and a similar view in Billing (1959).
101. Livingstone (1899):363; Schapera (1960):145–6, 207.
102. Anderson (1919).
103. Myers (1927).
104. Colson (1960):167–8.
105. Smith and Dale (1920):II, 180–1; Jaspan (1953):41; Fielder (1965).
106. Fagan (1963):157–77, especially 174f.
107. Fagan (1963); Fagan and Phillipson (1965):274–5.
108. Siddle (1971); Phillipson (1968).
109. Fagan and Phillipson (1965).
110. Fagan *et al.* (1969):II, 135–9, 142f; Fagan and Phillipson (1965).
111. Miracle (1959).
112. Mukuni (n.d.); Muntemba (1970).
113. Colson (1970). A highly interesting group for further research is the ethnic cluster of the 'Baluba', whom Smith and Dale ((1920):I, xxvii, 25f., 40, 123, 313) report as living at the periphery of the Ila, and as Ila-speaking.
114. Melland (1923):29–30. The Kaonde are generally considered to be of Luba extraction.
115. Smith and Dale (1920):II, 180ff.
116. Smith and Dale (1920):II, 181ff.
117. Van Binsbergen (1971a); (1971b); (1980).
118. Archer (1971) summarizes the pattern of rainfall in Zambia. Towards the south there is a considerable decrease in average annual rainfall and a considerable increase in annual fluctuations in rainfall (i.e., greater uncertainty and unpredictability).

Chapter 4 Religious change and the problem of evil in western Zambia

1. I am indebted to T.O. Ranger, R.J. Papstein, M.S. Muntemba, J.M. Schoffeleers, and the participants of Leiden Africa Seminar (1976), for their comments on earlier drafts of this chapter, and for more general discussions on parts of the argument. In this chapter the word 'region' is employed in its usual geographical sense, without any of the implications this term would have in regional-cults theory (cf. chapters 5 and 7).
2. With the exception of the Totela and Subiya to the south-west, on whom very little is known.
3. Relevant general sources for the region include Brelsford (1965): 14f., 49–68, 74–7; Chibanza (1961); Clay (1946); Doke (1931);

Fielder (1968–9); Ikacana (1971); Jaspan (1953); McCulloch (1951);
Mainga (1973):148f. and *passim;* Melland (1923); Shimunika
(n.d.), claimed to be an African National Congress publication
from Kaoma, cf. Mainga (1973):225, 242f; Smith and Dale
(1920); Turner (1952); Whiteley (1950):55f., 65f. In addition,
there is a wealth of general information available in the
Zambia National Archives, e.g., district notebooks of Mankoya,
Kasempa, Namwala, Mumbwa; the reports of the Gielgud-
Anderson expedition to the Kafue Hook, BS1/93 and KTJ1/1;
G.H. Nicholls, Notes on the Natives Inhabiting the Baluba Sub-
District, 1906, enclosure in KTJ2/1; J.G. Hall, A Paper on the
Origin of the Baila, 1917, KSF 3/1 and KSF 2/1/I, p. 173f.
(one of the best pieces of sociological and historical analysis to
be produced by the colonial administration of Zambia). All
file references are to the Zambia National Archives, Lusaka. The
identification of two main ethnic and linguistic clusters in the
area, which admittedly represents a very rough and tentative
classification, is based on Fortune (1959):26f., 33f. More recent
historical and linguistic work on the area (e.g., Kashoki, 1978:
18 f.) seems to suggest more subtle distinctions within the non-
Tonga group.

4. In the region, joking relations include those between Tonga/Nkoya,
    Ila/Nkoya (although Nkoya may claim that due to the massive
    assimilation of Nkoya among the Ila, relations are more like
    'brothers' than like 'grandfathers'), Ila/Kaonde, Lenje/Kaonde,
    and Lenje/Nkoya (my field-notes).

5. Trapnell and Clothier (1937).

6. At present the Kafue National Park, an uninhabited fly-infested
    area of some 20,000 km^2, forms the empty heart of the region,
    and wrongly suggests sharp cultural and linguistic discontinuity
    between the Kaoma (formerly Mankoya) and Kasempa districts
    to the west, and the Mumbwa and Namwala districts to the
    east. A game reserve was gazetted in the Hook of the Kafue in
    1908, but occupation and hunting by the local population
    never ceased until 1933, when the much larger Park was created
    to the west and north of the former reserve. Before that time
    the area was in parts densely populated (it had formed a sanc-
    tuary against the Kololo, Ngoni, Chikunda and Yeke raids in the
    nineteenth century). It was intimately linked (through marriage,
    trade, migration, raiding, against a common cultural and lin-
    guistic background) with the areas to the west and east. Mean-
    while, game preservation has led to a marked increase of
    tsetse-fly, affecting the areas bordering on the present park.
    (Gielgud, Nicholls (see note 3); KDB1/2; ZA1/9/37/4.)

7. Sources on the religion of the region include: Doke (1931);

Kuntz (1932); Mainga (1972); Melland (1923); Reynolds
(1963); Smith and Dale (1920); Smith (1935); Turner
(1952):48f; Nicholls (see note 3): 7f. Primarily relevant for the
study of the missions' impact, but occasionally reflecting on the
pre-mission religious situation, are the publications of missionary
societies working in the region, particularly: *Herald of the
Primitive Methodist Missionary Society* (cf. Fielder 1965), and
The S.A.G.M. [South Africa General Mission] Pioneer. While
all these sources provide ample comparative evidence for the
claimed religious homogeneity of the region, the description
in the present section is largely based on my own participatory
research among the Mashasha (eastern Nkoya). Since most
aspects of nineteenth-century religion are still in existence, I
use the present tense.

8. Smith and Dale (1920):II,181f; Namwala Station daybook: 6,
127 (KSF 2/1/I); Hall (see note 3):6; 'Extract from an Old
Report of Mr Dale's' (enclosure in KTJ 2/1); ' "Mukamwani" and
of Mr Dale's' (enclosure in KTJ 2/1); ' "Mukamwani" and
"Bamowa" ' (Lenje possession cults), Native Commissioner
Ndola, 17 April 1923 (enclosure in U1/3); Chilanga district
notebook: 226f, under the heading 'Lenje Religion', KSA 6/1;
also pp. 117–18, 128–32 below.

9. See pp. 18–19, 65.

10. Sources on creation myths in the region are very scarce. I
follow here a Nkoya version, disclosed to me by the prophet
Lubumba, and later corroborated by the Mutondo royal
council (my field-notes).

11. Melland (1923):155f. and Smith and Dale (1920):II, 209
mention rain ritual directed to God, but imply that this was
resorted to very infrequently. The Kaonde rain ritual which
Melland describes as 'traditional' may well have been an
innovation pertaining to Mupumani's cult (see below), which
reached the Kaonde at about the same time that Melland
became their administrator. Despite the common origin between
the Lozi (*Luyi*) and the Nkoya (as manifested by their languages
and historical traditions: Givon, 1971; Fortune, 1963; Mainga
(1973):15f; field-notes), among the Nkoya I found no traces of
a High-God cult similar to the one hinted for the early Lozi
in the Kalabo area (Mainga, 1972:95f.).

12. Hunting ritual (led by, but rarely confined to, accomplished
hunters) is well developed in this region (field-notes; Melland,
1923:258, 286f; Smith and Dale, 1920:II,209; Gatti, 1932:39f.)
and at least two of the religious innovators to be discussed below
were great hunters: Mwepya and Lubumba (see notes 73 and 79).

13. Van Binsbergen (1979b); this volume, chapter 3.

14. For the common Central African institution of the inheritance of a deceased's social person, cf. Munday (1948); Stefaniszyn (1954); Colson (1962):1f; (1960):123f.

15. Turner's analyses of reconciliatory shrine ritual among the Ndembu of north-western Zambia apply to some extent to our region: Turner (1957):123f., 288f; (1968) *passim*. It should, however, be pointed out that among the Nkoya the actual contribution of religious institutions (divination, shrine ritual, cults of affliction) to intra-group conflict resolution is limited, and presupposes non-religious factors working towards reconciliation. Moreover, the one other major religious institution, sorcery, when encountered in a situation of personal social conflict, usually implies the escalation of such conflict to a point where the only way out is fission; cf. Van Binsbergen (1974):4f.

16. Cf. Van Binsbergen (1979c): postscript.

17. In the most comprehensive sociological study of central African sorcery, Marwick (1965a:94f., 289f. and *passim*; 1965b) concentrates entirely on sorcery as an expression of direct conflict in personal, 'multiplex' relationships.

18. Cf. Gluckman (1967):423: 'the old fears that no man advances save by using witchcraft to kill his own kin'; Melland (1923): 204f; Smith and Dale (1920): I, 260f; Smith (1935):477f; Doke (1931); Mainga (1972):102f; Holub (1881):II, 241; Chibanza (1961):50; Shimunika (n.d.):1f; Turner (1968): 136f.

19. Cf. burials suggesting social stratification in the late first millennium: Fagan (1967):124; Fagan *et al.* (1969):58f.

20. Field-notes; Smith and Dale (1920): I, 20f; Ikacana (1971):1f. The views of Miller (1972) as to the very early rise of central African states may not be applicable to central western Zambia.

21. Cf. Roberts (1970):717f., 723f.

22. Smith and Dale (1920):I, 299f; Fielder (1968-9):11 and *passim*; Van Binsbergen (1979b); this book, chapter 3.

23. Smith and Dale (1920):II, 181f; Van Binsbergen (1979b); pp. 117-18, 128-32 below.

24. Muntemba (1972a):2f; (1970).

25. Brelsford (1935).

26. Melland (1923):36f; Chibanza (1961):43f; Copeman, MS papers, enclosure in CO 3/4/2; Nicholls (see note 3):3f.

27. Field-notes; Shimunika (n.d.):1f; Smith and Dale (1920):I, 25; Nicholls, (see note 3):3f.

28. Field-notes; Tuden (1958): especially 71f; Gielgud (see note 3); U 1/2; KDE 2/36/3. Slavery was still an important topic in the Mankoya district correspondence, 1931-5 (KSX 1/1/1).

29. The association of high status with *both* terror *and* supernatural benevolence (the latter aspect exemplified by the central place hunting occupies in the ecologico-religious system, and by the conception of God as the first archetypal chief of the heavenly village) can be partly explained as an attempt at supernatural legitimation on the part of high-status groups; but beyond this, the ambivalence seems a universal feature of the sacred (cf. Durkheim 1912:584f; Otto, 1917: *passim*).

30. Nkoya names for these beings include: *Byamulishaka* ('forest things'), *Lube, Mwendanjangula* ('tree-top walker'), *Shibinda* ('hunter'); cf. Reynolds (1963):50, 64f; Ikacana (1971):34; Melland (1923):226; Doke (1931):242f. (on *moba*). Apart from the mythical snakes, another major manifestation of these forces of the deep forest is what we might call the *halfling*, using a term coined by Tolkien (1975) for very different mythical beings. In the Central African context, the halfling is a being in the shape of a human person, but having only the right or the left side of a normal body.

31. E.g., Doke (1931):242f; Stefaniszyn (1964):156f. The complex seems closely related to the *ngulu* complex of northern Zambia: cf. Whiteley (1950); Slaski (1951):93f; Werner (1971).

32. A good summary of the doctor's role in Melland (1923):199.

33. Livingstone (1899):75; Smith and Dale (1920):I, 31; II, 144f., 347f; Schlosser (1949):29f; Mushindo (1973):59f.

34. Colson (1960):164–6 and *passim*; (1962):92f., 100; Scudder (1962):111f; Doke (1931):244f; Cunnison (1959):220f; Torrend (1906–9). Melland (1923: 149), referring to the time when Mupumani's movement swept over Kaondeland (see below, and Chibanza, 1961:80f.), explicitly denies the existence of prophets among the Kaonde!

35. Smith and Dale (1920):II, 140f; Schlosser (1949):44f; specific sources on Mupumani are cited below. In addition to those discussed by Smith and Dale and Schlosser, there is archival evidence on the following prophets in the Ila and Sala area, in the early twentieth century: Njebe (a prophet who took the name of a deceased *boma* messenger allegedly withholding the rain: Namwala Station daybook, p. 209, KSF 2/1/I); Ntambo and Shikariabwizu ('two descendants of one Zhingu, a chief of Basala origin to the East': 'Extract. . .', see note 3); Tambakuwa ('who said he was God'; enclosure in ZA 1/10/vol. 3, no. 4: statement by chief Lilanda).

36. While Rotberg (1967:135f.) is anxious to claim religious roots for later mass nationalism, Henderson (1970b, especially 673f.) is probably right in largely denying such roots. For a theoretical discussion on the difficulties involved in the analysis of modern

Central African religion in terms of protest and deprivation, see Van Binsbergen (1972b; see pp. 87–8, also 15, 58–9 below).

37. Cf. Mainga (1973):149f; Holub (1881); Stokes (1966). There is abundant archival material on Lozi influence among the Ila; e.g., Gielgud (see note 3); ZA 1/13; KSF 1/6.

38. Fielder (1968–9); Tuden (1958).

39. Gielgud, 5 July 1901, 9 October 1901, 21 February 1902 (BS 1/93); Copeman describes the Ila attack on the trader Rankin (enclosure in C03/4/2). Tensions also existed at the Kansanshi mine, north of the region, as became manifest in an alarming rate of desertions amongst the African workers, apparently related to an early anti-white religious movement. As Copeman, the Kasempa district officer, made investigations, he 'learned that the Head Capitao and some of his friends appeared to keep the remainder of the native employees in a state of terror'. The Head Capitao turned out to be in the possession of 'a gruesome collection of skulls and human bones and all the paraphernalia of a witch doctor . . .. The Capitao by claiming supernatural powers had sought to make as many as possible join in a horrible brotherhood of which he was the leader. Those who refused to have anything to do with it he used his position to ill-treat. It came out that he had boasted that he would live for ever, and that presently all the white men would die and he and his friends would take possession of their belongings. Those whom he persuaded to join his brotherhood were promised that they would share these benefits, but before they were qualified to do so they had to go to the burial place and dig up the latest buried corpses and possess themselved of certain portions, they also had to break the arm and leg bones and suck out the marrow and indulge in other loathsome practices'. Copeman publicly destroyed the Capitao's sorcery kit and humiliated him; with their leader, 'several of the Capitao's neophytes were sentenced to periods of imprisonment, but the mass desertions ceased from this date' (enclosure in C03/4/2).

40. Du Plessis (n.d.):312f; Kafue District Annual Report 1914–15 (ZA 7/1/2/5, p. 8); Namwala District Annual Report 1915 (KSF 3/2/1).

41. Gielgud, 8 February 1901 (BS 1/93); Namwala District Annual Report 1913–14 (ZA 7/1/1/5) and 1915 (KSF 3/2/1).

42. Stokes (1966):281f; 'Native Unrest Kafue District' (KDE 2/32/3); Rotberg (1967):73f.

43. Smith and Dale (1920):II, 143; Schlosser (1949):46.

44. Smith and Dale (1920):II, 147f; Fielder (1965):294, 302f; Schlosser (1949):47f; 'Observer' (1914) and *Livingstone Mail*

(1914); articles by E.W. Smith and J.W. Price, in the *Herald of the Primitive Methodist Society*, as cited in Fielder (1965):303f; Chibanza (1961):78f. Chibanza's account is largely literal plagiarism from Smith and Dale (1920) but as an eye-witness to the episode he adds some revealing personal observations. See also Mumbwa Annual Report 1913–14 (ZA 7/1/1/5); Harris (1914); the latter publication shows how Mupumani's movement, though in a rather distorted form, had a heavy impact in the area bordering on Zaïre (then Belgian Congo).

45. This standard biographical pattern has so far been recorded, apart from Mupumani, for the affliction prophets Moya (field-notes, see note 95 below), Simbinga and his rival Kapata (Van Binsbergen, 1972a:4f), and Chief Katota (Muntemba, 1972b:1f); for the eschatological prophet Nasilele (cf. note 79); and for several leaders of Zambian independent churches (field-notes), including Lenshina (Lehmann, 1961:267; cf. chapter 8 of this volume).

46. Smith and Dale (1920):II, 149.

47. Smith and Dale (1920):II, 148, 152.

48. In this respect Mupumani gave a formal expression to tendencies that had already existed before his appearance as a prophet; as J.W. Price, the Primitive Methodist missionary in the area, writes in 1911, 'Many have practically given up ancestor worship. God seems nearer to them' (quoted in Fielder, 1965:289).

49. Fielder (1965):304f., based on the articles by Smith and Price.

50. Fielder (1965):299f.

51. Cf. map enclosed in ZA 1/9/53/2/1.

52. Hall p. 9 (see note 3); 'Report on the Chiefs and Divisional Headman of the Namwala Subdistrict', 1917, enclosure in KTJ 2/1.

53. Fielder (1968–9).

54. Fielder (1968–9):5, 11; Smith and Dale (1920):II, 110; Namwala Station Daybook: 131f. (KSF 2/1/I).

55. Field-notes.

56. Mumbwa Annual Report 1913–14; 'Cases Tried April 1st 1913–31st March 1914, Magistrate's Court, Mumbwa Station', KTJ 1/2, p. 196; L.M., 1914.

57. That there was a discrepancy between the prophet's original vision and the followers' redefinition is suggested by: Smith and Dale (1920):II, 149; Schlosser (1949):48; Fielder (1965): 304.

58. Chibanza (1961):80f.

59. Chibanza (1961):80.

60. Chibanza (1961):79; cf. Smith and Dale (1920):II, 149: 'had to yield to their insistence. He gave them drugs, and they gave him money in return'.

61. While shrines in the form of miniature huts are a-typical in the region, they are standard in the neighbouring areas to the south and east: Doke (1931):230f; Stefaniszyn (1964):153f; Colson (1962):87f; Von Rosen (1916):422f.
62. 'It was ultimately known that they were only being provided with some ordinary roots of a thorned tree called "kankoma" ' (Chibanza, 1961:80).
63. Smith and Dale (1920):II, 152; Chibanza (1961):80.
64. General descriptions, attempts at synthesis and interpretation, and bibliography in: Carter 1972; Van Binsbergen (1972b), this volume, chapter 2; further sources particularly for (central) western Zambia include: Kuntz (1932); Gluckman (1951):85f; Turner (1952):52f; (1957):288f; (1968):52f., 156f; White (1949b); (1961):46f; McCulloch (1951):92f; Symon (1959); Reynolds (1963):62f.
65. This aspect was first emphasized by White (1949b):331.
66. Sources include: Colson (1962):92f; (1960):164f; (1969):70f; Scudder (1962):111f; Doke (1931):244f; Smith and Dale (1920):II, 136f; Garbett (1966; 1969); Hugo (1935); Kuper (1955):34f; Tracey (1934); Editor (1918); see also note 8.
67. Van Binsbergen 1979b, this volume, chapter 3.
68. Cf. White (1949b):328f; (1961):49f., (1949a):30; Reynolds (1963):64f.
69. Reynolds (1963):134; Muntemba (1972b):*passim*; Van Binsbergen (1972a):*passim*; cf. this volume, chapter 5; field-notes.
70. Alexander and Rau (1972).
71. Lehmann (1961):267.
72. Field-notes.
73. Cf. Gann (1964):231f; Ranger (1975; 1972a); Buell (1928):I, 243; Cross (1970); Greschat (1967):46f., 49f., 68f. and *passim*; Taylor and Lehmann (1961):227–46; Shepperson and Price (1958):147f., 323f., 417 and *passim*; Hooker (1965), cf. below, chapter 8, note 45. Abundant archival material is available on the Watchtower and *mchape* movements in general, on government attitudes concerning them, and on their impact on central western Zambia. For the Kasempa district: e.g., KDD1/4/1; enclosures in ZA 1/9/181/(3): Secretary Native Affairs to Chief Secretary, 14 August 1933: '*Mchape*'; Chief Secretary to Provincial Commissioner, Ndola, 6 October 1933; Secretary Native Affairs to Chief Secretary, 23 September 1933: 'Watchtower Preacher Jacob Nkunda and Suspension of Chief Ingwe'; and further reports on investigations on Chief Ingwe. In the same district the very well-documented case of Mwepya (1930): a skilful though physically handicapped hunter,

who preached on God and Jesus Christ (without claiming to
represent Watchtower), and who divined and exorcized
tuyevera (sorcery familiars) with the aid of a church hymnal,
hymn singing, a reed applied to the ear, a broken mirror, and
game that he killed (KDD 1/2/1). For the Mankoya District:
the witch-cleansers Kapila and Swana Mukulwane, Mankoya
District Annual Report 1926 (KDE 8/1/18); enclosures in
KSX 1/1/1: District Commissioner Mankoya to Provincial
Commissioner Mongu, 18 August 1934; District Commissioner
Mankoya to District Commissioner Mumbwa, 29 January 1935:
'Joseph Pili, Watchtower Preacher'; District Commissioner
Mankoya to Provincial Commissioner Mongu, 2nd May 1935,
'Watchtower Preachers [at] Afumba and Kumina'; Mankoya
District Annual Report 1933 (ZA 7/1/16/3), 1934 (ZA 7/1/
17/5), 1935 and 1936 (SEC/NAT/66A). For Mumbwa district:
Assistant Inspector Mazabuka to Acting Commissioner Northern
Rhodesian Police, Livingstone, 7 December 1934, enclosure in
ZA/1/15/M/2; enclosures on a Kaonde and a Henga preacher,
1935, in ZA 1/9/62/1/6; and, as mentioned above, J. Pili. S.
Cross made available to me his 1969 seminar paper on Watchtower in western Zambia, which helped me to direct my own
archival research into this topic; his paper also contains information on Watchtower in the Namwala district.
74. Law Department Circular no. 2, 1925, neatly sums up the
various pretexts available to magistrates who were loath to per-
secute the preachers and dippers on purely religious grounds. The
approach was later denounced by the Governor (Chief Secretary
to Provincial Commissioner Kasempa, 4 April 1932) and the
Secretary for Native Affairs (to Chief Secretary, 16 January
1932, 'Watch-tower Adherents', section 17) (enclosures in ZA
1/15/M/1).
75. Gann (1964):231f.
76. Mankoya Annual Report 1935; Barotse Annual Report 1936:
5f; enclosures in SEC/NAT/66A.
77. For Barotseland, see: District Commissioner Lealui to Provincial
Commissioner Mongu, 4 October 1934 (enclosure in ZA 1/15/
M/1), and in note 73 the references relating to the Mankoya
district. The material about Chief Ingwe (cf. note 73) illustrates
the general government attitude concerning chiefs sympathizing
with Watchtower outside Barotseland. The material cited offers
ample evidence that in many cases chiefs and senior headmen
invited the preachers and dippers to their areas, in order to
obtain their services as witch-finders.
78. Field-notes.
79. The only case from central western Zambia so far documented is

my informant, the prophet and hunter Lubumba, to whom I hope to devote a separate study. A Mashasha, he was active as an eschatological prophet in the Kayingu area (Namwala district), about 1950. Further: the prophet Nasilele in the Kalabo district (Native Commissioner Kalabo, 'Quarterly Report for the Period Ending 30 September 1926. Confidential Annexure', in ZA 1/10/file no. 62); and two Angolan prophets closely associated with the eschatological movement in the Mwinilunga area, 1931–2 (District Commissioner Mwinilunga to Provincial Commissioner Kasempa, 8 February 1932 (enclosure in SEC/NAT/393); Provincial Commissioner Kasempa to Secretary Native Affairs, 19 February 1932, and Chief Secretary to Provincial Commissioner Kasempa, 4 April 1932 (enclosures in ZA 1/15/M/1); Provincial Commissioner Kasempa to Chief Secretary, 19 April 1932 (enclosure in KDD 1/4/1); the same materials partly also in ZA 1/9/181/(3)).

80. Cf. the much-cited case of the six self-accused female witches in Mwinilunga: Provincial Commissioner Kasempa to Secretary Native Affairs, 15 July 1933; Secretary Native Affairs to Provincial Commissioner Kasempa, 4 August 1933 (enclosures in ZA 1/9/181/(3)).

81. Barotse Annual Report 1935 (SEC/NAT/66A).

82. In the Mankoya district, Watchtower preachers imposed food taboos on groundnuts (claiming that these were 'God's eyes') and on cassava leaves (field-notes).

83. Field-notes; a well-documented example of the common claim of medicine for an exceptionally long or eternal life is the doctor Bumpila in Kalomo, 1926 (enclosure in ZA 1/9/44/(3)). Cf. the Head Capitao's claims, note 39.

84. Field-notes; an example from the documents is the Barotse cattle cordon incident in 1926, when policemen intimidated and pillaged returning labour migrants, under, among others, the following pretexts: 'they told us they had orders to search us for white man's medicine which the law forbade us to take to Barotse' (enclosure in ZA 1/5/1–8).

85. Field-notes; District Commissioner Feira to Provincial Commissioner Lusaka, 26 November 1932; Provincial Commissioner Lusaka to Secretary Native Affairs, 6 December 1932; Secretary Native Affairs to Provincial Commissioner Lusaka, 17 December 1932, all enclosures in ZA 1/9/98.

86. Fielder (1965):294f; Anderson (1919):304f.

87. Durkheim (1912):428f, has characterized this aspect of religion as a 'negative cult'.

88. Field-notes, cf. note 110; the ritual in question is the annual ant-hill ritual.

89. Field-notes.
90. Van Binsbergen (1979b), pp. 124–32 below.
91. Harding (1905):367; Gielgud (see note 3).
92. In central western Zambia, the *muba* cult of affliction is considered as the first of its kind to have been introduced, from the Lenje to the east (field-notes) or from the related Totela to the south (Gluckman, 1951:85). Kuntz (1932; cf. Turner, 1952:51) claims that such major cults of affliction as *maiymbwe, liyala, macoba* and *kayongo* are locally considered to derive each from one particular ethnic group and to affect neighbouring other groups (respectively Nkoya, Lozi, Kaonde and Luvale). The Songo affliction is named directly after the Songo people of eastern Angola; the very widespread *bindele* affliction concentrates on 'white people' (White, 1949b:329; 1961:49f; Reynolds, 1963:133f; Muntemba, 1972b:1f.). Identical 'white people' appear as dream symbols in the Bituma prophetic cult of affliction (field-notes). They are strangers clad in white cloth but not necessarily Europeans: cf. the myths concerning the 'white doctor' Luchele in Hall (1968):11f, Roberts (1973):346, and references given there. Several modern cults of affliction concentrate on such European-introduced symbols of alienness (and novelty) as 'guitar', 'airplane', 'steamer' (Colson, 1969:79f; White, 1949b:330; 1961:50; field-notes).
93. Field-notes.
94. Cf. the Bituma cult (Van Binsbergen, 1972a: 5f); another cult of the Angel is reported by Colson (1971: 101).
95. The Moya cult, which since *c.* 1970 has spread over central western Zambia, from Mongu (field-notes). Its contemporary prophet, Moya, revitalized and still spreads a cult which in fact had been introduced into western Zambia several decades earlier by Luvale immigrants (Ikacana, 1971:33).
96. A similar argument, with emphasis on West Africa, in Horton (1971). See pp. 28–42 below.
97. The missionary position is well known, cf. *Proceedings*, etc. (1927):169. Watchtower in the Mankoya district advocated the demolition of village shrines (field-notes) – in line with similar events, e.g., in the Chilanga area, where in the course of a massive dipping campaign in 1925 one of the leaders, Mutale (a Bemba), asked headman Shikoswe to destroy his spirit huts (enclosure in ZA 1/10/vol. 3, no. 4). As part of an eschatological prophetic movement, people in the Mwinilunga district in 1931–2 uprooted their village shrines (cf. note 79); Mupumani's more subtle attack on the cult of the dead has been discussed above.

98. This was a dominant theme in the major rural Rhodes–Livingstone studies, e.g., Turner (1957); Colson (1962); Marwick (1965a); Van Velsen (1964); Mitchell (1956b); cf. Gluckman (1955, 1963).

99. Such a date is perhaps suggested by archeological findings concerning social stratification (chieftainship) and ironworking in Central Africa; cf. Phillipson (1977):169f. (however, see also 144f; where the possibility of social stratification in the early Iron Age is discussed). For a general exploratory study of the association between chieftainship and ritual, see: Van Binsbergen (1979b), this volume, chapter 3. That ironworking in the past was a doctor's cult is strongly suggested by: Brelsford (1949) and Melland (1923):136f.

100. E.g., Turner (1968):300f; Van Binsbergen (1977a):8; my field-notes; Kuntz (1932, as quoted in Turner, 1952:51); especially the *kayongo* cult; Lamba possession by Lenje chiefs, Doke (1931):244f; a similar pattern among the Ambo, Stefaniszyn (1964):153, 156f; see also note 8.

101. Field-notes; Van Binsbergen (1972a); cf. this volume, chapters 5 and 7; Colson (1969):88f.

102. One possible model for the relation between cults of affliction and healing churches is developed in Van Binsbergen (1977a), this volume, chapter 5.

103. Eschatological movements have been found to intensify rather than collapse when their initial prophecies fail to materialize (cf. Festinger *et al.*, 1969). An obvious Zambian example is the continuous shifting of the date for the imminent end of the world as predicted by Watchtower (Hooker, 1965:91; Rotberg, 1967:136f.).

104. Field-notes; Long (1968:200f.) described for the Serenje district a pattern similar to that of central western Zambia; equally relevant is the case study by Cross (1970).

105. Melland (1923):131; Werner (1973):23. Lala myths, along with those of central western Zambia, place the invention of sorcery at the beginning of human society (Munday, 1961:1f.).

106. Gluckman (1955):42f; (1963):86f., 110f.

107. E.g., the Kwangwa (Ikacana, 1971: 3f.) and the Luvale (Papstein, 1978: chapters 3 and 4).

108. Vansina (1966):216, 234f., 242.

109. A related argument in: Apthorpe (1960).

110. For the eastern Nkoya, the range of chiefly terror included punitive expeditions and enslavement (cf. Gielgud, 9 October 1901, BS 1/93), a man – particularly a chief – having the right to commit his sister's son to slavery. Moreover, ritual murders were staged to procure medicine at the following occasions:

at a chief's accession; at the completion of his new capital and
royal fence; and at a chief's burial. Also, the chief's agents
(*tupondwa*) would secretly murder people in order to procure
parts of the body (particularly brains) for the chief's day-to-day
medicinal requirements. An echo of this is in Westbeech
(1963):60f. Human medicine was also required for the annual
ant-hill ritual that chiefs and senior headmen would perform
for the newly-harvested millet and maize; this ritual was later
completely modified within the Bituma cult. A deceased chief
was (and is) held to indulge in 'post-mortal sorcery' (see p. 141
above). Too little is known on similar ritual in other parts of Zambia
(but cf. note 18). Ritual murder, however, did surround the
royal cult of the Lozi (Shimunika, n.d.:1f; Gann, 1964: 231f;
field-notes) and the not dissimilar Bemba (Brelsford, 1944:36).

111.   Melland (1923):214f; Gielgud (cf. Van Binsbergen, 1974:12f.);
       field-notes; some very interesting Zaïrese parallels in Bentley
       (1887):70f.
112.   Field-notes; Muuka (1966):259.
113.   Livingstone (1899); Schapera (1960):184; Ikacana (1971):31f.
       Symon (1959:72) identified as syphilis the affliction underlying
       the important *manyanga* cult (cf. Van Binsbergen, 1972a:4,
       6, 8).
114.   Field-notes; Nicholls (1906, see note 3 of this chapter).
115.   Newson, 'Report on Investigation of Disease Mumbwa-Kasempa
       – July/August 1932' (ZA 1/9/28/12/1); Kee (1974);
       Mangango Mission Hospital Annual Report 1973.
116.   Cf. note 92; a further example is the *lubuku* cult among the
       Chokwe traders; cf. Pogge (1880):47f; Vansina (1966):220f.
117.   Field-notes. The sorcery connotations of game guards, most
       significant in view of the ecological importance of hunting,
       became particularly manifest in the very widespread beliefs
       concerning *Banyama* ('Game People') said to be engaged in
       man-hunting in order to procure medicine (especially as
       prepared from human blood) for modern hospitals; Gann
       (1964):231f; field-notes. A letter from Secretary for Native
       Affairs to Provincial Commissioner, Kasama, 1 April 1931
       (enclosure in ZA 1/9/62/2/1), suggests the occurrence of the
       Banyama belief throughout Zambia, from the Northern
       Province to Livingstone. In modern years the belief has
       developed in man-hunting strangers hiding in the forest,
       a belief associated with the alleged traffic in medicine of human
       origin between rural areas and the line of rail where such
       medicine is rumoured to be used for the magical boosting of
       African private enterprise (field-notes).
118.   Field-notes. The Secretary for Native Affairs (to Chief

Secretary, 16 January 1932, 'Watchtower Adherents',
enclosure in both SEC/NAT/393 and KDD 1/4/1) characterized
the Watchtower preachers applying for licences to preach, as
'natives of the Clerk and store-boy type'. Elsewhere Watchtower preachers are said to 'emanate from the mining areas',
i.e. returning labour migrants (District Commissioner Balovale
to Secretary Native Affairs, 6 December 1934, enclosure in
ZA 1/9/62/1/6); the same suggestion is carried by the mass
deportation of alleged Watchtower members from Elisabethville
(e.g., ZA 1/15/M1). Other references mention a houseboy (ZA
1/10/vol. 3, file 4), the dipper Mutale (see note 97) and a
fishmonger (ZA 1/15/M/2). These data certainly suggest that
preachers and dippers were 'modern achievers', but a more
systematic and precise analysis is required, distinguishing
between various categories of preachers and dippers that are
likely to have existed.

119. Mainga (1972):102f; the chapters by M. Wright and Rau in
Ranger and Cross (in preparation). Chiefs were generally eager
to enlist the services of the new-style witch-finders (normally
strangers to the local community), and occasionally issued
them with written permits (field-notes; cf. notes 73, 77);
besides the intention of making the community benefit from
the new witch-finders' valued services, private interests of the
chiefs (the elimination of rival foci of power in their areas)
are likely to have played a role.

120. Cf. Parkin (1968).

121. Mainga (1972):102f; Chibanza (1961):47f. Colonial legislation
(Witchcraft Ordinance, 1914, amended in 1948, 1952, 1963
and 1964, and now chapter 30 of the *Laws of the Republic
of Zambia*) made not witchcraft and sorcery, but witchcraft
and sorcery *accusations* the main offence in the sphere of
witchcraft and sorcery, and thus added to the vulnerability
of the doctor and witch-finder in the overall political structure of village society. A clear example of a religious innovatory
movement explicitly attacking old-style doctors is encountered
in the Bituma cult: the prophet Simbinga denounced the 'dirty'
medicine of the local doctors and urged the latter to dispose of
all their material apparatus, although he did not stage any ritual
witch-cleansing. Later, however, Simbinga was forced to give
doctors, particularly his cousin and main rival Kapata, leading
functions in the new movement (Van Binsbergen, 1972a:6f., cf.
this volume, pp. 203–5). The confusion in the doctors' ranks upon
the introduction of modern cults of affliction is also hinted by
White (1949b:331).

122. Cf. Mitchell (1955).

123. Cf. Ranger (1972a, 1975). The Chilanga episode (ZA 1/10/vol. 3, no. 4) is a typical example of massive, peaceful dipping. The cases from central western Zambia (cf. note 73) were mainly of the same category, although occasionally violence, in a few cases resulting in death, did occur (e.g., Mankoya Annual Report 1926, enclosure in KDE 8/1/18; and Mankoya Annual Report 1935, enclosure in SEC/NAT/66A).
124. This applies particularly to the South Africa General Mission (formerly the Andrew Murray Memorial Mission, cf. Du Plessis n.d.:239f; this mission is now known as the Africa Evangelical Fellowship, and Evangelical Church of Zambia). In our region, this organization established missions and excellent hospitals at Luampa and Mukinge Hill. Although conversion is not a condition for treatment, in practice much of the evangelization work takes place in the medical context, and leprosy outposts are manned by local church leaders. In the first years of the Luampa mission (started 1923), before the medical work gained momentum, the mission presented itself even more directly as a cult of affliction. Its founder (Mr Jakeman) 'fancied himself at casting out devils' (Jones, 1959:157).
125. Northern Rhodesia 1937:section P.
126. Van Binsbergen (1972a); cf. this volume, chapter 5.
127. Van Binsbergen (1972a):4f; Mankoya District Annual Report 1931, 1932, 1933, 1934, 1935, and the general reports for Barotse province of the same years (to which the Mankoya reports are attached): ZA/7/1/14/2, ZA/7/1/15/2, ZA/7/1/16/3, ZA/7/1/17/5, and SEC/NAT/66A. A description of the incredible destruction caused by the locusts is in: District Commissioner Mankoya to Chief of Agriculture, 'Locust report', 24 January 1935 (enclosure in KSX 1/1/1), e.g., 'Libinga, Induna on the Lalafuta, reports that his people have planted seed four times and that the fourth and last crop has just been destroyed like its predecessors. Kalamba reports to the same effect'. The 1933 report emphasized the population's 'well-behaved response to the hardship', as exemplified by the fact that for the first time in years the district had had no witchcraft cases and that criminality was low. The 1936 Report (SEC/NAT/66A) describes the economic recovery of the area.
128. Reynolds (1963):*passim*; Gluckman (1967):423f; field-notes.
129. Van Binsbergen (1972a):8; cf. chapter 5 of this volume.
130. This might be one adequate alternative for the deprivation hypothesis, as regards the interpretation of female preponderance in modern cults of affliction in Central Africa; cf. Colson (1969): 97f; Lewis (1966, 1971); Harris (1957).

131. Cf. Fielder (1965), who concentrates on the interaction between Ila society and the Primitive Methodist Mission.
132. Prior to his appearance as a prophet, Simbinga had been a labour migrant to Johannesburg, had amassed considerable wealth (including ten head of cattle), and had been an evangelist with Luampa mission.
133. Lepers were not eligible for recruitment as labourers and formed the main category of adult males exempted from tax (cf. ZA 1/9/43/1/3, ZA 1/9/43/vol. 3).
134. Fielder (1965):307, and J.W. Price, as quoted there.
135. Cf. Horton's remarks (1971:103) on religious innovation as an active concern of traditional religious leaders facing modern change.
136. White (1949b):331. Van Binsbergen (1972a):6; cf. this volume, pp. 203-7. Before they returned as prophets after a period of absence (claimed to have been a visit to heaven), the Angolan religious innovators associated with the eschatological movement in the Mwinilunga area (cf. note 79) were renowned doctors (District Commissioner Mwinilunga to Provincial Commissioner Kasempa, 8 February 1933, enclosure in SEC/NAT/393).
137. Since 1973 Keith Rennie has been engaged on a historical study of Namwala district. Much to my surprise, in a recent seminar paper he seems to conclude that there were no 'exploited or underprivileged groups within the society' of Namwala district in the early twentieth century (Rennie, 1978, as quoted in Ranger, 1978c:115). Concerning young men, women, slaves, the cattle-less peripheral Ila groups, and the non-Ila Batwa, quite the contrary is suggested in the works of, e.g., Smith and Dale (1920), Tuden (1958), Fielder (1965, 1968-9), as well as in the wealth of data contained in the Zambia National Archives – only a tiny fraction of which has been cited in this chapter. However, I have not seen Rennie's original paper, and rely on Ranger's rendering of its contents.
138. This mechanism also applies to the rise of independent churches in general, which, for lack of data relating to central western Zambia, have not specificially been dealt with in this chapter.
139. For a critique of the deprivation hypothesis as applied to modern Central African religious history, cf. Van Binsbergen (1972b):4-14; this volume, pp. 77-88.
140. The alternative view, in the line of Weber's 'Protestant ethic thesis' (Weber, 1976) is pursued by Long (1968):200f.
141. A discussion along these lines in H. W. Turner (1969).
142. Cf. Melland (1923):206; Reynolds (1963):26f; for a case of hereditary witchcraft in the Ndola area, see: Secretary

Native Affairs to Provincial Commissioner Kasempa, 4 August
1933 (enclosure in ZA 1/9/181/(3)).

Chapter 5 Cults of affliction in western Zambia

1. I am indebted to R.P. Werbner for his most stimulating
   editorial efforts towards the production of this chapter.
2. Turner (1957, 1962, 1967, 1968).
3. Kuntz (1932); White (1949b); Gluckman (1943, 1951);
   McCulloch (1951):72f; Turner (1952).
4. Christian churches are cults in terms of my definition of cult.
   However, they would be distinguished from cults in the
   dominant sociological approach to types of religious organization, which has been developed on the basis of the writings of
   Troeltsch, Von Wiese, Becker and Yinger (cf. Kolb, 1964;
   O'Dea, 1968).
5. Van Binsbergen (1976a, 1979b); cf. this volume, chapters 3 and
   4.
6. Carter (1972); Van Binsbergen (1972b, 1976a); cf. this volume,
   chapters 2 and 4.
7. Cf. Shorter (1972):141.
8. White (1949b, 1961).
9. Turner (1957):296f.
10. Chapter 4, cf. Van Binsbergen (1976a).
11. Clay (1946); McCulloch (1951); Fortune (1959):26f; Symon
    (1959); Van Binsbergen (1975a, 1975b (cf. this volume, chapter
    6), 1977c, 1978, 1979c, in preparation·(a).)
12. The following associations between non-regional cults of affliction
    and ethnic groups are recognized in western Zambia: the
    songo cult is associated with the Songo people of Angola
    (McCulloch, 1951), and introduced into western Zambia by the
    Luvale (Ikacana, 1971); *chimbandu* with the Angolan Ovim-
    bundu (McCulloch, 1951); *kayongo* with the Luvale (Kuntz,
    1932) or in general with Angolan immigrants (my field-notes);
    kalendamawulu with the Lozi (my field-notes); *viyaya* or
    siaya with the Luvale (Ikacana, 1971; my field-notes); *liyala*
    with the Lozi (Kuntz, 1932; Gluckman, 1951); *macoba* with
    the Kaonde (Kuntz, 1932); *mayimbwe* with the Nkoya (Kuntz,
    1932; Gluckman, 1951; Ikacana, 1971; my field-notes);
    kasheba with the Kaonde (my field-notes); *muba* with the Totela
    (Gluckman, 1951; Ikacana, 1971, who also mentions the
    neighbouring Toka), Lenje (my field-notes), or even groups
    further to the east, like the Lamba (Doke, 1931) and the
    Ambo (Stefaniszyn, 1964).

13. Symon (1959).
14. 'Anamnesis' is used here in the technical, medical sense of a patient's own account of the history of his complaint.
15. Van Binsbergen (1977c) discusses judicial aspects of the social process among the Nkoya; (1979c) is a lengthy analysis of Nkoya actors' decision patterns in the social process, illustrated by an extended case revolving on health and disease.
16. See Werbner (1971); (1972):235.
17. In this context one should bear in mind that most cult leaders are women, who in extra-religious public settings are not supposed to sit on chairs.
18. This might be read to constitute a moral aspect, in contrast with what I have said above about the a-moral nature of these cults. However, this concern with fair play points in a different direction – just as the ethics of fair play do not turn soccer or the retail trade into a predominantly moral institution.
19. Reynolds (1963):133f.
20. Mongu district files; the report could not be consulted.
21. Muntemba (1972b).
22. Cf. Van Binsbergen (1972a) for a preliminary account of the cult.
23. Ranger (1972b).
24. Ikacana (1971):33.
25. Weber (1969):358f.
26. Van Binsbergen (1976a):71; cf. this volume, p. 147.
27. Van Binsbergen (1976a), cf. this volume, chapter 4.
28. Muntemba (1972b):2.
29. Muntemba (1972b):5f.
30. Reynolds (1963):135, 138.
31. Muntemba (1972b):7f. Reynolds (1963:133f) suggests the contrary.
32. Weber (1969):361.
33. Weber (1969):363f.
34. Reynolds (1963:133) mentions the date of 1944, Muntemba (1972b:1) 1940.
35. Muntemba (1972b): *passim*; Reynolds (1963):137.
36. Reynolds (1963):136f.
37. Reynolds (1963):137.
38. Muntemba (1972b):3.
39. Initially a jar of chalk, and church bells (Reynolds, 1963:135, 137); later also a sacred cup for the administering of medicine (Muntemba, 1972b:6, 11).
40. B.R. Wilson (1975).
41. B.R. Wilson (1975):92f.

42. B.R. Wilson (1975):93f.
43. B.R. Wilson (1975):94f.
44. Roberts (1972):3; see also Ranger (1973a) for a critical review
    of Wilson's approach, and Van Binsbergen (1976c, this volume,
    chapter 8). However, later work by Calmettes (1978) has
    considerably enhanced our knowledge of the internal
    organization of Lumpa (see pp. 305–13 below).
45. The paraphernalia which Simbinga brought from his journey,
    and which to this day are in possession of his widow (one of my
    chief informants), were mainly the following. In three differently-
    coloured bottles (allegedly brought from Johannesburg by some-
    body else, and for secular purposes) Simbinga had collected
    water from three rivers: the Zambezi, the Kabompo and the
    Lungwebungu. These bottles he used as a divining device: only
    a patient who managed to indicate which bottle contained water
    from which river could be considered to suffer from Bituma,
    and thus be eligible for treatment. In addition Simbinga
    brought a round grey stone (about 10 cm diameter); a
    mpande shell partly covered with copper wire; a fly-switch made
    of eland-tail; a number of cowrie shells; a genet skin (*mbomba*);
    a circular ornament, made of parts of white water-lily sown into
    strings of white beads; a small copper bell of European manu-
    facture; and a leather-bound copy of an Afrikaans hymnbook
    (*Die Berijmde Psalms,* 1936). For the healing ritual, Simbinga
    would dress completely in white clothes. Although I cannot
    elaborate on this point here, to one familiar with the material
    culture and symbolism of western Zambia it will be clear that
    Simbinga's choice of paraphernalia was largely based on wide-
    spread conventional symbolism in this area, and reflected personal
    idiosyncrasies only to a limited degree – except in their
    combination, which brought together the insignia of both
    political and religious office, both historical and modern.
46. Some individual leaders did keep record of their own patients,
    along with a price-list of various treatments available.
47. Reynolds (1963):137.
48. Reynolds (1963):136.
49. Muntemba (1972b):11f.
50. Davies (1971).
51. Davies (1971):42-7.
52. In the 1969 census Mongu had 10,700 inhabitants, Livingstone
    43,000 inhabitants, and the other centres mentioned fewer
    than 4,000 (Davies, 1971:126).
53. The sex ratio obtaining in a given area is defined as $R = (A/B)$
    $\times 100$, where A = number of men, and B = number of women,
    actually resident in that area at a given moment. In a context of

labour migration, R > 100 suggests an area where (typically male) migrants go to work; R < 100 suggest an area from which male migrants have departed in order to work elsewhere. Despite increase in population, the relative demographic difference between the Bituma and Nzila regions was of essentially the same nature as in the 1930s, when Mongu and Livingstone had already been provincial and national capitals respectively for several decades, and (cf. Merle-Davis, 1933: appendix map) population density in western Zambia showed variations similar to the present-day distribution.

54. Parkin (1966); cf. Sundkler (1961): 302f., and chapter 2 above.
55. Cf. Van Binsbergen (1978, 1979c, forthcoming (a)).
56. Map 3 gives, *inter alia*, an overview of the size, growth and distribution of Christianity in western Zambia between the years 1929 and 1948, the crucial period for the emergence and early development of Nzila and Bituma. Basic figures were derived from Northern Rhodesia (1929, 1937, 1948).
57. Muntemba (1972b):12f.
58. Clay (1946); Colson (1970).
59. Muntemba (1972b):3.
60. Cf. Van Binsbergen (1975a, forthcoming (a)).

Chapter 6 Ritual, class and urban-rural relations

1. I am indebted to S. van der Geest, S. Simonse, W. Koot, M.L. Creyghton and R.P. Werbner for comments on an earlier draft of this paper.
2. Cf. Parkin (1975); Gerold-Scheepers and Van Binsbergen (1978): 22.
3. Van Binsbergen (1972a).
4. One important difference is, however, that the Ndembu are more strongly matrilineal, whereas among the Nkoya the historical matrilineal kinship structure has over the past 150 years developed in a bilateral direction.
5. Turner (1957, 1967, 1968, 1969).
6. Published, with considerable delay, as Turner (1964); reprinted in Turner (1967):19–47.
7. *Nkang'a* among the Ndembu. Among the Nkoya, *Nkanga* is the name of the polluting spirit associated with female puberty and menstruation; the aims of the girls' puberty ritual (*kutembuka kankanga*) are to appease this spirit, and to prepare the girl for her sexual, domestic and kinship roles as an adult woman.
8. It is within the same theoretical tradition that I, for one, have previously studied the religion of the highlands of north-western

Tunisia; cf. Van Binsbergen (1968, 1971a, 1971b, 1976d, 1980).
9. Turner (1957): 301; (1964):50, and throughout his work.
10. Cf. Van Binsbergen (1975a).
11. Cf. Colson (1968); Gutkind (1970); Lancaster (1974); Van Binsbergen (1975a).
12. Kay (1967):78f.
13. Turner (1957):17; (1968):59, 101, 104f., 118f., 128, 152, 194.
14. Van Binsbergen (1972a, 1976a) and chapters 4, 5 and 7 of the present volume.
15. Not only is the forked branch, from which the bark has been stripped, the main type of shrine in both the Bituma cult and in pre-existing ecological ritual; Bituma also incorporated and redefined the annual ant-hill ritual celebrating the harvesting of the new crop; cf. Van Binsbergen (1979b) also chapter 3 note 110 and *passim* and chapter 4 below.
16. The same point is made in Werbner's stimulating re-interpretation of Turner's analyses of similar Ndembu cults of affliction, as compared to Kalanga data from Southern Africa; see Werbner (1971).
17. Van Binsbergen (1975a).
18. Cf. Gluckman (1945, 1960, 1961).
19. Cf. Mitchell's (1956b) discussion of joking relations and apparently tribal dances in town.
20. Despite occasional remarks, cf. note 13.
21. Durkheim (1912); Parsons (1937, 1951); Geertz (1966); Berger and Luckmann (1963).
22. Bohannan (1964).
23. Worsley (1956b, 1967).
24. Worsley (1956a).
25. Fortes (1945, 1949a, 1959).
26. Van Velsen (1964).
27. Van Binsbergen (1975a).
28. For a general discussion along the same lines, see Cohen (1974b).
29. Geertz (1956); Wertheim (1964):3f.
30. The distinction is, of course, mainly a matter of emphasis. As I admit below, economic determinism alone cannot build an acceptable theory of religion and ritual; once the economic, and kinship-political, aspect is fully acknowledged, indispensable further insights can be gained from the idealist-Durkheimian, the psycho-analytic and other major 'ultimate' explanations of religion.
31. Durkheim (1912):327f; Parsons (1937):*passim*.
32. Geertz (1966):4 and *passim*.
33. Van Binsbergen (1976a); cf. this volume, chapter 4.
34. Cf. Van Binsbergen (1975a, 1975b).
35. 'We may speak of a "class" when (1) a number of people have

in common a specific causal component of their life chances, in so far as (2) this component is represented exclusively by economic interests in the possession of goods and opportunities for income, and (3) is represented under the conditions of the commodity of labour markets': Weber (1968):21.

36. Cf. Van Binsbergen (forthcoming (a)); the present volume, chapters 5 and 7. Van Binsbergen (1979c) offers a very lengthy description and analysis of one extended case relevant in this context.

37. Apthorpe (1960); Van Binsbergen (1976a):74f., 79f; cf. this volume, chapter 4.

38. Van Binsbergen (1976a, 1977a); cf. this volume, chapters 1, 4, 5 and 7.

39. Cf. Van Binsbergen (1977c); for a more extensive discussion precisely on this point, see the original conference paper: Van Binsbergen (1974):11-17, 23f.

Chapter 7 Cults of affliction in town

1. I am indebted to S. Simonse and the other members of the Amsterdam Work-Group for Marxist Anthropology, T.O. Ranger, R.P. Werbner, the Leiden Africa Seminar (February 1979), and the participants in the Department of Social Anthropology Seminar, University of Manchester (March 1979), for valuable criticism of earlier drafts of this chapter.

2. Carter (1972); Van Binsbergen (1972b, this volume, chapter 2); cf. Papstein (1978):218.

3. Van Binsbergen (1976a, 1977a, this volume chapters 4 and 5) and references cited there.

4. E.g., the *songo* cult, named after the Songo ethnic group in Angola; the *bindele* cult, *bindele* meaning 'white people' or 'people clad in white' (Swahili traders); and the *ndeke* (airplane) and *guitar* cults.

5. Cf. Van Binsbergen (1977a).

6. These Western Province languages include Lozi, Luvale, Mbunda, Luchazi and Chokwe, in addition to Nkoya; cf. chapter 3, note 87. Most Nkoya urban immigrants learn Nyanja in the first months after their arrival in town. But usually they can, after years, still be detected as non-native speakers of that language. On *linguae francae* in Zambia, see Kashoki (1978):31f.

7. A white pole (usually forked at the top), adorned with white beads, and with white meal sprinkled at its base. Some urban healers have permanent cult shrines on their premises; in some cases (in fact, *always* when the session takes place at the

patient's or sponsor's place of residence) a shrine is erected for that specific occasion.

8. Van Binsbergen (1977a), this volume, chapter 5.

9. Something she had still not done as this book was going to press; for detailed accounts of stages in her progress towards inheriting her sister's ritual status, cf. Van Binsbergen (1979c).

10. The Lenje are the north-eastern neighbours of the Nkoya. Since the creation of Kafue National Park in the 1930s they are separated from the vast majority of the Nkoya by a hundred miles of uninhabited forest. Infrequent rural inter-marriage does, however, still exist between these ethnic groups, whereas in the late pre-colonial period there were contacts in the form of itinerant Nkoya elephant-hunters, royal emissaries, and a few Lenje slaves at Nkoya chiefly courts. Formal joking still exists between Nkoya and Lenje, as is usual in Central Africa between groups which have a common history of warfare and raiding. Within the Bituma cult there are some puzzling Lenje elements, like the occasional use of Lenje songs, and one major leader's claim to be able to speak Lenje when in trance. Although I have been unable as yet to get conclusive evidence on this, it appears that the Lenje element in Bituma is due to the fact that Bituma has absorbed many elements of the *muba* cult, which probably was an ancient cult of the wilds among several groups in central Zambia (Doke, 1931:235, 253f; Stefaniszyn, 1964:156) before it was transformed into a new, non-prophetic cult of affliction, and in that form reached the Nkoya some time between the World Wars, via the Lenje. Gluckman (1951) and Ikacana (1971) suggest, in addition, other ethnic groups of the Tonga-speaking cluster: Toka, Totela, as transmitters of this cult.

11. Whose rural forms have been described by Colson (1969).

12. Cf. White (1949b, 1961) for a description of rural forms; Turner's work (1953, 1957, 1962, 1967, 1968, 1969) describes similar rural cults among the Ndembu, on whose presence and cultic practice in Lusaka I have, however, no data.

13. Instruments sometimes have to come all the way from Chief Mungule's area in Kabwe rural district, at some distance from Lusaka's Matero township, where at the end of the last century a group of Nkoya (here called: Mbwera) elephant-hunters settled, hundreds of miles east of their homelands at that time.

14. Reference is to the early 1970s, when K1 equalled about Hfl. 4 (and in US dollars, $1.70).

15. Discussed at much greater length in Van Binsbergen (1979c).

16. Cf. Hansen (1977).

17. Gluckman (1972b).

18. Cf. Van Binsbergen (in press).
19. Cf. Bates (1976):175.
20. Cf. Van Binsbergen (forthcoming (a)).
21. Van Binsbergen (in press).
22. One important set of options I have not considered here: modes of analysis developed in studies of rural-derived urban rituals outside Central Africa. The comparative African material is scanty and theoretically very uninspiring; it includes Mayer and Mayer (1974:150f), Mitchell (1965) and Hammond-Tooke (1970) for Southern Africa: Rigby and Lule (1975) for East Africa (the latter article also cites the main West African references, which are even more descriptive and less penetrating). Outside Africa, the main area which has yielded studies relevant in this context seems to be south-east Asia (Jay, 1963; Geertz, 1956, 1960; Peacock, 1968). All these works have a strong cultural orientation and therefore are difficult to relate to my present argument, as long as the more comprehensive symbolic theory, hinted at in the conclusion of the present chapter, has not yet been developed.
23. Gluckman (1960):57.
24. Mitchell (1956b).
25. Epstein (1958).
26. Turner (1953); (1974b):336.
27. Colson (1962, 1969).
28. Long (1968):200–49; Wylie (1969); Cross (1973); Jules-Rosette (1975, 1977); Dillon-Malone (1978).
29. G. Wilson (1968, first published in 1942).
30. Wilson and Wilson (1945).
31. G. Wilson (1968):I, 35.
32. Gluckman (1960).
33. Van Velsen (1961).
34. Richards (1940); Barnes (1951).
35. Watson (1959).
36. Watson (1959):225.
37. Watson (1959):228.
38. Long (1968).
39. Long (1968):227f.
40. Long (1968):227f.
41. Harries-Jones (1975):101f; for a related discussion, focusing however on urban network mobilization in time of bereavement, see Boswell (1969).
42. Cf. Bates (1976); Van Binsbergen (1977b); Gerold-Scheepers and Van Binsbergen (1978).
43. Werbner (1977c):xviiif.
44. Fortes (1959).

45. Geertz (1966).
46. K. Marx, *Theses on Feuerbach*, in Bottomore and Rubel (1974): 84.
47. Van Binsbergen (1976b, this volume, chapter 6); cf. Neckebrouck (1978):453f.
48. Turner (1957).
49. It is on this point that in an earlier publication (1976b; this volume, chapter 6) I failed to do justice to Turner's work, although some of my other points of criticism, there and elsewhere (1972b, 1977a; this volume, chapters 2 and 5), appear to remain valid.
50. Turner (1957):303.
51. Turner (1967, 1968, 1969).
52. Werbner (1977a).
53. Turner (1974a); Turner and Turner (1978); Werbner (1977a, 1977c, 1979a); on Turner's crucial impact on this development, cf. Werbner (1977c):xif and *passim*.
54. Werbner (1979a):2.
55. Van Binsbergen (1977a; this volume, chapter 5).
56. Muntemba (1972b); Reynolds (1963).
57. Which I admitted at the time: Van Binsbergen (1977a):164 (this volume, p. 208).
58. Werbner (1977b):215.
59. Werbner (1977a).
60. Schoffeleers (1979b).
61. Schoffeleers (1979c):2f; Van Binsbergen (1979b); this volume chapter 3).
62. Cf. Poulantzas (1974).
63. Gellner (1963, 1969); O'Brien (1971).
64. Stokes and Brown (1966); Vansina (1966); Langworthy (1972); Roberts (1976).
65. Ranger and Kimambo (1972a); Ranger and Weller (1975); Schoffeleers (1979a); Van Binsbergen (1976a), cf. this volume, chapter 4 and *passim*.
66. E.g., Clarence-Smith (1979a, 1979b); Papstein (1978):206f. Along with other Marxist and radical approaches the modes-of-production approach has inspired many of the authors of the important recent collection *The Roots of Rural Poverty in Central and Southern Africa* (Palmer and Parsons, 1977); but in line with the theoretical eclecticism characteristic of that book, and indeed of much work in African history, this approach is never pursued there with the rigour and consistency found in many French studies of similar topics. On this and related problems, see Ranger (1978c).
67. Meillassoux (1975); Rey (1973, 1976); Terray (1969); Amin (1973); Godelier (1973, 1975a, 1975b); useful summaries of

current debates are given in Pouillon (1976). Seddon (1978) offers a collection of significant articles translated into English; Bloch (1975) and Hindess and Hirst (1975) are English-language contributions to the same debates. In this body of literature, only Godelier's work contains more than passing references to religion.

68. Cf. the extensive bibliography in Maduro (1975a); see also Feuchtwang (1975); Godelier (1975b).

69. Houtart and Lemercinier (1977a).

70. Houtart and Lemercinier (1977b).

71. One Africanist example is Schoffeleers (1978). My own previous attempt (1976c; this volume, chapter 8), presented without reference to the relevant theoretical literature, remained somewhat unconvincing, for instance in its awkwardly rigid distinction between infrastructure and superstructure, as more than one critic has pointed out (Werbner, 1979b; Fernandez, 1978a:212-15; however, cf. Fernandez, 1978c.)

72. Cf. Wallerstein and Gutkind (1976); Gutkind and Waterman (1977). For specific applications to African migration and urban-rural relations, see most of the contributions in Van Binsbergen and Meilink (1978).

73. The term 'branch of production', for a complex of productive activities that can be meaningfully distinguished within a mode of production, derives from Terray (1969). Beach applied this term successfully to the pre-colonial Shona economy (1977), although his argument is essentially non-Marxist. A related concept is that of 'form of production', defined by Le Brun and Gerry (1975: 20) as existing, for instance, 'at the margins of the capitalist mode of production, but . . . nevertheless integrated into and subordinate to it'. For a preliminary description of branches of production in the social formation at Kaoma district, see Van Binsbergen (1978); however, that analysis is theoretically still very defective. A much revised version is forthcoming in *Africa*.

74. Oral evidence on this institution and its historical development is scanty, but we may surmise that what was involved was actually a local version of the institution of pawnship, postulated by Douglas (1964a) to form a general feature of clan structures in the Central African matrilineal belt.

75. In addition to oral traditions I collected myself, there are four collections systematized by their collectors/authors: Clay (1946); Ikacana (1971); Shimunika (n.d.); Shimunika (forthcoming). Extensive treatment of this material and relevant archival data, is in my forthcoming book (Van Binsbergen (a)).

76. Mainga (1973); Papstein (1978); Van Horn (1977); Clarence-Smith (1979a).

77. This is, of course, an echo of Horton's (1971, 1975) intellectua-

list theory of African religious change; see pp. 28–41 below
for a critical review.
78. Amin (1973):11.
79. There are some interesting parallels between chiefs and healers
which however are too imperfectly documented to be discussed
in greater detail. Various musical instruments (the *njimba* xylo-
phone and the *mukupele* hour-glass drum), and other paraphernalia (like the *hefu* eland-tail fly-switch and the *mpande* conus-
shell disc) were associated with the new dynasties coming from
the north and establishing Lunda-style chieftainship. Possession
of these items was prohibited among commoners, yet these items
were appropriated by cult leaders (cf. Simbinga's case, chapter 5,
note 45 above), without the chiefs taking offence. Likewise, the
formal respect paid to chiefs (*ku bombela*) is similar to the
attitudes towards the cult leaders during sessions (cf. the song
quoted above). This seems to corroborate the association between the cults and the linking of the domestic and the tributary
mode of production, although there remains room for other
explanations, such as: competition between chiefs and cult
leaders, in which it was not a matter of the healers' appropriating
healers' symbols of ritual authority. Such competition, as I have
attempted to demonstrate elsewhere (in Van Binsbergen 1979b,
this volume, chapter 3), is a recurrent theme in Central African
religious history.
80. They favoured chiefs and paid formal respect to them; in the
course of trading expeditions they would stop for months in
order to cultivate. Cf. Soremekun (1977):87; Papstein
(1978):236f.
81. Stokes (1966); Caplan (1970); Van Horn (1977):155f.
82. Van Horn (1977):154f.
83. Obviously the space is lacking here for a convincing discussion
on this point. Let it therefore suffice to say that the compatibility
between early twentieth-century mission Christianity and the
capitalist mode of production is strongly suggested by the fact
that they were intimately linked in the North Atlantic societies
from where capitalism expanded (Weber's Protestant ethic
thesis: Weber, 1976), and that by and large they jointly
expanded into Africa. This is not to deny that individual
missionaries have raised their voice against the expansion of
capitalism and some of its undesirable effects on the African
people.
84. Van Binsbergen (1977a; pp. 195–9 below).
85. This volume, p. 254.
86. Van Binsbergen (1977a; this volume, chapter 5).
87. Reynolds (1963); Muntemba (1972b).

88. Most cogently by Amselle (1976a); cf. Gerold-Scheepers and Van Binsbergen (1978).
89. Cf. map in Van Binsbergen (1977a:168; this volume, Map 3).
90. The best theoretical discussion of the mechanism through which labour migration exploits the domestic sector, is Meillassoux (1975); cf. Gerold-Scheepers and Van Binsbergen (1978).
91. Carter (1972); Beattie and Middleton (1969a).
92. Epstein (1958).
93. Epstein (1978):112.
94. To avoid misunderstanding: neither would Epstein.

Chapter 8 The Lumpa rising

1. Given the circumstances described in the opening section of this chapter, I could not carry out local field-work specifically on the Lumpa Church. The general argument is backed up by prolonged research in Zambia, both in the Zambian National Archives and in various urban and rural field-work settings. Moreover, while in Zambia I informally interviewed a limited number of people with first-hand knowledge of the Lumpa Church, some of them personally involved in its history. However, the specific argument on Lumpa is primarily based on published sources (including the Zambian press) and secondary analyses, most of which are listed in the bibliography. My purpose is not to present new data but to attempt a new interpretation on the basis of available data. For the present chapter, I am indebted to R. Buijtenhuijs, C. Holzappel, A. Kuper and G. Verstraelen-Gilhuis for comments on an earlier draft, and to L. Lagerwerf for bibliographical assistance. My greatest debt is to S. Simonse, who took a keen interest in this study and generously contributed towards its leading ideas.
2. *Times of Zambia*, 20 September 1969, as quoted in Gertzel (n.d.):41.
3. Tordoff and Molteno (1974):12; Sklar (1974):359; Pettman (1974):95.
4. Legum (1966):209.
5. Mwanakatwe (1968):253f; Phiri (1975); Hodges (1976); Sklar (1974):359; Pettman (1974):29, 96f; Assimeng (1970):110f.
6. Meebelo (1971):141.
7. Interestingly, the comparison was suggested to Meebelo by the influential Nestor of Zambian Protestant ministers of religion, the late Rev. Mushindo, whose refusal to accommodate Alice any longer within the Lubwa Mission congregation formed the

occasion for the founding of Lumpa as an independent Church.
On early Watchtower, see note 45.

8. Hall (1968):229f.
9. Legum (1966):xii.
10. For detailed studies of Zambia's attainment of independence,
    see: Mulford (1967); Hall (1968); Krishnamurty (1972).
11. Mulford (1967):330.
12. Cf. Hall (1968:209) for some conservative figures on the death
    toll of 'Chachacha'. Macpherson (1974:340f) gives a more vivid,
    lengthy description suggestive of a large number of casualties,
    but does not actually provide an estimate. On the basis of
    confidential government reports to which Short, a former
    district officer, had access at the time, he quotes a number of
    about fifty fatal casualties (Short, 1978).
13. *Report* 1965, as quoted in Gertzel (n.d.):40, and in *Times of
    Zambia*, 22 September 1965; Kaunda in Legum (1966):108;
    Roberts (1972):39f.
14. *Zambia Mail*, 4 and 21 June 1968.
15. E.g., *Daily Mail* (Zambia), 2 June and 17 July 1972; *Times of
    Zambia*, 21 March; 1, 5, 20 and 25 April; and 14, 16 and 20
    May 1972.
16. *Mirror* (Zambia), 45, February 1976: 3. Lenshina died on 7
    December 1978 (*Zambia Daily Mail*, 8 December 1978).
17. Report (1965).
18. Hall (1968); Mulford (1967); Macpherson (1974); Rotberg
    (1967); Krishnamurty (1972).
19. For fuller bibliographical references, particularly to more
    obscure publications and journalistic pieces, see: Roberts
    (1972); Calmettes (1970); Mitchell and Turner (1966);
    Ofori (1977).
20. Rotberg (1961); Lehmann (1961); Macpherson (1958); Stone
    (1958); Oger (1960); Chéry (1959, 1961). Oosthuizen (1968:65)
    refers to an article by Audrey I. Richards on the subject, which
    however does not appear in Gulliver's (1972) bibliography of
    the principal writings of Audrey Richards, and most probably
    does not exist.
21. Anonymous (1964); Emanuel (1964); Fernandez (1964b);
    Martin (1964); Douglas (1964b); Welbourn (1964); Heward
    (1964); B.R. Wilson (1964); Roberts (1964).
22. Lanternari (1965–6); Greschat (1968); Calmettes (1970,
    1972); Roberts (1972).
23. While this was written, J.–L. Calmettes was working on his
    MSc Econ thesis on the subject, for University College of Wales;
    cf. Calmettes (1978) and below.
24. B.R. Wilson (1975):94f; Greschat (1965):101f.

25. Shepperson (1970):48; Lehmann (1963):68.
26. Banton (1970):225.
27. Henderson (1970a):591.
28. Barrett (1968):246f; Peel (1973):349.
29. Tordoff (1974); Pettman 1974.
30. Pettman (1974):94.
31. Molteno (1974):85f.
32. Molteno (1974):85.
33. Molteno (1974):86.
34. I have myself studied a similar peasant situation in western Zambia (Van Binsbergen, 1975a, 1975b, 1976b, 1977c, 1978, 1979c, and forthcoming (a)).
35. Vansina (1966):19f.
36. Van Binsbergen (forthcoming (a)).
37. Van Binsbergen 1979b, this volume, chapter 3.
38. Carter (1972).
39. Van Binsbergen (1972b, this volume, chapter 2); 1976a (cf. chapter 4), 1977a (chapter 5); cf. this volume, chapters 1 and 7.
40. Van Binsbergen (1976a); cf. this volume, chapter 4.
41. Eliade (1949).
42. Gluckman (1971).
43. Rotberg (1965).
44. Cf. this volume, chapters 6 and 7.
45. On Nzila, see Muntemba (1972b); Van Binsbergen (1977a, this volume, chapter 5). On Watchtower in the period indicated, see, e.g., Hooker (1965); Assimeng (1970); Rotberg (1967):136f; Greschat (1967); Cross (1970, 1973) and by that same author a number of unpublished papers which I have no authority to cite. Hooker's reference (1965:99) to Watchtower in Kasempa district, north-western Zambia, as early as 1913 (instead of the correct date of the 1930s) is based on a mis-reading of Chibanza (1961:81). In the 1910s, African Watchtower in Zambia was confined to the extreme north-east, where it was closely connected with the military campaign against the Germans in Tanzania, during the First World War (Meebelo, 1971:133f; Rotberg, 1967:136f.). Much of African Watchtower in Zambia indirectly derived from the movement of John Chilembwe in Malawi, which ended in the 1915 rising (Shepperson and Price, 1958; for a recent reinterpretation cf. Linden and Linden, 1971). My views on the rural adaptation process in Watchtower are based not only on secondary literature, but also on the events in rural western Zambia in the 1920s and 1930s, as documented in Zambia National Archives files: KDD 1/4/1; ZA 1/9/181/(3); KDD 1/2/1; KDE 8/1/18; ZA 7/1/16/3; KSX 1/1/1; ZA 7/1/17/ 5; SEC/NAT/66A; ZA 1/15/M/1; SEC/NAT/393; ZA 1/9/62/1/6;

ZA 1/10/file no. 62; ZA 1/10/vol. 3, no. 4; ZA 1/15/M/2.
46. Rotberg (1967):142f; Ranger (1975).
47. Ranger (1972a); Willis provides a lengthy bibliography (1970), including all the classic references; specifically for north-eastern Zambia – the area of the Lumpa Church – cf. Roberts 1972:4f., 8f.
48. Willis (1970).
49. Douglas (1963).
50. Aptly summarized in B.R. Wilson (1975):56.
51. Henderson (1970a). A fascinating study could be written on the use of socialist catchwords, the adoption of Zambian humanism as a conveniently evasive ideology and the yielding to capitalist constraints and temptations among the Zambian nationalist leaders; cf. the useful remarks in Molteno (1974):80f., and Molteno and Tordoff (1974):388f.
52. Examples of such successful latterday Watchtower communities are described by Long (1968) and Cross (e.g., 1970).
53. See the literature cited in notes 19–28.
54. Rotberg (1961):63.
55. Information Department (1964):941; however, as, e.g., the number of emigrant Lumpa-adherents in Zaïre demonstrates, these are very conservative estimates.
56. Rotberg (1961):75f; Macpherson (1974):238, cf. 180; Mulford (1967):40; Kaunda as quoted in Emanuel (1964):198; *Northern News* (Zambia), 19 June 1965, which contains Nkumbula's statement.
57. Balandier (1965):443.
58. Rotberg (1961); Lehmann (1961).
59. Rotberg (1961):71; Lehmann (1961):253; Gertzel (n.d.) 36; Warren, as quoted in Information Department (1964):940; cf. below, note 99.
60. Roberts (1972):43, 47.
61. Lehmann (1961):266.
62. Calmettes (1970); Roberts (1972).
63. Roberts (1973).
64. Rotberg (1961):76f; Roberts (1972):32.
65. Clairmonte (1964).
66. Chéry (1959); Calmettes (1970, 1972).
67. Rotberg (1961):76; Roberts (1972):22.
68. Source: Report (1965) as quoted in *Times of Zambia,* 22 September 1965.
69. Roberts (1972):55.
70. Ranger (1968a):639; Ranger quoted from an earlier version of Roberts's analysis than the 1972 one used for the present study.
71. Roberts (1972):45.

72. Roberts (1972):35.
73. Such an explanation would come close to the views of those writers who have interpreted UNIP/Lumpa feuding as a clash between rival religions: Anonymous (1964); Franklin (1964). A similar suggestion in relation to the clashes between Zambian Watchtower and UNIP in Assimeng (1970):112.
74. E.g., M. Chona, the later Vice-President, as quoted in Information Department (1964):940f. Charlton (1969:140) quotes almost identical statements by Rev. Colin Morris. Morris has been one of Kaunda's main advisers. In 1964, as president of the United Church of Zambia (UCZ), he organized the churches' rehabilitation mission to the area where the final conflict was fought. In 1965 he campaigned to draw Lenshina into the UCZ fold – which failed.
75. Roberts (1972):35f; Macpherson (1974):410.
76. Legum (1966):109.
77. Legum (1966):109.
78. Weber (1969):328.
79. E.g., Caplan (1970):191 f.
80. Lanternari (1965–6) made an interesting attempt to interpret Lumpa, along with similar movements, in terms of urban-rural relations. In his view, 'les villages . . . représentent des "groupes de pression" contre la politique de déculturation et de dépersonalisation de certaines élites dirigeantes. . . . Les mouvements religieux à tendance néo-traditionaliste de la période post-coloniale renferment un avertissement à l'adresse des élites insuffisamment décolonisées. Ils sont la manifestation d'un besoin pressant d'intégration des valeurs que la civilisation occidentale a exportées en Afrique Noire, sans réussir à les intégrer dans l'arrière-plan culturel des sociétés indigènes' (1966:110). While thus recognizing that incorporation processes lie at the root of such conflicts as between Lumpa and the state, Lanternari only stresses superstructural elements and ignores the fundamental issues of class and the distribution of power.
81. Cf. Kuper (1979).
82. Weber (1969):363f.
83. A recent example that shows that the established churches do occasionally antagonize, rather than legitimize, the Zambian state, is the protest by the Zambia Council of Churches against the banning of the Kimbanguist Church (*Mirror* (Zambia), 50, July 1976: 1).
84. E.g., in the Gondwe Watchtower community (Cross, 1970), or in some Lusaka unauthorized settlements (Jules-Rosette, 1977).
85. Calmettes (1978).

86. In its emphasis on political, economic and class issues Calmettes's latest work also represents a remarkable step forward as compared to his earlier Lumpa pieces (1970, 1972).
87. Van Binsbergen (1976c): 109; cf. p. 275 above.
88. Calmettes (1978):193.
89. Rey (1973, 1976).
90. Calmettes (1978):195.
91. *Report* (1965):9; cf. Roberts (1972):39.
92. Roberts (1972):39.
93. Short (1973):267.
94. Calmettes (1978):193; cf. Oger (1960):17.
95. Calmettes (1978):172.
96. Van Binsbergen (1976c):121; cf. p. 292 above.
97. Roberts (1972):3; cf. Van Binsbergen (1977a:161, this volume, p. 202).
98. Werbner (1977a).
99. 'Lumpa Church is an organisation in which to worship God and his son Jesus Christ. *It is not an organisation to make unruly behaviour with the laws of the Country'*, Laws of the Lumpa Church, Lehmann (1961):253; my italics.
100. Cf. Poulantzas (1974).
101. Calmettes (1978):197; it would be interesting to know what specific pre-colonial wars or primary resistance movements Calmettes is referring to here.
102. Lehmann (1961).
103. Calmettes (1978):196.
104. Calmettes (1978):198.
105. Roberts (1973).
106. Richards (1939, 1969); Brelsford (1942, 1944); Werbner (1969).
107. Cross (1978):307.
108. Calmettes (1978):109f.
109. Van Binsbergen (1976c):126; cf. p. 297 above.
110. Calmettes (1978):145f.
111. Mamdani (1976); Shivji (1976); Alavi (1972); Saul (1974); Geschiere (1978); Buijtenhuijs and Geschiere (1978).
112. Cf. Miliband (1969) and especially Poulantzas (1974).
113. Short (1973):267.
114. Short (1973):267.

Bibliography

Aberle, D.F. (1970), 'A note on relative deprivation theory as
    applied to millennarian and other cult movements', in Thrupp
    (1970): 209–14.
Alavi, H. (1972), 'The state in post-colonial societies: Pakistan and
    Bangla Desh', *New Left Review*, 74:25–39.
Alexander, D. and W. Rau (1972), 'Spirit Possession at Chalumbwe
    Primary School', paper presented at Conference on the History
    of Central African Religious Systems, University of Zambia/
    University of California Los Angeles, Lusaka.
Allen, C.H. and R.W. Johnson (eds) (1970), *African Perspectives*,
    Cambridge University Press.
Alpers, E.A. (1972), 'Towards a history of the expansion of Islam
    in East Africa', in Ranger and Kimambo (1972a): 172–201.
Amin, S. (1973), *Le Développement inégal*, Paris: Editions de
    Minuit.
Amselle, J.-L. (1976a), 'Aspects et significations du phénomène
    migratoire en Afrique', in Amselle (1976b):9–39.
Amselle, J.L. (ed.) (1976b), *Les Migrations africaines*, Paris: Maspéro.
Anderson, W.H. (1919), *On the Trail of Livingstone*, San Francisco:
    Pacific Press.
Anonymous (1964), 'Postscript to the Lumpa movement',
    Newsletter (London: Institute for Race Relations), September
    1964; 25–8.
Anonymous (1973), 'Remarkable trees in Zambia', *Orbit* (Lusaka),
    2, 1:10–11.
Apthorpe, R.J. (ed.) (1959a), *From Tribal Rule to Modern
    Government*, Thirteenth Conference Proceedings, Lusaka:
    Rhodes–Livingstone Institute.
Apthorpe, R.J. (1959b), 'Northern Rhodesia: clanship, chieftainship
    and Nsenga political adaptation', in Apthorpe (1959a):69–98.

Apthorpe, R.J. (1959c), Introduction, in Rhodes–Livingstone Communication no. 15. Lusaka: Rhodes–Livingstone Institute: i–vii.

Apthorpe, R.J. (1960), 'Mythical African political structures, Northern Rhodesia', in Dubb (1960):18–37.

Apthorpe, R.J. (1961), (ed.) *Central Bantu Historical Texts*, I, Lusaka: Rhodes-Livingstone Institute, Communication no. 22.

Archer, D.R. (1971), 'Rainfall', in Davies (1971):20–1.

Arrighi, G. and J.S. Saul (1973), *Essays on the Political Economy of Africa*, New York/London: Monthly Review Press.

Assimeng, J.M. (1970), 'Sectarian allegiance and political authority: the Watch Tower Society in Zambia 1907–35', *Journal of Modern African Studies*, 8:97–112.

Augé M. (1975), *Théorie des pouvoirs et idéologie*, Paris: Hermann.

Balandier, G. (1965), 'Messianism and nationalism in black Africa', in Van den Berghe (1965):443–60.

Banda, J. (n.d.), 'The history of the Tumbuka-speaking people of Lundazi district', n.p., MS in the University of Zambia Library, Lusaka.

Banton, M. (ed.) (1966), *Anthropological Approaches to the Study of Religion*, London: Tavistock, ASA Monograph no. 3.

Banton, M. (1970), 'African prophets', in Middleton (1970):222–33.

Baré, J.F. (1977), *Pouvoir des vivants, langage des morts*, Paris: Maspéro.

Barnes, J. (1951), *Marriage in a Changing Society*, Oxford University Press for Rhodes-Livingstone Institute, Rhodes–Livingstone Paper no. 20.

Barnes, J. (1962), 'African models in the New Guinea Highlands', *Man*, 62:5–9.

Barrett, D.B. (1968), *Schism and Renewal in Africa*, Nairobi: Oxford University Press.

Bates, R.H. (1976), *Rural Responses to Industrialization*, Yale University Press.

Beach, D. (1977), 'The Shona economy: branches of production', in Palmer and Parsons (1977):37–65.

Beattie, J. and J. Middleton (eds), (1969a), *Spirit Possession and Society in Africa*, London: Routledge & Kegan Paul.

Beattie, J. and J. Middleton (1969b), Introduction, in Beattie and Middleton (1969a):xvii–xxx.

Bendix, R. and S.M. Lipset (eds) (1968), *Class, Status and Power*, London: Routledge & Kegan Paul, 2nd edition.

Bentley, W.H. (1887) *Life on the Congo*, London: Religious Tract Society.

Benz, E. (ed.) (1965), *Messianische Kirchen, Sekten und Bewegungen im Heutigen Afrika*, Leiden: Brill.

Berger, P. and T. Luckmann (1963), 'Sociology of religion and sociology of knowledge', *Sociology and Social Research,* 47:417–27.

Billing, M.G. (1959), 'Government policy in the utilization of indigenous political systems', in Apthorpe (1959a):1–16.

Bloch, M. (ed.) (1975), *Marxist Approaches and Social Anthropology,* London: Malaby Press, ASA Studies.

Bloch, M. (1977), 'The past and the present in the present', *Man,* 12:278–92.

Bohannan, P. (1964) ' "Conscience collective" and culture', in Wolff (1964):77–96.

Bolink, P. (1967) 'Towards Church Union in Zambia', PhD thesis, Free University, Amsterdam.

Boswell, D.M. (1969), 'Personal crisis and the mobilization of the social network', in Mitchell (1969):245–96.

Bottomore, T.B., and M. Rubel (eds) (1974), *Karl Marx: Selected Writings in Sociology and Social Philosophy,* Harmondsworth: Penguin Books.

Bourgignon, E. (ed.) (1973), *Religion, Altered States of Consciousness and Social Change,* Ohio State University Press.

Bourgignon, E. (1976), *Possession,* San Francisco: Chandler & Sharp.

Brelsford, W.V. (1935) 'History and customs of the Basala', *Journal of the Royal Anthropological Institute,* 65:205–15.

Brelsford, W.V. (1942), 'Shimwalule: a study of a Bemba chief and priest', *African Studies,* 1:207–23.

Brelsford, W.V. (1944), *Aspects of Bemba Chieftainship,* Livingstone: Rhodes–Livingstone Institute, Communication no. 2.

Brelsford, W.V. (1946), *Fishermen of the Bangweulu Swamp,* Oxford University Press for Rhodes–Livingstone Institute, Rhodes–Livingstone Paper no. 12.

Brelsford, W.V. (1949), 'Rituals and medicines of the Chisinga iron-workers', *Man,* 49:27–9.

Brelsford, W.V. (1950), 'Insanity among the Bemba of Northern Rhodesia', *Africa,* 20:46–54.

Brelsford, W.V. (1965), *The Tribes of Zambia,* Lusaka: Government Printer.

Bruwer, J.P. (1952), 'Remnants of a rain cult among the Acewa', *African Studies,* 11:179–82.

Buell, R. (1928), *The Native Problem in Africa,* I, New York: Bureau of International Research.

Buijtenhuijs, R. and P.L. Geschiere (eds) (1978a), *Social Stratification and Class Formation, African Perspectives 1978/2,* Leiden: Afrika-Studiecentrum.

Buijtenhuijs, R. and P.L. Geschiere (1978b), Introduction, in Buijtenhuijs and Geschiere (1978a):7–18.

Burridge, K. (1971), *New Heaven, New Earth,* Oxford: Blackwell.

Calmettes, J.-L. (1970), *Lumpa Church*: I, *The Genesis and Development 1953–1964,* Ilondola Mission, Chinsali.

Calmettes, J.-L. (1972), 'The Lumpa Church and Witchcraft Eradication', paper read at Conference on the History of Central African Religious Systems, University of Zambia/University of California Los Angeles, Lusaka.

Calmettes, J.-L. (1978), 'The Lumpa Sect, Rural Reconstruction, and Conflict', MSc (Econ) thesis, University of Wales.

Caplan, G.C. (1970), *The Elites of Barotseland 1878–1969,* London: Hurst.

Carter, M. (1972), 'Origin and Diffusion of Central African Cults of Affliction', paper read at Conference on the History of Central African Religious Systems, University of Zambia/University of California Los Angeles, Lusaka.

Charlton, L. (1969), *Spark in the Stubble,* London: Epworth Press.

Chéry, H.C. (1959), 'Les sectes en Rhodésie du Nord', *Parole et Mission,* 2:278–94.

Chéry, H.C. (1961), 'Visage des sectes et motifs de dissidence', in Masson (1961):28–51.

Chibanza, S.J. (1961), 'Kaonde history', in Apthorpe (1961):41–114.

Chimba, B. (n.d.), 'A History of the Baushi of Zambia', n.p., MS in the University of Zambia Library, Lusaka.

Chiwale, J.C. (1962), *Royal Praises and Praise Names of the Lunda Kazembe of Northern Rhodesia,* Lusaka: Rhodes–Livingstone Institute, Communication no. 25.

Clairmonte, P. (1964), 'Lumpa church based on fear', *The Times,* 6 August 1964.

Clarence-Smith, G. (1979a), 'Slaves, commoners and landlords in Bulozi, *c.* 1875 to 1906', *Journal of African History,* 20:219–34.

Clarence-Smith, G. (1979b), *Slaves, Peasants and Capitalists in Southern Angola 1840–1926,* Cambridge University Press.

Clarke, J.D. (1950), 'A note on the Pre-Bantu inhabitants of Northern Rhodesia and Nyasaland', *Northern Rhodesian Journal,* 1:4–52.

Clay, G.C.R. (1946), *History of the Mankoya District,* Livingstone: Rhodes–Livingstone Institute, Communication no. 4.

Cohen, A. (ed.) (1974a), *Urban Ethnicity,* London: Tavistock, ASA. Monograph no. 12.

Cohen, A. (1974b), Introduction: 'The lesson of ethnicity', in Cohen (1974a):ix–xxiv.

Cohen, R., and J. Middleton (eds) (1970), *From Tribe to Nation in Africa,* Scranton: Chandler.

Colson, E. (1951), 'The plateau Tonga of Northern Rhodesia', in Colson and Gluckman (1951):94–162.

Colson, E. (1958), *Marriage and the Family among the plateau Tonga of Northern Rhodesia*, Manchester University Press for Rhodes–Livingstone Institute.

Colson, E. (1960), *Social Organization of the Gwembe Tonga*, Manchester University Press for Rhodes–Livingstone Institute.

Colson, E. (1962), *The Plateau Tonga of Northern Rhodesia*, Manchester University Press for Rhodes-Livingstone Institute.

Colson, E. (1964), 'Social Change and the Gwembe Tonga', *Rhodes–Livingstone Journal*, 35:1–13.

Colson, E. (1968), 'Contemporary tribes and the development of nationalism', in Helm (1968):201–6.

Colson, E. (1969), 'Spirit possession among the Tonga of Zambia', in Beattie and Middleton (1969):69–103.

Colson, E. (1970), 'The assimilation of aliens among Zambian Tonga', in Cohen and Middleton (1970):35–54.

Colson, E. (1971), *Social Consequences of Resettlement*, Manchester University Press for Institute for Social Research.

Colson, E. and M. Gluckman (eds) (1951), *Seven Tribes of British Central Africa*, Oxford University Press for Rhodes–Livingstone Institute.

Cross, S. (1970), 'A prophet not without honour: Jeremiah Gondwe', in Allen and Johnson (1970):171–84.

Cross, S. (1973), 'The Watch Tower Movement in S. Central Africa 1908–1945', DPhil. thesis, Oxford.

Cross, S. (1978), 'Independent churches and independent states: Jehovah's Witnesses in East and Central Africa', in Fasholé-Luke *et al.* (1978):304–15.

Cunnison, I.G. (1950), *Kinship and Local Organization on the Luapula*, Livingstone: Rhodes–Livingstone Institute, Communication no. 5.

Cunnison, I.G. (1951), *History of the Luapula*, Oxford University Press for Rhodes-Livingstone Institute, Rhodes-Livingstone Paper no. 21.

Cunnison, I.G. (1959), *The Luapula Peoples of Northern Rhodesia*, Manchester University Press for Rhodes–Livingstone Institute.

Cunnison, I.G. (ed.) (1961), *Historical Traditions of the Eastern Lunda*, Lusaka: Rhodes–Livingstone Institute, Communication no. 23.

Daneel, M.L. (1970a), *The God of the Matopos Hills*, The Hague/Paris: Mouton for Afrika-Studiecentrum.

Daneel, M.L. (1970b), *Zionism and Faith-Healing in Rhodesia*, The Hague/Paris: Mouton for Afrika-Studiecentrum.

Daneel, M.L. (1971), *Old and New in Shona Independent Churches*, I: *Background and Rise of the Major Movements*, The Hague/Paris: Mouton for Afrika-Studiecentrum.

Daneel, M.L. (1974), *Old and New in Shona Independent Churches*,

II: *Causative Factors and Recruitment Techniques,* The Hague/
Paris, Mouton for Afrika-Studiecentrum.
Davidson, S. (1949), 'Psychiatric work among the Bemba',
Rhodes–Livingstone Journal, 7:75–86.
Davies, D.H. (ed.) (1971), *Zambia in Maps,* London: Athlone Press.
Declé, L. (1898), *Three Years in Savage Africa,* New York: M.F.
Mansfield.
De Craemer, W., J. Vansina and R. Fox (1976), 'Religious movements
in Central Africa', *Comparative Studies in Society and History,*
18:458–75.
De Heusch, L. (1964), 'Mythe et société féodale: le culte de kubandwa
dans le Rwanda traditionnel', *Archives de sociologie des religions,*
18:133–46.
De Heusch, L. (1966), *Le Rwanda et la civilisation interlacustre,*
Université Libre de Bruxelles, Institut de Sociologie.
De Heusch, L. (1972), *Le Roi ivre ou l'origine de l'état,* Paris:
Gallimard.
De Leeuwe, J. (1973), 'Why leave so much unsaid and unargued',
Bijdragen tot de Taal-, Land- en Volkenkunde, 129:144–50.
Dillon-Malone, C.M. (1978), *The Korsten Basketmakers,* Manchester
University Press for Institute for African Studies.
Doke, C.M. (1931), *The Lambas of Northern Rhodesia,* London:
Harrap.
Douglas, M. (1963), 'Techniques of sorcery control in Central Africa',
in Middleton and Winter (1963):123–41.
Douglas, M. (1964a), 'Matriliny and pawnship in Central Africa',
Africa, 24:301–13.
Douglas, M. (1964b), 'Against witchcraft', *New Society,* 4.
Douglas, M. (ed.) (1970a), *Witchcraft Confessions and Accusations,*
London: Tavistock, ASA Monograph no. 9.
Douglas, M. (1970b), *Natural Symbols,* London: Barrie & Jenkins.
Dubb, A. (ed.) (1960), *Myth in Modern Africa;* Fourteenth
Conference Proceedings, Lusaka: Rhodes–Livingstone Institute.
Du Plessis, J. (n.d.), *The Evangelisation of Pagan Africa,* Cape Town/
Johannesburg (*c.* 1930).
Durkheim, E. (1897), *Les Règles de la méthode sociologique,* Paris:
Alcan.
Durkheim, E. (1912), *Les Formes élémentaires de la vie religieuse,*
Paris: Presses Universitaires de France.
Editor (1918), Editorial, *Zambesi Mission Record,* 6:82.
Eliade, M. (1949), *Le Mythe de l'éternel retour,* Paris: Gallimard.
Emanuel, P.A. (1964), 'De zwarte Hemel', *Kroniek van Afrika,* 4:
196–9.
Epstein, A.L. (1958), *Politics in an Urban African Community,*
Manchester University Press for Rhodes–Livingstone Institute.

Epstein, A.L. (1978), *Ethos and Identity*, London/Chicago: Tavistock/Aldine.

Evans-Pritchard, E.E. (1940), *The Nuer*, Clarendon Press.

Evans-Pritchard, E.E. (1965), *Theories of Primitive Religion*, Clarendon Press.

Fabian, J. (1971), *Jamaa: a Charismatic Movement in Katanga*, Northwestern University Press.

Fabian, J. (1978), 'Popular culture in Africa: findings and conjectures', *Africa*, 48:315–34.

Fagan, B.M. (1963), 'The Iron Age sequence in the Southern Province of Northern Rhodesia', *Journal of African History*, 4:157–77.

Fagan, B.M. (1967), *Iron Age Cultures of Zambia*, I, London: Chatto & Windus for National Museum of Zambia.

Fagan, B.M. and D.W. Phillipson (1965), 'Sebanzi: the Iron Age sequence at Lochinvar, and the Tonga', *Journal of the Royal Anthropological Institute*, 95:253–94.

Fagan, B.M., D.W. Phillipson and S.G.H. Daniels (1969), *Iron Age Cultures in Zambia*, II, London: Chatto & Windus for National Museum of Zambia.

Fasholé-Luke, E.R., R. Gray, A. Hastings and G. Tasie (eds) (1978), *Christianity in Independent Africa*, London: Rex Collins.

Fernandez, J.W. (1964a), 'African religious movements: types and dynamics', *Journal of Modern African Studies*, 2:531–49.

Fernandez, J.W. (1964b), 'The Lumpa uprising: Why?', *Africa Report*, 9:30–2.

Fernandez, J.W. (1978a), 'African religious movements', *Annual Review of Anthropology*, 7:198–234.

Fernandez, J.W. (1978b), 'Imageless Ideas in African Inquiry', paper read at Social Science Research Council Conference on Cultural Transformations in Africa, Elkridge.

Fernandez, J.W. (1978c), 'African religious movements: the worst or the best of all possible microcosms', *Issue*, 8:50–2.

Festinger, L., H.W. Riecken and S. Schachter (1969), *When Prophecy Fails*, New York: Harper & Row.

Feuchtwang, S. (1975), 'Investigating religion', in Bloch (1975): 61–82.

Fielder, R.J. (1965), 'Social Change among the Ila-Speaking Peoples of Northern Rhodesia, with particular Reference to their Relations with the Primitive Methodist Mission', MA thesis, University of Manchester.

Fielder, R.J. (1968–9), 'Economic Spheres in Pre- and Post-Colonial Ila Society', paper read at Universities Social Sciences Conference, Kampala.

Firth, R. (1959), 'Problems and assumptions in an anthropological study of religion', *Journal of the Royal Anthropological Institute*, 89:129–48.

Firth, R. (1969), Foreword, in Beattie and Middleton (1969a):ix–xiv.

Fisher, H.J. (1973), 'Conversion reconsidered: Some historical aspects of religious conversion in black Africa', *Africa*, 43:27–40.

Fortes, M. (1945), *The Dynamics of Clanship among the Tallensi*, Oxford University Press for International African Institute.

Fortes, M. (1949a), *The Web of Kinship among the Tallensi*, Oxford University Press for International African Institute.

Fortes, M. (ed.) (1949b), *Social Structure*, Oxford University Press.

Fortes, M. (1953), 'The structure of unilineal descent groups', *American Anthropologist*, 55:17–41.

Fortes, M. (1959), *Oedipus and Job in West African Religion*, Cambridge University Press.

Fortes, M. (1965), 'Some reflexions on ancestor worship in Africa', in Fortes and Dieterlen (1965):122–44.

Fortes, M. and G. Dieterlen (eds) (1965), *African Systems of Thought*, Oxford University Press for International African Institute.

Fortune, G. (1959), *A Preliminary Survey of the Bantu Languages of the Federation*, Rhodes–Livingstone Communication no. 14, Lusaka: Rhodes–Livingstone Institute.

Fortune, G. (1963), 'A note on the languages of Barotseland', in Proceedings of Conference on the History of Central African Peoples, Lusaka: Rhodes–Livingstone Institute.

Frankenberg, R. (1969), 'Man, society and health', *African Social Research*, 8:573–87.

Franklin, H. (1964), 'Zambia's holy war', *Spectator* (London), 213, 7 August 1964: 173.

Fromm, E. (1952), *The Forgotten Language*, London: Gollancz.

Gamitto, A.L.P. (1960), *King Kazembe*, trans. I. Cunnison, Lisbon: Junta de Investigações do Ultramar, Centro de Estudios Politícos e Sociais.

Gann, L.H. (1964), *A History of Northern Rhodesia*, London: Chatto & Windus.

Garbett, G.K. (1966), 'Religious aspects of political succession among the valley Korekore', in Stokes and Brown (1966):137–70.

Garbett, G.K. (1969), 'Spirit mediums as mediators in Korekore society', in Beattie and Middleton (1969a):104–27.

Gatti, A. (1932), *Tom-Toms in the Night*, London: Hutchinson.

Geertz, C. (1956), 'Religious beliefs and economic behaviour in a central Javanese town', *Economic Development and Cultural Change*, 4:134–58.

Geertz, C. (1960), *The Religion of Java*, Glencoe: Free Press.

Geertz, C. (1966), 'Religion as a cultural system', in Banton (1966): 1–46.

Gellner, E. (1963), 'Saints of the Atlas', in Pitt-Rivers (1963):145–57.

Gellner, E. (1969), *Saints of the Atlas,* London: Weidenfeld & Nicolson.

Gerold-Scheepers, T.J.F.A. and W.M.J. van Binsbergen (1978), 'Marxist and non-Marxist approaches to migration in Africa', in Van Binsbergen and Meilink (1978):21–35.

Gertzel, G. (ed.) (n.d.), *The Political Process in Zambia: Documents and Readings,* Part I: *The Socio-Economic Background,* University of Zambia (*c.* 1972).

Geschiere, P.L. (1978), 'Stamgemeenschappen onder Staatsgezag', PhD thesis, Free University, Amsterdam.

Gilsenan, M. (1972), 'Myth and the history of African religion', in Ranger and Kimambo (1972a):50–69.

Givon, T. (1971), *The Si-Luyana Language,* Lusaka: Institute for African Studies, Communication no. 6.

Gluckman, M. (1935), 'Zulu women in hoecultural ritual', *Bantu Studies,* 9:255–71.

Gluckman, M. (1942), 'Some processes of social change illustrated from Zululand', *African Studies,* 1:243–60; reprinted in Gluckman (1958):53–77.

Gluckman, M. (1943), 'Notes on the social background of Barotse music', in Jones (1943); reprinted in Occasional Papers (1974): 103–6.

Gluckman, M. (1945), 'Seven-year research plan of the Rhodes–Livingstone Institute of Social Studies in British central Africa', *Rhodes–Livingstone Journal,* 4:1–32.

Gluckman, M. (1949), 'The role of the sexes in *Wiko* circumcision ceremonies', in Fortes (1949b):145–67.

Gluckman, M. (1950), Introduction, in Mitchell and Barnes (1950): 1–20.

Gluckman, M. (1951), 'The Lozi of Barotseland, N.W. Rhodesia', in Colson and Gluckman (1951):1–93.

Gluckman, M. (1955), *Custom and Conflict in Africa,* Oxford: Blackwell.

Gluckman, M. (1958), *Analysis of a Social Situation in Modern Zululand,* Manchester University Press for Rhodes–Livingstone Institute, Rhodes–Livingstone Paper no. 28.

Gluckman, M. (1960), 'Tribalism in modern British Central Africa', *Cahiers d'études africaines,* 1:55–70.

Gluckman, M. (1961), 'Anthropological problems arising from the African industrial revolution', in Southall (1961):67–82.

Gluckman, M. (1963), *Order and Rebellion in Tribal Africa,* London: Cohen & West.

Gluckman, M. (ed.) (1964), *Closed Systems and Open Minds*, Edinburgh: Oliver & Boyd.

Gluckman, M. (1967), *The Judicial Process among the Barotse of Northern Rhodesia*, 2nd edition, Manchester University Press for Rhodes-Livingstone Institute.

Gluckman, M. (1971), 'Tribalism, ruralism and urbanism in South and Central Africa', in Turner (1971):127–66.

Gluckman, M. (ed.) (1972a), *The Allocation of Responsibility*, Manchester University Press.

Gluckman, M. (1972b), Personal communication, 12 September 1972.

Godelier, M. (1973), *Horizon, trajects marxistes en anthropologie*, Paris: Maspéro.

Godelier, M. (1975a), 'Modes of production, kinship, and demographic structures', in Bloch (1975):3–27.

Godelier, M. (1975b), 'Towards a Marxist anthropology of religion', *Dialectical Anthropology*, 1:81–5.

Godelier, M. (1977), 'Infrastructures, sociétés, historie', *Dialectiques*, 21:41–53.

Goody, J. (1961), 'Religion and ritual: The definitional problem', *British Journal of Sociology*, 12:142–64.

Gould, J. and W.L. Kolb (1964), *A Dictionary of the Social Sciences*, New York: UNESCO.

Graham, I.M. and B.C. Halwindi (1970), *Guide to the Public Archives of Zambia*, Lusaka: National Archives of Zambia.

Greenbaum, L. (1973) 'Societal correlates of possession trance in sub-Saharan Africa', in Bourguignon (1973):39–57.

Greschat, H.J. (1965), ' "Witchcraft" und Kirchlicher Separatismus in Zentral-Afrika', in Benz (1965):89–104.

Greschat, H.J. (1967), *Kitawala*, Marburg: Marburger Theologische Studien, 4.

Greschat, H.J. (1968), 'Legend? fraud? reality? Alice Lenshina's prophetic experience: notes from some sources', *Africana Marburgensia*, 1:8–13.

Groff, D. (1978), 'Kouao Bile's Water: The Rationality of Religious Conversion in a West-African Town', paper read at 21st Annual Meeting, African Studies Association, Baltimore.

Gulliver, P.H. (1972), 'Bibliography of the principal writings of Audrey Richards', in La Fontaine (1972):285–9.

Gutkind, P.C.W. (ed.) (1970), *The Passing of Tribal Man in Africa*, Leiden: Brill.

Gutkind, P.C.W. and P. Waterman (eds) (1977), *African Social Studies*, London: Heinemann.

Gwassa, G.C.K. (1972), 'Kinjikitile and the ideology of Maji Maji', in Ranger and Kimambo (1972a):202–17.

Hall, R. (1968), *Zambia*, London: Pall Mall Press.

Hammond-Tooke, W.D. (1970), 'Urbanization and the interpretation of misfortune', *Africa*, 40:25–39.

Hansen, K.T. (1977), 'Prospects for wage labor among married women in Lusaka, Zambia', paper presented at 20th Annual Meeting, African Studies Association, Houston.

Harding, C. (1905), *In Remotest Barotseland*, London: Hurst & Blackett.

Harries-Jones, P. (1975), *Freedom and Labour*, Oxford: Blackwell.

Harris, E.A.M. (1914), 'A harvest to be reaped: Chisalala Mission Station, Northern Rhodesia', in *S.A.G.M. Pioneer*, 37:149–51.

Harris, G. (1957), 'Possession "hysteria" in a Kenya tribe', *American Anthropologist*, 59:1046–65.

Hayward, V.E.W. (ed.) (1963), *African Independent Church Movements*, London: Edinburgh House Press.

Helm, J. (ed.) (1968), *Essays on the Problem of Tribe*, Proceedings of the 1967 Annual Spring Meeting of the American Ethnological Society, Seattle/London: University of Washington Press.

Henderson, I. (1970a), 'The origins of nationalism in East and Central Africa: the Zambian case', *Journal of African History*, 11:591–603.

Henderson, I. (1970b), 'Pre-nationalist resistance to colonial rule in Zambia', *African Social Research*, 9:669–80.

Heward, C. (1964), 'The rise of Alice Lenshina', *New Society*, 4, 98, 13 August 1964: 6–8.

Hindess, B. and P.Q. Hirst (1975), *Pre-Capitalist Modes of Production*, London: Routledge & Kegan Paul.

Hodges, T. (1976), *Jehovah's Witnesses in Central Africa*, London: Minority Rights Group.

Holub, E. (1881), *Seven Years in South Africa*, London: Low.

Hooker, J.R. (1965), 'Witnesses and Watchtower in the Rhodesias and Nyasaland', *Journal of African History*, 6:91–106.

Horton, R. (1967), 'African traditional thought and western science', *Africa*, 37:50–71, 155–87.

Horton, R. (1971), 'African conversion', *Africa*, 41:85–108.

Horton, R. (1975), 'On the rationality of conversion', *Africa*, 45:219–35, 373–99.

Horton, R. and J.D.Y. Peel (1976), 'Conversion and confusion: a rejoinder on Christianity in Eastern Nigeria', *Canadian Journal of African Studies*, 10:481–98.

Houtart, F. (1977), 'Mouvements religieux du Tiers Monde: Formes de protestation contre l'introduction des rapport sociaux capitalistes', *Civilisations*, 27:81–101, 245–260.

Houtart, F. and G. Lemercinier (1977a), 'Religion et mode de production tributaire', in Houtart and Lemercinier (1977b):157–69.

Houtart, F. and G. Lemercinier (eds) (1977b), *Religion and Tributary Mode of Production, Social Compass*, 24, 2-3, Louvain: Centre de Recherches Socio-Religieuses.

Hugo, H.C. (1935), 'The Mashona spirits', *NADA*, 13:52-8.

Ifeka-Moller, C. (1974), 'Social structural factors in conversion to Christianity: Eastern Nigeria 1921-66', *Canadian Journal of African Studies*, 8:55-72.

Ikacana, N.S. (1971), *Litaba za Makwanga*, Lusaka: Neczam (reprint of 1952 edition).

Information Department of the Government of Northern Rhodesia (1964), 'Official Description of the Development of the Lumpa Church, etc.', *East Africa and Rhodesia*, 40 (2080), 20 August 1964: 940-1.

Janzen, J.M. (1978), 'Ideologies and institutions in the history of Equatorial African medical systems', paper read at Social Science Research Council on Cultural Transformations in Africa, Elkridge.

Jaspan, M.A. (1953), *The Ila-Tonga Peoples of North-Western Rhodesia*, Oxford University Press for International Africa Institute, Ethnographic Atlas of Africa.

Jay, R.R. (1963), *Religion and Politics in Rural Central Java*, New Haven: Southeast Asia Studies, Cultural Reports Series no. 12.

Johnson, W.R. (1977), *Worship and Freedom*, New York: Africana Publishing Company.

Jones, A.M. (1943), *African Music*, Livingstone: Rhodes-Livingstone Museum; 2nd edition (1949) reprinted in Occasional Papers (1974):71-106.

Jones, S. (1959), 'Mankoya in 1925 to 1927', *Northern Rhodesia Journal*, 4, 2:153-8.

Jules-Rosette, B. (1975), *African Apostles*, Cornell University Press.

Jules-Rosette, B. (1977), 'Grass-roots ecumenism', *African Social Research*, 23:185-216.

Kashoki, M.E. (1978), 'The language situation in Zambia', in Ohannessian and Kashoki (1978):9-46.

Kay, G. (1964), *Chief Kalaba's Village*, Manchester University Press for Rhodes-Livingstone Institute, Rhodes-Livingstone Paper no. 35.

Kay, G. (1967), *A Social Geography of Zambia*, University of London Press.

Kee, A. (1974), Personal communication.

Kjekshus, H. (1977), *Ecology Control and Economic Development in East African History*, London: Heinemann.

Köbben, A.J.F. (1960), 'Prophetic movements as an expression of social protest', *International Archives of Ethnography*, 49:117-64.

Köbben, A.J.F. (1961), 'New ways of presenting an old idea', in Moore (1961):175-92.

Köbben, A.J.F. (1970), 'Comparativists and non-comparativists in anthropology', in Naroll and Cohen (1970):581–96.

Kolb, W.L. (1964), 'Cult', in Gould and Kolb (1964).

Krishnamurty, B.S. (1972), *Chachacha,* Lusaka: Oxford University Press and Neczam.

Kuntz, M. (1932), 'Les rites occultes et la sorcellerie sur le Haut-Zambèze', *Journal de la Société des Africanistes,* 2:123–38.

Kuper, A. (1970), 'Lévi-Strauss comes to Africa, speaking French', *African Social Research,* 10:769–88.

Kuper, A. (1973), *Anthropology and Anthropologists: the British School 1922-72,* Harmondsworth: Penguin Books.

Kuper, A. (1979), 'The magician and the missionary', in Van den Berghe (1979):77–96.

Kuper, H. (1955), 'The Shona', in H. Kuper *et al.* (1955):9–40.

Kuper, H., A.J.B. Hughes and J. van Velsen (1955), *The Shona and Ndebele of Southern Rhodesia,* Oxford University Press for International Africa Institute, Ethnographic Atlas of Africa.

La Fontaine, J.S. (ed.) (1972), *The Interpretation of Ritual,* London: Tavistock.

Lancaster, C.S. (1974), 'Ethnic identity, history and "tribe" in the Middle Zambezi valley', *American Ethnologist,* 1:707–30.

Langworthy, H.W. (1969), 'A Political History of Undi's Kingdom to 1890: Aspects of Pre-Colonial Chewa history in East Central Africa', PhD thesis, Boston University.

Langworthy, H.W. (1971), 'Conflict among rulers in the history of Undi's Chewa kingdom', *Transafrican Journal of History,* 1:1–23.

Langworthy, H.W. (1972), *Zambia before 1890,* London: Longman.

Lanternari, V. (1965-6), 'Syncrétismes, messianismes, néo-traditionalismes: Postface à une étude des mouvements religieux de l'Afrique noire', *Archives de Sociologie des Religions,* 19:99–116, and (II: 'La situation post-coloniale') 20:101–110.

Leach, E. (ed.) (1967), *The Structural Study of Myth and Totemism,* London: Tavistock, ASA Monograph no. 5.

Le Brun, O. and C. Gerry (1975), 'Petty commodity producers and capitalism', *Review of African Political Economy,* 3:20–32.

Leeson, J. (1969), 'Paths to medical care in Lusaka, Zambia: Preliminary findings', *African Urban Notes,* 4:8–19.

Legum, C. (1966), *Zambia: Independence and Beyond,* London: Nelson.

Lehmann, D. (1961), 'Alice Lenshina Mulenga and the Lumpa Church', in Taylor and Lehmann (1961):248–68.

Lehmann, D. (1963), 'Women in the independent African churches', in Hayward (1963):65–9.

Lévi-Strauss, C. (1949), *Les Structures élémentaires de la parenté,* Paris: Presses Universitaires de France.

Lewis, I.M. (1966), 'Spirit possession and deprivation cults', *Man*, n.s. 1:307–29.

Lewis, I.M. (1971), *Ecstatic Religion*, Harmondsworth: Penguin Books.

Linden, I. (1979), 'Chisumphi theology in the religion of central Malawi', in Schoffeleers (1979b):187–207.

Linden, J. and I. Linden (1971), 'John Chilembwe and the New Jerusalem', *Journal of African History*, 12:629–51.

Livingstone, D. (1899), *Missionary Travels and Researches in South Africa*, London: Murray.

Livingstone Mail (1914), Editorial statement, 6 February 1914:3.

Long, N. (1968), *Social Change and the Individual*, Manchester University Press for Institute for Social Research.

McCracken, J. (1968a), 'The nineteenth century in Malawi', in Ranger (1968b):97–111.

McCracken, J. (1968b), 'African politics in twentieth-century Malawi', in Ranger (1968b):190–209.

McCracken, J. (1978), Review article: 'Rethinking rural poverty', *Journal of African History*, 19:611–15.

McCulloch, M. (1951), *The Southern Lunda and Related Peoples*, Oxford University Press for International Africa Institute, Ethnographic Atlas of Africa.

McKillop Wells, M. (1978), 'A Comparison of Three Societal Correlates in Possession and Non-Possession Groups', paper presented at 21st Annual Meeting, African Studies Association, Baltimore.

Macpherson, F. (1958), 'Notes on the beginning of the movement', *Occasional Papers* (London, International Missionary Council), 1:2–5.

Macpherson, F. (1974), *Kenneth Kaunda of Zambia*, Lusaka: Oxford University Press.

Maduro, O. (1975a), 'Marxist analysis and sociology of religions: an outline of international bibliography up to 1975', in Maduro (1975b):401–79.

Maduro, O. (ed.) (1975b), *Marxism and the Sociology of Religion*, Social Compass, 22, 3–4, Louvain: Centre de Recherches Socio-Religieuses.

Magubane, B. (1971), 'A critical look at the indices used in the study of social change in colonial Africa', *Current Anthropology*, 12:419–45.

Mainga, M. (1972), 'A history of Lozi religion to the end of the nineteenth century', in Ranger and Kimambo (1972a):95–107.

Mainga, M. (1973), *Bulozi under the Luyana Kings*, London: Longman.

Malinowski, B. (1954), *Magic, Science and Religion, and Other Essays*, Garden City: Doubleday Anchor Books.

Bibliography

Mamdani, M. (1976), *Politics and Class Formation in Uganda*, London: Heinemann.

Mangango Mission Hospital (1973), Annual Report, Kaoma: Mangango Mission Hospital.

Martin, M.L. (1964), 'The conflict between the Lumpa church and the government of Zambia (Northern Rhodesia)', *Ministry* (Marija), 5:46-8.

Marwick, M.G. (1965a), *Sorcery in its Social Setting*, Manchester University Press for Rhodes-Livingstone Institute.

Marwick, M.G. (1965b), 'Some problems in the sociology of sorcery and witchcraft', in Fortes and Dieterlen (1965):171-95.

Masson, J. (ed.) (1961), *Devant les Sectes non-chrétiennes*, Louvain: Desclée de Brouwer.

Mayer, P. and I. Mayer (1974), *Townsmen or Tribesmen*, Cape Town: Oxford University Press, 2nd ed.

Meebelo, H.S. (1971), *Reaction to Colonialism*, Manchester University Press for Institute for African Studies.

Meillassoux, C. (1964), *Anthropologie économique des Gouro de Côte d'Ivoire*, Paris/The Hague: Mouton for Ecole Pratique des Hautes Études.

Meillassoux, C. (1975), *Femmes, greniers et capitaux*, Paris: Maspéro.

Melland, F. (1923), *In Witchbound Africa*, London: Cass.

Merle-Davis, J. *et al.* (1933), *Modern Industry and the African*, London: Macmillan.

Middleton, J. (ed.) (1970), *Black Africa*, London: Collier-Macmillan.

Middleton, J. and D. Tait (eds) (1958), *Tribes without Rulers*, London: Routledge & Kegan Paul.

Middleton, J. and E.H. Winter (eds) (1963), *Witchcraft and Sorcery in East Africa*, London: Routledge & Kegan Paul.

Miliband, R. (1969), *The State in Capitalist Society*, London: Weidenfeld & Nicolson.

Miller, J.C. (1972), 'The Imbangala and the chronology of early central African history', *Journal of African History*, 13:549-74.

Miller, J.C. (1976), *Kings and Kinsmen*, Clarendon Press.

Miracle, M.P. (1959), 'Plateau Tonga entrepreneurs in historical inter-regional trade' *Rhodes-Livingstone Journal*, 26:34-50.

Mitchell, J.C. (1955), 'The African middle classes in British central Africa', in *INCIDI Conference on the Development of the Middle Classes in Tropical Countries*, London: INCIDI: 222-32.

Mitchell, J.C. (1956a), *The Yao Village*, Manchester University Press for Rhodes-Livingstone Institute.

Mitchell, J.C. (1956b), *The Kalela Dance*, Manchester University Press for Rhodes-Livingstone Institute, Rhodes-Livingstone Paper no. 27.

Mitchell, J.C. (1965), 'The meaning of misfortune for urban Africans', in Fortes and Dieterlen (1965):192-203.

Mitchell, J.C. (ed.) (1969), *Social Networks in Urban Situations,* Manchester University Press.

Mitchell, J.C. and J.A. Barnes (1950), *The Lamba Village,* Cape Town University Press, Communication from the School of African Studies, New Series, no. 24.

Mitchell, R.C. and H.W. Turner (1966), *A Comprehensive Bibliography of Modern African Religious Movements,* Northwestern University Press.

Molteno, R. (1974), 'Cleavage and conflict in Zambian politics: a study in sectionalism,' in Tordoff (1974):62–106.

Molteno, R. and W. Tordoff (1974), Conclusion: 'Independent Zambia: achievements and prospects', in Tordoff (1974):363–401.

Moore, F.W. (ed.) (1961), *Readings in Cross-Cultural Methodology,* New Haven: Human Relations Area Files.

Mukuni, Chief Silocha II (n.d.), 'A Short History of the Baleya People of Kalomo District', MS in University of Zambia Library, Lusaka.

Mulford, D.C. (1967), *Zambia: The Politics of Independence 1957–1964,* Oxford University Press.

Munday, J.T. (1948), 'Spirit names among the central Bantu', *Africa,* 7:39–44.

Munday, J.T. (1961), 'Kankomba', in Apthorpe (1961):1–40.

Muntemba, M.S. (1970), 'The political and ritual sovereignty among the Mukuni Leya of Zambia', *Zambia Museum Journal,* 1:28–39.

Muntemba, M.S. (1972a), 'Indirect Rule and its Impact on Lenje Chieftainship', Seminar Paper, University of Zambia, Institute for African Studies, Lusaka.

Muntemba, M.S. (1972b), 'Zambia Nzila Sect and Christian Churches in the Livingstone Area', paper read at Conference on the History of Central African Religious Systems, University of Zambia/ University of California Los Angeles, Lusaka.

Murdock, G.P. (1949), *Social Structure,* New York: Macmillan.

Murphree, M.W. (1969), *Christianity and the Shona,* London: Athlone Press.

Mushindo, P.B. (1973), *The Life of a Zambian Evangelist,* edited by J. van Velsen, Lusaka: Institute for African Studies, Communication no. 9.

Muuka, L.S. (1966), 'The colonization of Barotseland in the 17th century', in Stokes and Brown (1966):248–60.

Mvula, A. (1973), 'Exclusive report from our tense southern border', *Sunday Times of Zambia,* 15 April 1973.

Mwanakatwe, J.M. (1968), *The Growth of Education in Zambia since Independence,* Lusaka: Oxford University Press.

Mwondela, W.R. (1972), *Mukanda and Makishi,* Lusaka: Neczam.

Myers, J.L. (1927), 'A religious survey of the Batonga', in *Proceedings* (1927):127–32.

Nader, L. (ed.) (1969), *Law in Culture and Society*, Chicago: Aldine.

Naroll, R. and R. Cohen (eds) (1970), *A Handbook of Method in Cultural Anthropology*, Columbia University Press.

Neckebrouck, V. (1978), *Le Onzième Commandement*, Immensee: Nouvelle revue de science missionaire.

Northern Rhodesia (1929), *Blue Book for the Year Ended 31st December 1929*, Livingstone: Government Printer.

Northern Rhodesia (1937), *Blue Book for the Year Ended 31st December 1937*, Lusaka: Government Printer.

Northern Rhodesia (1948), *Blue Book for the Year Ended 31st December 1948*, Lusaka: Government Printer.

O'Brien, D. Cruise (1971), *The Mourides of Senegal*, Clarendon Press.

'Observer' (1914), 'The native god', *Livingstone Mail*, 6 February 1914: 3.

Occasionai Papers (1974), *Occasional Papers of the Rhodes-Livingstone Museum* nos 1-16, Manchester University Press for Institute for African Studies.

O'Dea, T.F. (1968), 'Sects and cults', in *International Encyclopaedia of the Social Sciences*, New York: Macmillan.

Ofori, P.E. (1977), *Christianity in Tropical Africa: a Selective Annotated Bibliography*, Nendeln: KTO Press.

Ogburn, W.F. and M.F. Nimkoff (1947), *A Handbook of Sociology*, London: Routledge & Kegan Paul.

Oger, L. (1960), 'Lumpa Church: the Lenshina Movement in Northern Rhodesia', (n.p.) (Serenje), MS in University of Zambia Library, Lusaka.

Oger, L. (1972a), 'Spirit Possession among the Bemba: a Linguistic Approach', paper read at Conference on the History of Central African Religious Systems, University of Zambia/University of California, Los Angeles, Lusaka.

Oger, L. (1972b), Personal communication, 5 September 1972.

Ohannessian, S. and M.E. Kashoki (eds) (1978), *Language in Zambia*, London: International African Institute.

Oosthuizen, G.C. (1968), *Post-Christianity in Africa*, London: Hurst.

Otto, W. (1917), *Das Heilige*, Munich: C.H. Beck.

Palmer, R. and N. Parsons (eds) (1977), *The Roots of Rural Poverty in Central and Southern Africa*, London: Heinemann.

Papstein, R.J. (1978), 'The Upper Zambezi: a History of the Luvale People 1000-1900', PhD thesis, University of California, Los Angeles.

Parkin, D. (1966), 'Voluntary associations as institutions of adaptation', *Man*, n.s. 1:90-94.

Parkin, D. (1968), 'Medicines and men of influence', *Man*, n.s. 3:424-39.

Parkin, D. (ed.) (1975), *Town and Country in East and Central*

Africa, Oxford University Press for International African Institute.

Parsons, T. (1937), *The Structure of Social Action*, New York: McGraw-Hill.

Parsons, T. (1951), *The Social System*, Glencoe: Free Press.

Peacock, J.L. (1968), *Rites of Modernization*, University of Chicago Press.

Peel, J.D.Y. (1968), *Aladura*, Oxford University Press.

Peel, J.D.Y. (1973), 'The religious transformation in Africa in a Weberian perspective', in CNRS/CISR, *The Contemporary Metamorphosis of Religion?*, Lille: 337–52.

Peters, E.L. (1967), 'Some structural aspects of the feud among the camel-herding Bedouin of Cyrenaica', *Africa*, 3:261–82.

Pettman, J. (1974), *Zambia: Security and Conflict*, Lewes: Julien Friedmann.

Phillipson, D.W. (1968), 'The early Iron Age in Zambia: Regional variants and some tentative conclusions', *Journal of African History*, 9:191–211.

Phillipson, D.W. (1977), *The Later Prehistory of Eastern and Southern Africa*, London: Heinemann.

Philpott, R. (1936), 'Mukumba – The Baushi tribal god', *Journal of the Royal Anthropological Institute*, 66:189–208.

Phiri, A. (1975), 'No salute, No school', *Target*, 147:4, 10.

Pitt-Rivers, J.A. (ed.) (1963), *Mediterranean Countrymen*, The Hague/Paris: Mouton.

Pogge, P. (1880), *Im Reich des Muata Jamvo*, Berlin; cited in Vansina (1966).

Posnansky, M. (1972),.'Archaeology, ritual and religion', in Ranger and Kimambo (1972a):29–44.

Pouillon, F. (ed.) (1976), *L'Anthropologie économique*, Paris: Maspéro

Poulantzas, N. (1974), *Les Classes sociales dans le capitalisme aujourd'hui*, Paris: Seuil.

Prins, G. (1978a), 'Grist for the mill: On researching the history of Bulozi', *History in Africa*, 5:311–25.

Prins, G. (1978b), Review of: Werbner (1977a), *African Social Research*, 26:506–9.

Proceedings of the General Missionary Conference of Northern Rhodesia, (1927), Lovedale: Lovedale Institute Press.

Radcliffe-Brown, A.R. and D. Forde (eds) (1950), *African Systems of Kinship and Marriage*, Oxford University Press for International African Institute.

Ranger, T.O.,(1966), 'The Role of Ndebele and Shona religious authorities in rebellions of 1896 and 1897', in Stokes and Brown (1966):94–136.

Ranger, T.O. (1967), *Revolt in Southern Rhodesia 1896–1897*, London: Heinemann.

387

Ranger, T.O. (1968a), 'Connexions between "primary resistance movements" and modern mass nationalism in East and Central Africa', *Journal of African History*, 9:437–53, 631–41.

Ranger, T.O. (ed.) (1968b), *Aspects of Central African History*, London: Heinemann.

Ranger, T.O. (1968c), 'The nineteenth century in Southern Rhodesia', in Ranger (1968b):112–53.

Ranger, T.O. (ed.) (1968d), *Emerging Themes of African History*, Dar es Salaam: East African Publishing House.

Ranger, T.O. (1970), *The African Voice in Southern Rhodesia*, London: Heinemann.

Ranger, T.O. (1972a), 'Mcape', paper read at Conference on the History of Central African Religious Systems, University of Zambia/ University of California Los Angeles, Lusaka.

Ranger, T.O. (1972b), Report on Proceedings of the Conference [on the History of Central African Religious Systems, Lusaka], *African Religious Research*, 2:6–35.

Ranger, T.O. (1973a), Review article: 'Magic and the Millenium', *African Religious Research*, 3:27–33.

Ranger, T.O. (1973b), 'Territorial cults in the history of Central Africa', *Journal of African History*, 14:581–97.

Ranger, T.O. (1974), Report on Conference on the Historical Study of East African Religion, June 1974, *African Religious Research*, 4:6–46.

Ranger, T.O. (1975), 'The Mwana Lesa movement of 1925', in Ranger and Weller (1975):45–75.

Ranger, T.O. (1977), 'The people in African resistance: a review', *Journal of Southern African Studies*, 4:125–46.

Ranger, T.O. (1978a), 'The churches, the nationalist state and African religion', in Fasholé-Luke *et al.* (1978):479–502.

Ranger, T.O. (1978b), *Witchcraft Belief in the History of Three Continents: An Africanist Perspective*, Wiles Lectures, Belfast, October 1978; publication forthcoming.

Ranger, T.O. (1978c) 'Growing from the roots: Reflexions on peasant research in Central and Southern Africa', *Journal of Southern African Studies* 5:99–133.

Ranger, T.O. (1979a), Preface to the first paperback edition: *Revolt in Southern Rhodesia*, London: Heinemann: ix–xviii.

Ranger, T.O. (1979b), 'Developments in the Religious History of Central Africa: Relations of Production and Religious Change', paper presented at Seminar on Religion and Change in African Societies, Edinburgh.

Ranger, T.O. and S. Cross (eds) (in preparation) *The Problem of Evil in Central and East Africa*.

Ranger, T.O. and I. Kimambo (eds) (1972a), *The Historical Study of*

African Religion, London: Heinemann.
Ranger, T.O. and I. Kimambo (1972b), Introduction, in Ranger and Kimambo (1972a):1–26.
Ranger, T.O. and J. Weller (eds) (1975), *Themes in the Christian History of Central Africa*, London: Heinemann.
Reefe, T.Q. (1977), 'Tensions of genesis and the Luba diaspora', *History in Africa*, 4:183–206.
Rennie, K. (1978), 'Traditional Societies and Modern Developments in Namwala District', seminar paper, Department of History, University of Zambia, Lusaka.
Report (1965), *Report of the Commission of Inquiry into the Former Lumpa Church*, Lusaka: Government Printer.
Rey, P.-P. (1973), *Les Alliances de classes*, Paris: Maspéro.
Rey, P.-P. (ed.) (1976), *Capitalisme négrier*, Paris: Maspéro.
Reynolds, B. (1963), *Magic, Divination and Witchcraft among the Barotse of Northern Rhodesia*, London: Chatto & Windus.
Richards, A.I. (1939), *Land, Labour and Diet in Northern Rhodesia*, Oxford University Press.
Richards A.I. (1940), *Bemba Marriage and Present Economic Conditions*, Oxford University Press for Rhodes–Livingstone Institute, Rhodes–Livingstone Paper no. 4.
Richards, A.I. (1950), 'Some types of family structure among the central Bantu', in Radcliffe-Brown and Forde (1950):207–51.
Richards, A.I. (1951), 'The Bemba of north-eastern Rhodesia', in Colson and Gluckman (1951):164–93.
Richards, A.I. (1969), 'Keeping the king divine', *Proceedings of the Royal Anthropological Institute of Great Britain and Ireland for 1968:* 23–35.
Rigby, P. and F.D. Lule (1975), 'Continuity and change in Kiganda religion in urban and peri-urban Kampala', in Parkin (1975): 213–27.
Roberts, A. (1964), 'The Lumpa tragedy', *Peace News*, no. 1471, 4 September.
Roberts, A. (1970a), 'Pre-colonial trade in Zambia', *African Social Research* 10:715–46.
Roberts, A. (1970b), 'The Lumpa Church of Alice Lenshina', in Rotberg and Mazrui (1970):513–68.
Roberts, A. (1972), *The Lumpa Church of Alice Lenshina*, Lusaka: Oxford University Press; reprint of Roberts (1970b).
Roberts, A. (1973), *A History of the Bemba*, London: Longman.
Roberts, A. (1976), *A History of Zambia*, London: Heinemann.
Roberts, S.A. (ed.) (1977), *Law and the Family in Africa*, The Hague/Paris: Mouton for Afrika-Studiecentrum.
Rotberg, R.I. (1961), 'The Lenshina movement of Northern Rhodesia', *Rhodes–Livingstone Journal*, 29:63–78.

Bibliography

Rotberg, R.I. (1965), *Christian Missionaries and the Creation of Northern Rhodesia, 1880-1924*, Princeton University Press.

Rotberg, R.I. (1967), *The Rise of Nationalism in Central Africa*, Harvard University Press.

Rotberg, R.I. and A. Mazrui (eds) (1970), *Protest and Power in Black Africa*, New York: Oxford University Press.

Runciman, W.R. (1972), *Relative Deprivation and Social Justice*, Harmondsworth: Penguin Books.

Sahlins, M. (1976), *Culture and Practical Reason*, University of Chicago Press.

Sangambo, M.K. (1979), *The History of the Luvale People and their Chieftainship*, A. Hansen and R.J. Papstein, eds, Los Angeles: Africa Institute for Applied Research.

Saul, J.S. (1974), 'African peasants and revolution', *Review of African Political Economy*, 1:41-68.

Saul, J.S. and R. Woods (1973), 'African peasantries', in Arrighi and Saul (1973):406-16.

Savage King, F. (1972), Personal communication, 14 February 1972.

Schapera, I. (1956), *Government and Politics in Tribal Societies*, London: C.A. Watts.

Schapera, I. (ed.) (1960), *Livingstone's Private Journals, 1851-53*, London: Chatto & Windus.

Schlosser, K. (1949), *Propheten in Afrika*, Brunswick: A. Limbach.

Schoffeleers, J.M. (1972a), 'The history and political role of the M'bona cult among the Mang'anja', in Ranger and Kimambo (1972):73-94.

Schoffeleers, J.M. (1972b), 'Attempt at a Synthesis of the Material on Territorial Cults', oral presentation, Conference on History of Central African Religious Systems, University of Zambia/ University of California Los Angeles, Lusaka.

Schoffeleers, J.M. (1972c), 'The Chisumphi and M'bona Cults in Malawi: a Comparative History', paper read at Conference on the History of Central African Religious Systems, University of Zambia/University of California Los Angeles, Lusaka; in: Schoffeleers (1979b):147-86.

Schoffeleers, J.M. (1974), 'Crisis, criticism and critique: An interpretative model of territorial mediumship among the Chewa', *Journal of Social Science* (University of Malawi), 3:74-80.

Schoffeleers, J.M. (1978), 'A martyr cult as a reflection on changes in production: The case of the lower Shire Valley, 1590-1622 AD', in Buijtenhuijs and Geschiere (1978a):19-33.

Schoffeleers, J.M. (1979a), 'Voorlopige Samenvatting van het Onderzoek Gedaan te Nsanje, December 1978-Januari 1979', MS, Amsterdam: Free University, Department of Religious Anthropology.

Schoffeleers, J.M. (eds) (1979b), *Guardians of the Land,* Gwelo: Mambo Press.

Schoffeleers, J.M. (1979c), Introduction, in Schoffeleers (1979b): 1–46.

Scudder, T. (1962), *The Ecology of the Gwembe Tonga,* Manchester University Press for Rhodes–Livingstone Institute.

Seddon, D. (ed.) (1978), *Relations of Production,* London: Cass.

Shepperson, G. (1970), 'The comparative study of millennarian movements', in Thrupp (1970):44–52.

Shepperson, G. and T. Price (1958), *Independent African,* Edinburgh University Press.

Shimunika, J.M. (n.d.), *Muhumpu wa Byambo bya Mwaka-Nkoya,* (n.p.) (Kaoma): no publisher's name (South African General Mission); the name of the author does not appear on this pamphlet, which was written in the 1950s.

Shimunika, J.M. (forthcoming), *Likota lya Bankoya/History of the Nkoya,* trans. M.M. Malapa and W.M.J. van Binsbergen, ed. W.M.J. van Binsbergen, Leiden: Afrika Studiecentrum.

Shivji, I.G. (1976), *Class Struggles in Tanzania,* London: Heinemann.

Short, R. (1973), *African Sunset,* London: Johnson Publications Ltd.

Short, R. (1978), Personal communication, 1 April 1978.

Shorter, A. (1972), 'Symbolism, ritual and history: an examination of the work of Victor Turner', in Ranger and Kimambo (1972): 139–49.

Siddle, D.J. (1971), 'Land use and agricultural potential', in Davies (1971):76–7.

Sklar, R. (1974), 'Zambia's response to the Rhodesian unilateral declaration of independence', in Tordoff (1974):320–62.

Skorupski, J. (1975), *Symbol and Theory,* Cambridge University Press.

Slaski, J. (1951), 'Peoples of the Lower Luapula Valley', in Whiteley (1951):76–100.

Smith, E.W. (1935), 'Inzuikizi', *Africa,* 8:473–80.

Smith, E.W. and A.M. Dale (1920), *The Ila-Speaking Peoples of Northern Rhodesia,* 2 vols, London: Macmillan.

Soremekun, F. (1977), 'Trade and dependency in central Angola', in Palmer and Parsons (1977):82–95.

Sorokin, P. (1928), *Contemporary Sociological Theories,* New York: Harper.

Southall, A.W. (1956), *Alur Society,* Cambridge: Heffer.

Southall, A.W. (ed.) (1961), *Social Change in Modern Africa,* Oxford University Press.

Spring Hansen, A. (1972), 'Fertility, Marriage and Ritual Participation among the Luvale of Northwestern Province, Zambia', seminar paper, University of Zambia, Institute for African Studies, Lusaka.

391

Bibliography

Stefaniszyn, B. (1954), 'African reincarnation re-considered', *African Studies*, 13:131-46.

Stefaniszyn, B. (1964), *Social and Ritual Life of the Ambo of Northern Rhodesia*, Oxford University Press for International African Institute.

Stokes, E., (1966), 'Barotseland: survival of an African state', in Stokes and Brown (1966):261-301.

Stokes, E. and R. Brown (eds) (1966), *The Zambesian Past*, Manchester University Press for Institute for Social Research.

Stone, W.V. (1958), 'The "Alice Movement" in 1958', *Occasional Papers*, London: International Missionary Council, 1:5-10.

Sundkler, B.G. (1948), *Bantu Prophets in South Africa*, London: Butterworth.

Sundkler, B.G. (1961), *Bantu Prophets in South Africa*, 2nd ed., Oxford University Press.

Swanson, G.E. (1964), *The Birth of the Gods*, University of Michigan Press.

Symon, S.A. (1959), 'Notes on the preparation and uses of African medicine in the Mankoya District, Northern Rhodesia', in *Rhodes-Livingstone Communication* no. 15, Lusaka: Rhodes-Livingstone Institute: 21-77.

Tabler, E.C. (ed.) (1963), *Trade and Travel in Early Barotseland*, London: Chatto & Windus for Rhodes-Livingstone Museum.

Taylor, J.V. and D.A. Lehmann (1961), *Christians of the Copperbelt*, London: SCM Press.

Terray, E. (1969), *Le Marxisme devant les sociétés 'primitives'*, Paris: Maspéro.

Thrupp, S.L. (ed.) (1970), *Millennial Dreams in Action*, New York: Schocken.

Tolkien, J.R.R. (1975), *The Hobbit*, London: Unwin.

Tordoff, W. (ed.) (1974), *Politics in Zambia*, Manchester University Press.

Tordoff, W. and R. Molteno (1974), Introduction, in Tordoff (1974): 1-39.

Torrend, J. (1906-9), 'A mysterious visitor to Batongaland', *Zambesi Mission Record*, 3:548-9.

Tracey, H. (1934), 'What are Mashawi spirits?' *NADA*, 12:39-52.

Trapnell, C.J. and J. Clothier (1937), *Ecological Survey of North-Western Rhodesia*, Lusaka: Government Printer.

Tuden, A. (1958), 'Ila slavery', *Rhodes-Livingstone Journal*, 24:68-78.

Turner, H.W. (1969), 'The place of independent religious movements in the modernization of Africa', *Journal of Religion in Africa*, 2:43-63.

Turner, V.W. (1952), *The Lozi Peoples of North-West Rhodesia*, Oxford University Press for International African Institute,

Ethnographic Atlas of Africa.

Turner, V.W. (1953), *Lunda Rites and Ceremonies,* Livingstone: Rhodes–Livingstone Museum: reprinted in Occasional Papers (1974):336–88.

Turner, V.W. (1957), *Schism and Continuity in an African Society,* Manchester University Press for Rhodes–Livingstone Institute.

Turner, V.W. (1962), *Chihamba the White Spirit,* Manchester University Press for Rhodes–Livingstone Institute, Rhodes–Livingstone Paper no. 31.

Turner, V.W. (1964), 'Symbols in Ndembu ritual', in Gluckman (1964):20–51.

Turner, V.W. (1966), 'Colour classification in Ndembu ritual', in Banton (1966):47–84.

Turner, V.W. (1967), *The Forest of Symbols,* Cornell University Press.

Turner, V. W. (1968), *The Drums of Affliction,* Oxford University Press for International African Institute.

Turner, V.W. (1969), *The Ritual Process,* London: Routledge & Kegan Paul.

Turner, V.W. (ed.) (1971), *Profiles of Change* (*Colonialism in Africa 1870–1960,* part III, general editors L. Gann and P. Duignan), Cambridge University Press.

Turner, V.W. (1974a), *Dramas, Fields and Metaphors,* Cornell University Press.

Turner, V.W. (1974b), See Turner (1953).

Turner, V.W. and E. Turner (1978), *Image and Pilgrimage in Christian Culture,* Oxford: Blackwell.

Tweedie, A. (1966), 'Towards a history of the Bemba from oral tradition', in Stokes and Brown (1966):197–225.

Van Binsbergen, W.M.J. (1968), 'Durkheim's begrippenpaar "sacré/profane" ', *Kula,* 8:14–21.

Van Binsbergen, W.M.J. (1971)a, 'Religie en samenleving: een studie over het bergland van N.W. Tunesië', Doctoraal-scriptie, University of Amsterdam.

Van Binsbergen, W.M.J. (1971b), 'Saints of the Atlas: Ernest Gellner', *Cahiers des arts et traditions populaires,* 4:203–11.

Van Binsbergen, W.M.J. (1972a), 'Bituma: Preliminary Notes on a Possession Healing Cult among the Nkoya', paper read at Conference on the History of Central African Religious Systems, University of Zambia/University of California Los Angeles, Lusaka.

Van Binsbergen, W.M.J. (1972b), 'Possession and Mediumship in Zambia: Towards a Comparative Approach', paper read at Conference on the History of Central African Religious Systems, University of Zambia/University of California Los Angeles, Lusaka; this volume, chapter 2.

Bibliography

Van Binsbergen, W.M.J. (1974), 'Kinship, Marriage and Urban-Rural Relations', paper read at International Seminar on New Directions in African Family Law, Afrika-Studiecentrum, Leiden.

Van Binsbergen, W.M.J. (1975a), 'Ethnicity as a Dependent Variable: The "Nkoya" Ethnic Identity and Inter-Ethnic Relations in Zambia', paper read at 34th Annual Meeting, Society for Applied Anthropology, Amsterdam.

Van Binsbergen, W.M.J. (1975b), 'Labour Migration and the Generation Conflict: An Essay on Social Change in Central Western Zambia', paper read at 34th Annual Meeting, Society for Applied Anthropology, Amsterdam.

Van Binsbergen, W.M.J. (1976a), 'The dynamics of religious change in western Zambia', *Ufahamu*, 6:69–87.

Van Binsbergen, W.M.J. (1976b), 'Ritual, class and urban-rural relations', *Cultures et développement*, 8:195–218; this volume, chapter 6.

Van Binsbergen, W.M.J. (1976c), 'Religious innovation and political conflict in Zambia', in Van Binsbergen and Buijtenhuijs (1976a): 101–35; this volume, chapter 8.

Van Binsbergen, W.M.J. (1976d), 'Shrine Cult and Society in North and Central Africa: a Comparative Analysis', paper read at Annual Conference, Association of Social Anthropologists, Manchester.

Van Binsbergen, W.M.J. (1977a), 'Regional and non-regional cults of affliction in western Zambia', in Werbner (1977a):141–75; this volume, chapter 5.

Van Binsbergen, W.M.J. (1977b), 'Occam, Francis Bacon, and the transformation of Zambian society', *Cultures et développement*, 9:489–520.

Van Binsbergen, W.M.J. (1977c), 'Law in the context of Nkoya society', in Roberts (1977):39–68.

Van Binsbergen, W.M.J. (1978), 'Class Formation and the Penetration of Capitalism in a Zambian Rural District', paper read at Seminar on Social Stratification and Class Formation in Africa, Afrika-Studiecentrum, Leiden.

Van Binsbergen, W.M.J. (1979a), 'Anthropological fieldwork: "There and back again" ', *Human Organization*, 38:205–9.

Van Binsbergen, W.M.J. (1979b), 'Explorations in the sociology and history of territorial cults in Zambia', in Schoffeleers (1979b): 47–88; this volume, chapter 3.

Van Binsbergen, W.M.J. (1979c) 'The infancy of Edward Shelonga: an extended case from the Zambian Nkoya', in Van der Geest and Van der Veen (1979):19–90.

Van Binsbergen, W.M.J. (1980) 'Popular and formal Islam, and supra-local relations: the Highlands of north-western Tunisia, 1800–1970', *Middle Eastern Studies*, 20:71–91.

Van Binsbergen, W.M.J. (forthcoming (a)), *Ritual, Class and Urban-Rural Relations.*

Van Binsbergen, W.M.J. (forthcoming (b)), *Shrines and Ecstasy in the Social Structure of North-Western Tunisia.*

Van Binsbergen, W.M.J. and R. Buijtenhuijs (eds) (1976a), *Religious Innovation in Modern African Society, African Perspectives 1976/2*, Leiden: Afrika-Studiecentrum.

Van Binsbergen, W.M.J. and R. Buijtenhuijs (1976b), 'Religious innovation in modern African society': Introduction, in Van Binsbergen and Buijtenhuijs (1976a):7–11.

Van Binsbergen, W.M.J. and H.A. Meilink (eds) (1978), *Migration and the Transformation of Modern African Society, African Perspectives 1978/1*, Leiden: Afrika-Studiecentrum.

Van den Berghe, P. (ed.) (1965), *Africa: Problems of Change and Conflict*, San Francisco: Chandler.

Van den Berghe, P. (ed.) (1979), *The Liberal Dilemma in South Africa*, London: Croom Helm.

Van der Geest, J.D.M. and K.W. van der Veen (eds) (1979), *In Search of Health*, University of Amsterdam.

Van Horn, L. (1977), 'The agricultural history of Barotseland 1840–1964', in Palmer and Parsons (1977):144–69.

Vansina, J. (1966), *Kingdoms of the Savanna*, Wisconsin University Press.

Vansina, J. (1968), 'The use of ethnographic data as sources for history', in Ranger (1968d):97–124.

Vansina, J. (1973), *The Tio Kingdom of the Middle Congo, 1880–1892*, Oxford University Press for International African Institute.

Vansina, J. (1978), *The Children of Woot*, University of Wisconsin Press/Folkestone: Wm Dawson.

Van Teeffelen, T. (1978), 'The Manchester School in Africa and Israel: a critique', *Dialectical Anthropology*, 3:67–83.

Van Velsen, J. (1961), 'Labour migration as a positive factor in the continuity of Tonga tribal society', in Southall (1961):230–41.

Van Velsen, J. (1964), *The Politics of Kinship*, Manchester University Press for Rhodes–Livingstone Institute.

Van Wetering, W. (1973), 'Hekserij bij de Djuka', PhD thesis, University of Amsterdam.

Von Rosen, E.C.G.B. (1916), *Traskfolket: Svenska Rhodesia-Kongo Expeditiones Etnografiska Forskningsresultat*, Stockholm: A. Bonnier.

Wallerstein, I. and P.C.W Gutkind (eds) (1976), *The Political Economy of Contemporary Africa*, London/Beverly Hills: Sage.

Watson, W. (1954), 'The Kaonde village', *Rhodes–Livingstone Journal*, 15:1–29.

Watson, W. (1959), *Tribal Cohesion in a Money Economy*, Manchester University Press for Rhodes–Livingstone Institute.

Weber, M. (1968), 'Class, status and party', in Bendix and Lipset (eds)
(1968):21-8.
Weber, M. (1969), *The Theory of Social and Economic Organization*,
Glencoe: Free Press.
Weber, M. (1976), *The Protestant Ethic and the Spirit of Capitalism*,
London: Allen & Unwin, 2nd ed.
Welbourn, F.B. (1964), "Lumpa and Zambia', *Venture* (London), 16,
9-10 September 1964: 41.
Werbner, R.P. (1969), 'Constitutional ambiguities and the British
administration of royal careers among the Bemba of Zambia', in
Nader (1969):245-72.
Werbner, R.P. (1971), 'Symbolic dialogue and personal transactions
among the Kalanga and Ndembu', *Ethnology*, 10:311-328.
Werbner, R.P. (1972), 'Sin, blame and ritual mediation', in Gluckman
(1972a):227-55.
Werbner, R. P. (ed.) (1977a), *Regional Cults*, London: Academic Press,
ASA Monograph no. 16.
Werbner, R.P. (1977b), 'Continuity and policy in Southern Africa's
High God cult', in Werbner (1977a):179-218.
Werbner, R.P. (1977c), Introduction, in Werbner (1977a):ix-xxxvii.
Werbner, R.P. (1979a), 'Central Places in History: Regional Cults and
the Flow of West African Strangers, 1860-1960', paper read at
Seminar on Religion and Change in African Societies, Edinburgh.
Werbner, R.P. (1979b), Review of Van Binsbergen and Buijtenhuijs
(1976a), *Africa*, 49:431.
Werner, D. (1971), 'Some developments in Bemba religious history',
Journal of Religion in Africa, 4:1-24.
Werner, D. (1973), 'The Coming of the "Iron Age" to the Southern
Lake Tanganyika Region: a Discussion of the Linguistic Evidence',
seminar paper, University of Zambia, Institute for African Studies
Lusaka.
Werner, D. (1979), '*Miao* spirit shrines in the religious history of the
southern Lake Tanganyika region', in Schoffeleers (1979b):
89-130.
Wertheim, W.F. (1964), *East-West Parallels*, The Hague: Van Hoeve.
Westbeech, G. (1963), 'The diary of G. Westbeech 1885-1888', in
Tabler (1963):23-101.
White, C.M.N. (1948), 'Witchcraft, divination and magic among the
Balovale tribes', *Africa*, 18:81-104.
White, C.M.N. (1949a), 'The Balovale peoples and their historical
background', *Rhodes-Livingstone Journal*, 8:26-41
White, C.M.N. (1949b), 'Stratification and modern changes in an
ancestral cult', *Africa*, 19:324-31.
White, C.M.N. (1956a), 'Factors in the social organisation of the
Luvale', *African Studies*, 14:97--112.

White, C.M.N. (1956b), 'The role of hunting and fishing in Luvale society', *African Studies*, 15:75–86.

White, C.M.N. (1959), *A Preliminary Survey of the Luvale Rural Economy*, Manchester University Press for Rhodes–Livingstone Institute, Rhodes–Livingstone Paper no. 29.

White, C.M.N. (1960), *An Outline of Luvale Social and Political Organisation*, Manchester University Press for Rhodes–Livingstone Institute, Rhodes-Livingstone Paper no. 30.

White, C.M.N. (1961), *Elements in Luvale Beliefs and Rituals*, Manchester University Press for Rhodes–Livingstone Institute, Rhodes–Livingstone Paper no. 32.

White, C.M.N. (1962), 'The ethno-history of the Upper Zambezi', *African Studies*, 21:10–27.

Whiteley, W. (1951), *The Bemba and Related Peoples of Northern Rhodesia*, Oxford University Press for International African Institute, Ethnographic Atlas of Africa.

Whiting, J.W.M. and I.L. Child (1953), *Child Training and Personality*, Yale University Press.

Willis, R.G. (1970), 'Instant millennium: The sociology of African witch-cleansing cults', in Douglas (1970a):129–39.

Wilson, A. (1978), 'The Kongo Kingdom to the Seventeenth Century', PhD thesis, London.

Wilson, B.R. (1964), 'Peril in martyrdom', *Observer*, 16 August 1964.

Wilson, B.R. (1975), *Magic and the Millennium*, Frogmore: Paladin/ Granada Publishing (reprint of 1973 edition).

Wilson, G. (1936), 'An introduction to Nyakyusa society', *Bantu Studies*, 10:253–91.

Wilson, G. (1939), *The Constitution of the Ngonde*, Livingstone: Rhodes–Livingstone Institute, Communication no. 1.

Wilson, G. (1968), *The Economics of Detribalization in Northern Rhodesia*, I & II, Manchester University Press for Institute for Social Research, Rhodes–Livingstone Papers nos 5–6 (reprint of 1942 edition).

Wilson, G. and M. Wilson (1945), *The Analysis of Social Change*, Oxford University Press.

Wilson, M. (1957), *Rituals of Kinship among the Nyakyusa*, Oxford University Press.

Wilson, M. (1959), *Communal Rituals of the Nyakyusa*, Oxford University Press for International African Institute.

Wilson, M. (1971), *Religion and the Transformation of Society*, Cambridge University Press.

Wilson, P. (1967), 'Status ambiguity and spirit possession', *Man*, n.s. 2:366–78.

Wolff, K.H. (ed.) (1964), *Essays on Sociology and Philosophy by Emile Durkheim et al.*, New York: Harper & Row.

Worsley, P.M. (1956a), 'The kinship system of the Tallensi: a revaluation', *Journal of the Royal Anthropological Institute*, 86:36–75.

Worsley, P.M. (1956b), 'Emile Durkheim's theory of knowledge', *Sociological Review*, 4:47–62.

Worsley, P.M. (1967), 'Groote Eylandt totemism and "Le Totémisme aujourd'hui" ', in Leach (1967):141–59.

Wright, M. (1972), 'Nyakyusa cults and politics in the later nineteenth century', in Ranger and Kimambo (1972a):153–170.

Wylie, D. (1969), 'Religion in an African Municipal Township', PhD thesis, University of Wisconsin.

Archival materials consulted

All files cited below are in the Zambia National Archives, Lusaka. For a general description of the organization of these archives, and an explanation of file numbers, see Graham and Halwindi (1970).

BS 1/93	Reports on the Gielgud-Anderson Hook of the Kafue Expedition.
CO 3/4/2	Copeman Papers (box 6), in HM 6 Historical Manuscripts Collection.
KDB 1/2/1	Kafue Game Reserve
KDD 1/2/1	Mwepya Witchdoctor (Kasempa District)
KDD 1/4/1	Kasempa Province Correspondence: Watchtower Movement
KDD 5	Kasempa District Notebook
KDE 2/36/3	Slavery 1914-1924 (Barotseland)
KDE 2/32/3	District Commissioner and Resident Magistrate Barotse Province, Correspondence: Native Unrest, Kafue District
KDE 8/1/18	Mankoya District Annual Report 1926
KSA 6/1	Chilanga District Notebook
KSF 1/6	Barotse in Namwala
KSF 2/1	Namwala District Notebook
KSF 2/1/vol.1	Namwala Station Daybook
KSF 3/1	J. Hall, 'A Paper on the Origin of the Baila' (also in KSF 2/1 vol. 1:173f.)
KSF 3/2/1	Namwala District Annual Reports 1912-15
KSX 1/1/1	Mankoya District Correspondence 1931-5
KSX 4	Mankoya District Notebook
KTJ 1/1	Mumbwa Out-letters (includes the reports of the Gielgud-Anderson Hook of the Kafue Expedition)

KTJ 1/2	Mumbwa Out-letters and Circulars (includes 'Cases Tried April 1st 1913–31st March, 1914, Magistrate's Court, Mumbwa')
KTJ 2/1	Mumbwa, Some Important Papers (includes Nicholls, 'Notes on Natives Inhabiting the Baluba Sub-District', and 'Extract from an Old Report of Mr Dale's')
KTJ 3/1	Mumbwa District Notebook
SEC/NAT/66A	Barotse Annual Report 1935, 1936 (includes Mankoya Annual Report 1935, 1936)
SEC/NAT/393	Watchtower 1931–2
U 1/2	Slavery
U 1/3	Witchcraft
ZA 1/5/1–8	Barotse Cattle Cordon
ZA 1/9/28/12/1	Newson, 'Report on Investigation of Disease, Mumbwa-Kasempa July-August 1932'
ZA 1/9/37/4	Game Reserves
ZA 1/9/43/1/3	Lepers
ZA 1/9/43/vol.3	Lepers
ZA 1/9/44/(3)	Natives' Medicines, Charms and Poisons
ZA 1/9/53/2/1	Census of Native-Owned Cattle
ZA 1/9/62/1/6	Watchtower from 4 September 1934
ZA 1/9/62/2/1	Banyama
ZA 1/9/98	Reports on Interesting Phenomena
ZA 1/9/181/(3)	Witchcraft
ZA 1/10/file no.62	Watchtower (includes: 'Quarterly Report for the Period Ending 30th September 1926, Confidential Annexure, Kalabo')
ZA 1/10/vol. 3 no.4	Watchtower Movement
ZA 1/13	Barotse Influence
ZA 1/15/M/1	Deportation of Watchtower Natives
ZA 1/15/M/2	Mchape
ZA 7/1/1/5	Kafue Province Annual Report 1913–14 (includes Namwala District Annual Report 1913–14 and Mumbwa District Annual Report 1913–14)
ZA 7/1/2/5	Kafue Province Annual Report 1914–15
ZA 7/1/14/2	Barotse Annual Report 1931 (includes Mankoya District Annual Report 1931)
ZA 7/1/15/2	Barotse Annual Report 1932 (includes Mankoya District Annual Report 1932)
ZA 7/1/16/3	Barotse Annual Report 1933 (includes Mankoya District Annual Report 1933)
ZA 7/1/17/5	Barotse Annual Report 1934 (includes Mankoya District Annual Report 1934)

Plates

Plate 1

Plate 2

Plates 3a, b

Plates 4a, b

Plate 5

Plate 6

Plate 7

Plate 8

Plate 9

Notes to plates

1 A village shrine The picture shows a typical village shrine at the eastern outskirts of a Nkoya village, Kaoma district, 1977. The two forked sticks form the core of the shrine. In the larger, dead tree in front, a gourd and a manufactured tin can be seen; they contain hunter's medicine. This photograph was taken in the early morning after the nocturnal part of a name-inheriting ritual. The soil in the foreground bears the imprints of the night's dancing. Drums used during the ritual have been temporarily put away in the shrine. In the background participants in the ritual can be seen chatting and drinking beer. (*Unless otherwise stated, photographs are by the author.*)

2 Name-inheriting ritual: an aspect of the ancestral cult The final phase of a name-inheriting ritual, as staged in a Nkoya village, Kaoma district, 1977. In the turmoil of music and dancing during the previous night, the young girl now seated in the centre has been forcibly appointed to inherit the name of her deceased aunt. Subsequently she has been dressed in white (the checkered sleeves are a concession to economic hardship). Leaning against a small forked shrine erected for the purpose of this particular ritual, she holds the deceased's youngest child. For along with the name she inherits the deceased's specific kinship relationships, including the latter's children and (if heir and widower are thus inclined) husband. The man seated next to the heir on a separate mat is the widower. In this particular case he will only be the heir's husband for the duration of the ritual. He holds an older child from his marriage with the deceased. All participants in the ritual are lining up to sprinkle meal on the heads of the heir and the widower, as public confirmation

403

of the fact that the deceased's name (if not she herself) has returned to
society.

3 a,b The shrine of a chief's capital An elaborate shrine in the eastern
part of the fenced yard around the palace of a major Nkoya chief,
Kaoma district, 1974. The top of the shrine is adorned with imposing
hunting trophies and a maize-cob. The pointed poles of the fence in the
background proclaim this palace to be that of a *royal* chief – only a
handful of chiefs in western Zambia being entitled to this type of
fence. Though of poor quality, *plate 3b* shows a unique set of paraphernalia: under the shadow of the trophies in the top of the shine,
we can make out the dual royal bells, as well as a saucer containing an
offering of meal to the chief's ancestors. This royal shrine has a triple
function: it serves as an individual hunting shrine for the chief, as a
ritual focus in the life of all inhabitants of the palace, and as the place
where one day the heir of the present incumbent of the chieftainship
will be enthroned.

4a A harvest ceremony: an aspect of the chiefly cult among the Bemba
The picture shows delegates bringing beer to the chiefs, Mpika district,
1933. Note the small chiefs' shrines in the form of miniature huts, the
gourd containing beer, and the man about to roll on his back to salute
the dead chiefs. In the religious history of Zambia, the Bemba were
unusual in that the chiefly cults which, from the seventeenth century
onwards, were imposed upon pre-existing territorial and ecological cults,
were capable of entirely encapsulating and partly eclipsing these older
cults. (*Photo: A. I. Richards; source: Richards 1939*)

4b An aspect of the ancestral cult among the Bemba Shrines for ancestral
spirits built outside a village, north-eastern Zambia, early 1930s. The
miniature hut is a widespread type of village shrine throughout Central
Africa. (*Photo: A. I. Richards; source: Richards 1939*)

5 The prophet Mupumani A leper from the area around Nanzela Mission,
Namwala district, Mupumani was the founder of a short-lived but massive
prophetic movement in 1913. Claiming to have visited heaven during a
temporary death, Mupumani preached the futility of human sorrow in
the light of the erratic omnipotence of God, 'The Creator of Pestilence'.
His movement was a major step in the rise to ever greater prominence
of the High God throughout Central Africa, as from the late pre-colonial
period. Spread by labour migrants and pilgrims, who significantly altered

the prophet's original message, Mupumani's movement had an impact over all central and western Zambia, as far as the Angolan and Zaïrese borders. (*Photo: E. W. Smith; source: Smith and Dale (1920) II*)

6 *The prophet Lubumba* Born c. 1915 in the eastern part of Kaoma district, Lubumba was a labour migrant to Mozambique in the late 1930s and early 1940s. Having settled in the eastern part of Namwala district, among his maternal kin, he was there active as a witch-finder and eschatological prophet, c. 1950. Forced by the colonial administration to leave that district, he has since been active as an eminently skilful hunter (despite being disfigured in a hunting accident), and an ecological prophet. His prophetic message is an idiosyncratic mixture of western Zambian traditions, and Watchtower teachings. As a prophet, he is emphatically not honoured in his own area, where he returned to become a village headman in 1968, and where this picture was taken in 1974.

7 *A Bituma shrine* This picture, taken in Kaoma district in 1974, shows a simple adept's shrine. This shrine had been erected only a few days before, on the occasion of a Bituma cult session staged for the benefit of a mature Nkoya woman, wife of a village headman. The tying of bark rope around the root of the fork is a characteristic feature. Note the similarity with the village shrine and the name-inheriting shrine, Plates 1 and 2.

8 *A senior cult leader of the Bituma cult* She is dressed in her white ceremonial robes, and stands beside her officiant's shrine in the eastern outskirts of her husband's village, Kaoma district, 1974. The shrine, whose forked top is obscured by the foliage, is adorned with long strings of white beads. Wielding an eland fly-switch to which she is entitled by virtue of her office, the priestess goes through a typical movement of the Bituma possession dance. The two saucers in front of the shrine contain coins, beads and meal offered to the Bituma spirit. This cult leader was one of the few Bituma leaders in the area to co-operate intensively with a colleague of equally senior standing in the cult; in fact, the shrine shown here was jointly owned by both cult leaders. The little girl is the priestess's granddaughter; she has no function in the Bituma ritual.

9 *Alice Lenshina Mulenga* Born c. 1920 near Lubwa mission, Chinsali district, Lenshina had her first visions in 1953. When her prophetic

activities could no longer be accommodated within the Mission church, she became the founder of the Lumpa Church, the largest independent church which Zambia has yet seen. Numbering about 100,000 members at its peak, a succession of clashes with the authorities, the established churches, chiefs and the United National Independence Party culminated in the annihilation of the Lumpa Church in armed confrontation with the Zambian state, 1964. Released from custody in 1975, Lenshina was a marketeer in Lusaka until her death in 1978. (*Photo: unknown; source: Short 1973; this photograph was originally published in the Zambian newspaper* Northern News *(Ndola), 1964)*

Indexes

Author index

Author index

Subject index

412

169; and cults of affliction,
153, 186-7; eradication of, 29,
147, 166-70, 270, 284-5,
289-90, 293-4; and evil, 162-7;
and game guards, 349; Lumpa
portrayed as, 300-1; measure-
ment of, 285, 367; and prophecy, 149-50; and trade, 162-5;
and Watchtower, 167
Witchcraft Ordinance, 294, 350
women: bridewealth, 233, 261-2;
in churches, 270; in cults of
affliction, 185-94, 198-9, 201,
208, 239-48, 262; deprived, 87,
251; exclusion of, 106, 114;
fertility, 150; and men, 88,
95-6; in possession cults, 233-

4, 328-9; powerful, 192;
puberty ritual, 216, 247, 356;
as rain-mediums 88; reproductory problems, 88; sex-ratio,
208-10, 355-6; as 'spirit-wife',
106; in towns, 244-6
wowa cult, 105

Yeke people, 146, 177

Zaïre, 27, 33, 266-7, 269, 299,
336, 343
Zambezi (river), 322, 355
Zambezi (town), 153, 198
Zimbabwe, 27, 238, 289, 317
Zulu people, 87